CAUSATION AND RISK IN THE LAW OF TORTS: SCIENTIFIC EVIDENCE AND MEDICINAL PRODUCT LIABILITY

Causation and Risk in the Law of Torts: Scientific Evidence and Medicinal Product Liability

RICHARD GOLDBERG, LLB, LLM, PhD
Solicitor
Lecturer in Law
University of Birmingham

·HART·
PUBLISHING
OXFORD – PORTLAND OREGON
1999

Hart Publishing
Oxford and Portland, Oregon

Published in North America (US and Canada) by
Hart Publishing c/o
International Specialized Book Services
5804 NE Hassalo Street
Portland, Oregon
97213-3644
USA

Distributed in the Netherlands, Belgium and Luxembourg by
Intersentia, Churchillaan 108
B2900 Schoten
Antwerpen
Belgium

Distributed in Australia and New Zealand by
Federation Press
John St
Leichhardt
NSW 2000

Hart Publishing Ltd is a specialist legal publisher based in Oxford, England.
To order further copies of this book or to request a list of other
publications please write to:

Hart Publishing Ltd, 19 Whitehouse Road, Oxford, OX1 4PA
Telephone: +44 (0)1865 434459 or Fax: +44 (0)1865 794882
e-mail: hartpub@janep.demon.co.uk

British Library Cataloguing in Publication Data
Data Available
ISBN 1 901362 85–X (cloth)

Typeset by Hope Services (Abingdon) Ltd.
Printed in Great Britain on acid-free paper
by Biddles Ltd, Guildford and Kings Lynn.

Preface

This book arose as a consequence of my research on a doctoral thesis on *Causation, Risk and Scientific Evidence in Medicinal Product Liability* at King's College London.

Several people have provided assistance to me in the preparation of this book. In particular, I wish to thank my supervisor at King's, Professor Gerald Dworkin, who provided helpful criticism throughout my researches. In addition, I am grateful to the following academic colleagues, who have given me considerable guidance whilst the book was being written. Professor Ian Kennedy and Professor Andrew Grubb provided me with helpful advice on Chapter 3 and Professor Jane Stapleton was able to offer helpful criticism of Chapters 1 and 6. Other academics who provided helpful advice were Professor David Miller, Professor Alec Elliott, Professor Edmund Kitch, Professor Wendy Mariner and Professor Louis Lasagna.

Many colleagues in Birmingham have assisted me. Thanks are particularly due to Professor Tony Arnull, Mr Peter Cook, Professor David Feldman, Mr Ray Hodgin, Dr Julian Lonbay, Mr Frank Meisel and Professor C. J. Miller for their continued support and encouragement. I am most grateful for the secretarial assistance that has been provided for the book. Mrs Mirella Wells has been of great assistance throughout the book's development. I have also been excellently assisted by Mrs Nadene Bryan, who took over the role of Mrs Wells when I arrived in the Birmingham Law Faculty. To both of these secretaries, I owe special thanks. I also wish to thank Laurence Bebbington of the Harding Law Library, who has responded to all requests on the location of important material, and to Miss Maureen Black for her continued support throughout the work.

Thanks are also due to the School of Law at King's College London for a King's College London School of Law Research Scholarship, which I held from 1993 to 1996, and to Professor Joe Thomson of the University of Glasgow for his encouragement in pursuing the topic. I am also grateful for the helpful advice of Mr Ian Dodds-Smith of Cameron McKenna, London, and Mr Richard Kingham of Covington and Burling, London and Washington DC. SmithKline Beecham Pharmaceuticals, in particular Mr Brian Russell, have been most helpful in assisting with research funding.

Richard Goldberg

Birmingham
November 1998

Contents

Table of Cases

Table of Statutes

Introduction

The central issue in product liability litigation concerning medicinal products is causation. This book attempts to provide a comparative account of the legal and scientific issues relating to proof of causation in alleged cases of drug-induced injury, principally in the UK, Europe and North America. In essence, it seeks to assess whether, by using probabilistic approaches, the courts may more accurately and efficiently determine the cause of adverse reactions contentiously associated with drugs.

A multitude of new drugs has emerged, as a harvest of the scientific and technological revolution in the twentieth century. It is therefore not surprising that scientific methods, including statistics, have been increasingly utilised to establish the cause of adverse reactions allegedly associated with drugs. Closely related to causation are the concepts of "risk" and "probability" of adverse reactions.

Whenever a new drug is licensed, not many more than 2,000 patients will have been screened for possible adverse effects, but many important and potentially fatal effects can be missed in these pre-licensing clinical trials. The drug manufacturers are thus vulnerable to the so-called "development risks" of undiscoverable defects in medicinal products causing dangerous side effects, which may only emerge after general distribution to patients.

The book examines several topics concerning product liability, causation and medicinal products. The legal and probability aspects of causation are explored in Chapter 1, including the role of causation in negligence in the context of medicinal products, the position surrounding drug injuries to unborn children, such as thalidomide, and the effect of the EC Product Liability Directive, together with its UK implementing statute, the Consumer Protection Act 1987. Alternative approaches to the problem of causation are examined from a probability perspective, namely (1) the imposition of liability in proportion to the probability of causation by a single medicinal product and (2) compensation for loss of a chance of recovery or loss of a chance of avoiding damage in cases involving medicinal products. The chapter concludes with an attempt to support probabilistic approaches to causation by the use of a statistical device, known as the Baye's Theorem, to help generate more certainty in the process of attributing cause.

In four case studies (DES, Bendectin, vaccine damage and "Gulf War Syndrome"), the deficiences of orthodox approaches to causation are revealed. Using the example of Diethylstilbestrol (DES), Chapter 2 examines the difficulties of causal link when the effects occur many years after administration of the drug. DES was used as an œstrogenic hormone for the prevention of miscarriage in early pregnancy. It was discovered to cause vaginal cancer in adolescence or young adulthood in daughters who were fœtuses *in utero* at the time their mothers had been administered the drug. The defect was of a latent nature, occurring between 12 and 25 years after birth, and this increased the difficulties of establishing an actual causal link with DES and of distinguishing it from illnesses of natural origin. The difficulties are addressed when traditional and alternative causation solutions are used to deal with a drug of this nature, including the problem of identifying the specific manufacturer of DES.

In contrast to the overwhelming epidemiological evidence establishing causality with thalidomide and, to a lesser extent, with DES is the case study of Bendectin (Debendox), an anti-nausea drug used in early pregnancy which was claimed to be associated with congenital birth defects. The evidence supporting such claims was weak and highly controversial. On the basis of this dilemma, Chapter 3 explores the increasing importance of using scientific evidence in ascertaining causation, including the role and choice of the expert witness.

Difficulties in establishing causation are most prominent in cases involving alleged damage caused by vaccines. The position is further complicated by the fact that such medicinal products have not only been actively promoted by government as a prophylactic measure for the individual, but also have been recommended for the benefit of the community at large. Chapter 4 compares the difficulties in establishing causation in vaccine damage litigation in the UK, Republic of Ireland, Canada and the USA. There are considerable differences between the American approaches and those of the other three countries to this difficult social and legal problem.

Chapter 5 focuses on an ongoing case study into the possible link between medicinal products and adverse effects suffered by veterans of the Gulf War (the so-called "Gulf War Syndrome"). It illustrates the importance of the use of epidemiological evidence in allocating causative responsibility.

Any analysis of product liability and drugs cannot be divorced from the economic issues. Chapter 6 thus undertakes an economic analysis of causation and medicinal products in both theory and practice to address the hypothesis that a probabilistic approach to causation and drugs promotes economic efficiency.

Closely related to the issue of economics, product liability and medicinal products is the question of liability for undiscoverable defects. The role of the development risk defence of the Consumer Protection Act 1987 in denying liability *irrespective* of causation is examined in Chapter 7. This chapter attempts to distinguish, first, between "probabilistic risk", i.e. the probability of a drug causing an adverse effect in an individual patient, and another form of risk, "development risk", *viz.* the inherent risk of a defective product being undiscoverable at the time of supply. It then proceeds to examine the development risk defence in the context of drugs associated with adverse reactions and tries to predict the way that courts might resolve such cases.

A sustained argument is presented throughout Chapters 1 to 7 in favour of according greater weight to epidemiological evidence in ascertaining causation.

Chapter 8 confronts the various possible scenarios which could emerge as a result of the application of epidemiological approaches to establishing causation. The question is addressed whether injury costs would be reduced or increased in such circumstances, at the same time as considering the effect of the development risk defence on costs, irrespective of the establishment of causal link. Where large injury costs have been sustained in product liability litigation by a pharmaceutical company, in circumstances where the hurdles of causation, defectiveness and the defence have been overcome by the plaintiff, the potential role of intellectual property rights in protecting innovation through an increase in patent life is addressed.

It is hoped that the book makes a contribution to the resolution of the legal problems in this complex area of tort law. In a wider sphere, it aims to contribute to the continuing debate concerning the importance of scientific evidence involving controversies which bestride both medical and legal disciplines.

1

Causation and Medicinal Products: A Legal and Probability Analysis

1. INTRODUCTION

This chapter[1] proposes to examine causation and medicinal products from both a legal and a probability perspective. First, a critical analysis is made of the role of causation in negligence in the context of medicinal products, as reflected in case law and the Congenital Disabilities (Civil Liability) Act 1976. Secondly, there is a discussion of the effect of the EC Product Liability Directive and its implementing statute, the Consumer Protection Act 1987, in relation to causation. Thirdly, alternative approaches to the causation problem are looked at from a probability perspective, namely the imposition of liability in proportion to the probability of causation by a single medicinal product in each case and the idea of compensation for loss of a chance of recovery or avoiding loss in cases involving medicinal products.

The chapter recognises the problematic nature of statistics that are not personal to the particular individual in each case, and it concludes with an attempt to re-examine the justification for probabilistic causation by the use of a statistical device, the Bayes' Theorem, to personalise statistics, so that a more accurate assessment can be made of the probability of a causal link between a drug and an injury in an individual case or class of cases before the court. It is suggested that such an approach may assist in establishing causal link in other drug-induced injury or medical negligence cases.

[1] This chap. is an expanded version of an article published by the author: R. Goldberg, "Causation and Medicinal Products. A Legal and Probability Analysis" [1996] *Consumer Law Journal* 57 and elements of R. Goldberg, "The Role of Scientific Evidence in the Assessment of Causation in Medicinal Product Liability Litigation: A Probabilistic and Economic Analysis" (1998) 1 *Current Legal Issues* 55.

2. THE ROLE OF CAUSATION IN NEGLIGENCE

(i) Importance of Causation in Medicinal Product Liability Litigation

In the context of actual decisions that have come before the courts in respect of causation and medicinal products[2] in negligence law,[3] the position presented from the point of view of the plaintiff is an unenviable one. The difficulties in proving causation are magnified in the context of medicinal products. As Teff and Munro have observed:

> "Drugs are always potentially dangerous due to their toxicity. They are often taken by people who are already ill and who may be unusually susceptible to further ailments. Unlike many other products, they may cause injury in unpredictable ways, depending on the individual user's constitution. They may not be taken according to the instructions. The user may be allergic to a particular drug. Alternatively, what appears to be an allergy may in fact be a toxic reaction."[4]

The practical importance of establishing causation in a medicinal product liability case is enormous. Causation, if proved, will probably lead to settlement or victory.[5] In *D and R* v. *Schering Chemicals*,[6] counsel for the plaintiffs obtained leave from Bingham J (as he then was) to discontinue actions alleging that, as a

[2] The term "medicinal product" is used in conformity with the definition in the Medicines Act 1968, s. 130(1). It is defined as a substance or an article (not being an instrument, apparatus or an appliance) which is used for administration to human beings or animals for a medicinal purpose. The definition encompasses drugs and biological products such as vaccines and blood products.

[3] It has been argued that negligence in the legal sense of a breach of a duty of care is in fact an element of causation: Harari, *The Place of Negligence in the Law of Torts* (Sydney: The Law Book Co. of Australia Pty. Ltd., 1962):

> "the statement that a man has caused damage always implies that he was under a duty of care and broke that duty, that is that he was negligent": *ibid.*, 55.

In this work, however, it will be submitted that the concept of causation is a complex but crucial element of both negligence liability and strict liability in respect of medicinal products. In one sense, therefore, the work is sympathetic to the view of Harari that liability in both negligence and strict liability "is based simply on causal principles": *ibid.*, 170.

[4] Teff and Munro, *Thalidomide: The Legal Aftermath* (Farnborough, Saxon House, 1976), 135–6: "[c]learly it is often harder to prove that one's injuries are due to an adverse drug reaction than that they have been caused by a faulty machine": Teff, "Regulation Under the Medicines Act 1968 : A Continuing Prescription for Health" (1984) 47 *MLR* 303, 322. Professor Teff also notes "[t]he synergistic effects of certain combinations (for example, barbiturates and alcohol, anti-histamines and cheese)": Teff, "Products Liability in the Pharmaceutical Industry at Common Law" (1974) 20 *McGill LJ* 102, 115. See below for further discussions of the problem of synergistic reactions.

[5] Mildred, "Representing the Plaintiff" in Howells (ed.), *Product Liability, Insurance and the Pharmaceutical Industry: An Anglo-American Comparison* (Manchester, Manchester University Press, 1991), 27. However, this may not necessarily be so. For example, in the HIV Haemophilia Litigation, although the causal agent of the infection was clear, i.e. HIV-infected blood fractions, the question still remained whether the provision of the product or its prescription by a doctor "*at the time the infection was caused*" was negligent: Mildred, "Class Actions", para. 147, in Division IIIA, Miller, *Product Liability and Safety Encyclopædia* (London, Butterworths, 1997).

[6] (2 July 1982, unreported).

result of the hormone pregnancy test drug Primodos taken by mothers during pregnancy, their children were born with serious congenital defects. The basis of Bingham J's decision was that, after an exchange of expert evidence, counsel for the plaintiffs concluded that on the evidence available the actions stood no reasonable prospect of establishing that the products were teratogenic as alleged.[7]

(ii) "But For" Test

It is clear that a person will not be subject to liability in tort unless it is shown that " 'but for' that person's tort, the plaintiff's loss would not have occurred [the 'but for' test]; or, in other words, the defendant's conduct was a necessary condition of the plaintiff's loss; or . . . the defendant's conduct caused or contributed to the plaintiff's damage".[8]

The "but for" test has been described by Lovell and Griffith Jones as "useless and circular" in operation in certain circumstances involving drugs and causation.[9] First, the drug may be the only operative cause of the adverse reaction. Secondly, the drug may have had "no appreciable influence" on the injuries which would have occurred in any event. Thirdly, there are cases where the drug has caused harm but it is not clear whether the drug is the only contributing cause.[10] In the last scenario the "but for" test would only prove circular, presumably because the patient may well have suffered the injury anyway. The court's task there would be to determine whether the other "causes" ought to be rejected, leaving the medicinal product as the legal cause.[11] It could be argued that the first scenario of Lovell and Griffith Jones is actually a classic vindication of the "but for" test, since but for the drug the adverse drug reaction would

7 (2 July 1982, unreported), *per* Bingham J at 2,3 of Official Transcript.

8 P. Cane, *Atiyah's Accidents Compensation and the Law* (5th edn., London, Dublin, Edinburgh, Butterworths, 1993), p94–5. Causation is a difficult term to define, principally due to the abstract nature of the concept. Nevertheless, Professor Walker has made such an attempt. He defines causation as:

> "The concept of relationship between two events based on the belief that they have not only happened fairly close in time and space but are related as cause and consequence in that the one has brought about or necessitated the happening of the other": Walker, *The Oxford Companion to Law* (Oxford, Clarendon Press, 1980), 192.

9 Lovell and Griffith Jones, " 'The Sins of the Fathers'—Tort Liability for Pre-Natal Injuries" (1974) 90 *LQR* 531, 536.

10 *Ibid.*: "[i]t is in situations where there are two independent factors, each being sufficient to produce the injury, that the test proves unsatisfactory": Strachan, "The Scope and Application of the 'But For' Causal Test" (1970) 33 *MLR* 386 at 391. The "but for" test's requirement of the identification of precise links with a particular defendant, and the prevention of recovery unless the factors linking to a particular defendant are essential to the onset of a condition, necessitate the existence of a detailed aetiology of the alleged disease, and this is often not available: Adeny, "The Challenge of Medical Uncertainty: Factual Causation in Anglo-American Toxic Tort Litigation" (1993) 19 *Monash University Law Review* 23, 29.

11 Lovell and Griffith Jones, n. 9 above, 536.

not have been caused, but it is unclear whether the test adds anything informative to what is already known. In the second scenario, where the injuries would have occurred in any event, the "but for" test is being used in a similar manner to that in *Barnett* v. *Chelsea & Kensington Hospital*[12] where the hospital, in refusing to treat a poisoned patient, was not a cause of the harm since the nature of the poison introduced into the patient's tea (i.e. arsenic) was such that he would have died anyway.[13] It has been argued, however, that this should not be treated as a ground for completely rejecting liability, but merely one for reducing damages.[14]

(iii) Representative Cases: *Bonnington Castings*; *McGhee*; *Kay*

Nevertheless, it has been submitted that difficulties of proof appear to have been reduced by the law seeming to require the plaintiff to prove only that his injury or damage was "more probably than not" caused by the defendant's negligence,[15] i.e. on a balance of probabilities the injury or damage was so caused.

Before the case of *Wilsher* v. *Essex AHA*,[16] a small number of House of Lords decisions had shaped the law in this area. In *Bonnington Castings* v. *Wardlaw*,[17] the House of Lords held that the onus of proof was on the pursuer to prove on a balance of probabilities that negligence or breach of duty caused or materially contributed to his injury.[18] This position was elaborated on in *McGhee* v. *National Coal Board*.[19]

In *McGhee*, the pursuer was sent by his employers (the defenders) to clean out brick kilns, and in the process was exposed to clouds of abrasive brick dust. The defenders failed to provide washing facilities at the works, with the result that the pursuer had to cycle home every evening caked in brick dust. The pursuer contracted dermatitis from the dust and the defenders' failure to provide washing facilities was held to be negligent. Although the defenders admitted

[12] [1969] 1 QB 428, 434, 439.

[13] See also the case of *Rich* v. *Pierpont* (1862) 3 F & F 35, where Erle CJ, in summing up the case to the jury, stated that the wrongful administration of tartaric acid to a pregnant woman "turned out to be of no consequence": *ibid.*, 40. *Barnett* was upheld in *Robinson* v. *Post Office* [1974] 1 WLR 1176 where Orr LJ, delivering the judgment, held that although a doctor had been negligent in not following the correct dose procedure for administering a test dose of anti-tetanus serum, even if the test dose had been administered there would have been no observable reaction in the patient, and so the doctor would have gone on to administer the injection: *ibid.*, 1188. In *Vernon* v. *Bloomsbury Health Authority* [1995] 6 Med. LR 297, Tucker J held that even if the plaintiff had found that the defendants had been negligent in failing to monitor his treatment while being administered gentamicin, further assays would probably not have recorded any danger signals of ototoxicity: *ibid.*, 307.

[14] P. Cane, *Atiyah's Accidents, Compensation and the Law* (4th edn., London, Weidenfeld & Nicolson, 1987), 101.

[15] See Cane, n. 8 above, 96 and *Wilsher* v. *Essex AHA* [1988] 1 AC 1074.

[16] [1988] 1 AC 1074.

[17] [1956] AC 613.

[18] *Ibid.*, 620, *per* Lord Reid.

[19] [1973] 1 WLR 1 (HL).

negligence they contended that their failure had not been proved to have caused the pursuer's dermatitis. The pursuer's expert witness was unable to confirm that the pursuer would not have contracted dermatitis if he had been able to wash the dust off, but was able to state that the absence of washing facilities had materially increased the risk of disease. The House of Lords held that it was sufficient for a pursuer to show that the defender's breach of duty *materially increased the risk* of injury, even though there were other factors, for which the defender was not responsible, which had contributed to the injury,[20] and that there was no difference in practice between materially increasing the risk of harm and materially contributing to that harm.[21] Stapleton regards the situation in which *McGhee* is able to come into operation as being when the relative contributions of risk of the defendant's fault and the background risk are inassessable and when the mechanism of an effect such as a disease is unknown, i.e. where there is an "evidential gap".[22] For example, there may be two sources of risk independently capable of producing a particular outcome, e.g. one being a drug (say an oral contraceptive), another being a human risk factor (obesity) to varying degrees of severity. However, Stapleton's criticism of *McGhee* is that the defenders had to pay for injuries which they had not been shown to have caused on the balance of probabilities. In *McGhee* the gist of the claim was formulated in terms of the entire outcome, whilst the causation requirement that the pursuer is asked to satisfy is limited only to a fraction of that gist damage. The purseur is able to recover for a part of the overall injury to which he has been unable on a balance of probabilities to show a causal connection.[23] Notwithstanding this criticism, *McGhee* has been defended as a justifiable tool in the context of the difficulties of proving causation in medicinal product liability cases provided there is *prima facie* evidence about the creation of a risk, a duty of care is owed by the defenders to the pursuer and a predicted harm to the pursuer has occurred.[24] The case is also defended on the ground that a profit-making pharmaceutical company is better able to carry and redistribute the cost of accidents than the injured user of a product.[25]

[20] [1973] 1 WLR 1 (HL), *per* Lord Salmon at 12.

[21] *Ibid.*, *per* Lord Reid at 5 and *per* Lord Salmon at 12–13; see Weinreb, "A Step Forward in Factual Causation" (1975) 38 *MLR* 518, 523.

[22] Stapleton, "The Gist of Negligence Part II: The Relationship Between Damage and Causation" (1988) 104 *LQR* 389, 401, 402.

[23] *Ibid.*, 404, 405.

[24] Hutchinson and Hodgson, "Who's Zoomin' Who? Comments on Liability for Pharmaceutical Products in Canada" in Howells, n. 5 above, 104.

[25] *Ibid.* See also the Canadian case of *Buchan* v. *Ortho Pharmaceutical (Canada) Ltd* (1986) 25 DLR (4th) 658 where the Ontario CA refused to review the trial judge's finding that Mrs Buchan's use of oral contraceptives probably caused or, at least, materially contributed to her stroke; cf the Scottish case, *Ingram* v. *Ritchie*, 1989 GWD 27–1217 (no convincing causal connection between pill and non-hæmorrhagic stroke suffered after six days of beginning first course of pills). Note also the unreported decision of *Vadera* v. *Shaw* (Case No. 95/NJ/1196, QBD (unreported)), where Alliot J held, in the light of statistical evidence, that an oral contraceptive (Logynon) did not cause or materially contribute to the plaintiff's stroke. I am grateful to Mr Ian Dodds-Smith, Cameron McKenna, for providing me with a copy of the draft judgment in this case.

In *McGhee*, Lord Wilberforce[26] appeared to reverse the burden of proof of causation. He said that in cases where neither the pursuer nor the defender could prove the precise causes of a disease, and where the pursuer had proved that the defender had failed to observe a precaution designed to safeguard the pursuer against a particular risk of injury and that injury materialised, *it was for the defender to prove that the injury did not result from his negligence*. It has been stated that this arrangement was suitable when the risk was the creation of one party alone and medical or scientific evidence was not clearly linked to a single defendant.[27] However, the applicability of the concept where a number of potential multifactorial causes were responsible for the risk in question but only one or some had caused the damage was ruled out by Lord Bridge in *Wilsher* v. *Essex AHA*[28] who, *a fortiori*, rejected Lord Wilberforce's concept in all circumstances.[29] The limitations of *McGhee* are apparent when it is not known that a drug is capable of causing or aggravating a particular reaction.[30] In *Kay* v. *Ayrshire and Arran Health Board*,[31] Mr Kay's son went to a hospital managed by the respondent health authority suffering from pneumococcal meningitis. In the course of treatment he was administered with a gross overdose of penicillin and became deaf. Evidence that the penicillin itself would damage the auditory nerve was rejected. No known case existed where deafness had been caused by a penicillin overdose but very many where deafness had been caused by meningitis. The issue was whether the overdose was a cause of his deafness. The House of Lords held, distinguishing *McGhee* v. *National Coal Board*, that where two competing causes of damage existed (meningitis and the overdose of penicillin) the law would not presume that the wrongful act (overdose) was responsible if it was not proved that it was an accepted fact that the wrongful

[26] [1973] 1 WLR 1 at 6.

[27] Newdick, "Strict Liability for Defective Drugs in the Pharmaceutical Industry" (1985) 101 *LQR* 405 at 426. Weinreb notes that materially increasing the risk and materially contributing to the injury were two elements that were traditionally distinct in factual causation but that the HL elided the two elements: Weinreb, "A Step Forward in Factual Causation" (1975) 38 *MLR* 518 at 523. He also states that it is unlikely that the HL in *McGhee* adopted the "incredible position" that the defender would have been liable even if he had proved that his conduct had not in fact caused the injury. Such an incredible position transpired in the American case of *Hymowitz* v. *Eli Lilly*, 541 NYS 2d 941 (CA 1989) at 950. A lack of universal and uniform allocation of the onus of proof indicates that such an allocation is subject to policy and fairness considerations: Weinreb, above, at 528. Where evidence one way or the other on causation is unavailable, Hart and Honoré suggest that rules in respect of the incidence of the burden of proof embody issues of legal policy since such rules are determinative where legal decision making is at its most difficult: H. L. A. Hart and A. Honoré, *Causation in the law* (Oxford, Clarendon Press, 1985), pp. liii, liv.

[28] [1988] 1 AC 1074. The HL has recently reaffirmed its rejection of the reversal of the burden of proof of causation in *Pickford* v. *Imperial Chemical Industries plc* [1998] 1 WLR 1189 (HL), where it held that the onus was on the plaintiff to prove that the cause she alleged was the correct one. Although it was open for the defendants to lead evidence in rebuttal, they did not have to do so: *ibid.*, 1199–1201 *per* Lord Hope of Craighead.

[29] [1988] 1 AC 1074, 1087.

[30] See Jones, *Medical Negligence* (2nd edn., London, Sweet & Maxwell, 1996), 416.

[31] [1987] 2 All ER 417 (HL).

act was capable of causing or aggravating such damage and it had not been so proved.[32] This case has been subject to trenchant criticism.[33]

The Law Lords rejected the Lord Ordinary's view in the Court of Session that the boy (Kay) had stood a good chance of recovery on admission to the hospital. Such evidence, according to Lord Griffiths, "was based on a mistaken view of the efficacy of the drug" that the pursuer's son "had been given at an early stage in the illness and a mistaken belief as to the date upon which the glucose present in the cerebro spinal fluid was at an abnormal level".[34] A low level of glucose early in the disease's development was indicative of the relative severity of the attack and was correlated with residual deafness caused by meningitis, but the records for the day when the disease had reached its peak were missing.[35] A normal level was recorded just before the administration of the overdose (29 November) and on 30 November the glucose level was normal. The doctor did not recall what the sugar level had been on the 28th, "but it may be inferred that it was below the normal level".[36] This has been heavily criticised as "*ex post facto* reasoning"[37] and uncommendable, being based on the fact that the patient suffered deafness and that it could not have been caused by the penicillin. Also, "no important significance" could reasonably be attached to the fact that the pursuer's son was two years and five months old at the material time, in spite of the prospects for full recovery from meningitis being better in the age band between six months and 22 years.[38] Such a negligence claim is unlikely to succeed in similar circumstances,[39] but a possibility was clearly left open that if it was shown that a drug was capable of causing or aggravating damage in the face of competing causes, the court might be willing to presume in favour of the plaintiff.[40]

(iv) Reversal of Burden of Proof in Diethylstilbestrol (DES) Cases

A parallel response, albeit to a different causal problem, has developed in the United States of reversing the burden of proof in cases of difficulty in identifying which manufacturer's product was used; the burden is imposed on each manufacturer of showing on the balance of probabilities that the product used

32 [1987] 2 All ER 417 (HL), *per* Lord Griffiths at 422.
33 See Logie, "Proof of Causation in Medical Negligence Cases", 1988 SLT (News) 25.
34 [1987] 2 All ER 417, 422.
35 *Ibid.*, *per* Lord Keith at 420.
36 *Ibid.*
37 Logie, n. 33 above, 26.
38 [1987] 2 All ER 417, *per* Lord Keith at 420; Logie, n. 33 above, 26,27.
39 *Ibid.*, 27.
40 Hutchinson and Hodgson, n. 24 above, 102; cf Mildred, n. 5 above, 30, who suggests that *McGhee* survives where there is only one possible cause of injury, i.e. *McGhee* would survive when a manufacturer supplied a patient with a product which on the balance of probabilities caused or materially contributed to the adverse drug reaction and there was no other identifiable cause. This seems to ignore the potential scenario of competing causes in the *Kay* decision.

was not his own. In the absence of proof, damages are apportioned on the basis of the market share of the sales of the particular compound in question. This approach was pioneered in the Diethylstilbestrol (DES) cases. DES, which was used as an œstrogenic hormone, is possibly the classic paradigm of the potential for generational drug-induced defects. The principal established adverse drug reaction associated with DES is that of second-generation vaginal adenosis and vaginal clear cell adenocarcinoma. A causal link between DES and vaginal adenocarcinoma and adenosis has been established for over 20 years.[41]

In respect of second-generation vaginal adenosis and vaginal clear cell adenocarcinoma, problems in such cases have been about establishing liability in the absence of knowledge of the identity of the manufacturer. Unlike *McGhee*, factual causation was not disputed in the DES cases, but what became an issue was the identification of the particular manufacturer of the product and a causal link between it and the damage. The American courts dispensed with traditional causation and invariably resorted to market share liability as the remedy, even in circumstances where a pharmaceutical company could show that its DES product did not cause the particular plaintiff's injury since it had not been used.[42]

[41] Herbst, Ulfelder and Poskanzer, "Adenocarcinoma of the Vagina. Association of Maternal Stilbestrol Therapy with Tumour Appearance in Young Women", 284 *N Eng. J Med.* 878, at 878, 879 (1971). In the Herbst study, it was found that seven out of eight of the mothers of patients with vaginal adenocarcinoma had been treated with diethylstilbestrol commenced during the first trimester of pregnancy. The maternal ingestion of stilbestrol during early pregnancy was found to have enhanced the risk of vaginal adenocarcinoma, developing years later in the offspring who were exposed as foetuses in utero at the time their mothers were administered the drug.

[42] See the discussion of market share liability and the American cases of *Sindell* v. *Abbott Laboratories*, 26 Cal. 3d 588, 607 P 2d 924 (1980) and *Hymowitz* v. *Eli Lilly*, 541 NYS 2d 941 (CA 1989), in Chap. 2. Many American courts, however, have rejected the *Sindell* approach and its progeny as being inconsistent with liability based on fault, e.g. the highest courts of Missouri and Iowa: *Zafft* v. *Eli Lilly and Co.*, 676 SW 2d 241 (Mo. banc 1984) and *Mulcahy* v. *Eli Lilly & Co.*, 386 NW 2d 67 (Iowa 1986). Market share liability has been excluded from applying to cases involving vaccines by the NJ Sup. Ct. in *Shackil* v. *Lederle Laboratories*, 561 A 2d 511, 528 (NJ 1989). A ceasefire on the application of market share liability to non-DES products appears to have been broken with its application by the Hawaiian Sup. Ct. to Factor VIII in *Smith* v. *Cutter Biological Inc.*, 823 P 2d 717, 729 (Hawaii 1991). In the recent Dutch DES decision of *Van Ballegooijen* v. *Bayer Nederland BV* (Rvdw 1992, No 219), the Dutch Sup. Ct. accepted the plaintiffs' theory of alternative causation liability (Section 3.71 of the decision, as numbered by the Sup. Ct.), rejected market share liability (sect. 3.8) and imposed liability for all injuries caused by DES on every DES producer notwithstanding the fact that each producer could not have caused all the damages of which it was made liable (sect. 3.73). See Teulings, Note, "DES and Market Share Liability in the Netherlands" (1994) 110 *LQR* 228; Bergkamp, "Compensating Personal Injuries Caused by DES: 'No Causation Liability' in the Netherlands", World Pharmaceuticals Report, BNA International Inc., London, Jan. 1993; Hondius, "A Dutch DES Case: Pharmaceutical Producers Jointly and Severally Liable" [1994] *Consum. LJ* 40; Dodds-Smith and Spencer, "Product Liability for Medicinal Products" in Powers and Harris (eds.) *Medical Negligence* (2nd edn., London, Butterworths, 1994), 512, 513. Interestingly, the German Ministry of Justice has noted problems of causation, including the burden of proof of causation, in respect of litigation concerning HIV infection of hæmophiliacs by contaminated blood products, a problem germane to pharmaceuticals. This is due to the fact that hæmophiliacs were given blood products over a period of time from a number of manufacturers. It is believed to be impossible to identify whether and which of the products were contaminated. There has been a consequent ongoing debate in Germany over where the burden of proof of causation should rest: Hodges, *Report for the Commission of the European Communities on the Application of Directive 85/374/EEC on Liabilty for Defective Products* (London, McKenna & Co, 1994).

(v) Competing Causes: Benzodiazepine Litigation; *Wilsher*

The question of possible competing causes has specific relevance to medicinal product liability cases involving competing drugs with potentially similar adverse drug reactions and in cases involving other potential causes. For example, in cases involving the alleged dependence effects of Benzodiazepines, it is most likely that some of the patients have consumed other drugs such as anti-depressants and other substances such as alcohol, which makes the causal connection between the Benzodiazepine and the alleged adverse drug reaction harder to ascertain.[43] Such difficulties of proving causation in the Benzodiazepine litigation were recently noted by the Court of Appeal in an appeal by the plaintiffs against prescribers of these drugs from the judgment of Ian Kennedy J, who had struck out their actions against prescribers of these drugs, on the basis that they were vexatious and an abuse of the process of the court.[44] Stuart-Smith LJ observed[45] that there were "very considerable problems on causation". Such problems involved "distinguishing between the effects of the drug and the underlying condition for which it was prescribed, the problems caused by previous addiction to Benzodiazepine drugs other than those prescribed by the defendants, and distinguishing between symptoms due to the drugs, or in some cases, other drugs or excess alcohol, and the fact that many plaintiffs may suffer at least some withdrawal symptoms in any event".[46]

In a similar appeal, recently brought against the manufacturers of Benzodiazepines (John Wyeth & Brother Ltd (Wyeth) and Roche Products Ltd (Roche)) from the judgment of Ian Kennedy J in which he struck out group actions against Wyeth and Roche, again on the basis that there was an abuse of process of the court and for want of prosecution, further reference was made to the difficulty of proving causation in these actions.[47] In dismissing the appeal, Stuart-Smith LJ continued to note the difficulties of causation as presenting "formidable problems" in prosecuting the group action.[48]

[43] The complications of proving the cause of drug-induced injury may be aggravated by inadequate notification of side-effects by practitioners.E.g. it has been said that the delay in ascertaining a causal link between thalidomide and phocomelia was responsible for the delay in the drug's withdrawal from the market. McLean, "Ante-Natal Injuries" in McLean (ed.), *Legal Issues in Medicine* (Aldershot, Gower, 1981), 159. On the other hand it can be said that there was no organisation at that time established for voluntary notification of side-effects. The Yellow Card system for such voluntary notification was brought about in 1964 with the establishment of the Committee On Safety of Drugs, something which came into being only *as a result of* the thalidomide tragedy and not before it. Moreover, the findings of phocomelia were so rare and were such a gross escalation of what was a very rare natural phenomenon that it required a period of time to establish a causal link between thalidomide and phocomelia.

[44] *A B and others* v. *John Wyeth & Brother Ltd and others (No 2)* [1994] 5 Med. LR 149.

[45] *Ibid.*, at 153.

[46] *Ibid.*

[47] *A B and others* v. *John Wyeth & Brother Ltd*; *A B and others* v. *Roche Products Ltd* (LEXIS, 13 Dec. 1996).

[48] He observed: "[s]o far as causation is concerned there were also likely to be formidable problems. Few if any of the plaintiffs had evidence from the general practitioners that they would have

Wilsher v. *Essex AHA*[49] was a similar case of an evidential gap to *McGhee*,[50] where the mechanism was unknown and not all sources of risk were under the defendant's control; indeed, there were a number of possible competing causes. In such circumstances it must be shown that the breach of duty, on a balance of probabilities, was an operative cause of the loss. In *Wilsher*, the plaintiff was born prematurely suffering from various illnesses including oxygen deficiency. He was incorrectly catheterised (venous rather than arterial) as a result of negligence and excess oxygen was administered. The baby was subsequently found to be suffering from an incurable condition of the retina (retrolental fibroplasia (RLF)) resulting in near blindness. RLF could have been caused by excess oxygen tension, but could also have been caused by any of five other conditions from which he was suffering, which were common in prematurity. The House of Lords held[51] that *McGhee* v. *National Coal Board* laid down no new principle of law since the burden remained on the plaintiff to prove the causal link between the defendant's negligence and his injury, and that there had been no clear finding of fact by the trial judge in *Wilshire* that the excess oxygen administered to the plaintiff caused or materially contributed to the plaintiff's retinal condition. As a matter of law it was not open for the onus to be shifted onto the defendants to show that the excess volume of oxygen did not cause or materially contribute to the blindness.[52] There was "no satisfactory evidence"[53] that excess oxygen was more likely than any of the other possible causative agents to have caused or to have materially contributed to the RLF.

Lord Bridge regarded *McGhee* as inferring, as a matter of common sense, cumulative causation.[54] It has been said that the mere proof of an increased risk

taken a different course if the defendant had given more adequate advice and warnings. Clinical experience is often a major reason for prescribing drugs. The symptoms alleged to be caused by Benzodiazepine addiction or withdrawal are not easily distinguishable from the underlying or endogenous condition that gave rise to the prescription. In those cases which Wyeth investigated, where they were able to trace the general practitioner concerned, there were marked discrepancies between the recollection of the plaintiff and the complaints and treatment recorded by the doctors. Not infrequently there were problems of alcohol or drug abuse, or the ingestion of other drugs which could cause similar symptoms. After 1985 when brand name drugs of this sort became a thing of the past in the NHS, there is the difficulty of proving that the drug ingested was manufactured by one of the defendants": *ibid.*

49 [1988] 1 AC 1074.

50 Stapleton, n. 22 above, 401, 403–407.

51 [1988] 1 AC 1074, 1090–1. It is now appreciably clear that in circumstances where there is more than one potential cause, the correct test of causation is the material contribution test: *Page* v. *Smith* (No 2) [1996] 1 WLR 855, 857–8, 863, *per* Sir Thomas Bingham MR.

52 [1988] 1 AC 1074, 1087.

53 *Ibid.*, at 1091, quoting Sir Nicolas Browne-Wilkinson V-C in the CA [1987] QB 730, 779.

54 [1988] 1 AC 1074 at 1088; cumulative causation is where both sources in aggregate cause the effect: Stapleton, n. 22 above, 401. Stapleton argues that the inference could equally have been in favour of an alternative cause mechanism where the outcome was produced by one of the sources alone: *ibid.*, 401, 404. In *Basko* v. *Sterling Drug Co.*, 416 F 2d 417 (1969), the plaintiff was treated with three drugs for eight years for a skin disease, lupus erythematosus. The drugs were sold under the trade names Avalen, Atabrine and Triquin. The plaintiff began experiencing blurring of her vision having been prescribed the drugs for three years. After ceasing taking the drug for a period of four years, her vision deteriorated badly. The plaintiff suffered from chloroquine retinopathy and

of an injury does not itself establish causation, and this is probably true, but it has been argued that *Wilsher* "did not disturb the doctrinal fact that proof of a substantial increase in risk does not only lead to evidence of causation but actually amounts to proof of causation".[55] It thus appears that the basic principles of *McGhee* (other than the reversal of the burden of proof) may well have remained intact since *Wilsher*. In the context of an evidential gap of unassessability of relative contribution of risk and a lack of knowledge of a mechanism of an effect, *McGhee* may well continue to operate to ameliorate the difficulties of establishing proof of causation. However, it is also arguable that the future significance of *McGhee* is open to doubt and it will, at the very least, be applied less frequently.[56]

(vi) Omission, Failure to Warn and Causation

The complex issues in cases involving tort and causation with medicinal products is that an adverse drug reaction may often be due to an omission[57] rather than a positive act.[58] Regarding an omission, the plaintiff would claim that the manufacturer failed to issue warnings on the product label or in the data sheet supplied to GPs.[59] It would be necessary for the plaintiff to show that she would

became almost blind. This was thought to be an idiosyncratic side-effect of drugs made from chloroquine and both Avalen and Triquin were made from chloroquine: *ibid.*, 419–20. The US CA, Second Circuit, held that where it was assumed that the plaintiff's blindness could have been caused by either Avalen or Triquin and where the jury could arguably have found a breach of duty in respect of Triquin but not Avalen, the defendant's negligence in respect of Triquin would be found, if the assumption was correct, to be a substantial factor in bringing the blindness about: *ibid.*, 430. Note that Stapleton (Stapleton, "Law, Causation and Common Sense" (1988) 8 *OJLS* 111, 126) describes the case of *Basko* as one of multiple cumulative causation, similar to *Bonnington Castings* v. *Wardlaw* [1956] 1 AC 613, whereas Hart and Honoré discuss it as a case of additional causation: Hart and Honoré, n. 27 above, 235–6. Stapleton states that *Basko* only qualifies as additional causation if one makes "the added assumption that the retina was *ruined* and that each drug was sufficient to achieve *that* result" (author's italics): Stapleton, above, 126. It is submitted, however, that it was the Court that assumed that the plaintiff's blindness in that case could have been caused by either Avalen or Triquin: *Basko* v. *Sterling Drug Co.*, 416 F 2d 417, 430 (1969). In reality, it could be because of additional causation, cumulative causation, a synergistic reaction or multiple possible causes, including lupus erythematosus.

[55] Hutchinson and Hodgson, n. 24 above, 103.

[56] Grubb, "Causation and Medical Negligence" (1988) 47 *Camb. LJ* 350, 352. It has been held that where the plaintiff's case is that because of delay he is worse off, and he seeks to obtain damages for loss of amenity by contending that a delay caused a general increment in injury, it is not sufficient to show that delay materially increased the risk of injury or that delay could cause injury. The plaintiff had to prove that damage was actually caused, i.e. that delay caused the injury. It was insufficient to show a general increment from the delay since the plaintiff had to prove "some measurable damage": *Tahir* v. *Haringey Health Authority* [1998] Lloyd's Rep. Med. 104, 108 *per* Otton LJ. See also *Taylor* v *West Kent Health Authority* [1997] 8 Med LR 251, 257.

[57] The "but for" test leads to difficulties in the case of omissions: Cane, n. 8 above, 98.

[58] Kvjatkovski, "Obstacles Facing Victims of Drug-Induced Injuries in Civil Litigation, with Particular Reference to Users of Minor Tranquillisers" (unpublished), 18.

[59] Note the fact that patient information is compulsory in the EC: Council Dir. 92/27/EEC on the labelling of medicinal products for human use and package leaflets ([1992] OJ L113/8) as

have followed the warning if it had been provided.[60] With prescription drugs, in Canada it is presumed that a reasonable doctor would not ignore an adequate warning or fail to disclose a material risk or otherwise act negligently.[61] However, in an unreported judgment of Ian Kennedy J in the English Benzodiazepine litigation, it was decided that, although evidence of the effect of a different warning on a reasonable practitioner might not be strictly inadmissible, such evidence would be given less weight than evidence directed to the individual circumstances of the case.[62] This seems to suggest that the plaintiff may be required to produce *subjective* evidence of what her actual doctor would have done in the individual circumstances.[63]

implemented by The Medicines (Labelling) Amendment Regs. 1992 (Sl 1992 3273) and the Medicines (Leaflets) Amendment Regs. 1992 (Sl 1992 3274). The labelling dir. establishes minimum requirements for the labelling of packages and containers of medicinal products and for the form and content of leaflets supplied with medicinal products: see Roche, "The Advertising Labelling, Classification & Distribution Directives", 7th Annual Canadian Law Conference, "Pharmaceuticals and the Law: European, US & Canadian Developments", London, Nov. 1992, 3. To some extent these requirements will overrule the significance of the learned intermediary rule, i.e. that the duty of a manufacturer to supply information about a medicinal product is discharged by providing the relevant information to a responsible intermediary: *Kuback* v. *Hollands* [1937] 3 All ER 907; *Holmes* v. *Ashford and Others* [1950] 2 All ER 76 (CA); Miller and Lovell, *Product Liability* (London, Butterworths, 1977), 245–6; Forte, "Medical Products Liability", in McLean (ed.), *Legal Issues in Medicine* (Aldershot, Gower, 1981), 72; *Buchan* v. *Ortho Pharmaceutical (Canada) Ltd* (1986) 25 DLR (4th) 658 at 669, 670, *per* Robins JA; *H* v. *The Royal Alexandra Hospital for Children and the Commonwealth Serum Laboratories Commission and the Australian Red Cross (NSW Division)* (SC of NSW) (1990) 1 Med. LR 297. It has been submitted by Hart and Honoré that this has little bearing on causation principles in negligence: Hart and Honoré, n. 27 above, 150. See, *per contra*, Jones, n. 30 above, 425–6.

60 The burden of proof lies on the plaintiff in such circumstances: *McWilliams* v. *Sir William Arrol & Co.* [1962] 1 WLR 295, 306, (HL), *per* Lord Reid. In *Goorkani* v. *Tayside Health Board*, 1991 SLT 94, Goorkani suffered from Behcet's disease and lost the sight of one eye. When the other eye became infected he was treated with a drug to prevent deterioration of that eye. This drug in the longer term had a risk of infertility. His doctor did not warn him that the drug carried such a risk of infertility. Goorkani became infertile. Lord Cameron of Lochbroom held that the doctor had failed in his duty of care to warn the patient of the risk of infertility arising from the extended course of treatment with the drug: *ibid.*, 95. However, he was not satisfied that had the patient been so warned, any different course of treatment would have taken place. Thus damages as a consequence of failure to warn were restricted to the degree of distress and anxiety which arose through the discovery of the possibility that the patient was infertile in 1983 and the length of time during which the uncertainty remained, together with the shock and anger at the discovery of his infertility and the frustration which that discovery brought to the marital relationship. Effectively, *Goorkani* gives damages for the fact of learning of the infertililty without being forewarned, not for becoming infertile. See Blackie, Book Review, Jackson, Powell and others, *Professional Negligence* (3rd edn., London, Sweet & Maxwell, 1992), 1992 SLT (News) 253.

61 *Buchan* v. *Ortho Pharmaceutical (Canada)* (1986) 25 DLR (4th) 658, 682 (Ont. CA).

62 Mildred, "Class Actions", n. 5 above, 151–60.

63 In *H* v. *The Royal Alexandra Hospital for Children* [1990] Med LR 297 (NSWSC), Badgery-Parker J held that the second and third defendants, i.e. the manufacturers of concentrate and creoprecipatate of anti-hæmophilic factor (AHF), were negligent in 1983 in failing to warn of the risk of AIDS from the AHF. However, the warning would have no effect on the attitude of the doctors to the use of the products for treatment of a hæmophiliac with a joint bleed. The doctors in question were aware of the risks of transmission of AIDS and had already taken it into account. Thus failure to warn was not a cause of the plaintiff's infection with the HIV virus: *ibid.*, 317. See also *Gregory* v. *Pembrokeshire HA* [1989] 1 Med LR 81, 85–7.

(vii) Summary

It thus appears that the traditional negligence position surrounding causation and medicinal products presents a scenario to the effect that the causation hurdle will be almost impossible to overcome in the majority of cases. The suggested approach of Hutchinson and Hodgson,[64] that of awarding a proportion of damages to plaintiffs equivalent to the extent that a defendant increased a risk[65] seems potentially workable in tort but it appears to amount to an elision of traditional tort principles. If this solution is equivalent to the reformulation of the gist of the action by Stapleton then it may be fraught with the difficulty that the solution will not operate when the combined background risk and the defendant's negligent act are synergistic.[66] It would seem that we may only be left with the support of *McGhee* v. *National Coal Board*[67] and the establishment of a material increase in risk/material contribution analysis in cases where there is an evidential gap. Strictly this could be ruled out under the Stapleton analysis without an acceptance of the severance of the traditional link between damage on which the causation issue operates (a *proportion* of the gist damage in *McGhee*) and damage forming the gist of the action (ie the entire damage).[68]

It should be noted, however, that in *Snell* v. *Farrell*,[69] the Supreme Court of Canada has taken the view that when relevant facts lie particularly within the knowledge of the defendant, the drawing of an inference of causation from little affirmative evidence presented by the plaintiff is justified in the absence of evidence to the contrary.[70] The Supreme Court indicated that if it was convinced that the defendants were escaping liability under currently applied principles, it would have no hesitation in adopting a test that the plaintiff prove

[64] Hutchinson and Hodgson, n. 24 above, 104, 105.

[65] See below. See also the discounting of damages in the Canadian case of *Janiak* v. *Ippolito* (1985) 16 DLR (4th) 1; Hudson, "Mitigation and Refusal of Medical Treatment Again" (1986) 49 *MLR* 381.

[66] Stapleton, n. 22 above, 390. See below.

[67] [1973] 1 WLR 1 (HL).

[68] N. 22 above, 405. Stapleton suggests that acceptance of such a severance may have been the intention of the HL in *Bonnington Castings* v. *Wardlaw* [1956] AC 613 but that very little evidence was addressed on the issue: n. 22 above, 406. She also states that apart from a short passage in Lord Keith's judgment in *Bonnington Castings* there was "little to indicate that such a startling doctrine [as material contribution] was being formulated": *ibid.*, n.39. It is submitted that dicta of Lord Reid ([1956] AC 613, 622) regarding a "substantial contribution" and a "material contribution" and those of Lord Keith of Avonholm regarding "material contribution" (*ibid.*, 627) are sufficient to establish a material contribution doctrine in *Bonnington Castings* and that Hart and Honoré correctly confirm this position: Hart and Honoré, n. 27 above, 410.

[69] (1990) 72 DLR (4th) 289.

[70] It was recognised by the Sup. Ct. that the traditional approach to causation had been challenged in cases of products widely manufactured and marketed by many corporations, but that this challenge had had little impact on common law jurisdictions, the court referring to the apportionment of liability among defendant manufacturers of a medicinal product by market share in *Sindell* v. *Abbott Laboratories* 607 P 2d 924 (Cal. 1980): *Snell* v. *Farrell* (1990) 72 DLR (4th) 289, 300: See also Forbes, "Product Liability and the Medical Practitioner", 23rd IBA Biennial Conference, 19–23 Sept. 1990, New York, 15–17.

simply that the defendant created a risk that the injury would occur or that the defendant had the burden of disproving causation[71] It is suggested that this approach "sanctions a benign 'interference'" in medical malpractice cases to compensate the parties' inequality in access to evidence, which is little different from a reversal of the burden of proof.[72] It is unclear what the effect of such a case on an English court would be. In the light of *Wilsher* v. *Essex AHA*,[73] the assertions of the Supreme Court of Canada would be unlikely to be embraced.

3. DRUG INJURIES TO UNBORN CHILDREN

It is important, in the context of assessing the role of causation in negligence, to consider the position surrounding drug injuries to unborn children.

(i) Thalidomide

The piecemeal developments in product liability reform have their origins in the tragic events surrounding the drug thalidomide and its effect on the fœtus. The tragedy of thalidomide focused lawyers' and the public's minds on both the susceptibility of the fœtus to harm[74] and the importance and difficulty of establishing the cause of congenital disability, although liability in England was never established in the thalidomide case.[75]

A number of factors have been considered in attempting to establish a causal link between an adverse effect and a drug,[76] but in respect of thalidomide many lines of evidence showed that the drug caused the malformations in question.[77]

Criminal proceedings, however, were brought against nine persons at Chemie Grünenthal, the initial developers of thalidomide, and they lasted two and a half

[71] (1990) 72 D.L.R. (4th) 289, 299.

[72] Fleming, "Probabilistic Causation in Tort Law: A Postscript" (1991) 70 *Can. Bar Rev*. 136, 139.

[73] [1988] AC 1074.

[74] Brazier, *Medicine, Patients and the Law* (2nd edn., Harmondsworth, Penguin, 1992), 233.

[75] *S* v. *Distillers Co. (Biochemicals) Ltd* [1970] 1 WLR 114. In that case a compromise was approved by the court of the defendants paying 40% of the damages decided by the court in return for the plaintiffs unreservedly withdrawing all allegations of negligence: See Hinchcliffe J at 117. A settlement was reached but not every child was compensated because of disagreement whether the injuries were due to the administration of the drug: Brazier, n. 74 above, 233.

[76] See below.

[77] Sjöström and Nilsson, *Thalidomide and the Power of Drug Companies* (Harmondsworth, Penguin, 1972), 156–9. However, the variation in the kinds of adverse effects shown by the children (principally phocomelia (seal limbs), but also microtia (abnormally small ears) and ectromelia (an absence or partial absence of limbs)) has resulted in difficulties in distinguishing genuine thalidomide-induced injuries from others: Teff and Munro, n. 4 above, 4–5. It has been suggested that in the USA (where the drug did not receive authorisation from the Food and Drug Administration (FDA)), thalidomide placed future mass tort plaintiffs in a worse position, "having set up perilous ideas of individualism, self-congratulation and unattainable certainty about causation": Bernstein, "Formed by Thalidomide: Mass Torts As a False Cure for Toxic Exposure" (1997) 97 *Colum L Rev*. 2153, 2176.

years. The trial was eventually suspended, but the German court made a declaration with the prosecution that a causal connection had been established between thalidomide and nerve damage and also thalidomide and malformation in the human fœtus.[78]

During the criminal proceedings, Ernst Chain, the Nobel Prize winner for the discovery of penicillin along with Fleming and Florey in 1945,[79] was questioned and stated that clinical trials had proved thalidomide did not cause nerve damage. This was more than the defendants had claimed; they had said that there was insufficient judicial proof that thalidomide caused nerve damage. Chain took his maverick viewpoint notwithstanding that, on questioning, he had admitted never to have done an experiment with thalidomide, nor to have had clinical experience with toxic polyneuritis. He also opined that there was no proof that thalidomide caused malformations.[80] However, in its declarations, the court rejected Professor Chain's evidence.[81]

The thalidomide disaster, though now more than 30 years ago, has remained of topical interest. For example, in the past few years there have been further second-generation children who have been the victims of the drug, particularly in the Brazil and Amazon areas. Some families in these areas have had at least one parent (often the male) being treated for leprosy (the drug being purchased as an over-the-counter drug) whilst the other parent (often female) has taken the drug as an hypnotic in the knowledge that thalidomide had that property. A number of women have taken the drug in these circumstances whilst pregnant and have given birth to malformed children.[82] It also appears that the legacy of phocomelia associated with thalidomide children may have continued into a subsequent generation. On 26 July 1993, a girl was born with similar malformations to the hands and feet of her father, who had received compensation from the Thalidomide Trust in the 1970s for damage caused by the drug. It has been mooted that such a reappearance of a deformity in the child of a thalidomide victim suggests that the parent's congenital abnormality was not caused by thalidomide in the first place. Most evidence seems to be against thalidomide causing second-generation genetic deformities.[83] It would appear that the effect in the father and child (a) could be genetic; (b) could be caused by the drug; or

[78] Sjöström and Nilsson, n. 77 above, 207–70, in particular 260. However, it should be noted that the mechanism of teratogenic effects of thalidomide remains unclear: Sherman and Strauss, "Thalidomide: A Twenty-Five Year Perspective" (1986) 41 *Food Drug & Cosmetic Law Journal* 458, 461.

[79] Bender, *Great Moments in Medicine* (Detroit, Ill., Northwood Institute Press, 1966), 381.

[80] Sjöström and Nilsson, n. 77 above, 225–36.

[81] *Ibid.*, 261. The principal lesson to be learned from the evidence of E. B. Chain is that an "expert witness", however eminent he may be in another field—and Chain was very eminent—is a danger to himself and the legal process when transposed to an area in which he has little experience. The expert witness must be very carefully chosen. For a further discussion of the expert witness and causation, see Chap. 4.

[82] See Cutler, Letter, "Thalidomide Revisited" (1994) 343 *Lancet* 795–6.

[83] See Laurence, "Thalidomide Man's Daughter Deformed", *The Times*, 6 Aug. 1993. It should be noted that in July 1998, thalidomide finally received its authorisation from the US FDA for non-pregnancy uses: "Thalidomide—A Necessary Evil", *Horizon*, BBC 2, 29 Oct. 1998.

(c) could be a mixture of the effect of the drug and a genetic trait. In 1978, the Pearson Commission almost prophetically stated that there was "no evidence that causation [was] becoming easier to establish". They continued: "[o]n the contrary, we understand that birth defects do not all have the same basis. The effect of a drug may be to cause a pre-existing and latent genetic defect to become manifest rather than to act directly on the unborn child. Goya, who lived some 200 years ago, portrayed a child with the same malformations as those of some of the thalidomide children".[84] (See Illustration.) However, when the Pearson Report was published, no evidence existed of thalidomide causing third-generation malformations and the effect continues to be uncertain.

Illustration: Infant with phocomelia (seal limbs), depicted by Francisco de Goya (1746–1828), in his drawing "Mother with deformed child" (1814–1817) (Louvre, Paris) (Courtesy of Réunion des Musées Nationaux Agence Photographique)

(ii) Congenital Disabilities (Civil Liability) Act 1976

The Law Commission's report on Injuries to Unborn Children[85] included a draft bill of what became the Congenital Disabilities (Civil Liability) Act 1976, which applies to England but does not extend to Scotland.[86] The Act has been

[84] Royal Commission on Civil Liability and Compensation for Personal Injury, Cmnd. 7054–1/1978, para. 450, hereafter Pearson Report.

[85] Report on Injuries to Unborn Children, Law Com., No. 60, Cmnd 5709/1974.

[86] S. 6(2).

strongly criticised as being "ambitious, complex and now largely irrelevant".[87] Although ambitious in that the scheme introduced was to protect children against any act at any stage of either parent's life resulting in a disability affecting a child, Brazier regards the Act as irrelevant because it still requires causation to be proved.[88] Professor Brazier considers that both the mother's and the child's claims where a child has been born disabled will fail on the grounds of inability to prove causation and that Parliament needs to consider whether the burden of proof of causation in such actions is workable in practice.[89]

The Law Commission concluded, after considering the views of, *inter alia*, the Bar Council[90] and the President of the Family Division,[91] that legislation should exclude a right of action by a child against its mother for ante-natal injury,[92] except where the mother caused such pre-natal injury by the negligent driving of a car.[93] The exclusion of a right of action was introduced into statute by section 1(l) of the Congenital Disabilities (Civil Liability) Act 1976 and the exception to the rule in the case of the woman driving a motor vehicle was introduced by section 2. It was, however, noted by the Bar Council that the most likely cause of injury to a fœtus by the mother was the taking of excessive or unsuitable drugs or food, usually with a warning. They considered that there would be great difficulties of proof.[94] However, since the Act does not apply to Scotland, it would appear that in Scots law an action could be brought by a child against her mother if the injuries were allegedly caused by the mother's negligence.[95] For example, if a child's mother was a drug addict taking heroin[96] and she took the drug warfarin (which was administered by her doctor during her pregnancy and which has the potential to cause mental retardation, as does heroin) the child could sue the drug company and the mother in Scots law as a

[87] Brazier, n. 74 above, 235.

[88] "[The Act] fails to address the central problem in this type of claim. How do you prove that the disability resulted from an identifiable act of negligence": *ibid.*

[89] *Ibid.*

[90] Who said it would be logical but socially unacceptable for a mother to be liable to her unborn child: Law Com., No. 60, n. 85 above, para. 55.

[91] It would be "cruel" to allow an action by a child against her mother for ante-natal injuries: *ibid.*, para. 56.

[92] *Ibid.*, paras, 58, 63.

[93] *Ibid.*, paras. 61, 64.

[94] *Ibid.*, para. 55.

[95] Certainly it has been held, by 5 of a court of 7 judges, that a son can sue his father for damages for personal injuries: *Young* v. *Rankin*, 1934 SC 499. Lord Hunter, however, in dissent argued that the exercise of a right of action on behalf of an infant in suing a parent might well have "disastrous effects upon the child's own welfare and the welfare of the other members of the family who constitute the social unit": *ibid.*, 511. See also Liability for Antenatal Injury, Scot. Law Com., No.30, Cmnd 5371/1973 paras. 25, 26; Thomson, *Family Law in Scotland* (3rd edn., Edinburgh, Butterworths/Law Society of Scotland, 1996), 151 and Walker, *Delict* (2nd edn., Edinburgh, W. Green and Son Ltd, 1981), 86. The Pearson Commission desired uniformity on this issue throughout the UK: Pearson Report, n. 84 above, para.1483.

[96] It is now known that excessive alcohol intake in a pregnant mother can result not infrequently in the so-called fœtal alcohol syndrome in which a child is born with certain physical and indeed mental abnormalities. Pregnant women who smoke cigarettes are more likely to have smaller children than non-smoking mothers. The legal position in these cases has yet to take shape.

co-defender. Subject to the extreme difficulties of showing proof of a causal link between each drug and the mental retardation, or proof of a contribution by each drug to the retardation, the drug company could end up being jointly and severally liable to the child and may then be able to recover an appropriate proportion of damages from the mother, reflecting the contribution made by the heroin to the damage.[97] It could be argued that through the strain of family relations the English position is preferable to that of the Scottish one.

The grounds of liability in the Congenital Disabilities (Civil Liability) Act 1976 are established in section 1. This states that a person who is responsible for an occurrence which affected either parent of the child in his or her ability to have a normal healthy child (pre-conception injury) or which affected the mother during her pregnancy (ante-natal injury) or the mother or child in the course of its birth (perinatal injury) and which causes a child to be born disabled as a result of such an occurrence, will be answerable to the child if he was liable in tort to the parent.[98] The words "as a result of such an occurrence" emphasise the critical nature of proving causation. It is clear from section 1(3) of the 1976 Act that the person will be answerable to the child if he was liable in tort to the parent, establishing derivative rights of the child. It is likely that a teratogenic drug may have, by virtue of the idiosyncrasies of causation and drugs, caused no harm to the mother but have harmed only the fœtus. Indeed, the Law Commission envisages the situation where the thalidomide drug benefited the mother (by being an efficient hypnotic) but caused injury to the child.[99] The 1976 Act responds to this problem by establishing that it is no answer that there was no liability to the parent since there was no suffering of actionable injury by the parent, providing there was a breach of legal duty which, accompanied by injury, would have resulted in such liability.[100] Section 1(3)'s establishment of derivative accountability to the child is tantamount to a statutory recognition of the "eggshell skull rule" in remoteness of damage since the defendant must take the mother as he finds her.[101] The fact that she is pregnant is treated as one of her characteristics and constitution.[102] Ignorance of the mother's pregnancy or the argument that damage to the child was unforeseeable are no defences.[103]

97 This, of course, assumes that the mother could afford to pay compensation. The basis of joint and several liability in such circumstances, where one party can seek recovery of an appropriate proportion of damages from a co-delinquent, stems from an extension of the rationale that a child's claim cannot ordinarily be affected by contributory negligence of a parent: Scot Law Com. No.30, n. 95 above, para. 26, citing *Taylor* v. *Dumbarton Tramways Co.*, 1918 SC (HL) 96, in respect of which see Viscount Haldane at 107.

98 Congenital Disabilities (Civil Liability) Act 1976 s. 1(1) to (3), hereafter the 1976 Act.

99 Law Com. No.60, n. 85 above, para 46.

100 S. 1(3).

101 Law Com. No.60, n. 85 above, para. 74.

102 *Ibid.*, para. 73.

103 *Smith* v. *Leech Brain* [1962] 2 QB 405; *Robinson* v. *Post Office* [1974] 1 WLR 1176, *per* Orr LJ at 1191–2; cf *Alston* v. *Marine and Trade Insurance* 1964 (4) SA 112 (w). In that case the plaintiff suffered brain injury as a result of a road accident for which the defendant was responsible. The plaintiff then suffered manic depression brought about by the brain injury and was treated with parstellin, an effective and recognised cure for manic depression. The plaintiff ate some cheese and

4. STRICT LIABILITY AND CAUSATION

(i) Introduction

The EC Product Liability Directive[104] and the UK Consumer Protection Act 1987 Part 1,[105] which gives effect to it, adopt a strict liability scheme for defective products. Strict liability has widely been described as "liability without fault".[106]

The claimant in a medicinal product liability case will have to prove for products supplied from 1 March 1988[107] that (a) the product was defective; (b) the plaintiff's injury was caused by the defective product;[108] and (c) the defendant either produced the product or was a party with the same liability as the actual producer.[109]

The person injured by a defective medicinal product must prove the damage, the defect and the causal relationship between them.[110] The damage must have been caused "wholly or partly by a defect" in the medicinal product.[111] Thus the difference from negligence is that breach of duty under a negligence action must cause the harm, whereas the *defect* under the Consumer Protection Act 1987

suffered a stroke as a result of an adverse drug interaction between the drug and cheese. At the time of the plaintiff's treatment the stroke was "not predictable by medical science" in these circumstances. The issue was whether the stroke suffered by the plaintiff was caused by the accident so as to render the stroke compensatable in law. Hiemstra J purportedly applying the "direct consequences" test concluded that the stroke was due to a "superseding cause", namely the eating of the cheese, and that it was too remote a consequence of the accident: *ibid.*, at 117. The eating of the cheese was a "superseding cause" since it was the act of the victim independent of the wrongdoer's negligent act and not a "normal response" to the situation created by the wrongdoer: *ibid.*, at 116. Honoré had noted (A. Honoré, "Remoteness of Damage" (1964) 81 *SALJ* 410) that Hiemstra J applied the direct consequences test wrongly since a "common sense" analysis indicates that eating cheese was not an abnormal act: *ibid.*, 411, 412. On the correct application of either the direct, consequences test or "foreseeability test" the plaintiff would recover: *ibid.*, 413. See also Turpin, "Roman-Dutch Law—Remoteness of Damage—*Wagon Mound* not followed" [1965] *CLJ* 34, in particular at 38 and note the fact that contrary to Weir's view (Weir, *A Casebook on Tort* (8th edn., London, Sweet & Maxwell, 1996), 234), the plaintiff did not die in this case.

104 Council Dir. 85/374/EEC on the approximation of the laws, regulations and administrative provisions of the Member States concerning liability for defective products [1985] OJ L210/29, hereafter "the Dir.".

105 Hereafter "CPA".

106 The preferable and, it is submitted, more accurate definition, is that of Professor Walker: "a standard of liability which is more stringent than the ordinary one of liability for failure to take reasonable care, yet not absolute, which is the standard sometimes set by statute, where liability arises if the harm to be prevented takes place, whatever care and precautions have been taken. Where strict liability exists there are certain, though limited, defences to liability—but having taken reasonable care is not among them": Walker, *The Oxford Companion to Law*, (Oxford, Clarendon Press, 1980), 1193.

107 When the CPA came into effect. S. 50(7) CPA states that no person is to be liable for a defective product supplied by its producer before the coming into force of Part 1, i.e. 1 Mar. 1988.

108 S. 2(1).

109 Ss. 1(2), 2(2), and (3).

110 S. 2(1), implementing Art. 4 of the Dir.

111 S. 2(1).

must cause the damage.[112] It seems that each Member State will rely on its own theory of causation as established in its civil liability system, though it has been noted that some kind of semi-autonomous European understanding of causation could be established from common elements of the Member States' legal systems.[113]

There are several issues involving problems in establishing causation in this area: first, "but for" causation; secondly, contributory causes; and thirdly the scenario when a patient has taken several drugs and the isolation of innocent from harmful drugs.

(ii) "But For" Causation

It must be shown that the medicinal product's defect was a *sine qua non* of the plaintiff's harm, i.e. would the damage have occurred "but for" the defendant's product.[114] In the context of product liability it seems that where there are inadequate warnings about a product's dangers, e.g. an insufficient patient package insert or warning on the medicine's box, it could be argued that the product is defective in terms of section 3(1) and (2) of the Consumer Protection Act 1987.[115] If the defectiveness of the product was based on the inadequacy of warnings in respect of potential dangers it is arguable that, on the balance of probabilities, the defect had not caused the plaintiff's adverse drug reaction since, even if an adequate warning had been provided, the plaintiff would not have read the warning or would have ignored it.[116] This "unattractive" scenario would amount to an exculpation from liability of the producer for his defective medicinal product on the basis of "what looks very much like the plaintiff's *hypothetical*[117] contributory negligence".[118] A suggestion has not been followed in the implementing legislation that the legislation would make the producer bear the risk of whether the users of his products would have noticed or followed his warnings, combining a causation analysis and one "imposing

[112] It is therefore incorrect to state, as has one author, that under the CPA, "a plaintiff is still required to establish a causal link between the *defendant's act or omission* and the former's loss" (italics added): Ferguson, *Drug Injuries and the Pursuit of Compensation* (London, Sweet & Maxwell, 1996), 125.

[113] Whittaker, "The EEC Directive on Product Liability" (1985) 5 *Ybk. Eur. Law* 233, 247, hereafter Whittaker.

[114] E.g. see *McWilliams* v. *Sir William Arrol & Co.* [1962] 1 WLR 295 (HL); *Barnett* v. *Chelsea & Kensington Hospital* [1969] 1 QB 428, 434, 439; Cane, n. 8 above, 98.

[115] A drug is defective if it does not provide the safety that persons generally are entitled to expect (s. 3(1)) taking all circumstances into account, including the manner in which and purposes for which the product has been marketed, its "get up", the use of warnings or instructions, what might reasonably be expected to be done with or in relation to the product, and the time when the product was supplied by its producer to another (s. 3(2)).

[116] Whittaker, n. 113 above, 248.

[117] Author's own italics.

[118] Whittaker, n. 113 above, 248.

liability for damage 'within the risk' of the defendant's activity", following Hart and Honoré in chapter 1X of *Causation in the Law*.[119]

(iii) Contributory Causes

A victim of a product liability accident, allegedly a drug-induced injury, will have great difficulty in showing that the defective drug caused his injury. In the case of drugs, the question to be asked is whether "the medical condition from which the plaintiff suffers [is] a side-effect of the defendant's drug or an extraneous disease or personal allergy".[120] There is a considerable degree of uncertainty surrounding the answers to such questions. However, Whittaker[121] has distinguished between two situations in this area: first, where the plaintiff's harm seems to be due to a product and partly to an "extraneous cause"; secondly, where the harm seems to be due to the product and partly the plaintiff's own fault.[122]

The first example reflects the CPA, in that under section 2(1) the damage may be caused partly by the defect and partly by an innocent event or third party's faulty conduct, e.g. failing to examine or test the product or heed the manufacturer's warnings. Under the Act and the Directive, if the plaintiff can show that the defect played *some* role in causing his harm the manufacturer and third party will in all probability be jointly and severally liable,[123] and an apportionment of responsibility can be made under the Civil Liability (Contribution) Act 1978.[124]

The plaintiff must show that the defect caused the damage but the *defendant*, to avoid liability, must prove that he did not cause the defect, either through the defect not existing at the time when the product was supplied[125] or through the defect (i) constituting a defect in a subsequent product in which the product in question had been comprised, and (ii) being wholly attributable to the design of the subsequent product or to compliance by the producer of the product with instructions given by the producer of the subsequent product.[126] But if the manufacturer had reasonable grounds for contemplating an intermediate inspection or the following of instructions by an intermediary, the product will not be

[119] Whittaker, n. 113 above, citing Hart and Honoré, n. 27 above, chap. 1X. Whittaker here seems to be alluding to Hart and Honoré's foreseeability in the theoretical sense, where ulterior harm, i.e. "harm the risk of which was not a reason for calling the defendant's act negligent" (*ibid*,, 263–5) is theoretically foreseeable.

[120] Whittaker, n. 113 above, 248.

[121] *Ibid*.

[122] *Ibid*., 249.

[123] CPA, s. 2(5); Dir., Art. 8.

[124] See Ss. 1(1), 2(1), (2). It seems that the application of the Civil Liability (Contribution) Act to multi-party situations which may arise under the CPA is unclear: Stapleton, *Product Liability* (London, Butterworths, 1994), 299–302.

[125] CPA s. 4(1)(d); Dir., Art. 7(b).

[126] CPA s. 4(1)(f); Dir., Art. 7(f).

defective.[127] This is because section 3(2) takes into account instructions, use of warnings and what might reasonably be expected to be done with or in relation to the product in ascertaining its defectiveness. Intermediate examination is no longer a causation issue under strict liability,[128] but an issue arising at the stage when one decides whether the product is defective. Once the product is regarded as defective the omission of an intermediate examination will not defeat the action on causation grounds.[129]

In the second example, the harm is due partly to the product and partly to the plaintiff's own fault. Article 8(2) of the Directive and section 6(4) of the Act envisage the operation of contributory negligence to reduce the producer's liability. Here the producer's liability may be reduced if the plaintiff's (victim's) conduct is careless. Article 8(2) is potentially a wider defence than English law, since it applies not only to the injured person's fault but also to "any person for whom the injured person is responsible".[130] This seems to amount to a reduction through a defence of "vicarious contributory negligence" caused by the plaintiff's own employee or perhaps by the plaintiff's own child.[131] Whittaker notes that it would be "undesirable" for damages to be reduced which are available to a parent injured partly by a defective product and partly by his own child's carelessness.[132] So if a plaintiff buys a bottle of corn solvent from a manufacturer who fails to provide an adequate cork and to warn of the corn solvent's dangers and a child runs into a bathroom with the open bottle when his father is drying himself and hits his father, some of the corn solvent then spilling on to the father's abdomen, injuring his genitals, under this rule the father could end up being vicariously contributorily negligent. Since the preparation had a strong concentration of acid in it the producer should have anticipated danger to more tender parts of the body by providing an adequate cork and warning, but the father would be liable for the child's negligence in opening the bottle and running into his father with it.[133] If the plaintiff misuses the product with conduct which is not reasonably foreseeable by the producer or merely disregards a warning it may be that the product is not defective.[134] If the product is defective, the plaintiff's conduct would probably amount to contributory negligence.[135]

[127] Jones, n. 30 above, 449.

[128] See, *per contra*, Hart and Honoré who say that it never was an issue based on causal principles in the common law of torts: Hart and Honoré, n. 27 above, 150.

[129] Jones, n. 30 above, 449.

[130] Cf CPA s. 6(4), which refers to the fault of the person "suffering the damage".

[131] Whittaker, n. 113 above, 252.

[132] *Ibid.*, 253.

[133] Cf *Devilez* v. *Boots Pure Drug Co. Ltd* (1962) 106 Sol. Jo. 552; Miller and Lovell, n. 59 above, 234; Whincup, *Product Liability Law* (Aldershot, Gower, 1985), 130.

[134] Jones, n. 30 above, 321.

[135] *Ibid.*

(iv) Where a Patient has Taken a Number of Drugs and the Separation of Innocent from Harmful Drugs

One of the most problematic issues involving causation and medicinal products is where there are plaintiffs whose adverse drug reactions are the result of the prescription of many drugs in situations where it is impossible to find the cause of the harm, or when drugs have interacted with each other in a damaging combination.[136] Under the law before the 1987 Act, this would be a situation involving competing causes where the background risk and the competing causes are unassessable in terms of risk and the mechanism involved is unclear or unknown.[137] In such cases of competing causes it would have to be shown that a breach of duty in relation to the administration of a particular drug was the operative cause of the loss on a balance of probabilities.[138] Under the 1987 Act, a causal link would have to be shown between the particular competing defective drug and the damage, again on a balance of probabilities.

(v) Summary

It seems that the area of strict liability and causation is affected by the same sort of complexity as existed prior to the Consumer Protection Act 1987. Indeed, it has been argued that the lack of clarity concerning the operation of causation under the Consumer Protection Act might result in a greater obstacle to the securing of compensation than even the inclusion of the Act's development risk defence.[139] With the difficulties of both causation in negligence and strict liability in mind, we now turn to alternative approaches to the causation problem looked at from a probability perspective.

[136] Newdick, n. 27 above, 428.

[137] Stapleton, n. 22 above. It has already been noted, however, that in relation to synergistic effects, Stapleton's analysis is of doubtful assistance. See also below.

[138] *Wilsher* v. *Essex AHA* [1988] 1 AC 1074.

[139] B. S. Markesinis and Deakin, *Tort Law* (3rd edn., Oxford, Clarendon Press, 1994), 553. For the development risk defence, see Chap. 7. It should be noted that, in respect of the Product Liability Dir., the European Parliament's Committee on the Environment has proposed a reversal of the burden of proof of causation in that, where the existence of a defect and causal link between the defect and damage can be inferred, this should be sufficient for consumers to prove that the damage occurred. It would be up to the manufacturer to produce evidence to the contrary: Draft Report of the European Parliament Committee on the Environment, Public Health and Consumer Protection, 3 Mar. 1998.

5. PROPORTIONAL LIABILITY

(i) The Role of Proportional Liability in the Context of Causation and Medicinal Products

The problematic nature of drug-induced causation poses the question whether the traditional standard of proof on a balance of probabilities is really an appropriate and indeed accurate way of assessing drug causality. Professor David Kaye has examined the usefulness of both the balance of probabilities standard (in the USA the preponderance of evidence standard) and that of proportional liability[140] using the concept of what he terms as an expected loss function (f).[141] It is his conclusion that the preponderance of evidence standard minimises expected losses and error in single defendant cases[142] and in cases involving multiple defendants.[143] Among the latter cases, he suggests that these are subject to important exceptions, most particularly the Diethylstilbestrol (DES) cases, where the preponderance of evidence standard produces "biased results".[144] In such cases, Professor Kaye submits that proportional liability is the only approach that does not compensate undeserving victims and awards an accurate sum to each victim in question.[145]

In cases involving alleged adverse drug reactions associated with DES there were many potential defendants and the type of harm became increasingly difficult to attach to the drug. The proportional liability approach to establishing causal link, also referred to as a "statistical analysis of probabilities",[146] is more often than not looked to as a solution to this difficult conundrum. Rosenberg moots proportional liability as a replacement for the traditional preponderance of the evidence rule requirement in tort:

> "Under such a standard, courts would impose liability and distribute compensation in proportion to the probability of causation assigned to the excess disease risk in the exposed population, regardless of whether that probability fell above or below the 50 per cent threshold and despite the absence of individualised proof of the causal connection."[147]

The probability of causation would be derived from dividing excess risk[148] by the total risk, i.e. by the sum of excess and background risk. The principal

140 See D. Kaye, "The Limits of the Preponderance of the Evidence Standard: Justifiably Naked Statistical Evidence and Multiple Causation" (1982) 2 *American Bar Foundation Research Journal* 487.

141 *Ibid.*, 498, 514.

142 *Ibid.*, 498–502.

143 *Ibid.*, 504, 507, 508.

144 *Ibid.*, 509.

145 *Ibid.*

146 Newdick, n. 27 above, 423.

147 Rosenberg, "The Causal Connection in Mass Exposure Cases: A 'Public Law' Vision of the Tort System" (1984) 97 *Harv. L Rev.* 851, 856.

148 Also known as "attributable risk", calculated by subtracting the level of risk of the unexposed population (background risk) from the level of risk of the exposed population (total risk): see

justifications for a scheme of proportional liability are deterrence[149] and the fact that the producer is subject to no greater degree of liability than that for which he is responsible.[150] Variations of this approach have been tried yet subsequently rejected in the courts.[151] The main objections to this concept of proportional liability are, first, the requirement of identification of risks that might be difficult to quantify[152] and, secondly, a form of class action would be required,[153] regarded as "unknown to the English courts" in the Opren

Sanders, "From Science to Evidence: The Testimony on Causation in the Bendectin Cases" (1993) 46 *Stan. L Rev*. 1, 23; Brennan, "Causal Chains and Statistical Links: The Role of Scientific Uncertainty in Hazardous Substance Litigation" (1988) 73 *Cornell L Rev*. 469, 508.

149 Rosenberg, n. 147 above, 866.

150 The proportionality rule thus comes as close as possible to preserving the value of individual entitlements to personal security and autonomy: *ibid*., at 860–2.

151 See *Hotson v. Fitzgerald* [1985] 1 WLR 1036 (first instance); *Hotson v. East Berks. AHA* [1987] 2 WLR 287 (CA), reversed by *Hotson v. East Berks. AHA* [1987] 1 AC 750 (HL). See below.

152 Newdick, n. 27 above, 424. Indeed Stapleton submits that the conceptual refinement of causal apportionment in respect of medical causation is ultimately of little use to disease victims since it hinges on the very estimates of relative contributions to risk, which are typically unavailable in such cases: Stapleton, *Disease and the Compensation Debate* (Oxford, Clarendon Press, 1986), 47–8. By virtue of problems in relation to proof of causation tort law is rarely used to compensate the victims of man-made disease. The main problems are that diseases may be gradually contracted and their symptoms may take time to manifest. Also, other conditions may be a cause of the disease. Statistics may be the only way to prove medical causation, and they are often not available: Stapleton, "Compensating the Victims of Diseases" (1985) 5 *OJLS* 248, 250–2, 267 n. 54. It has been said that there is little justification for imposing collective responsibility in non-signature disease cases since often there is no identifiable collective action, no incentive effects are apparent and often the data to support probabilistic measures of causation are non-extant: Abraham, "Individual Action and Collective Responsibility: The Dilemma of Mass Tort Reform" (1987) 73 *Va. L Rev*. 845, 865, 867. (A signature disease is one in which there is an accepted direct causal link between a substance and a disorder). However, Abraham notes vaginal carcinoma as a signature disease amenable to market share liability: *ibid*,, 860 n. 38, but seems to confuse market share liability with collective responsibility when collective responsibility in the form of enterprise liability in respect of DES manufacturers was rejected in *Sindell v. Abbott Laboratories*, 607 P 2d, 924, 935 (1980) . It is therefore submitted that collective responsibility is an inappropriate term to use when discussing cases involving DES, and also that DES has associated data problems, particularly in the context of assessing relative contributions to risk in vaginal adenocarcinoma DES cases and also with the problems of third-generation birth defects allegedly caused by the drug. It is still being questioned whether clear cell adenocarcinoma is in fact a signature disease of DES: American Law Institute Reporters' Study, *Enterprise Responsibility for Personal Injury Vol II: Approaches to Legal and Institutional Change* (Philadelphia, Penn., American Law Institute, 1991),322, although the evidence seems to suggest that it is: see Buitendijk, "Diethylstilbestrol and the Next Generation: A Challenge to the Evidence?" in Dukes and Beeley (eds.), *Side Effects of Drugs Annual 12* (Amsterdam, New York and Oxford, Elsevier, 1988), 347–8. However, the value of signature disease evidence seems not to be very high: American Law Institute Reporters' Study, above, 322. The most technical and useful way to characterise signature diseases is by referring to the epidemiological concept of attributable fraction (or risk) of disease: Brennan, "Environmental Torts" (1993) 46 *Vand. L Rev*. 1, 15. DES causes a high attributable risk of disease but is not very potent, requiring relatively high doses to cause harm: *ibid*.

153 Newdick, n. 27 above, 424. It has been submitted that this is because the private law process ends up excluding most mass exposure cases by treating "all claims as if they arose from unrelated, stochastic, factually unique and temporally and physically immediate interactions between individuals": Rosenberg, n. 147 above, 905–6. Rosenberg argues that class actions allow the victims of mass exposure cases to litigate in numbers and achieve utilitarian, rights-based and compensation objectives: *ibid*., 907.

case.[154] Class actions are regarded by some with inherent scepticism on the basis that they encourage "gold diggers" to join actions for a potential share of the takings, and also lawyers who represent plaintiffs to pressurise people into joining actions despite the weakness of their claims. It has been recently noted that class actions in America "have not been invoked with any consistent success in personal injury litigation".[155] Indeed, a major criticism of proportional liability recovery, by which each class member is compensated in proportion to the damages sustained by the class as a whole, is that it tends to under-compensate those who have suffered effects from the background risk and the toxic agent and that it tends to over-compensate those who have solely suffered from the background risk and have not suffered from the risk of the toxic agent, although this cannot be proved.[156] Newdick lays down the requirement of eligibility to the class as being "membership of a group for which the relative incidence of the risks had been assessed and the presence of disability or illness for which the product is said to be responsible".[157] Relative incidence of the risks is probably "attributable risk",[158] but it may not truly be known whether the disease in each member of the class was caused by the drug or background risk.

In the Opren case it was said that "of the more than 1400 claims received by the company, nearly two thirds [had] no medical report and in relatively few [had] . . . complete medical records" been given.[159] It has been noted that in the Benzodiazepine litigation, of the 10,800 claims notified to Roche Products Ltd, one defendant, 2,336 claimants had served writs. However, legal aid support

154 *Davies* v. *Eli Lilly & Co.* [1987] 1 WLR 1136, *per* Sir John Donaldson MR at 1139. Co-ordinated proceedings for multi-claimant cases as in Opren and the Benzodiazepine litigation are, however, accepted. The majority of co-ordinated proceedings have master pleadings on generic issues together with separate individual statements of claim adopting the appropriate part of the master pleadings in the individual case. However, master pleadings are no more than vehicles "for setting out parts of a claim that may be common to a large number of individual actions and can be conveniently adopted by such actions—[they have] no life of [their] own": Dodds-Smith, "Product Liability Iissues Arising out of the Introduction of Strict Liability Procedures for Dealing with Multi-claimant Cases" in Goldberg and Dodds-Smith (eds.), *Pharmaceutical Medicine and the Law* (London, Royal College of Physicians, 1991), 55. A series of actions must be selected to determine the various issues of the case. However, in medicinal product liability cases there is rarely a common issue which, when tried, will determine the outcome of proceedings. Such a rare case, however, may emerge when an issue of general causation arises as in the pertussis litigation: see *Loveday* v. *Renton* [1990] 1 Med. LR 117. This can be contrasted with questions of individual causation which present many issues and sub-issues developing with time. Any decision in such a case will be determined by the facts of the individual case.

155 "A Legal Perspective" in Foster, Bernstein and Huber (eds.), *Phantom Risk: Scientific Inference and the Law* (Cambridge, London, MIT Press, 1993), 28. They have been criticised as being an "especially unwieldy method" for compiling the group of victims associated with any one substance: Brennan, "Causal Chains and Statistical Links: The Role of Uncertainty in Hazardous-Substance Litigation" (1988) 73 *Cornell L Rev*. 469, 522.

156 Fleming, "Probabilistic Causation in Tort Law" (1989) 68 *Can. BR* 661 at 680. Courts would require proof of use of DES so that the latter scenario would be unlikely. Fleming, however, states that proportional liability is contended to be better than either compensating none or compensating all for the full amount of their injuries: *ibid*.

157 Newdick, n. 27 above, 423–4.

158 See Sanders, n. 148 above.

159 Lilly Industries Limited Communication regarding Opren Litigation, 3 Mar. 1988.

was suspended in January 1993 for 2,319 claimants on the basis that they were unworthy of funding.[160]

The Legal Aid Board has recently suspended support on 1,200 claims over Ativan (cases being run against John Wyeth and Brother Ltd), thus effectively bringing an end to the Benzodiazepine litigation, since the Board concluded that the final costs would grossly exceed any damages awarded and because of "the difficulty of establishing liability".[161] As previously noted, in respect of actions by the plaintiffs against prescribers, which had been struck out by Kennedy J in the High Court on the basis that they were vexatious and an abuse of the process of the court, as the costs incurred and likely to be incurred by the prescribers were out of proportion to the benefit that the plaintiffs could obtain from litigation against them, the Court of Appeal held that the court was entitled to strike out the actions on a cost-benefit analysis.[162] Stuart-Smith LJ noted the "very considerable problems on causation".[163]

(ii) **Liability for the Tortious Creation of Risk**

It is thus clear that there remains great difficulty surrounding the use of traditional and alternative causation solutions to resolve such complex issues, though proportional liability has been increasingly proposed as an appropriate response to many medicinal product liability cases.[164] Indeed, the most radical version of probability mooted is that of liability for the tortious creation of risk, which eliminates the actual harm requirement of tort law by assessing liability according to the degree of risk imposed on the plaintiff as opposed to the amount of harm suffered by the plaintiff.[165] The most extreme form of such liability is imposed before anyone suffers physical harm, liability being measured by the product of the probability that a risk will result in harm and the expected magnitude of that harm.[166] The liability is assessed as an amount equal to the

[160] McIntosh, "When the Only Winners are the Lawyers", *The Times*, 6 Apr. 1993.

[161] See Barton, "Taxpayers Swallow a Bitter Pill", *The Times*, 19 Apr. 1994 and Dyer, "Sad Story of the Happy Pills", *The Guardian*, 5 Apr. 1994.

[162] *AB and Others* v. *John Wyeth & Brother Ltd and Others* (No 2) [1994] 5 Med. L.R. 149. See above, and the discussion of the similar case against the manufacturers of Benzodiazepines: *AB and Others* v. *John Wyeth & Brother Ltd*; *AB and Others* v. *Roche Products Ltd* (LEXIS, 13 Dec. 1996).

[163] *Ibid.*, at 153.

[164] See, e.g., in respect of Bendectin, Lasagna and Shulman, "Bendectin and the Language of Causation" in Foster, Bernstein and Huber (eds.), n. 155 above, 116. This seems, however, to conflict with the book's conclusion that traditional standards of proof should be maintained: *ibid.*, 434–5.

[165] See Abraham, "What is a Tort Claim? An Interpretation of Contemporary Tort Reform" (1992) 51 *Md. L Rev.* 172, 181.

[166] See Robinson, "Probabilistic Causation and Compensation for Tortious Risk" (1985) 14 *J Legal Stud.* 779, 783, 786. Robinson argues that from a fairness perspective, liability should be based on creation of an unreasonable risk, not on whether someone was injured by it: Robinson, "Multiple Causation in Tort Law. Reflections on the DES Cases" (1982) 68 *Va. L Rev.* 713, 739–40. On such a basis, the imposition of liability in the DES cases is regarded by him as fair, since each defendant made a "defective" product which created an unreasonable risk of harm, irrespective of whether the

expected harm at the moment an agent acts, an *ex ante* approach which translates future uncertain occurrences into risks which are then discounted to present values. This eliminates causation entirely and ensures that a factor of expected harm by the agent is taken into account, thus apparently eliminating the lottery characteristics of the present liability system and seemingly satisfying the corrective justice conditions of action based responsibility.[167] It is predicted that just compensation and internal financing will be achieved since pay-ins and pay-outs will ultimately be balanced. In such circumstances, there will be underpayments and over-payments when viewed *ex post*, but not over-payments or under-payments *ex ante*. In the long run it is said that such overages and underages would "cancel each other out" by a recalculation of the expected harm liability.[168] It is submitted that this would require a futuristic statistical refinement process which potentially could cause more difficulties than an *ex post* system using existing statistics as they emerge from medical monitoring which could then be more accurately refined.[169] The *ex ante* approach has been likened to

defendant's actions caused harm in the first place: *ibid.* In synopsis, his argument is that losses should be apportioned in multiple causation cases "among all defendants that created unreasonable risks according to the magnitude of the risks they created", where such measures of apportionment can be ascertained: *ibid.*, 754–5. According to Robinson, such scaling of liability in proportion to magnitude of risk fulfils the same functions as proximate cause since the principal role of proximate cause is to limit liability to results caused by particular risks which made the conduct tortious: *ibid.*, 755–6, cf Hart and Honoré, who submit that liability should not be limited by the scope of a risk tortiously created and that there can be liability for ulterior harm, harm the risk of which is not a reason for calling the defendant's act negligent: Hart and Honoré, n. 27 above, 263–6; see also Stapleton, n. 54 above, 122 (submitting that risk and foreseeability do not explain recovery for ulterior harm). Robinson finds Hart and Honoré "unconvincing": above, 756, 757, n. 144. It has been argued, however, by advocates of a philosophical approach to probability, that risk does not generally constitute harm in itself: Perry, "Risk, Harm and Responsibility" in Owen (ed.), *Philosophical Foundations of Tort Law* (Oxford, Clarendon Press, 1995), 321, 336–8.

167 Schroeder, "Corrective Justice and Liability for Increasing Risks" (1990) 37 *UCLA L Rev.* 439, 460–6 and Robinson, "Probabilistic Causation", n. 166 above, 790 (showing the fulfilment of corrective justice objectives in the context of a pharmaceutical company that produces a carcinogenic drug).

168 Schroeder, n. 167 above, 468.

169 Brennan advocates the use of attributable fraction concepts of disease compensation on an *ex post* basis (after the injuries have occurred and with medical monitoring from the time of exposure until the end of the latency period) as opposed to compensation on an *ex ante* basis (ascertaining the probability that some members *will* develop a disease or injury): Brennan, "Environmental Torts" (1993) 46 *Vand. L Rev.* 1, 61–70. This enables monitoring of exposed people for a longer period than the expected latency period for scientists to calculate true attributable fractions: *ibid*, 66. Brennan believes that such an approach will permit rational compensation and develop remedies to fit injuries and create rational deterrence: *ibid.*, 64, 72. The establishment of attributable fractions of proportionate compensation could be undertaken by a Federal Hazardous Substance Science Panel, though the evidence from the Science Panel would not necessarily be determinative, all evidence in court being weighed by the trier of fact. Such a panel would be able to instruct common law courts about probabilistic causation: Brennan, "Causal Chains and Statistical Links: The Role of Scientific Uncertainty in Hazardous-Substance Litigation", (1988) 73 *Cornell L Rev.* 469, 525–7, 529, 532. Cynics may also ask questions about how independent the Hazardous Substance Panel would be if it complemented and supplemented bodies such as the Food and Drug Administration: *ibid.*, 529 but it is submitted that such co-ordination would be beneficial in the move towards a goal of better pharmacovigilance and just compensation of those injured by medicinal products.

being a complement of losses of chance cases with virtually identical problems of causal determination and valuation.[170]

However, the less radical system of *ex post* use of proportional liability would seem to be the more reliable of the two approaches. The American Law Institute (ALI) advocates *ex post* use of proportional liability, i.e. only *after* epidemiological evidence is established and the actual disease victims are known. With such an approach, probabilistic causation is not applicable when a party is merely put at risk of a disease. The ALI also support a threshold for using attributable fractions in this area of 20 per cent and above, calculated by a science panel, to recognise the need for fairness to the defendants and economic predictability. Any injuries involving an attributable fraction greater than 80 per cent would be compensated at 100 per cent levels. This would seem to result in over-deterrence and over-compensation to those at such levels by conforming to a common law standard when an attributable fraction is greater than 80 per cent. Nonetheless, since most exposures to environmental toxins result in only slight increases in risk of about 2 to 3 per cent, they will most likely fall below the threshold resulting in a presumption of no causal link.[171]

At present, in the United Kingdom, there is no liability in tort/delict for increasing risks. Indeed, the courts have established that causal connection with the defendant's wrongful conduct is a requisite of liability, additional to the foreseeability of the type of harm.[172] It seems that English or Scottish courts would be considerably resistant to using probabilistic apportionment of risk without additional corroborative evidence indicating that the general statistics fairly represented the individual case in issue,[173] an argument pointing to a statistical chance/personal chance dichotomy, the answer to which is to refine the probabilities in respect of a class of persons or in respect of individual members

[170] Robinson, n. 166 above, both sitations, 792–3 and 752; see below in respect of loss of a chance and the Bayes theorem. Indeed, Hill, "A Lost Chance for Compensation in the Tort of Negligence by the House of Lords" (1991) 54 *MLR* 511, 511, submits that only a lost personal chance is compensatable and that this is a case which involves a "future hypothetical question", which seems to reflect the *ex ante* probabilistic approach of Robinson *et al*. It would seem that daughters or granddaughters of women who have taken DES but have not suffered any identifiable harm at present could obtain compensation under such a scheme, provided the *ex ante* epidemiological or other statistical measures were available to assess expected harm. This may substantially increase the number of claims filed in DES cases: Robinson, "Probabilistic Causation", n. 166 above, 796–9. It would therefore seem incorrect to argue that Robinson's paper only reflects cases where the undesirable outcome has transpired: cf Lunney, "What Price a Chance?" (1995) 15 *LS* 1, 6 n. 21. However, liability for tortious creation of a risk is only operable where direct evidence exists of a degree of risk imposed on the plaintiff by the defendant in the form of epidemiological or other statistical measures: see Abraham, "What is a Tort Claim? An Interpretation of Contemporary Tort Reform" (1992) 51 *Md. L Rev*. 172, 183–4.

[171] American Law Institute Reporters' Study, n. 152 above, 370–5. The Reporters' Study was criticised by academics and practising lawyers and the American Law Institute intended to draft a restatement of product liability, with the Reporters' Study evidently only serving as a background document: Brennan, "Environmental Torts", n. 169 above, 4. For further details, see Chap. 6.

[172] Hart and Honoré, n. 27 above, pp. lxvii, 282–3; *McKew* v. *Holland and Hannen & Cubitts (Scotland) Ltd* [1969] 3 All ER 1621, *per* Lord Reid at 1623.

[173] See Robinson, "Multiple Causation", n. 166 above, 765 for such resistance in the American courts.

of that class.[174] Robinson considers it unnecessary to establish absolute magnitudes of risk and regards rough estimates of relative magnitudes as being sufficient, since the task is to assess causal responsibilities to provide a fairer and more efficient method of apportioning losses in multiple causation cases.[175] However, in the absence of accurate prior probabilities it would seem that problems of over-compensation/over-deterrence or under-compensation/under-deterrence still remain.[176]

6. LOSS OF A CHANCE

The idea of compensation for loss of a chance of achieving a satisfactory outcome or of avoiding loss has been advocated more often than not by legal academics concerned with the apparent unfairness of the all-or-nothing preponderance of evidence standard of causation, in situations where it is simply impossible to prove that it is more probable than not that a breach of duty caused a particular injury.[177] Professor King[178] advocates loss of a chance despite that chance being not better than even and suggests a need to develop an appropriate method of assigning a value to such a lost chance for it to be a compensatable interest[179] and for precision and validity to be introduced into the loss-assigning process.[180] Professor King's thesis suggests the need to distinguish between causation, on the one hand,[181] and valuation, on the other[182] Although the English legal position is inconclusive after *Hotson* v. *East Berkshire AHA*,[183]

174 See below.

175 Robinson, "Multiple Causation", n. 166 above, 767.

176 It should be noted that the plaintiff should only recover a percentage of damages when the correlation coefficient between exposure and injury is less than one. If the correlation coefficient between the exposure and injury *was* one, the plaintiff would receive 100 per cent damages: see Sanders, "From Science to Evidence: The Testimony on Causation in the Bendectin Cases" (1993) 46 *Stan. L Rev*. 1, 17.

177 See the seminal article advocating loss of a chance by Professor Joseph King: King, "Causation, Valuation and Chance in Personal Injury Torts Involving Pre-existing Conditions and Future Consequences" (1981) 90 *Yale LJ* 1353.

178 *Ibid*.

179 *Ibid*., 1354, 1376, 1381, 1385.

180 *Ibid*., 1387.

181 Questions of causation "relate to the fact of a loss or of its source": *ibid*., 1354.

182 Valuation is a mechanism whereby loss caused by tortious conduct can be identified and measured: *ibid*. See, *per contra*, the view of Stapleton that Professor King fails to distinguish the identification/formulation of a loss from its quantification: n. 22 above, 393 n. 11. It seems that Professor King identifies the need to recognise the loss of a less than even chance as an actionable injury: King, n. 177 above, 1394 as well as its valuation: *ibid*., 1387.

183 [1987] 1 AC 750. In *Spring* v. *Guardian Assurance plc* [1995] 2 AC 296, the HL held that an employer who provides a reference in respect of one of his employees to a prospective future employer will owe a duty of care to his employee in respect of the preparation of a reference: *ibid*., 319, *per* Lord Goff. Lord Lowry stated that the plaintiff did not have to prove that but for the negligent reference Scottish Amicable (the prospective employer) would have employed him. The plaintiff only had to show that he had "lost a reasonable chance of employment (which would have to be evaluated)": *ibid*., 327. A recent legal professional negligence case in the CA, *Allied Maples Group* v. *Simmons & Simmons* [1995] 1 WLR 1602, rested on discussion of balance of probabilities and loss

American states have experimented in alterations to the preponderance of evidence standard in difficult cases of medical malpractice where plaintiffs are unable on a balance of probabilities to show a causal connection between the breach of duty and the injury.[184] One American case illustrates a hybrid of techniques available to the plaintiff. In *Scafidi* v. *Seiler*,[185] the plaintiff was suffering early labour complications, including cramping. Her doctor ordered the drug Vasodilian to calm the uterus. The plaintiff took three of the Vasodilian pills during the night but the cramping continued. Another doctor examined her the next morning, hospitalised her immediately and began tocolytic therapy, a means of arresting premature labour using magnesium sulphate solution intravenously. Later that day the plaintiff gave birth to a premature child who died two days later. The plaintiff alleged that her doctor's failure to examine and hospitalise the plaintiff resulted in the child's death. At trial, the plaintiff's expert witness gave evidence that Vasodilian administered orally was almost valueless as a tocolytic agent and that timely administration of tocolytic therapy was 75–80 per cent effective in stopping premature labour.[186] The Supreme

of a chance. Stuart-Smith LJ deemed that loss of a chance was only relevant in the context of hypothetical third-party actions. He indicated that where the plaintiff's loss depends on the hypothetical actions of an independent third party, the plaintiff must show that there was "a real or substantial chance, as opposed to a speculative one": *ibid.*, 1614 *per* Stuart Smith LJ that the third party would have acted so as to confer the benefit or avoid the risk to the plaintiff: *ibid.*, 1611, 1614 *per* Stuart-Smith LJ. *Allied Maples Group* was followed in *Stovold* v. *Barlows*, *The Times*, 30 Oct. 1995 (CA), in *First Interstate Bank of California* v. *Cohen Arnold & Co.*, *The Times*, 11 Dec. 1995 (CA), (establishing that the evaluation of the chance was taken account of at the quantification of damages stage), and in *Doyle* v. *Wallace*, *The Times*, 22 July 1998 (CA) (damages recoverable in personal injury action for loss of earnings as a result of loss of a chance to become a teacher.) See also the comments on *Hotson* in the Canadian case of *Lawson* v. *Laferrière* (1991) 78 DLR (4th) 609, 658 (rejecting loss of a chance in a medical context and requiring proof as to causal link to be established on a balance of probabilities): *ibid.*, 656–8. For the view that there should be no legal difference in negligence between loss of a chance to recover from a medical condition and loss of a chance to advance a legal claim, see Phillips, "Lost Chances in Delict: All or Nothing" [1995] *Jur. Rev.* 401.

184 See, e.g., the relaxation of the traditional cause in fact requirement in *O'Brien* v. *Stover*, 443 F 2d 1013 (1971) (holding expert evidence of a 30% survival rate in absence of the defendant's negligence sufficient to present a jury question under Iowa law: *ibid.*, 1018). The leading case on recovery for loss of chance would seem to be *Herskovits* v. *Group Health Cooperative of Puget Sound*, 664 P 2d 474 (Wash. 1983), where the Sup. Ct. of Washington, Dore J held that proof that a defendant's conduct had increased the risk of death by decreasing chances of survival by 14% was sufficient to allow the proximate cause issue of whether a physician's failure to diagnose was a proximate cause of death to go to the jury: *ibid.*, 476–7, 479 (similar to *McGhee* reasoning (see Lord Mackay in *Hotson*, n. 183 above, at 787)). Pearson J in *Herskovits* agreed with the majority but gave different reasoning. He viewed the injury or disability not as death but as a reduction in chance of the decedent's survival: 664 P 2d 474, 479, 481. He supported recovery for loss of less than an even chance of recovery, having reviewed the cases and noted academic support from King, n. 177 above, particularly 1363–4. Recovery for loss of a chance as a separate compensatable injury in its own right was recognised in *DeBurkarte* v. *Louvar*, 393 NW 2d 131, 137–8 (Iowa 1986). The percentage chance as a proportional measure of damages was recognised in *Falcon* v. *Memorial Hospital*, 462 NW 2d 44 (Mich. 1990) (loss of 37.5% opportunity of living constituted loss of a substantial opportunity of avoiding physical harm and 37.5 times damages recoverable for wrongful death was an appropriate proportional measure of damages since it was in proportion to the extent of the lost opportunity: *ibid.*, 56–7).

185 574 A 2d 398 (NJ 1990).

186 *Ibid.*, 399.

Court of New Jersey held that evidence showing that negligent treatment increases the risk of harm posed by a pre-existent condition raises a jury issue whether increased risk is a substantial factor in causing the ultimate result. The Court also added that the plaintiff's recovery in such cases should ordinarily be limited to lost-chance damages.[187] Thus the Court offered a hybrid of techniques in that it relaxed the traditional requirements of causation as a "complement"[188] to limiting the plaintiff's damages. However, loss of a chance as a separate common law cause of action has also been rejected outright in other cases.[189] Moreover the idea of extending loss of a chance "across the board" to limit the damages of a plaintiff who can show by a preponderance of evidence that the defendant caused his ultimate injury has been vigorously resisted on precedential, theoretical, deterrence and fairness grounds, since it would dispense with the "cause in fact" inquiry and disallow full recovery in medical malpractice diagnosis cases.[190]

Returning to the issue of causation and medicinal products, the concept of a market share liability action has been likened to a claim for a loss of a chance in tort[191] in terms of reformulation of the damage forming the gist of the action from being physical injury to being "lost chance of avoiding the physical injury".[192] In general terms, the plaintiff would be able to obtain damages for that lost chance if it could be established on the balance of probabilities that the defendant's fault had caused that reformulated damage.[193] In her recent text, *Product Liability*,[194] Professor Stapleton suggests that recovery on a market share basis "is like allowing the plaintiff to recover to the extent that it was *likely* [my emphasis] to have been this manufacturer who made the relevant product unit".[195] However, this theory seems to disappoint with the remarkably pro-plaintiff American decision of *Hymowitz* v. *Eli Lilly & Co*,[196] since in that case it was held that the manufacturer could be liable, in terms of its market share, despite showing that his DES product did not cause the particular plaintiff's injury as it had not been used. The *chance* of that product being used is thus

187 *Ibid.*, 405–7.

188 *Ibid.*, 408.

189 See *Kramer* v. *Lewisville Memorial Hospital*, 858 SW 2d 397, 398 (Tex. 1993) and also the rejection of loss of a chance and increased risk doctrines in favour of a "substantial factor" standard of proof for proving proximate causation in *Manning* v. *Twin Falls Clinic & Hospital*, 830 P 2d 1185, 1190 (Idaho 1992).

190 See Ellis, Note, "Loss of Chance as Technique: Toeing the Line at Fifty Percent" (1994) 72 *Tex. LR* 369, 372, 385, 395–402.

191 Stapleton, n. 124 above, 287, 288. *Sindell* v. *Abbott Laboratories*, 607 P 2d 924 (1980) has been interpreted as an "important signa", of an increased desire to integrate chance into resolving torts cases: King, n. 177 above, 1381.

192 Stapleton, n. 22 above, 391, 392.

193 *Ibid.*, 392.

194 Stapleton, n. 124 above, 287, 288.

195 She is supported in this argument by Fleming, who regards *Sindell* as being an example of liability being discounted by the statistical chance of a particular defendant's product being the actual cause: Fleming, "Probabilistic Causation in Tort Law" [1989] *Can. BR* 661 at 672.

196 541 NYS 2d 941 (CA 1989).

nil, and yet the plaintiff is nonetheless recovering to the extent of that manufacturer's share of the market. *A fortiori*, to that extent, the plaintiff must surely be overcompensated, which accords with Stapleton's major criticism of *McGhee* v. *National Coal Board*,[197] where the plaintiff was able to recover for a part of the overall injury to which he was unable on a balance of probabilities to show a causal connection.[198]

An important assumption of Stapleton's theory of reformulation of the damage forming the gist of the action, which presents difficulty, is that the combined background risk of an outcome (B per cent) and the defendant's fault (D per cent) are independent variables, i.e. that there is no synergistic relation between them.[199] However, it is clear that the uniqueness of drugs could prove an exception to the Stapleton analysis, since under certain circumstances drugs may react synergistically with a genetic propensity or a nutritional defect when these operate as a background risk. For example, a number of drugs affect people who have genetic abnormalities. Someone may react badly to an anæsthetic because they have a genetic defect which reacts synergistically with the drug. Prior to the therapeutic use of thalidomide, phocomelia existed as a background risk in the form of a pre-existing latent genetic defect. As the Pearson Commission noted, the "effect of a drug may be to cause a pre-existing latent genetic defect to become manifest rather than to act directly on the unborn child",[200] a clear suggestion of a genetic defect reacting synergistically with a drug. In such circumstances, the Stapleton reformulation of the gist of an action in terms of loss of chance would fail to assist the plaintiff.

This issue could perhaps only be resolved under the Consumer Protection Act 1987, Part 1. If the product reacted synergistically, the question would then turn on whether such a propensity to be synergistic would render the product defective in terms of the Act.[201] Stapleton argues that in *Hotson* v. *East Berkshire AHA*[202] the House of Lords focused on the irrelevant question whether the plaintiff had shown a causal connection on the balance of probabilities to his epiphyseal avascular necrosis which released it from determining whether loss of a chance could form the gist of the action in negligence.[203] However, it has recently been argued that as well as the House of Lords in *Hotson* leaving open the question whether loss of a chance of recovery or of avoiding loss will be recoverable in tort, the actual loss of a chance reformulation by Stapleton has been incorrectly applied.[204] This is now pursued.

197 [1972] 1 WLR 1 (HL).

198 N. 22 above, 404, 405.

199 *Ibid.*, 389, 390.

200 Royal Commission on Civil Liability and Compensation for Personal Injury, Cmnd 7054–1/1978, para. 1450.

201 See CPA, s. 3(1) and (2).

202 [1987] 1 AC 750.

203 Stapleton, n. 22 above, 393.

204 Hill, "A Lost Chance for Compensation in the Tort of Negligence by the House of Lords" (1991) 54 *MLR* 511, 511.

7. STATISTICAL CHANCES AND PERSONAL CHANCES

It has been submitted that there are two kinds of chance, one "statistical" and the other "personal". A statistical chance is a figure collected from "previous unconnected outcomes, giving a probability of that outcome in any non-individual case". A personal chance is "peculiar to a particular individual".[205] A loss of a chance of recovery or of avoiding loss requires a personal chance, which in turn requires an unresolvable future hypothetical question and not a question of past fact.[206] A statistical chance is insufficient since it is not personal to the plaintiff and the statistics do not relate to a particular case.[207] The basis of the decision in *Hotson* is reinterpreted to the extent that the plaintiff is regarded as failing to show that he had a 25 per cent personal chance of recovery. The 25 per cent was really a statistical chance, which has no real compensatory value.[208] "[U]nless and until the data is 'personalised', a statistical chance should not be sufficient to form a compensative loss or . . . the 'gist of a negligence action' ".[209]

8. ALTERNATIVE APPROACHES TO DRUG CAUSALITY

In respect of evidence about a specific causal link in an individual case, it must be ascertained whether there is a proximate causal relationship between the drug treatment and the illness or injury.[210] It is in this context that the use of existing causality assessment methods becomes relevant. Expert witnesses may disagree whether in a specific case there is an association between the drug and an injury. The simplest method is to rely on ordinary clinical judgment or "global introspection",[211] though being aware that this may be highly subjective. At the other end of the spectrum is the use of standardised assessment

[205] *Ibid.*, 512.

[206] *Ibid.*, 511, 523.

[207] *Ibid.*, 512–14.

[208] *Ibid.*, 514–16. See, *per contra*, Stapleton, n. 22 above, 395.

[209] *Ibid.*, 518. See *Hotson* v. *East Berkshire AHA* [1987] 2 WLR 287, 303 (CA), *per* Croom-Johnson LJ. Croom-Johnson LJ observed: "[i]f it is proved statistically that 25% of the population have a chance of recovery from a certain injury and 75% do not, it does not mean that someone who suffers that injury and who does not recover from it has lost a 25% chance. He may have lost nothing at all. What he has to do is to prove that he was one of the 25% and that his loss was caused by the defendant's negligence. To be a figure in a statistic does not by itself give him a cause of action": *ibid.*, 223. See also *Herskovits* v. *Group Health Cooperative of Puget Sound*, 664 P 2d 474, 490, *per* Brachtenbach J (dissenting), stating the need to obtain evidence connecting the statistics to the facts of the case. Contrary to the views of some, Hill does not rule out the possibility of a limited loss of a chance doctrine when personal chances can be established which are peculiar to a particular individual: cf Scott, "Causation in Medico-Legal Practice: A Doctor's Approach to the 'Lost Opportunity' Cases" (1992) 55 *MLR* 521, 523–4.

[210] Dukes and Swartz, *Responsibility for Drug-Induced Injury* (Amsterdam, New York, Oxford, Elsevier, 1989), 41.

[211] See Lane *et al.*, "The Causality Assessment of Adverse Drug Reactions Using a Bayesian Approach" (1987) 2 *Pharmaceutical Med.* 265–83, 266.

methods (SAMs), including algorithms,[212] to determine probability.[213] How dependable a given algorithm is can be ascertained by permitting a number of experts to employ it to assess the same case; but an algorithm which has proved reliable in assessing one kind of drug-induced reaction may be less reliable in assessing another one. Thus a method for assessing long term neurological complications (e.g. Parkinsonian effects induced by neuroleptics) may be inappropriate for assessing cases of acute anaphylactic shock, which is neither long-term nor neurological. A court admitting evidence based on an algorithm should require evidence that its reliability in the type of case in question has been established. Where a conflict emerges between the results of an algorithm and those of sound clinical judgement, the latter may be regarded as more dependable.[214]

However, Dukes and Swartz state that the most favoured method is a set of "simple criteria" to assess causality in a given case. They regard the best algorithms as being no more than a means of ensuring that these criteria are all considered. The criteria can be used as a starting point in a case or to test the relevance of existing clinical judgements or algorithms.[215] The criteria are:

(i) A temporal link between drug use and the event;
(ii) The dose–effect relationship;
(iii) A decline of the effect on drug withdrawal;
(iv) A reintroduction of the effect on rechallenge, i.e. restarting the drug;
(v) An absence of another reasonable cause in the same patient.[216]

By far the major criticisms of SAMs are their limited and inflexible nature, coupled with the fact that they tend to contradict the results of other calculations.[217]

There are thus several deficiencies in these alternative approaches to ascertaining whether there is a specific causal link in an individual case between the drug and an injury. In the light of such difficulties, an attempt can be made to gain the assistance of the Bayes' Theorem.

9. THE PROPOSED SOLUTION—THE BAYES' THEOREM

Eggleston[218] has examined the importance of Bayes' Theorem in questions involving probability. The theorem allows us to determine how our evaluation of probability based on initial assumptions can be modified in the light of more

[212] An algorithm may be defined as a flow chart of rules to deal with the resolution of a particular problem.

[213] See Lane *et al.*, n. 211 above, 266.

[214] Dukes and Swartz, n. 210 above, 42.

[215] *Ibid.*

[216] *Ibid.*, 43–5.

[217] See Lane *et al.*, n. 211 above, 266.

[218] Eggleston, *Evidence, Proof and Probability* (2nd edn., London, Weidenfeld and Nicolson, 1983), 22–4.

data. The author will endeavour to show that this methodology can be used in the context of medicinal products and causation,[219] in respect of refining statistical chances into personal chances.

Bayes' Theorem is a significant branch of applied statistics which can be developed out of conditional probability. It expresses the relationship between the probability of a proposition (A) evaluated *before* the utilisation of new data (B) (prior probability) and the probability of the same proposition evaluated *after* the utilisation of the new data (posterior probability).

Thus:

$$\text{Posterior Probability of A given B} = \frac{\text{Prior Probability of A}}{1} \times \frac{\text{Probability of B given A}}{\text{Unconditional Probability of B}}$$

$$\text{i.e. } P(A/B) = P(A) \times \frac{P(B/A)}{P(B)}$$

An appropriate application of the Bayes' Theorem is delineated in the appendix at the end of this chapter. The main possible utility of Bayes' Theorem in the context of causation and medicinal products is in refining statistics regarding evidence of general causal links between a drug and an injury into statistics establishing a specific causal link between the drug and the adverse drug reaction in the case in question. However, the biggest criticism of Bayes' Theorem is the difficulty of arriving at a sufficiently accurate evaluation of a pre-existing probability to which experimental data can be applied.[220]

As already indicated, perhaps the most interesting potential use of Bayes' Theorem is refining what may be termed statistical chances[221] into "personal chances" which are peculiar to a particular individual.[222] For example, if a defendant had not negligently given an overdose of anæsthesia to a child suffering from cancer resulting in that child's death, there might have been a 40 per cent statistical chance of recovery from the cancer if the anæsthesia had been correctly given.[223] It is arguable that the Bayes' Theorem could be applied to the 40 per cent statistical chance to obtain an accurate assessment of the personal chance in that case.

In the context of medicinal products and causation, the author has attempted to show that it is possible to obtain a measure of probability through the

[219] For a clear discussion of the use of this theorem in a scientific context see Wonnacott and Wonnacott, *Introducing Statistics* (5th edn., New York, Chichester, Brisbane, Toronto, Singapore, John Wiley & Sons, 1990), chap. 3. See also Lane *et al.*, n. 211 above. I am grateful to Professor Alec Elliot, Professor of Clinical Physics, and Professor D. M. Titterington, Professor of Statistics, both of the University of Glasgow, for their advice on the application of the Bayes' Theorem.

[220] Eggleston, n. 218 above, 171.

[221] Kennedy and Grubb, *Medical Law: Text with Materials* (2nd edn., London, Dublin, Edinburgh, Butterworths, 1994), 488; Hill, n. 204 above, 512.

[222] *Ibid.*

[223] See King, n. 177 above, 1370 (plaintiff claiming that, by virtue of intervention of defendant's tortious conduct, plaintiff lost chance to recover from the pre-existing condition or avoid an untoward consequence of it).

application of Bayes' Theorem. (In our example in the appendix, we looked at the establishment of a statistical probability that someone taking D will suffer a drug-induced headache.) It is possible that such a statistical chance could be refined and personalised into a "personal chance" unique to an individual, using specific factors embodied in the likelihood ratio.

The likelihood ratio (LR) of a test can be defined as:

$$\frac{\text{The true positive incidence of the test}}{\text{The false positive incidence of the test}}$$

The probabilities in the likelihood ratio (LR) can be decomposed into factors in the light of specific case information in respect of patient history LR(Hi), timing LR(Ti), characteristics of the adverse event LR(Ch), the response to dechallenge, i.e. discontinuing the drug LR(De) and the response to rechallenge, i.e. restarting the drug LR(Re). The likelihood ratio is found by obtaining the product of all the individual likelihood ratio factors.

Diagrammatically this can be expressed by:

$$LR = LR(Hi) \times LR(Ti) \times LR(Ch) \times LR(De) \times LR(Re)$$

(Caveat = components, i.e. Hi etc. must be statistically independent).

The use of all these factors is dependent on the specific case information available. If all specific case information in respect of the factors is available, the posterior odds[224] are calculated as follows:

$$\text{Posterior Odds} = \text{Prior Odds} \times LR(Hi) \times LR(Ti) \times LR(Ch) \times LR(De) \times LR(Re)$$

Thus the posterior odds can be further refined by combining the prior odds, based on background information and the likelihood ratios, based on case-specific information, to produce as accurate a posterior probability as possible.[225] This would seem to be a possible solution to the statistical chance–personal chance dilemma.

Particularly important known risk factors could be introduced into the calculation,[226] such as kidney and liver function, age,[227] gender, genetic aberration or nutritional deficiency.

224 The relationship between odds and probability is: Odds = Probability/1-Probability. Thus the probability of 0.9 = odds of 9:1.

225 Donatini *et al.*, "Causality Assessment of Spontaneous Reporting: Correlation Between Bayesian and Other Approaches" (1993) 7 *Pharmaceutical Med.* 255, 256.

226 See Dukes and Swartz, n. 210 above, 19.

227 In the case of Opren, the establishment that Opren was causative of an adverse drug reaction resulted from the fact that the drug excretion was diminished by older patients with impaired renal function. The incidence of illness through natural causes and the fact that drugs such as Opren would probably be taken by elderly patients often already taking other medication, and thus particularly susceptible to further illness, increases the problematic nature of drug causation: See Teff, "Proposals for Compensating the Victims of Drug Injury" (1984) 24 *Med. Sci. Law* 208 at 208. Uncertainty existed as to causation of some of the more frequently alleged side-effects of Opren which were highly controversial as shown by the medical evidence: Hirst J in *Randall* v. *Eli Lilly & Co.*, *The Independent*, 4 Feb. 1988, QBD.

The list of factors indicating a proximate causal relationship[228] will help personalise the data.

Finkelstein and Fairley, two of the early protagonists of the Bayes' Theorem, proposed its use in trials "in order to translate the data into a form congenial to scrutiny by jurors".[229] Although heavily criticised in a powerful rejoinder by Tribe,[230] in which he considered that the costs of trying to integrate mathematics into the fact-finding process of legal trials outweighed its benefits, he refrained from ruling out the "carefully limited use of probabilistic proof in special circumstances".[231]

In recent years, support for the use of the theorem in the resolution of legal problems has become increasingly prevalent.[232] Indeed, it is argued that Bayes' Theorem "offers an instrument for picking the thought process apart",[233] providing a convincing rejoinder to the criticism that a probability approach to dealing with legal issues does not interpret evidence.[234] It is able to provide a "normative approach" to legal decision making,[235] though implementation of it in legal practice is difficult. As one of the major protagonists of the Bayes' Theorem has argued, the Bayesian model's results are not inconsistent with those that emerge when a court or jury evaluates the weight of conflicting evidence in accordance with legal norms.[236] Although hardly a convincingly positive reason for using the Bayes' Theorem, it would seem to be one which would support its use in certain circumstances. It is arguable, however, that the

[228] Dukes and Swartz, n. 210 above, 41–5. See above. There are also the criteria of Sir Austin Bradford Hill to determine whether a reported association is causal or non-genuine, i.e. strength of association, consistency, specificity, temporality, biological gradient, plausibility, coherence, experiment and analogy: Hill, "The Environment and Disease: Association or Causation?" [1965] *Proc. R. Soc. Med.* 295, 295–300. Note also the recent application of Hill's criteria by French J in *Reay* v. *British Nuclear Fuels plc; Hope* v. *BNF* [1994] 5 Med. LR 1, 49.

[229] Finkelstein and Fairley, "A Bayesian Approach to Identification Evidence" (1970) 83 *Harv. L Rev.* 489, 517.

[230] Tribe, "Trial by Mathematics: Precision and Ritual in the Legal Process" (1971) 84 *Harv. L Rev.* 1329.

[231] *Ibid.*, 1377. However, such circumstances would have to be "extraordinary": *ibid.* Tribe objected to the use of the Bayes' Theorem at trial because its methods generated an "intrinsic bias" within the trial process. However, he conceded that the Bayesian approach might not display an intrinsic bias *outside* the trial process in circumstances where its use could be subjected to continuing scrutiny over time: *ibid*, 1356–7.

[232] For a comprehensive examination of the merits and demerits of using Bayes' Theorem when dealing with the uncertainty of factfinding, see Tillers and Green (eds.), *Probability and Inference in the Law of Evidence* (Dordrecht, Kluwer Academic Publishers, 1988).

[233] Robertson and Vignaux, "Probability—The Logic of the Law" (1993) 13 *OJLS* 457, 471.

[234] *Ibid.*, 459.

[235] Fienberg and Schervish, "The Relevance of Bayesian Inference for the Presentation of Statistical Evidence and for Legal Decision Making" (1986) 66 B.U.L. Rev. 771, 794.

[236] Lempert, "The New Evidence Scholarship: Analyzing the Process of Proof" in Tillers and Green, n.232 above, 76. Lempert observes that the arguments of those who reject Bayesian models in trials suggest that statistical evidence has no place at all in trials: *ibid.*, 63. His following reply indicates an awareness of the day-to-day practical importance of probabilistic evidence in trials: "[t]hose who criticise Bayesian models of the legal process and the suggested application of the Bayesian approaches at trial must confront the reality that statistical evidence is offered in trials every day": *ibid.*

standard of proof in England of a balance of probabilities is "even more susceptible to a probabilistic interpretation" than its American counterpart, the preponderance of the evidence standard,[237] and that the English courts should consider carefully the use of Bayes' Theorem as a working tool in fact-finding.[238] An attempt to correlate existing causality assessment methods and the Bayes' Theorem approach to drug causality suggests that a non-numerical approach is sufficiently accurate for a causality assessment based on spontaneous reports. Donatini *et al.* also suggest that the Bayes' Theorem should be used if there is doubt regarding causality using non-numerical approaches.[239] So it would seem that Bayes' Theorem, in the specific context of problems concerning causation and medicinal products, may assist where a non-numerical approach has failed.

Depending on the availability of data from a test or sample, Bayes' Theorem can thus help to establish more personalised chances, helping to satisfy criticisms[240] of the Stapleton analysis. However, as noted above, the assumption that there is no synergistic[241] relationship between the combined background risk and the defendant's fault remains a distinct problem in respect of causation and medicinal products.

Despite such difficulties, there thus seems to be potential in the use of such a statistical analysis in the attempt to improve probabilistic assessments of causal link, particularly in drug-induced injury cases. Nevertheless, the focus from the position of legal scholarship has mainly been on the use of logic, probability and inference to resolve issues of forensic science.[242]

[237] Fienberg and Schervish, n. 235 above, 780.

[238] See support for use of Bayes' Theorem in courts requiring an accurate assessment of a drug's causal role in particular cases: Lane *et al.*, n. 211 above, 265, 282.

[239] Donatini *et al.*, n. 225 above, 255–6, 262–4. The interdisciplinary Vaccine Safety Committee of the Institute of Medicine adopted an "informal Bayesian approach" to assessing case reports in its review of scientific and medical literature on specific risks to children associated with vaccines: Stratton, Howe and Johnston (eds), *Institute of Medicine, Adverse Events Associated with Childhood Vaccines: Evidence Bearing on Causality* (Washington, DC, National Academy Press, 1994), 3, 25.

[240] See Hill, n. 204 above. Allen has argued that civil trials should be reconceptualised to permit the parties to determine how far they wish the particularity of the relevant facts to be pushed but that it is the parties, and not the state, who must decide the extent to which they wish to explore a case's particularities: Allen, "A Reconceptualization of Civil Trials" in Tillers and Green, n. 232 above, 45–6. However, it is arguable that the state does have an interest in the particularity of evidence, since this will affect the quality of decision by the fact-finder. This would be of particular importance in the area of drug product liability and causation.

[241] Synergism's challenge to legal concepts is, however, contained by the difficulties in identifying such interactions: Stapleton, *Disease and the Compensation Debate* (Oxford, Clarendon Press, 1986), 58–9.

[242] See the masterly monograph of Robertson and Vignaux, advocating the use of Bayes' Theorem in assessing scientific evidence: Robertson and Vignaux, *Interpreting Evidence: Evaluating Forensic Science in the Courtroom* (Chichester, John Wiley & Sons, 1995). It is Robertson and Vignaux's thesis that expert evidence must be correctly interpreted by a court and that the best way of achieving this is to utilise the likelihood ratio to describe the evidence's strength: *ibid.*, 219. They also advocate that scientific evidence concerning an issue "should be combined with other evidence relating to the same issue" and that the most effective way of doing so is to express the evidence in likelihood ratio form for it to be subsequently combined with other evidence: *ibid.*, 220. In addition,

It seems that the Bayes' Theorem could be of the greatest potential use in medicinal product liability cases involving causation, since the epidemiological evidence associated with adverse reactions naturally lends itself towards being used as part of a statistical refinement process. Moreover, the fact that proof in a civil court must be established on a balance of probabilities suggests that the Bayesian approach to legal decision-making might be more appropriate in a civil arena than a criminal one, where the concept of certainty assumes much greater importance.[243] The Bayes' Theorem recognises that absolute certainty cannot be provided for by science. But there is, however, a need for greater accuracy in decision-making by the courts, and Bayes' Theorem may at least help to achieve that.[244]

10. THE LIMITATIONS OF EPIDEMIOLOGY, IN PARTICULAR PHARMACO-EPIDEMIOLOGY

(i) Definitions

Epidemiology is the study of disease and its distribution in defined populations. Pharmaco-epidemiology is a study of the effects of drugs, both beneficial and adverse, in populations and the application of this to the control of disease by drugs. The limitations of epidemiological and pharmaco-epidemiological studies are related to the quantity, quality and accuracy of the input of data.

(ii) Collection of Data

(a) Clinical Trials (Pre-marketing)

Clinical trials could include 2,000 or more patients in each trial. In respect of the limitations of clinical trials, Weed and McKeown have described the broad

Robertson and Vignaux have observed that the likelihood ratio's importance is that it determines relevance and probative value, the key determinants of admissibility of expert evidence: *ibid.*, 22, 29. See Chap. 3. Robertson and Vignaux have also argued that it is not essential to have precise numbers for each of the probabilities to assess the likelihood ratio: *ibid.*, 22. This seems, however, arguable in complex cases involving the establishment of causation with medicinal products. Indeed the need for statistics with a strong evidential foundation for the calculation of the likelihood ratio has recently been expressed: See Grevling, Book Review, Robertson and Vignaux *Interpreting Evidence: Evaluating Forensic Science in the Courtroom* (1996) 112 *LQR* 509, 510.

243 Allen, n. 240 above, 51.

244 For further reading, see Redmayne, Review Article, "Science, Evidence and Logic" (1996) 59 *MLR* 747. Redmayne provides a cautious recognition of Bayes' Theorem but regards it as problematic, since it assumes that the fact-finder will have "unlimited cognitive capabilities". However, he considers that it is a useful "analytical tool" in providing insights into the fact-finding process. The fact that Bayes' Theorem discloses the complexity of situations with which it "copes poorly" is ironically a positive value of it: *ibid.*, 756, 759. Cf this book's submission that Bayes' Theorem is most useful in dealing with *complex* situations involving causation and drugs that are recalcitrant to non-numerical solutions, above.

spectrum of inappropriate conduct and misconduct in the reporting of scientific data, from the "falsification, fabrication and plagiarism of scientific data at one extreme . . . to plain sloppiness and the honest mistake".[245] An unsubstantiated estimate of the prevalence of fraudulent science is between 0.1 per cent and 0.4 per cent.[246] The well-rewarded collection of data from clinical trials is not free from examples of misconduct.

(b) Post-marketing Surveillance of Committee on Safety of Medicines (CSM) (Yellow Card System)

There is a highly significant under-reporting in general practice of suspected adverse drug reactions to the CSM of newly marketed drugs.[247] The CSM is well aware of and makes allowances for this under-reporting.

(c) Case Control Studies

This starts with a group which has the disease under study and another group, comparable in every other way, but which does not have the disease. The presence of the suspected cause, e.g. a drug, is compared retrospectively in the members of each group, particularly noting whether the suspected cause is commoner in the "cases" than the "controls". This is a rapid and relatively cheap type of study.[248]

Important limitations in this type of study are the tricks of human memory that can invalidate the assessments to a particular risk factor. In addition, the biases and confounding factors, related to the retrospective collection of data, must be considered, e.g. people who drink alcohol also tend to smoke; also, there are confounding factors relating to poverty.

(d) Cohort Studies

This starts with a group of people (cohort) who have been exposed to a drug or other factor, suspected of being associated with a disease. A group or cohort, comparable in every other respect but which has not been exposed to the drug or other suspected factor, is identified. These groups or cohorts are carefully observed over a period of time, e.g. one year, ten years or more, to determine the

[245] Weed and McKeown, "Epidemiology and Virtue Ethics" (1998) 27 *International Journal of Epidemiology* 343, 344.

[246] Editorial, "Dealing with Deception" (1996) 347 *Lancet* 843.

[247] Martin, Kapoor, Wilton and Mann, "Under-Reporting of Suspected Adverse Drug Reactions to Newly Marketed ('Black Triangle') Drugs in General Practice: Observational Study" (1998) 317 *BMJ* 119.

[248] Goldacre and Vessey, "Health and Sickness in the Community" in Weatherall, Ledingham and Warrell (eds.) *Oxford Textbook of Medicine* (2nd edn., Oxford, Oxford Medical Publications, 1987), chap. 3, 10–17.

frequency of the suspected disease among the exposed and non-exposed cohorts.[249]

The principal limitations of the cohort study are that it is slow, expensive and normally requires large numbers of subjects. The case control and the cohort studies allows the derivation of the relative risk[250]

(e) Record-linkage Studies

The availability of powerful computers has facilitated the collection and analysis of very large databases acquired from hospital patients exposed to specific drugs. This study has been extended to general practice. The Boston (USA) Collaborative Drug Surveillance Programme and the Dundee (UK) Medicines Evaluation and Monitoring Unit have carried out such studies, but again they are inherently reliant on sufficient numbers of quality data.[251]

(iii) Limitations in Quality of Data

(a) Sufficiency of Numbers of Subject

This is essential since this is related to the ability of the exercise to determine the incidence rate of the adverse drug reactions (ADRs). Thus an ADR rate of one in 100 requires observations in at least 1,000 patients. An ADR rate of one in 10,000 requires observations of 100,000 exposed patients, who have taken the drug. The need for large numbers of subjects in the National Child Encephalopathy Study (NCES) was one of the principal reasons behind the continued uncertainty surrounding the alleged association between pertussis vaccine and permanent brain damage, and the choice of the case control approach over a cohort study.[252]

(b) Age of Patient

Subjects older than 60 years are more likely to suffer ADRs. Subjects in the age group 71–80 have a significantly greater chance of hospital admission from ADRs. The neonate (new-born), especially if born prematurely, is at particular danger from certain drugs, because some of the enzymes involved

[249] *Ibid.*

[250] The relative risk of acquiring a disease in association with an exposure to a drug or other suspected factor is given by the incidence rate of the disease in the exposed group, divided by the incidence rate in the non-exposed group: Goldacre and Vessey, n. 248 above, chap. 3, 16.

[251] See Lawson, "Epidemiology" in Davies (ed.) *Textbook of Adverse Drug Reactions* (4th edn., Oxford, Oxford University Press, 1991), 10.

[252] Miller, Ross, Aldersalde, Bellman and Rawson, "Pertussis Immunisation and Serious Acute Neurological Illness in Children" (1981) 282 *BMJ* 1595–9. See below, chap. 4.

in the metabolism and excretion of these drugs are not, by then, fully developed.[253]

(c) Gender

There are many studies which suggest that women are more likely than men to suffer ADRs from a large number of drugs.[254]

(d) Genetic Considerations

Many drugs are metabolised by enzymes of oxidation or acetylation, the activities of which are under genetic control. Individual subjects who are poor oxidisers or poor acetylators will take longer to degrade appropriate drugs, and this will lead to prolonged pharmacological activity of the drug, and thus to a greater chance of adverse drug reactions, in comparison with rapid oxidisers and acetylators.[255]

(e) Racial Considerations

Such individual differences of these enzymes may be part of racial enzymic differences. Thus rapid acetylators of drugs are more common amongst Eskimos and Japanese, and slow acetylators amongst Mediterranean Jews. Women in Scandinavia and Chile seem to be particularly vulnerable to hepatic jaundice associated with oral contraceptives: therefore, results of pharmaco-epidemiological studies carried out in one country may not be applicable to another, if such basic differences are operative.[256]

(iv) **Interpretation of Results**

Having achieved the data, hopefully ideal in quantity, quality and provenance, and having analysed them, there is still the final hurdle of assessment and interpretation of (a) the causal relation to disease and (b) the influence it should have on public health advice or litigation. Eminent experts have disagreed in their application of the same data to these two points. This may be due to personal bias of the "experts" and/or to the intrinsic inadequacy and uncertainty of the data to define causation.

Taubes[257] collected opinions on the interpretation of epidemiological results. The result of the relative risk would seem to be the favourite criterion for assess-

[253] Lawson, n. 251 above, 12.
[254] *Ibid.*, 10.
[255] *Ibid.*
[256] *Ibid.*
[257] Taubes, "Epidemiology Faces its Limits" (1995) 269 *Science* 164–9.

ing validity of results, by several eminent authorities. Angell of the *New England Journal of Medicine* and Temple, the Director of Drug Evaluation at the Food and Drug Administration, agreed that unless the study has produced a relative risk of more than 3:1, it falls short of immediate acceptance; but Bailar, epidemiologist of McGill University, points out the difficulty of identifying a dividing line in marginal cases.[258]

Meta-analysis is a technique for combining many ambiguous epidemiological studies on the same topic in order to achieve a decisive result. A questionnaire by Taubes[259] to a number of epidemiologists on the use of meta-analysis for this purpose revealed no consistency of opinion.

(v) Conclusion

While yet aware of these limitations of epidemiological evidence, it is submitted that the use of such evidence, particularly in circumstances where non-numerical solutions to causation have proved elusive, will lead to greater accuracy in litigation concerning adverse reactions, contentiously associated with drugs. The use of the Bayes Theorem in refining statistics to the individual case should help in this process.

However, without the sufficient evidence of prior probabilities, and quality of data, the use of Bayesian approaches in pharmaceutical product liability litigation could prove to be ineffective. It has been argued that the principal difficulty with epidemiology, particularly cohort studies, "is its inability to discover small increases of risk above a background rate".[260] Nevertheless, Green is careful to suggest that he is not trivialising the importance and probative value of epidemiological evidence:

> "Rather, the point is that the value of any given set of epidemiological studies in making causal inferences requires a careful consideration, assessment, and accounting for possible systematic biases and random sampling errors".[261]

He argues against the adoption of an epidemiological threshold in cases other than Bendectin[262] involving toxic substances on the grounds that in the majority of cases epidemiological evidence is lacking[263]. Green is critical of the limitations of statistical significance:

> "Statistical significances only protect against false positive error—concluding an association exists when there is no association. The more protection against false positive

[258] *Ibid.*, 168.

[259] *Ibid.*

[260] Green, *Bendectin and Birth Defects: The Challenges of Mass Toxic Substances Litigation* (Philadelphia, Penn., University of Pennsylvania Press, 1996), 33.

[261] *Ibid.*, 34.

[262] See Chap. 3.

[263] *Ibid.*, 311–12, 316–17.

error provided by significance testing, the greater the risk of . . . false negative [error]—concluding that no association exists when there is one".[264]

However, it is submitted that a reduction in the chance of false positivity and false negativity is reflected in the application of the likelihood ratio used in applying the Bayes' Theorem to epidemiological evidence. Although Green details the methodological flaws of epidemiological evidence (limited samples, chance, confounding, systematic biases), all of which are able to compromise a study's validity,[265] it is submitted that all types of evidence have methodological flaws. The point of the use of Bayes' Theorem is in refining the statistics to the individual and in reducing some of the uncertainty and limitations of epidemiological evidence.

11. THE PROPOSED USE OF EPIDEMIOLOGICAL APPROACHES TO ASCERTAINING CAUSATION IN THE LIGHT OF CURRENT TRENDS IN CIVIL JUSTICE

The Civil Justice System in England and Wales is presently subject to several recommendations for reform. Lord Woolf's Final Report on *Access to Justice*[266] highlighted the need for a fundamental transfer in the responsibility for management of civil litigation from litigants and their legal advisors to the courts.[267] This approach to judicial case management has been supported by Sir Peter Middleton's review of the reform proposals. He has stated that they constitute "a coherent programme that can improve the efficiency and flexibility of the courts system".[268] Despite Professor Zander's severe criticisms of the Woolf Report and the Middleton Review,[269] the view prevails that the civil justice system is too costly and inefficient.

Although it would seem that an increase in the use of epidemiological evidence could result in an increase in costs, particularly in the use of experts to interpret the evidence, it is submitted that this approach will lead to greater efficiency within the civil justice system. That view is taken for the following reasons.

[264] See Chap. 3, 317.

[265] *Ibid.*, 319.

[266] Rt. Hon. Lord Woolf MR, *Access to Justice: Final Report* (London, The Stationery Office, 1996).

[267] Rt. Hon. Lord Woolf, *Access to Justice: Interim Report* (London, Woolf Enquiry Team, 1995), Recommendation 1; Rt. Hon. Lord Woolf MR, *Access to Justice: Final Report*, n. 266 above, Recommendation 1.

[268] "Review of Civil Justice and Legal Aid": Reports to the Lord Chancellor by Sir Peter Middleton GCB (London, Lord Chancellor's Department, 1997).

[269] In respect of the Woolf Report, see M. Zander, "The Woolf Report: Forwards or Backwards for the New Lord Chancellor" (1997) 16 Civil *JQ* 208; in respect of the government's proposals on civil justice and a view on some of the recommendations of the Middleton Report, see M. Zander, Report, "The Government's Plans on Civil Justice" (1998) 61 *MLR* 382.

First, although strongly rejected by Professor Zander as being a mechanism that will lead to additional costs,[270] the prevailing view in legal practice, and certainly in the Woolf proposals, is in support of the use of judicial case management, both in the context of medical negligence cases and in multi-party actions, which would embrace the majority of cases involving medicinal product liability litigation. Judicial case management would arguably operate to increase efficiency in judicial decision-making. The Woolf Report established a three-tier system for judicial case management: first, an increased small claims jurisdiction; secondly, a new fast track for cases at the lower end of the scale; thirdly, a new multi-track for remaining cases.[271] The presumption is that clinical negligence cases should be in the multi-track.[272] Indeed, Lord Woolf considers that judicial case management should be particularly appropriate in medical negligence cases since it will eliminate hopeless cases, ensure control of discovery, restrict parties to the real issues and control expense through limited hearings.[273] However, the majority of cases involving pharmaceuticals and product liability would seem to come within what would be termed "multi-party situations" by Lord Woolf.[274] Here again, such actions with their inherent complexity would "invariably merit the full hands on judicial control".[275] Thus, despite the protestations of Zander, it would seem that judicial case management would be the most appropriate way to address pharmaceutical product liability litigation. *A fortiori*, the early experiences of the courts in multi-party actions were formulated from the group action litigation surrounding Opren[276] and the benzodiazepines.[277] Thus, much of the courts' experience in judicial case management, as recommended in Woolf, has spawned from medicinal product liability litigation. In addition, it is submitted that judicial case management should help in the interpretation and understanding of epidemiological evidence when ascertaining the merits of cases. A proper control over the use of statistical evidence will be necessary in such cases, and judges will be required to exercise their authority in narrowing and defining issues when such evidence is presented before the courts.[278]

[270] Zander, "The Woolf Report", n. 269 above, 219.

[271] Rt. Hon. Lord Woolf, *Access to Justice: Interim Report,* n. 267 above, Recommendation 2; Rt. Hon. Lord Woolf, *Access to Justice: Final Report,* n. 266 above, Recommendation 2.

[272] See the Consultation Paper, *Proposed New Procedures for Clinical Negligence* (London, Lord Chancellor's Department, 1997), para. 11. Clinical negligence is the term used in the above Consultation Paper since it is considered to be a broader and more accurate description of the types of case in this area than medical negligence.

[273] Rt. Hon. Lord Woolf MR, "Medics, Lawyers and the Courts" (1997) 16 *Civil JQ* 302.

[274] Rt. Hon. Lord Woolf MR, *Access to Justice: Final Report*, n.266 above, chap. 17, Multi-Party Actions.

[275] *Ibid.*, para. 14.

[276] *Davies* v. *Eli Lilly & Co* [1987] 1 WLR 1136.

[277] *AB and others* v. *John Wyeth & Brother Ltd and Others (No 2)* [1994] 5 Med. L.R. 149; *AB and others* v. *John Wyeth & Brother Ltd; AB and Others* v. *Roche Products Ltd* (LEXIS, 13 Dec. 1996).

[278] The Woolf Report referred to the need for trial judges to have training in medical issues in order that they acquire the technical knowledge to carry out their new role effectively, so that they

Secondly, the need to establish better ways of weeding out weak and/or hopeless claims and, if possible, to prevent them from beginning actions in the first place, has been stressed in the context of multi-party actions by Lord Woolf.[279] A similar view was given by Lord Woolf in his discussion of the pursuit of unmeritorious claims in medical negligence cases.[280] In the context of multi-party actions, it is submitted that the use of epidemiological evidence would help to identify the strongest and weakest cases on causation. The elimination of the weakest and the focus on the strongest would help to increase efficiency in decision-making in this area. In multi-party situations, issues such as the approach to causation would be determined at the first Case Management Conference by the managing judge.[281]

Thirdly, it seems that the use of epidemiological evidence would also be supported by the proposed changes to funding in civil litigation. The government takes the view that in the future conditional fee agreements should be entered into in any proceedings, except in the categories currently proscribed by statute.[282] A conditional fee agreement (also known as a no-win-no-fee agreement) is one which "allow[s] a lawyer to agree to take a case on the understanding that if the case is lost, he will not charge his client for the work he has done".[283] However, if "the case is won, the lawyer is entitled to charge a success fee calculated as a percentage of his normal costs, to recompense for the risk he has run of not being paid".[284] The success fee is set according to the risk the lawyer is taking. The higher the chance of winning, the lower the success fee.[285] Clearly, the risk of losing will have to be quantified. Since establishment of causation may well amount to settlement or victory,[286] the assessment of probability of causal link through epidemiological evidence should assist in the risk assessment. The government as yet does not intend to remove medical negligence claims from legal aid, "but will look to do so as the market develops and lawyers adapt to the greater use of conditional fee agreements".[287] It will therefore be necessary for lawyers to prepare for this transition. The Lord Chancellor's Department Consultation Paper on Conditional Fees observes the difficulty in proving causation in medical negligence cases, and attributes part of

are able to narrow and define issues as a case progresses and can exercise their power to exclude evidence: Rt. Hon. Lord Woolf MR, *Access to Justice: Final Report,* n. 266 above, chap. 15, paras. 61–2.

[279] Rt. Hon. Lord Woolf MR, *Access to Justice: Final Report*, n. 266 above, chap. 17, paras. 51–2, 71, 73.

[280] *Ibid.*, chap. 15, para. 1.

[281] See Multi-Party Situations: Proposed New Procedures: A Consultation Paper (London, Lord Chancellor's Department, 1997), para. 32.

[282] Namely criminal and family proceedings: s. 58 (10), Courts and Legal Services Act 1990. See *Access to Justice with Conditional Fees: A Lord Chancellor's Department Consultation Paper* (London, Lord Chancellor's Department, 1998), para. 2.7.

[283] *Ibid.*, para. 2.1.

[284] *Ibid.*

[285] *Ibid.*

[286] Mildred, "Representing the Plaintiff" in Howells (ed.), n. 5 above, 27.

[287] Lord Chancellor's Department Consultation Paper, n. 282 above, para. 3.16.

the failure of recovery in such cases[288] to them being pursued by lawyers with insufficient experience or knowledge to identify at the beginning those which lack merit. Such lawyers are also unable to appraise properly the evidence of medical reports that will allow them to stop cases earlier.[289] The government therefore proposes to limit the right of choice of solicitors who may undertake medical negligence cases under legal aid,[290] and the Legal Aid Board will only be able to give contracts to solicitors who have shown sufficient competence in this area.[291] Nevertheless, it may well be that pharmaceutical product liability cases will continue to be supported by a form of legal aid, at least under transitional arrangements, where cases excluded from legal aid show wider public interest.[292] The Consultation Paper states, for these purposes, that public-interest cases "are defined as those which affect, or potentially affect a wider group of people than those directly involved".[293] In order "[t]o justify legal aid funding a case would have to demonstrate the potential to produce *tangible* benefits for a *significant* number of people in a *definable* category", including cases involving novel points of law.[294] Since the use of epidemiological evidence and experts to interpret it could involve high investigative costs, it may well be that the government will be able to fund such costs with a transitional limited fund for such high-cost cases involving pharmaceutical products. Such cases might be unlikely to attract a conditional fee agreement and could be regarded as public interest cases .[295]

It is conceded that the increased use of epidemiological evidence and experts to interpret it may result in increased transaction costs. However, it is submitted that the use of such evidence will assist in the filtering out of weak cases and the identification of strong ones.[296] The hands-on judicial case management approach, as envisaged by Lord Woolf, could reveal the multi-claimant pharmaceutical product liability case as a suitable paradigm for the operation of its proposals.

12. CONCLUSION

This chapter has attempted to demonstrate the difficulties of proving that a drug caused an adverse effect under both the law of negligence and the Consumer

[288] In only 17% of cases was £50 or more recovered in 1996–7: *ibid.*, para. 3.17.
[289] *Ibid.*
[290] *Ibid.*, para. 3.18.
[291] *Ibid.*, para. 3.19.
[292] *Ibid.*, paras. 3.30–3.31.
[293] *Ibid.*, para. 3.32.
[294] *Ibid.*
[295] *Ibid.*, para. 3.35.
[296] Whatever the approach to funding taken, as Lord Woolf has indicated, "[t]he difficulty of proving . . . causation . . . which arises more acutely in medical negligence than in other personal injury cases, accounts for much of the excessive cost": Rt. Hon. Lord Woolf MR, *Access to Justice: Final Report,* n. 266 above, chap. 15, para. 5.

Protection Act 1987. In the context of assessing the role of causation in negligence, the position surrounding drug injuries to unborn children has been examined, including the thalidomide tragedy and the Congenital Injuries (Civil Liability) Act 1976. A description has been given of methods used to ameliorate causation difficulties, including the possibility in *McGhee* that a plaintiff might succeed if he could establish a material increase in risk of damage. Alternative probabilistic methods of establishing causation, including proportional liability, have also been discussed. The drawbacks of these approaches have been noted.

The other method discussed is Stapleton's reformulation of the damage forming the gist of an action from being a physical injury to being a lost chance of recovery or of avoiding a physical injury. However, it has been previously argued by Hill that such a reformulation has been incorrectly applied. This chapter has reaffirmed Hill's important distinction between statistical and personal chances, a distinction which is often blurred by insufficient knowledge to establish personal chances with certainty.

In response to such problems, the role of Bayes' Theorem has also been examined, including the extent to which it can help in the conversion of statistical chances to personal chances of drug causation: the limitations of epidemiological evidence, particularly pharmaco-epidemiology, have also been noted. This "personalising" of the data by the Bayes' Theorem depends on the availability of further data to apply to pre-existing probability, which itself must be sufficiently accurate before the theorem can be utilised. The focused answer of refined statistical evidence requires focused questions involving accurate prior probability and data to apply to it. However, the use of Bayes' Theorem as a tool to refine statistics to establish the most accurate specific causal link between a drug and an injury is potentially useful. Such techniques could be used to refine *ex ante* or *ex post* statistics in an attempt to improve probability methods of analysis such as proportional liability and to reduce the possibility of over-compensation or under-compensation for each individual. In relation to proportional liability, it is submitted that the *ex post* use of existing statistics as they emerge from medical monitoring[297] could be accurately refined by the Bayes' Theorem. Perhaps the use of the Bayes' Theorem may amount to a pragmatic response to the problem of proving causation in drug-induced injury litigation cases where proof of causation is recalcitrant to non-numerical solutions.

Although an increase in the use of epidemiological evidence could result in an increase in costs, particularly in the use of experts to interpret the evidence, it is submitted that this approach will in the long term lead to greater efficiency within the reformed civil justice system.

[297] E.g., the General Practice Research Database and also the Boston Collaborative Drug Surveillance Programme: Jick, *A Major Resource for Drug Safety Studies* (Carshalton, Surrey, Centre for Medicines Research, 1995).

APPENDIX: APPLICATION OF BAYES' THEOREM

Example

Sulphonomide (drug D) is used to treat acute pyelitis, an infection of the pelvis of the kidney, (the medical condition, M). An epidemiologic study indicates that approximately one in eight of patients who take D subsequently experience a severe headache (the adverse event, E) while one in ten patients with acute pyelitis who do not take D experience severe headache due to their illness. Such a headache occurs within one hour of the drug's administration, whilst an M-caused headache may occur at any time within two days following the onset of M. Indeed, the time-to-headache for an M-caused headache is uniformly distributed over the range (0,48) hours.

Problem

A patient takes D when symptoms of M begin and suffers a headache within 60 minutes. What is the chance that the headache is D-induced?

Solution

We have initially to calculate the probability that a given headache is drug-induced. Formulation of Bayes' Theorem is thus:

$$P(D \rightarrow E/E) = \frac{P(D \rightarrow E)}{1} \times \frac{P(E/D \rightarrow E)}{P(E)}$$

i.e.

$$\text{The probability of a drug-induced headache given the patient has a headache} = \text{The probability of a drug-induced headache} \times \frac{\text{The probability of a headache given the patient has a drug-induced headache}}{\text{The probability of a headache from any cause}}$$

Now $P(E/D \rightarrow E) = 1$, i.e. 100 per cent probability

To obtain P(E), seek first p (no headache)
Assuming that the causes of headache other than drug or pyelitis are very small and also that drug-caused headache occurs (or does not occur) independently of a pyelitis-caused headache.

p (no headache) = (1-1/10) × (1-1/8)
Because the probability of pyelitis headache is 1/10

Because the probability of drug headache is 1/8

$$
\begin{aligned}
p\,(\text{no headache}) &= (1-0.1) \times (1-0.125)\\
&= 0.9 \times 0.875\\
&= 0.79\\
\therefore\ p(E) &= 1-0.79\\
&= 0.21\\
\therefore\ p(D \rightarrow E/E) &= \frac{0.125 \times 1}{0.21}\\
&= \underline{0.59} \quad \text{(i.e. probability of a drug induced headache given patient has a headache)}\\
\therefore\ p(M \rightarrow E/E) &= \underline{0.41} \quad \text{(i.e .probability of a pyelitis-induced headache given patient has a headache)}
\end{aligned}
$$

To refine probability to include Timing (T_1), where T_1 denotes that the time to headache is less than one hour

$P(T_1/D \rightarrow E) = 1$ (because E occurred in first hour)
$P(T_1/M \rightarrow E) = 1/48$ (because pyelitis-induced headache can occur in any hour of 48 hours), assuming that the time to headache for an M-caused headache is uniformly distributed over the range (0,48) hours

$\therefore$ Odds on the headache being drug-induced against it being disease-induced

$$
\begin{aligned}
&= \frac{P(D \rightarrow (E/E,T1)}{P(M \rightarrow E/E,T1)}\\
&= \frac{0.59 \times 1}{0.41 \times 1/48}\\
&= 69{:}1
\end{aligned}
$$

$$
\begin{aligned}
\therefore\ P(D \rightarrow E) \text{ within 60 minutes} &= \frac{69}{69+1}\\
&= \underline{0.98}
\end{aligned}
$$

2

Diethylstilbestrol and Causation

1. INTRODUCTION

This chapter concerns problems of causation[1] associated with the drug Diethylstilbestrol (DES). After a background discussion in section 2, section 3 examines three main scenarios associated with the administration of DES, the first of which is second-generation vaginal adenosis and vaginal clear cell adenocarcinoma. Here, the principal causation problem is of identifying the particular manufacturer of DES to ensure a correct causal attribution between manufacturer and damage. The American and Dutch courts have overcome these difficulties by respectively two forms of liability, i.e. market share and alternative causation liability. Both of these approaches are critically examined by demonstrating their apparent failure to deal directly with the practical problems of defining market share, exculpation and ensuring that at least one of the parties to the case actually made the DES which caused the injuries to the plaintiffs.

The remainder of section 3 concerns the two other alleged adverse drug reactions associated with DES: first, the alleged association between DES and second-generation physical abnormalities of reproductive organs, also allegedly associated with third-generation physical disabilities, including cerebral palsy. Most of the cases in this area turn on the issue of whether a right of action exists for a preconception tort for the third generation, but it is shown that difficulties in establishing causation seem to have a bearing on the recognition of such a cause of action in the first place. Such difficulties, it is suggested, may be a reason for the refusal to recognise an action on behalf of third-generation victims of DES in the United States. It is arguable that a preconception right of action exists in English law, but judicial policy may operate to rule out the possibility of such actions for third-generation DES victims. Secondly, an examination is made of the alleged association between DES and second-generation chromosomal damage to sperm germ cells, allegedly in turn resulting in third-generation female offspring with clear cell vaginal adenocarcinoma. It is suggested that it is particularly difficult in such cases to establish causation, with recent English case law floundering on the causation issue in respect of genetic damage allegedly being passed on from a father's sperm.

[1] Elements of this chap. were originally published in R. Goldberg, "Causation and Drugs: The Legacy of Diethylstilbestrol" (1996) 25 *Anglo-American LR* 286.

However, it is observed that this does not rule out the possibility of future cases alleging genetic damage passed on through the father's sperm being successful and involving the ingestion of medicinal products such as DES. Unlike the first scenario in section 3, where a causal link between DES and vaginal adenocarcinoma and adenosis has been established for over 20 years, the association between DES and such other second- and third-generation effects remains uncertain.

Section 4 concludes with an examination of the current legal stance in the United Kingdom in respect of DES and causation. Causation seems to remain an inherently difficult problem under the law of negligence. *A fortiori*, English negligence law seems to restrict liability at an early stage through the judicial policy mechanism of the three-stage test of establishing a duty of care. It is arguable that the Congenital Disabilities (Civil Liability) Act 1976 is inapplicable in second-generation DES cases, though the theoretical argument of third-generation DES cases being covered by the Act is mooted. Finally, the lack of assistance of the strict liability regime for defective products under the Consumer Protection Act 1987 is noted, as is the increased importance of an understanding of medicinal products with alleged generational side-effects, in the light of the use of high risk drugs such as AZT, used in the treatment of AIDS.

2. BACKGROUND

> visiting the iniquity of the fathers upon the children
> unto the third and fourth generation . . . [2]

The drug DES was developed by an English researcher as an effective œstrogenic hormone taken in the first three months of pregnancy to prevent threatened abortion. As very few clinical trials were performed on the drug and the basis of its use was theoretical, much doubt has existed whether the drug was useful at all. Apart from the issue of the drug's efficacy, problems started to emerge with DES when it was discovered to cause vaginal cancer in adolescent or adult daughters, who were fœtuses *in utero* at the time their mothers had been administered the drug.[3] One of the key determinants of establishing cause and effect was the characteristic nature of the vaginal clear cell adenocarcinoma, a type of cancer which very rarely occurs spontaneously. Another characteristic has been the latent nature of the cancer, occurring between 12 and 25 years after birth.

[2] Exodus 20:5.

[3] Herbst, Ulfelder and Poskanzer "Adenocarcinoma of the Vagina. Association of Maternal Stilbestrol Therapy with Tumour Appearance in Young Women" (1971) 284 *N Eng. J Med.* 878, at 878, 879. In the Herbst study, it was found that 7 out of 8 of the mothers of patients with vaginal adenocarcinoma had been treated with diethylstilbestrol commenced during the first trimester. The maternal ingestion of stilbestrol during early pregnancy was found to have enhanced the risk of vaginal adenocarcinoma, developing years later in the offspring who were exposed as fœtuses in utero at the time their mothers were administered the drug.

Notwithstanding the overwhelming establishment of a causal link between vaginal clear cell adenocarcinoma and DES, strict epidemiological analyses of data have pointed to shortcomings in such evidence.[4]

The effect of DES on the second generation, i.e. the daughters who were fœtuses *in utero* when their mothers took the drug, can be distinguished from third-generation cases which have alleged that DES can cause reproductive abnormalities in the second generation, resulting in the premature birth of third-generation children with physical disabilities, including cerebral palsy. There are also alleged cases of DES causing chromosomal damage to germ cells in the sperm of second-generation male children, resulting in female offspring with clear cell vaginal adenocarcinoma.[5] Cases of second-generation injury and DES seem to be examples of prenatal torts, which occur when someone tortiously inflicts physical injury on an unborn child through the body of the mother,[6] whereas alleged cases of third-generation injury and DES appear to be illustrative of preconception torts where tortious acts of the defendant prior to conception cause resultant harm to the child.[7] Harm to the second-generation child may be prenatal (vaginal adenocarcinoma, manifesting many years later, or damage to reproductive organs, again appearing later). Harm to the third-generation child may be perinatal (cerebral palsy) or possibly pre-natal

[4] McFarlane, Feinstein and Horwitz, "Diethylstilbestrol and Clear Cell Vaginal Carcinoma. Reappraisal of the Epidemiologic Evidence" (1986) 81 *Am. J Med.*, 855–63. In the McFarlane *et al.* study the authors conclude that there are two possible alternative explanations of the association between DES and clear-cell vaginal carcinoma: *ibid.*, 862. First, there is the possibility of "susceptibility bias" arising from the reasons for the administration of a drug in a problem pregnancy. The authors express the need to obtain a history of prior pregnancy loss to match the cases and controls: *ibid.*. However, the McFarlane *et al.* study has been strongly criticised by Buitendijk: Buitendijk, "Diethylstilbestrol and the Next Generation: A Challenge to the Evidence?" in Dukes and Beeley (eds.), *Side Effects of Drugs Annual 12* (Amsterdam, New York and Oxford, Elsevier, 1988), 347–8. He concludes that none of the references cited by the authors supports a strong association between prior pregnancy problems or first trimester bleeding and clear cell adenocarcinoma of the cervix or vagina: *ibid.*, 347. Moreover, Buitendijk adds that for such pregnancy problems to account for an increased risk of adenocarcinoma of the cervix or vagina, such an association should be at least as strong as the association between diethylstilbestrol and adenocarcinoma of the cervix or vagina, which would be very unlikely. Thus it would seem that matching on prior pregnancy history is unnecessary: *ibid.* McFarlane *et al.*, in respect of their second alternative explanation, considered that the rates of previous exposure to DES in the previously published two case control studies may have been elevated by "interviewer bias or recall bias", since a relatively high incidence of clear cell vaginal carcinoma, which would have been expected from such case control studies, had not been observed in the cohort studies: McFarlane *et al.*, above, 862. However, Buitendijk counters this point by contending that McFarlane *et al.* confuse high incidence with high risk since the expected numbers are low, even with strong relative risk in the case control studies because the incidence of adenocarcinoma of the vagina and cervix in exposed and unexposed offspring is low: Buitendijk, above, 347–8. Buitendijk also concludes that McFarlane *et al.* ignored additional epidemiologic evidence showing an association between DES and adenocarcinoma of the vagina and cervix: *ibid.*, 348. Thus such an attempt to invalidate the initial case control studies would seem not to have succeeded.

[5] See 3. The Role of Causation with Diethylstilbestrol, below.

[6] Keeton, Dobbs, Keeton and Owen (eds.), *Prosser and Keeton on The Law of Torts* (5th edn., St. Paul, Minn., West Publishing Co., 1984), 367.

[7] Mascaro, "Preconception Tort Liability: Recognizing a Strict Liability Cause of Action for DES Grandchildren" (1991) XVIII *American Journal of Law & Medicine* 435,436–7.

(chromosomal damage in sperm of second-generation male causing damage to third-generation zygotes, manifesting many years later in clear cell vaginal adenocarcinoma).

3. THE ROLE OF CAUSATION WITH DIETHYLSTILBESTROL

Three main scenarios have emerged in respect of the administration of DES to women, which are illustrated in Figure 1.[8]

(i) Scenario 1: Second Generation Vaginal Adenosis and Vaginal Clear Cell Adenocarcinoma

(a) Introduction

First, the administration of DES to pregnant women has resulted in damage to the female second-generation fœtus causing vaginal adenosis and vaginal clear cell adenocarcinoma from the ages of 15 to 25 years.[9] Here, evidence of a causal link has been overwhelming and long accepted,[10] though shortcomings in the epidemiological evidence have been suggested.[11] Problems in the cases involving vaginal cancer have been about establishing liability in the absence of knowledge of who the manufacturer of the drug actually was, the courts invariably resorting to market share liability as the remedy, even in circumstances where a pharmaceutical company can show that its DES product did not cause the particular plaintiff's injury since it had not been used.[12]

In certain cases the identification of the manufacturer responsible for a particular drug can be difficult, e.g. where generic drugs have been prescribed over a period of time. There were about 200 to 300 manufacturers of DES by virtue

[8] A fourth scenario, briefly alluded to in the chap., is the alleged administration of DES to women, resulting in damage to the male fœtus *in utero* causing abnormalities of the male genital tract. This is also referred to in Figure 1.

[9] See Herbst, Ulfelder and Poskanzer, n. 3 above, 878–9.

[10] Buitendijk, n. 4 above, 347–8.

[11] McFarlane, Feinstein, and Horwitz, n. 4 above. The cases involving DES and adenocarcinoma of the vagina have been criticised for failing adequately to discuss the causation issue since the courts in such cases have taken the causation issue as being settled: Brennan, "Causal Chains and Statistical Links: The Role of Uncertainty in Hazardous-Substance Litigation" (1988) 73 *Cornell L Rev*. 469, 500. A worldwide registry of women suffering from adenocarcinoma shows that only 384 of the women who contracted this disease were born between 1940 and 1971. However, these are figures from a 1979 study quoted in a 1981 article and do not take account of new cases, including allegedly third-generation DES cases. 213 of these 384 cases are associated with DES use, which is criticised as being small, yet the number is more than 50%. The possibility of a second peak developing in the future was conceded: Fisher, "Products Liability—An Analysis of Market Share Liability" (1981) 34 *Vand. L Rev*. 1623, 1624.

[12] See *Sindell* v. *Abbott Laboratories*, 26 Cal. 3d 588, 607 P 2d 924 (1980) and *Hymowitz* v. *Eli Lilly & Co*, 541 NYS 2d 941 (CA 1989), below.

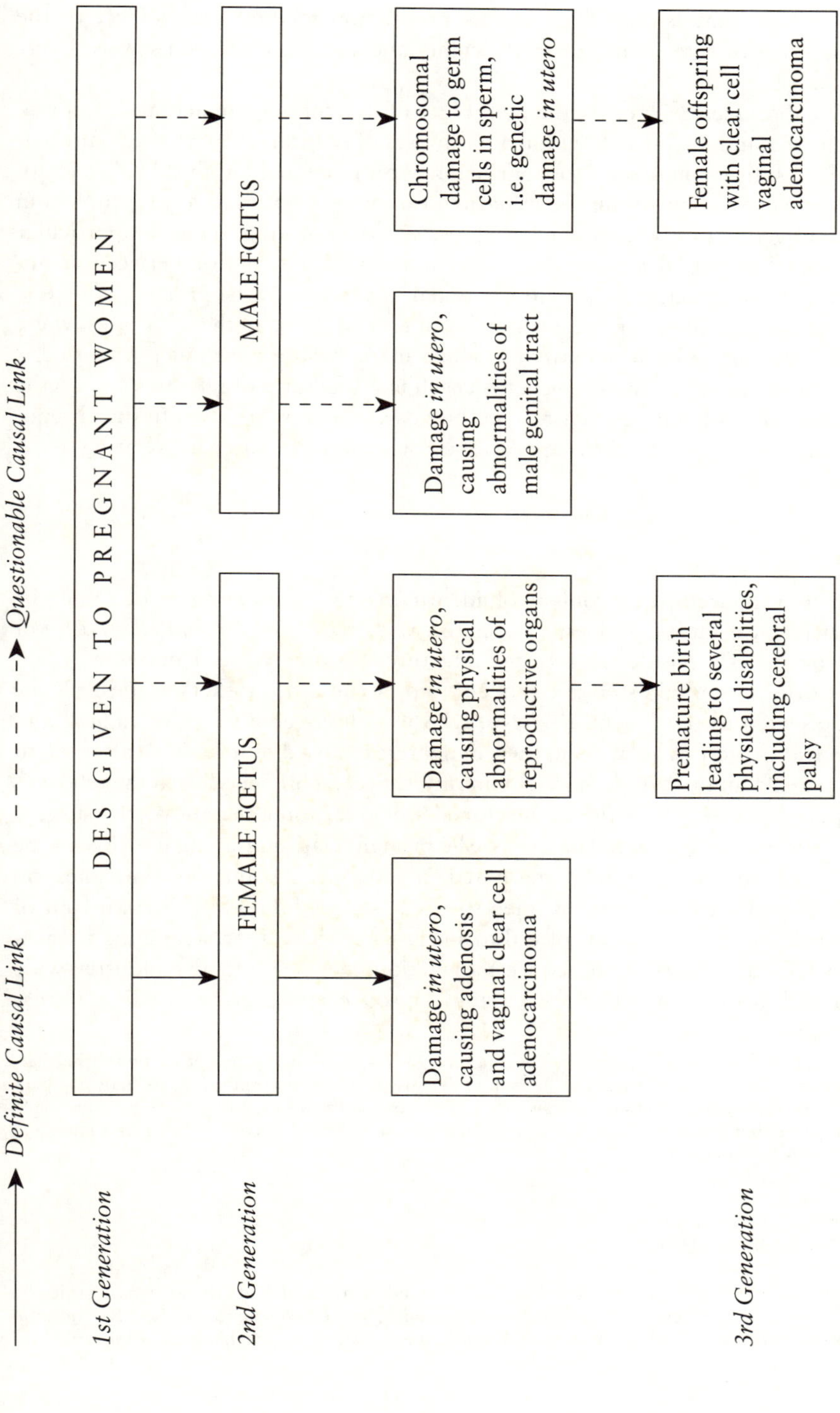

Figure 1: Generational Effects Associated with the Administration of DES to Pregnant Women

of the fact that neither DES nor its production method was subject to the protection of intellectual property rights and the basic materials were freely available.[13]

We discussed previously the possibility of determining an actual causal link with DES and distinguishing it from illnesses of natural origin through alternative causation solutions, most particularly proportional liability.[14] This chapter, however, concentrates in scenario 1 on the principal causation problem in second-generation vaginal cancer cases, *viz.* that of identifying the particular manufacturer of DES to achieve an accurate causal attribution between manufacturer and damage. As previously noted in Chapter 1, the practice of reversing the burden of proof of causation became established in the DES cases where there was difficulty in identifying which manufacturer's product was used.[15] The burden of proof was imposed on each manufacturer of DES to show on the balance of probabilities that the product used was not his own. In the absence of such proof damages were apportioned on a market-share basis relating to the sales of DES.

(b) Market Share Liability

We now address the problem of identifying the manufacturer of DES, the principal causation problem associated with the drug. In *Sindell* v. *Abbott Laboratories*[16] the defendants manufactured, promoted and marketed DES. The drug was administered to Sindell's mother and the mothers of the class she represented to prevent miscarriage. DES was discovered to cause vaginal and cervical cancerous growths in their daughters exposed to it *in utero* after ten to 12 years from birth and, more commonly, 20 years. Sindell alleged that she was exposed to the drug *in utero*, developed a bladder tumour removed by surgery and suffered from vaginal adenosis. She brought class actions against five of the producers of the drug, who amounted to between 200 and 300 companies, on behalf of herself and other women similarly situated. Holding 9:3 in favour of Sindell, the Supreme Court of California rejected three approaches; the alternative liability theory,[17] the concert of action theory[18] and the industry-wide liability theory.[19] It constructed a new approach to causation, holding it "rea-

[13] Rarely could there be a stronger case made for the justification of patent protection in the pharmaceutical industry than Diethylstilbestrol. In the absence of patent protection, so many companies marketed the product that it became impossible to identify any manufacturer's product which caused the injuries. See Sheiner, Comment, "DES and a Proposed Theory of Enterprise Liability" (1978) 46 *Fordham L Rev*. 963, 976.

[14] See Chap. 1.

[15] *Ibid.*

[16] 26 Cal. 3d 588, 607 P 2d 924 (1980).

[17] 607 P 2d 924, 930–1.

[18] *Ibid.*, 932–3.

[19] *Ibid.*, 934–5. This theory, otherwise known as the enterprise liability theory, was regarded by a student article, which was heavily relied on in *Sindell*, as the best solution to the DES causation problem: Sheiner, n. 13 above, 974–5, 1003. The Fordham Comment, as it has become known, based

sonable in the present context to measure the likelihood that any of the defendants supplied the product which allegedly injured the plaintiff by the percentage which the DES sold by each of them for . . . preventing miscarriage bears to the entire production of the drug sold by all for that purpose".[20] With the proviso that "a substantial share of the appropriate market" is present in the action, each defendant would be liable for the proportion of the judgment represented by its market share unless it demonstrated that it could not have made the product which caused the plaintiff's injuries.[21] The court recognised the problems of a defendant being liable for a somewhat different percentage of the damage than its share of the market would justify.[22] In conclusion, the court stated that "under the rule we adopt, each manufacturer's liability for an injury would be approximately equivalent to the damages caused by the DES it manufactured".[23] Richardson J in his dissent[24] said that in the present case it remained "wholly speculative and conjectural whether any of the five named defendants actually caused the plaintiff's injuries".[25] Recovery was permitted from a handful of defendants who individually might account for a comparatively small market share "so long as the aggregate business of those who have been sued is deemed substantial". So a particular defendant could be held proportionately liable "even though mathematically it is much more likely than not that it played no role whatever in causing plaintiffs' injuries".[26] "[T]hose defendants brought to trial . . . will bear effective joint responsibility for 100% of plaintiffs' injuries [notwithstanding] that their 'substantial' aggregate market share may be considerably less". This fact forced the majority to concede that "a defendant may be held liable for a somewhat different percentage of the damage than its share of the appropriate market would justify".[27]

It is clear, however, that *Sindell* leaves a number of problems unresolved.[28] It is possible but unrealistic to regard *Sindell* as merely shifting the burden of proof since the defendants are usually in no better position to disprove causation than the plaintiffs are to prove it.[29] Dodds-Smith, in an answer to a question by the

its argument on the belief that the pharmaceutical industry adhered to an inadequate industry-wide safety standard: *ibid.* In *Sindell*, however, the pervasive role of the Food and Drug Administration in formulating the criteria for testing and marketing drugs, combined with the fact that the theory was unreasonable when applied to a decentralised industry comprised mainly of small producers and that safety functions were not delegated to a trader association, were the principle reasons for not applying enterprise liability in *Sindell*: 607 P 2d 924, 934–5.

20 607 P 2d 924, 937.

21 *Ibid.*, cf *Hymowitz* v. *Eli Lilly & Co*, 541 NYS 2d 941 (CA 1989), below.

22 607 P 2d 924 at 930.

23 *Ibid.*, 938.

24 *Ibid.*, 938–43.

25 *Ibid.*, 939.

26 *Ibid.*

27 *Ibid.*, 940.

28 See Teff, "'Market Share' Liability—A Novel Approach to Causation" (1982) 31 *ICLQ* 840.

29 *Ibid.*, 842, 843; H. L. A. Hart and A. Honoré, *Causation in the Law*, (2nd edn., Oxford, Clarendon Press, 1985), pp. liv, 102, 424. *Sindell's* approach is tantamount to a shifting of the grounds of legal responsibility from the need to show cause and effect: *ibid.* at pp. liii–liv, lxii, 102, 424; Stapleton, "Law, Causation and Common Sense" [1988] *OJLS* 111 at 128.

author whether Lord Wilberforce's reversal of the burden of proof in *McGhee* would help ease the causation difficulty on plaintiffs, has stated:

> "If the burden of proof on causation is also reversed, I believe that the concept might just as well be abandoned. It is not reasonable to ask a defendant to prove a negative here, but it is reasonable to expect a plaintiff to show, on the balance of probability, that a drug has caused an injury. People involved in these cases know their complexity, and I believe that showing causation will remain a major problem whatever system is adopted".[30]

In *Sindell*, traditional causation principles are clearly abandoned and Richardson J's dissent highlights any administrative difficulties associated with market share.[31] The insistence on a "substantial share" of the market being joined, presumably to increase the probability that the causally responsible manufacturer is in fact sued is "[h]ardly consistent with . . . allocating responsi-

[30] Dodds-Smith, "Product Liability Issues Arising out of the Introduction of Strict Liability Procedures for Dealing with Multi-claimant Cases" in Goldberg and Dodds-Smith (eds.), *Pharmaceutical Medicine and the Law*, 61, 62. When the plaintiff is unable to prove what caused an accident and the circumstances are, in the absence of any other explanation, more consistent with negligence than any other cause, it is possible that the maxim *res ipsa loquitur* will apply. The principle is laid down by Erle CJ, in *Scott* v. *London and St. Katherine Docks Co.* (1865) 3 H & C 596 at 601: "where a thing is shown to be under the management of the defendant or his servants, and the accident is such as in the ordinary course of things does not happen if those who have the management use proper care, it affords reasonable evidence, in the absence of explanation by the defendants, that the accident arose from want of care". The defendant will be liable if he fails to explain the accident in terms consistent with the exercise of proper care: Brazier, *Medicine Patients and the Law* (2nd edn., Harmondsworth, Penguin, 1992), 156. In the context of drug-induced injury, the *res ipsa loquitur* principle can be applied if the injury is a self-evident consequence of an undeniable fault, but this is uncommon in prescribing and administering drugs. The closest examples to such a situation are incorrectly administered injections damaging nerve tissues or the demonstration of toxic residues of a drug in the body which should not have been given: Dukes and Swartz, *Responsibility for Drug-Induced Injury* (Amsterdam, New York, Oxford, Elsevier, 1989), 89. The *res ipsa loquitur* principle has, however, been successfully utilised in the case of a drug-induced injury using an anæsthetic. In *Saunders* v. *Leeds Western HA* (1985) 82 Law Soc. Gaz. 1491, a girl was administered an anæsthetic before undergoing an operation to correct a congenitally displaced hip, suffering cardiac arrest and consequent spastic quadriplegia, defective eyesight and mental retardation. In the course of judgment it was stated by Mann J that on the basis of the evidence called, the heart of a fit child would not arrest under anæsthesia if proper care was taken in the anæsthetic and surgical process: cf *Roe* v. *Minister of Health* [1954] 2 QB 66. However, the majority of cases are more subtle, requiring clinical, pharmacological and toxicological knowledge before a failure to perform a duty can be established, and that this was most likely, in the absence of further evidence, to have resulted in an injury which would have otherwise been avoided: Dukes and Swartz, above, 89. *Res ipsa loquitur*, however, is restricted to injuries of a kind that do not occur in the absence of negligence: see Delgado, "Beyond *Sindell:* Relaxation of Cause-in-Fact Rules for Indeterminate Plaintiffs" (1982) 70 *Cal. L Rev.* 881, 888. It is unlikely that it could apply to any situation involving diethylstilbestrol other than possibly the rare tumour of clear cell adenocarcinoma of the cervix and vagina in women exposed as fœtuses *in utero* to DES, and even an application in these circumstances is debatable: Brennan, "Causal Chains and Statistical Links: The Role of Scientific Uncertainty in Hazardous-Substance Litigation" (1988) 73 *Cornell L Rev.* 469 502; American Law Institute Reporters' Study, *Enterprise Responsibility for Personal Injury Vol. II: Approaches to Legal and Institutional Change*, (Philadelphia, Penn., American Law Institute, 1991), 322.

[31] Teff, n. 28 above, 843.

bility in proportion to the amount produced".[32] In Teff's view, the administrative difficulties of market share are "formidable". Such difficulties appear to stem from the uncertainty over the meaning of "substantial share" in respect of amount and geographical location. "Some companies were major national suppliers of DES; others operated only in a regional market, and their respective shares may have varied considerably over time and from place to place. An additional complication is that the drug was also prescribed for purposes other than preventing miscarriage".[33]

One of the major criticisms of *Sindell* is that it is unclear from which market the share is estimated and on what basis the share would be calculated.[34] In a caustic polemic,[35] market share has been criticised as being too wide a leap from the traditional elements in a tort action and the abrogation of causation in fact,[36] and has been regarded as unwarranted, due to insufficient data being in existence to develop market shares for all producers of DES, preventing an equitable allocation of liability[37] and due to the argument either that the underlying policies justifying market share liability's adoption are not achieved or that the policies provide insufficient reasons to adopt it.[38]

In particular, *Brown* v. *Superior Court (Abbott Laboratories)*[39] is regarded as being "patently unsound"[40] because it adopted market share liability on the basis of the policy considerations underlying strict liability,[41] and the fact that the court seemed to contradict itself by holding prescription drugs as exempt

32 *Ibid.* The substantial share requirement is pointless because the presence of all possible actors does not alter the probability that any *one* of them was the cause of the injury: Robinson, "Multiple Causation in Tort Law: Reflections on the DES Cases" (1982) 68 *Va. L Rev.* 713, 725–6, 753, 768.

33 *Ibid.*

34 Newdick, "Strict Liability for Defective Drugs in the Pharmaceutical Industry" (1985) 101 *LQR* 405, 428.

35 Schultz, "Market Share Liability in DES Cases: The Unwarranted Erosion of Causation in Fact" (1991) 40 *De Paul L Rev.* 771.

36 *Ibid.*, 773. "[T]here must be some reasonable connection between the act or omission of the defendant and the damage which the plaintiff has suffered": Keeton, Dobbs, Keeton and Owen (eds.), *Prosser and Keeton on The Law of Torts* (5th edn., St. Paul, Minn., West Publishing Co., 1984), 263.

37 An accurate determination of market share, reflecting the amount of DES supplied into the market by a manufacturer is unachievable: Schultz, n. 35 above, 803. Schultz states that for an accurate reconstruction of the market share "evidence must be presented detailing each defendant's percentage of the relevant market for a specific year, overlapping years, or span of years. For instance, if a plaintiff's mother . . . took DES intermittently over a period of three years before the plaintiff's birth, the trial court will have to reconstruct the market shares of each defendant for each year': *ibid.* Reconstructing such narrow markets is nearly impossible based on the fact that the data are unreliable or insufficient, resulting in great cost to both litigants and the court system: *ibid.*, 804. In many cases, sufficient evidence to present a complete and accurate picture of market share of all DES manufacturers may be non-existent. Statistics such as the amount of DES one manufacturer produced to prevent miscarriage, in comparison with the total amount of DES produced for that purpose by all other manufacturers may not be readily available: Fisher, n. 11 above, 1648–9.

38 Schultz, n. 35 above, 773, 801–811.

39 751 P 2d 470 (Cal. 1988).

40 Schultz, n. 35 above, 808.

41 751 P 2d 470 at 476 n. 5.

from strict liability,[42] so that market share liability could not be used in a strict liability action. However, *Sindell* v. *Abbott Laboratories*[43] says that the policy consideration that, as between the innocent plaintiff and manufacturer of defective products, the manufacturer of the product should bear the cost of injury, derives from *Summers* v. *Tice*,[44] a negligence case,[45] and not a strict liability one. The argument of non-achievement of policies thus appears to be not so strong on further analysis.

It is then stated that the policies provide insufficient reasons to adopt market share liability since, contrary to *Sindell*,[46] drug companies are not better able to absorb costs of injury through insurance and passing costs on, since some drug companies cannot obtain insurance or survive[47] and the ability of pharmaceutical companies to absorb costs is insufficient, given the unclear effect on the future availability of drugs.[48]

The national market has been regarded as the only suitable market;[49] but national market as a concept has been criticised as flawed due to the lack of reliable information available to the court because not all the companies went before each court. Many were not included as they were no longer amenable to suit.[50] However, it is arguable that a "pool of generally accepted data" for DES manufacturers emerges with a national market figure being established through regular decisions of the courts.[51] It has been suggested that a single standard should apply in the establishment of the local but not national market of the pharmaceutical manufacturer.[52] If a national market share is established through general acceptance in decisions across the United States it is submitted that it can be utilised. However, it is unlikely that any such general acceptance could be established with a local market.

The New York DES litigation favoured a scheme known as a matrix from San Francisco showing for each company and each dosage strength its share of the market per year.[53] The San Francisco matrix was commended to the defendants because it resulted in low market shares being associated with the companies. But there have been a series of problems with establishing the San Francisco

[42] 751 P 2d 470 at 482–3.

[43] 26 Cal. 39 588, 607 P 2d 924 (1980).

[44] 199 P 2d 1, 5 (Cal. 1948). The Restatement (Second) of Torts (1965) has codified *Summers* in § 433B(3), including *Summers* as Illustration 9: American Law Institute, *Restatement of the Law: Second: Torts*, 2d (St. Paul, Minn., West Publishing Co., 1965).

[45] See *Sindell*, 607 P 2d 924 at 936.

[46] 607 P 2d 924 at 936.

[47] Schultz, n. 35 above, 809.

[48] *Ibid.*, 811.

[49] *Hymowitz* v. *Eli Lilly* 541 NYS 2d 941 at 950, supported in Twerski, "Market Share—A Tale of Two Centuries" (1989) 55 *Brook. L Rev.* 869, 871.

[50] Schultz, n. 35 above, 805.

[51] Cf. *Ibid.*, 805.

[52] McGuire, Note, "Market Share Liability After *Hymowitz* and *Conley*: Exploring the Limits of Judicial Power" (1991) 24 *U Mich. JL Ref.* 759, 781.

[53] Rheingold, "The Hymowitz Decision—Practical Problems of New York DES Litigation" (1989) 55 *Brook. L Rev.* 883, 894.

matrix, most particularly the fact that no data exist for many years of DES production. The matrices have been described as being the "product of great time and expense, with many econometricians involved on all sides giving what apparently amounted to nothing more than educated guesses about what the market was".[54]

Thus the area of defining market share remains unclear and unconvincing, except for the pragmatic national market share, though one must concede the accuracy of any figure arrived at in respect of a national market.

Considerable uncertainty surrounded the question whether *Sindell* concluded that the defendants in the action were to be held jointly and severally liable for a plaintiff's damages or merely severally liable.[55] In *Brown* v. *Superior Court (Abbott Laboratories)*,[56] the Supreme Court of California held that the manufacturers' liability was several only and, where the manufacturers in the market are not joined for any reason, liability remains limited to market share which amounts to a less than 100 per cent recovery for a plaintiff. The court concluded that an imposition of joint liability on defendants would be inconsistent with the rationale of achieving a "reasonable approximation" of a manufacturer's responsibility for injuries caused by the DES it produced[57] and would frustrate *Sindell's* goal of achieving a balance between the interests of DES plaintiffs and manufacturers of the drug.[58]

This position was upheld in *Hymowitz* v. *Eli Lilly*:[59]

> [W]e hold that the liability of DES producers is several only, and should not be inflated when all participants in the market are not before the court in a particular case. We understand that, as a practical matter, this will prevent some plaintiffs from recovering 100% of their damages. However, we eschewed exculpation to prevent the fortuitous avoidance of liability, and thus, equitably, we decline to unleash the same force to increase a defendant's liability beyond its fair share of responsibility.

As Teff concludes, *Sindell,* while not resolving issues with "mathematical precision" does embody a notion of fault which is appropriate to the bizarre circumstances in question.[60] The main practical difficulties are evidentiary ones related to the production of fungible goods. An "administrative no-fault scheme" funded by all generic products manufacturers within a particular industry might be more workable but there could remain difficulties, e.g. the

[54] *Ibid*., 895.

[55] See *Sindell,* n. 16 above, 937; Teff, n. 28 above, 843; it has been argued that the case "seems" to establish several liability of the defendants: Clark, *Product Liability* (London, Sweet & Maxwell, 1989), 70. Several liability has been supported since it gives the plaintiffs an incentive to bring as many defendants as is feasible before the court, thus encouraging efficient loss spreading amongst the manufacturers and seemingly being administratively sensible: Note, "Market Share Liability: An Answer to the DES Causation Problem" (1981) 94 *Harv. L Rev*. 668, 673.

[56] 751 P 2d 470 (Cal. 1988).

[57] *Ibid*., 486.

[58] *Ibid*., 487.

[59] 541 NYS, 2d 941 (CA 1989) at 950.

[60] Teff, n. 28 above, 844.

determination of fungibility.[61] This, however, he regards as being preferable to "stretching already fragile causation principles to breaking point".[62]

Any remaining causation principles left in the market share concept of allocating responsibility appear to have been abrogated in *Hymowitz* v. *Eli Lilly & Co.*,[63] which has rendered identification of which manufacturer's product was used as unnecessary. *Hymowitz* is the first decision in the United States to recognise that a manufacturer can be liable for a percentage of damages caused by a product notwithstanding that the manufacturer can show that his product did not cause the particular plaintiff's injury since it had not been used.[64] In *Hymowitz*, the Court adopted a market share liability theory using a national market. It was conceded that problems could occur with a national market. First, the market would likely result in the disproportion between the liability of individual manufacturers and the actual injuries each manufacturer caused in New York State. Thus the theory could not ensure that liability would approximate causation in the state. Secondly, the use of a national market did not provide a reasonable link between liability and the risk created by a defendant to a particular plaintiff. However, the national market in *Hymowitz* is designed to "apportion liability so as to correspond to the over-all culpability of each defendant measured by the amount of risk of injury each defendant created to the public at large".[65]

Of the greatest importance was the court's abrogation of any causation requirement. Having held that a defendant could escape liability by not being part of the market of DES for pregnancy use the court then stated:

> "Nevertheless, because liability here is based on the over-all risk produced, and not causation in a single case, there should be no exculpation of a defendant who, although a member of the market producing DES for pregnancy use, appears not to have caused a particular plaintiff's injury. It is merely a windfall for a producer to escape liability solely because it manufactured a more identifiable pill, or sold only to certain drug stores. These fortuities in no way diminish the *culpability*[66] of a defendant for marketing the product, which is the basis of liability here."[67]

Thus it appears that if one goes to the trouble of making one's medicinal product more identifiable to avoid confusion with other products of the same sub-

[61] Teff, n. 28 above, 844; see also Newdick, n. 34 above, 428. It has been said that a no fault compensation scheme "is the only solution for the drug injury problem that would deal with generic prescribing": Diamond, "Product Liability and Pharmaceuticals in the United Kingdom", in Woodroofe (ed.), *Consumer Law in the EEC* (London, Sweet & Maxwell, 1984), 142. However, it is perhaps defeatist and over-preferential to suggest a generic restriction to drug indemnity.

[62] Teff, n. 28 above, 844.

[63] 541 NYS 2d 941 (CA 1989).

[64] Cf Hart and Honoré, who claim that though it remains open in theory for a firm to show that its product did not cause harm in an individual case, in practice it could not do so: Hart and Honoré, n. 29 above, pp. liv, 102, 424. Such a burden is by no means always insurmountable: Robinson, n. 32 above, 729.

[65] 541 NYS 2d 941 at 950.

[66] Author's italics.

[67] N. 65 above.

stance, one suffers if one is a member of the product's market. If the whole rationale behind market share liability is regarded as being a "practical solution to the problems created by harmful fungible goods which cannot be traced to any specific producer"[68] then this rationale has been ludicrously stretched to the point where showing that one's product was clearly not a cause is now totally irrelevant.

Twerski regards the need for exculpation of a defendant who can establish it was not responsible for the harm as "arrant nonsense",[69] since market share liability means that causation should be "viewed writ large" over a market.[70] He states that it is irrelevant to market share liability that a defendant establishes that it did not sell a particular pill to a patient and that such an approach would cut across an equitable administration of market share liability, since a defendant who exits the market by the chance of showing that it did not sell to a particular pharmacy "dumps" its percentage of harm upon defendants who cannot prove the negative. Thus such defendants end up paying a disproportionate share of the costs of DES-induced injury.[71] However, this argument ignores the fact that liability in DES cases is several in nature[72] and is reasoned as if liability were joint and several.[73] Twerski gives credit to *Hymowitz* for not "paying senseless obeisance to tradition"[74] and not paying its dues to the "nineteenth century causation club"[75] since it faced up to the fact that market share is irreconcilable with traditional causation theory.[76]

By contrast, other writers have been more taken aback by the *Hymowitz* approach to exculpation. One has stated that "[t]he stunning aspect of the New York theory is that it denies a defendant the opportunity to exculpate itself"[77] which is an "integral part"[78] of each of the other three variants of market share in *Sindell* v. *Abbott Laboratories*,[79] *Martin* v. *Abbott Laboratories*[80] and *Collins* v. *Eli Lilly*.[81]

The majority appeared to fail to clarify the legal justification for refusing to grant exculpation,[82] but the dissent notes that liability is premised upon the overall risk of injury which each defendant created to the public-at-large.[83]

68 Teff, n. 28 above, 182.
69 Twerski, n. 49 above, 872.
70 *Ibid.*
71 *Ibid.*
72 *Brown* v. *Superior Court*, 751 P 2d 470 (Cal 1988) at 486, 487.
73 Reflecting the erroneously argued *Martin* v. *Abbott Laboratories*, 698 P 2d 368 (Wash. 1984) at 383 and not *Brown*, cf Twerski, n. 49 above, at 874 in an apparent contradiction when he asks "[b]y what act of legerdemain can one defendant be held for the damage of another?".
74 Twerski, n. 49 above, 870.
75 *Ibid.*, 873.
76 *Ibid.*
77 McGuire, n. 52 above, 769.
78 *Ibid.*
79 607 P 2d 924, 937 (1980).
80 689 P 2d 368 at 382 (Wash. 1984).
81 342 NW 2d 37 at 52 (Wis. 1984).
82 *Hymowitz* v. *Eli Lilly*, 541 NYS 2d 941 at 950; see Rheingold, n. 53 above, 809.
83 541 NYS 2d 941 at 955.

However, the dissent claims that by adopting such a view the majority, whilst stating that it is adopting a market share theory of liability, is adopting a concerted action theory of liability, though this is expressly disclaimed by the majority.[84]

It could be argued that *Hymowitz* is consistent with the views of Rosenberg on market share liability. He states that courts have apportioned liability through market share when it is assumed that each firm's contribution to the excess risk of disease is directly related to the firm's market share for the disease-causing product.[85] In the event of a divergence between market share and excess risk "apportionment should accord with the firm's contribution to risk",[86] which would seem to be the case where a manufacturer could show that his product did not cause the particular plaintiff's injury since it had not been used. In such a situation the risk would reflect the national market, since this would be an appropriate measure of the risk of injury to the public at large, a situation reflected in the court's judgment in *Hymowitz* since they still impose liability on such a manufacturer according to the market share figure as a measure of risk. It is thus still correct to say that the wrongdoer is only liable for that which he is responsible and not greater.[87]

The court in *Hymowitz* examined two decisions which declined to follow *Sindell* v. *Abbott Laboratories*, *viz. Collins* v. *Eli Lilly & Co.*[88] and *Martin* v. *Abbott Laboratories*.[89] In *Collins* v. *Eli Lilly & Co.* the court held that it was prevented from following *Sindell* because of "the practical difficulty of defining and proving market share".[90] The court declined to link liability to the odds of actual causation, as had been attempted in *Sindell*, and held that each defendant was liable in proportion to the amount of risk it created that the plaintiff would be injured by DES.[91] In *Collins* the "risk" each defendant was liable for was a question of fact in each case,[92] taking into account market share, though the defendants were permitted to exculpate themselves by showing that their product could not have caused the injury.[93] The court in *Hymowitz* considered that

84 541 NYS 2d 945, 946.

85 Rosenberg, "The Causal Connection in Mass Exposure Cases: A Public Law Vision of the Tort System" (1984) 97 *Harv. L Rev*. 851, 867.

86 *Ibid*.

87 Cf Rosenberg, n. 85 above, 866.

88 342 NW 2d. 37 (Wis. 1984).

89 689 P 2d 368 (Wash. 1984).

90 342 NW 2d 37 at 48.

91 *Ibid*., at 49. The variation was based on the premise that "each defendant contributed to the risk of injury to the public" and consequently to individual plaintiffs such as the plaintiff in question. The court, however, still required it to be shown that the defendant drug manufacturer could reasonably have contributed in some way to the actual injury: *ibid*., partially rejecting Robinson's risk contribution theory: Robinson, n. 32 above, 739–40, 754–55. The court thus seemed to concern itself with linking liability to culpability, similar to courts adopting concert of action and enterprise liability: Klein, "Beyond DES: Rejecting the Application of Market Share Liability in Blood Products Litigation" (1994) 68 *Tul. L Rev*. 883 at 890, 891, 902. Cf Schultz, n. 35 above, 800, concluding that *Collins* contravenes the principle that a mere possibility that a defendant is the responsible party is not enough to satisfy causation.

92 342 NW 2d 37 at 50, 51.

93 The court also noted that the plaintiff need only sue one defendant: *ibid*., 50.

the *Collins* v. *Eli Lilly & Co.* approach of assessing the "risk" each defendant caused a plaintiff, to be litigated as a question of fact, was a theory requiring "the fact finder's individualised and open-ended assessment of the relative liabilities of scores of defendants in every case".[94] The theory would have resulted in delayed recoveries and inconsistent results in New York State, and so was rejected.[95] *Martin* v. *Abbott Laboratories*[96] rejected the *Sindell* market share theory due to the erroneous belief, as shown in *Brown* v. *Superior Court (Abbott Laboritories)*,[97] that California's approach inherently distorted liability by "arguably" inflating market shares to ensure the plaintiffs received 100 per cent damages from all named defendants.[98]

The *Martin* court adopted "market share alternative liability", a theory which presumed that all manufacturers had equal market shares totalling 100 per cent but gave each defendant the opportunity of rebutting the presumption by showing (a) that it was not the manufacturer of DES that injured the plaintiffs (which resulted in complete exculpation)[99] or (b) that its actual market share was less than presumed. If a defendant was successful in so rebutting, the liability shares of the remaining defendants, who could not prove their own market share, were inflated so that the plaintiff could recover 100 per cent.[100]

[94] 541 NYS 2d 941 at 949, 950.

[95] *Ibid.*

[96] 689 P 2d 368 (Wash. 1984).

[97] 751 P 2d 470 (Cal 1988). *Brown* clarified the uncertainty by ruling that liability in market share theory cases in California is several only: *ibid.* at 485–7.

[98] 689 P 2d 368 at 380–1. The court illustrated the distortion by an example: "[a]ssume that plaintiff's damages are $100,000 and she joins enough DES manufacturers to represent 60 percent of the relevant market. Defendant X occupies 20 percent of the relevant market and one-third of the market that all joined defendants represent. If defendant X is liable only for its share of the relevant market, it would be liable for 20 percent of the damages or $20,000. If defendants are required to pay 100 percent of the judgment, however, then defendant X must pay one-third of the judgment or $33,333, which is equivalent to one-third of the smallest that all the joined defendants represent. In other words, defendant X would have to pay 67 percent ($13,333)more than its share of the relevant market": *ibid.*, at 381. The court also stated that the smaller the percentage of the market that is required to be joined, the greater will be the ensuing distortion: *ibid.* The erroneous belief was also present in contemporaneous commentary with *Sindell*: see Fisher, 1644–78. It is submitted that the confusion that suggested that the joined plaintiffs would be liable for 100% of the damages was created by the statement by the majority in *Sindell* that once the plaintiff had met her burden of joining the required defendants they could file a cross-complaint against other manufacturers, alleging that they might have supplied the injury-causing product: 607 P 2d 924, 937. This seemed to imply that the defendants would be liable for 100% of the damages since the only reason for the defendants to cross-complain against third parties would be to seek a contribution, which can only happen when the joined defendants are liable for more than their *pro rata* share of the judgment: Fisher, above, 1645–6.

[99] "Individual defendants are entitled to exculpate themselves from liability by establishing, by a preponderance of the evidence, that they did not produce or market the particular type DES taken by the plaintiff's mother, that they did not market the DES in the geographic market area of plaintiff mother's obtaining the drug; or that it did not distribute DES in the time period of plaintiff mother's ingestion of the drug": *ibid.*, at 382.

[100] *Ibid.*, at 382–3. Thus under the *Martin* approach, defendants unable to exculpate themselves from potential liability are designated members of the plaintiff's market. These defendants are initially presumed to have equal shares of the market and are liable only for the percentage of the

The *Martin* approach became "more mathematically complex"[101] in the context of unavailable defendants and the solution of the court led to case management problems.[102] Market share had to be relitigated in each case, and since neither substantial share nor an initial limitation on liability was a requirement, a plaintiff was encouraged to sue one or two defendants, who then were pressured into impleading a host of others, resulting in administrative chaos.[103] *Martin* v. *Abbott Laboratories* was not adopted in court.

The major differences in the *Hymowitz* decision from *Sindell* were that *Sindell* required a "substantial share" of the market and *Hymowitz* did not embrace that requirement as part of the New York theory, despite the fact that it recognised it in its discussion of *Sindell,*[104] *Sindell* also stated that if a defendant could prove that it could *not* have been the manufacturer of the product which injured the plaintiff, the defendant could avoid liability. The New York State Court of Appeals did not permit this.

(c) Rejection of Market Share Liability

The implications of *Hymowitz* are to the effect that there has been no end to the causation requirement in US product liability law. Market share liability has been overshadowed by punitive damages and has not been embraced by the US courts.[105] Indeed, the traditional requirement to identify the manufacturer is the "majority rule". Many courts have rejected the *Sindell* approach and its progeny as being inconsistent with liability based on fault, e.g. the highest courts of Missouri and Iowa, *Zafft* v. *Eli Lilly & Co.*[106] and *Mulcahy* v. *Eli Lilly & Co.*[107]

In *Zafft* v. *Eli Lilly & Co.*, the Supreme Court of Missouri held that the court would not abandon Missouri tort law requiring a causal relationship between the defendants and the injury-producing agent as a precondition to maintaining their cause of action.[108] Market share liability was regarded as being unfair, unworkable and contrary to Missouri law, in addition to being unsound public

plaintiff's judgment that represents their presumptive share. These defendants are then provided with an opportunity to rebut such a presumption and to reduce their potential liability by proving that their true share of the relevant market is less than the presumptive share. The presumptive shares of those defendants unable to establish their proportionate share of the market are then increased to account for 100% of the market. However, if the plaintiff is unable to name all the members of the market, the plaintiff will recover less than 100% of the judgment if the named defendants prove a total aggregate share of less than 100%: *ibid.*, at 383. It should also be noted that, unlike *Sindell*, the plaintiff need only commence suit against one manufacturer to maintain a market share liability action: *ibid.*, at 382.

101 *Hymowitz,* n. 59 above, 949.

102 Mayer and Carter, "The Adoption of the Market Share Theory of Liability in New York", 20 (on file with Mr Ian Dodds-Smith, Solicitor, Health Care Group, Cameron McKenna, 160 Aldersgate St. London EC1A 4DD), hereafter Mayer and Carter.

103 *Ibid.*, 20, 21.

104 541 NYS 2d 941 at 948.

105 Mayer and Carter, n.103 above, 25.

106 676 SW 2d 241 (Mo. banc 1984).

107 386 NW 2d 67 (Iowa 1986).

108 676 SW 2d 241 at 247.

policy. Moreover, there were legitimate concerns that market share liability would discourage desired pharmaceutical research and development while providing little incentive to produce safe products. The shifting of the burden of proof of causation to the respondents was rejected as substantially altering the existing rights and liabilities of the litigants.[109] In *Mulcahy* v. *Eli Lilly* the Supreme Court of Iowa rejected market share liability on a broad policy basis since awarding damages to an admittedly innocent party by means of a court-constructed device that places liability on manufacturers who were not proved to have caused the injury involved "social engineering more appropriately within the legislative domain".[110] Market share liability has been excluded from applying to cases involving vaccines by the Supreme Court of New Jersey in *Shackil* v. *Lederle Laboratories*[111] because of the "regressive effect that collective liability would have on the social policy of encouraging vaccine production and research".[112] The imposition of collective liability theory would frustrate public policy and public health considerations by threatening the availability of needed drugs and prospects of the development of safer vaccines. In addition, compensatory relief was provided by the National Childhood Vaccine Injury Act 1986.[113] Market share liability has also recently been rejected in *Gorman* v. *Abbott Laboratories*,[114] where the Supreme Court of Rhode Island held that it would not adopt the market share doctrine to impose liability and opined that the establishment of liability required the identification of the specific defendant responsible for the injury.

The New York decision of *Hymowitz* has dispensed with the ability of a manufacturer to avoid liability by proving he could not have been the manufacturer of the product and has eliminated the requirement that the plaintiff sue a substantial market share. This, however, has been regarded as not necessarily inequitable, since very few DES manufacturers could justify exculpation by special marketing practices or types of pills. The elimination of the requirement of substantial share has no negative effect, since under several liability the plaintiff has an incentive to sue a substantial share of the market because that share has direct bearing on the percentage of her alleged damages she could recover.[115] The negative aspects of *Hymowitz* appear to be that industries with fungible products may be more susceptible to lawsuits. Secondly, the plaintiff may sue a number of defendants, putting the burden of identification on them, by saying she is unable to identify the manufacturer when her own preliminary investigation may have identified a manufacturer.[116] It has thus been argued that it is necessary for the law to proceed with caution and for the law to be limited under

109 *Ibid*., at 246–7.
110 386 NW 2d 67 at 75–6.
111 561 A 2d 511 (NJ 1989).
112 *Ibid*., at 528.
113 *Ibid*., at 512; see also 529.
114 599 A 2d 1364, 1364 (RI 1991).
115 Mayer and Carter, n. 103 above, 32, 33.
116 *Ibid*., 33.

these approaches to causation. For example, such approaches should relate to fungibles only, and where the plaintiff has tried and failed to identify the manufacturer. This problem of identifying the manufacturer must affect a "large majority of . . . similarly situated persons who constitute a significant percentage of the general population sufficient to merit this modification of the tort law".[117]

The decision of *Hymowitz* v. *Eli Lilly* clearly indicated that the New York court had no desire to expand market share into other areas which did not have the unique characteristics of DES.[118] Twerski concluded that *Hymowitz* was restricted to its facts and that DES was *sui generis*, particularly in the light of the fact that the court noted that DES had been the subject of a direct legislative response.[119]

(d) Market Share Liability and Factor VIII

However, such a ceasefire on application to non-DES products appears to have been broken with the application of market share liability by the Hawaiian Supreme Court to Factor VIII.[120] In *Smith* v. *Cutter Biological, Inc.*[121] the plaintiff, a hæmophiliac, claimed that he had been tested HIV positive with the AIDS virus as a result of injections of Factor VIII concentrate, an essential blood product enabling the blood to coagulate. The appellant filed suit against the four appellee manufacturers of Factor VIII for negligence and strict liability, but he was unable to prove specifically which manufacturer's product caused his infection.[122] The Supreme Court of Hawaii adopted market share liability,[123] utilising the *Hymowitz* version of it.[124] The court apportioned liability on the basis of the national market share of Factor VIII concentrate rejecting any narrower versions, and took on board the reasoning of *Hymowitz* that the national market is able to apportion liability so as to correspond to the amount of risk of injury each defendant created to the public at large.[125] As in *Hymowitz*, Factor VIII producers are unable to exculpate themselves by proving that their concentrate did not cause the plaintiff's illness.[126] A manufacturer can only be exculpated by proving that it did not have Factor VIII concentrate on the market at

[117] Mayer and Carter, n. 103 above, 34.

[118] See *Hymowitz* v. *Eli Lilly*, 541 NYS 2d 941 at 947: "[w]e stress, however, that the DES situation is a singular case, with manufacturers acting in a parallel manner to produce an identical, generically marketed product, which causes injury many years later and which has evoked a legislative response reviving previously barred actions".

[119] Twerski, n. 49 above, 876. Twerski indicated that it was highly unlikely that market share would extend to non-generic products, to products with no latency periods or where plaintiffs have failed to secure the evidence to identify the manufacturer: *ibid*.

[120] *Smith* v. *Cutter Biological, Inc.*, 823 P 2d 717 (Hawaii 1991).

[121] *Ibid.*

[122] *Ibid.*, at 721–2.

[123] *Ibid.*, at 729.

[124] *Ibid.*, at 728.

[125] *Ibid.*, quoting *Hymowitz* 541 NYS 2d 941 at 950.

[126] 823 P 2d 717 at 729.

the time of the plaintiff's injury.[127] The case was, however, marked by a strong dissent. Market share liability was said to be contrary to the rules of statutory construction and the intent of the Hawaii legislature in enacting Hawaii's statute relating to blood products.[128] It was also stated that market share liability required Factor VIII to be fungible and untraceable to specific manufacturers. However, Factor VIII was not fungible[129] and it was not impossible for Factor VIII users to identify manufacturers.[130] The final argument against the imposition of market share liability was that it required the existence and breach of a legal duty based on a provable standard of care which was factually impossible.[131] The dissent concluded that the broad imposition of liability was "wholly unjustified, unfair and likely to discourage the future development and sale of blood therapies".[132]

The *Smith* case has been subject to trenchant criticism, one writer regarding it as being a relaxation of what he terms the third of three links to individualism, adumbrated in *Summers* v. *Tice*.[133]

It is stated that because of the lack of risk equivalence associated with Factor VIII, *Smith* "represents an enormous expansion in the law of actual causation".[134] Such an extension of market share liability principles to blood

127 *Ibid.*

128 *Ibid.*, at 730 (Moon J dissenting).

129 This was conceded by the majority who explained that the donor source of the plasma was not a constant, so that Factor VIII was only harmful if the donor was infected: *ibid.*, at 724.

130 *Ibid.*, at 730, 733, 734 (Moon J dissenting).

131 *Ibid.*, at 730 (Moon J dissenting). The inability to prove when, or even how, the plaintiff was infected with the HIV virus, coupled with the fact that information in respect of AIDS and the techniques to detect the HIV virus were just being developed during the early 1980s, the pertinent period in question, evidently made it impossible for the plaintiff to prove the standard of care: *ibid.*, at 736, 738. It is arguable, however, that such standards ought to have been based on the state of scientific and technical knowledge at the time of supply, and that this information ought to have been available.

132 *Ibid.*, at 738.

133 199 P 2d 1 (Cal. 1948); see Klein, "Beyond DES: Rejecting the Application of Market Share Liability in Blood Products Litigation" (1994) 68 *Tul. L Rev*. 883, 885–6, 888. Klein states that three links to individualism were established in *Summers*. Under *Summers*, the burden of proving causation shifts from plaintiff to defendant if: (1) all culpable entities are joined in the action; (2) each defendant has an opportunity to exculpate itself by proving that its conduct did not cause the plaintiff's injury; and (3) each instrumentality that may have injured the plaintiff carried a uniform risk of harm: *ibid.*, 885–6. Such requirements connect *Summers* to the individualism tradition "by maximizing the possibility that a defendant will bear responsibility only for damages caused by its own actions": *ibid.*, 886. *Sindell* relaxed the first requirement by requiring a substantial share of culpable entities: 607 P 2d 924 at 937 (1980), with further relaxations in *Martin* v. *Abbott Laboratories*, 689 P 2d 368, 382 (Wash. 1984) and in *Collins* v. *Eli Lilly Co.*, 342 NW 2d 37, 50 (Wis. 1984), which held that plaintiffs could maintain actions by suing only one DES manufacturer. *Hymowitz* abandoned completely both the first and second links to individualism, allowing for market share liability even if a manufacturer could show that he did not produce the DES purchased and ingested by the plaintiff's mother: 541 NYS 2d 941 at 950. Klein argues that the final link to individualism, risk uniformity, is broken by *Smith* v. *Cutter Biological, Inc.*, which adopts *Hymowitz* liability without concern for risk uniformity: Klein, above, 888.

134 *Ibid.*, 912. It has been argued that without a uniform risk and without adjustment of the market share data in the light of such non-uniform risk, such data cannot be used: Note, "Market Share Liability: An Answer to the DES Causation Problem" (1981) 94 *Harv. L Rev*. 668, 679. Cf Robinson

products litigation is "illogical and unwise", incompatible with blood products and disregards the traditional tort requirement that the plaintiff establish a link with the defendant's conduct.[135] In a rejection of the application of market share liability to blood products, it is stated that both legislatures and courts have rejected strict liability in actions against blood products manufacturers to ensure the availability of blood products for those who require them. The corollary of that is that if the plaintiff can bring a tort action only by proving breach of duty against the manufacturer, it would be illogical for the plaintiff to recover for breach of duty without proof of cause in fact, since it would mean that a manufacturer would have to "assume liability for injuries caused by products over which he has no control".[136] Factor VIII is distinguished from DES on the basis that Factor VIII concentrate is depended on by hæmophiliacs at an affordable price. Such liability would result in the only Factor VIII concentrate being marketed as being the most risk-free product "without regard to cost for the full community of users".[137]

The author adopts a legislative substitute for market share liability in blood products litigation based on the US National Childhood Vaccine Injury Act 1986 as a model.[138] Awards, it is suggested, would be funded through an industry tax based on the sale of blood products; the legislation would only be used when plaintiffs were unable to prove traditional cause in fact.[139] It is submitted that this would depend on the number of manufacturers of the blood product and proof that a particular manufacturer's product was responsible for the injury which, as illustrated by *Smith*,[140] is often difficult or impossible to establish. In addition, because of the difficulty in proving breach of duty in blood products litigation, already recognised in *Smith*,[141] people would attempt to avoid tort and not try too diligently to identify a manufacturer. It is also suggested that manufacturers would be encouraged to improve product safety, knowing that they would answer in tort for their own actions as opposed to others over which they have no control,[142] but it is submitted that there will be no deterrence value in tort here by virtue of the difficulty of proving breach of duty. The author suggests that the "free rider" problem of market share liability would be eliminated, since less diligent firms no longer would benefit from

who argues that providing liability is proportionate to risks created to the defendant, the *Sindell* rule could be applied to cases involving multiple and different risk-creating activities: Robinson, n. 32 above, 750–1.

135 Klein, n. 133 above, 912.

136 *Ibid.*, 918–19.

137 Surely it could be argued that it is imperative for the most risk-free product to be available to hæmophiliacs, whatever the cost and, if need be, the government should help to subsidise this cost?

138 This is somewhat ironic when the dissenting judge in *Shackil* v. *Lederle Laboratories* described *Hymowitz* as being most similar to the National Childhood Vaccine Injuries Act: *Shackil*, 541 A 2d 511, at 533 (NJ 1989). See Chap. 4.

139 Klein, n. 133 above, 933.

140 823 P 2d 717 at 721–2.

141 *Ibid.*, 736.

142 Klein, n. 133 above, 933.

the actions of more responsible firms.[143] However, it is arguable that a plaintiff may be unable to prove traditional cause in fact by virtue of a less diligent firm's avoidance of identification of his product by some mechanism or other. Thus the compensation system would come into operation and the less diligent firm would be the "free rider" at the expense of the rest of the industry. This situation could occur with either blood products or DES.[144] Finally, the legislation will require evidence from the petitioner of a probable date of HIV infection through one of the blood products, the source of compensation determined by whether the date of infection was before or after the presumed negligent date of April 1984 when a scientific consensus emerged that HIV was transmissible through blood.[145] Klein, however, concedes the difficulty here of the court determining when each of the industry's members developed techniques to inactivate the HIV virus in its blood products, a complicated and potentially adversarial determination that might defeat its goal of quickly compensating victims.[146] It thus seems inconclusive to state that a traditional tort theory, in combination with legislative innovation, can address the concerns of all persons associated with either HIV transmission through blood products or any DES-induced injury.[147]

(e) Alternative Causation Liability

The recent Dutch decision involving medicinal product liability and DES[148] was decided by the Supreme Court of the Netherlands on 9 October 1992 and involved six daughters bringing a claim against ten producers of DES, having been exposed to the drug in the period from 1953 until the middle of 1967.[149] The plaintiffs claimed that despite the lack of evidence of safety and efficacy of DES, each defendant marketed and produced the drug during their mothers' pregnancies. The plaintiffs were unable to show which of the defendants produced the particular DES used by their mothers, arguing that each defendant was jointly and severally liable for all damages to each plaintiff.[150] The court accepted the plaintiffs' theory of alternative causation liability,[151] rejected

143 *Ibid.*, cf Twerski, n. 49 above, 872.

144 See Schultz's suggestion that legislation of the National Childhood Vaccine Injury Act should operate in DES cases: Schultz, n. 35 above, 814–17.

145 Klein, n. 133 above, 934.

146 *Ibid.*

147 Cf Klein, 936. Twerski thus seems to be correct in stating that "mass tort litigation cannot proceed with a pot-pourri of classic tort law and radical resolution of causation related problems": Twerski, n. 49 above, 882.

148 *Van Ballegooijen* v. *Bayer Nederland BV* (Rvdw 1992, No. 219). I wish to acknowledge the assistance of a translation of the judgment by Loeff Claeys Verbeke, on file with Cameron McKenna, Solicitors, London.

149 Teulings, Note, "DES and Market Share Liability in the Netherlands" (1994) 110 *LQR* 228. See also Bergkamp, "Compensating Personal Injuries Caused by DES: 'No Causation Liability' in the Netherlands", World Pharmaceuticals Report, BNA International Inc., London, Jan. 1993; Dodds-Smith and Spencer, "Product Liability for Medicinal Products" in Powers and Harris (eds.), *Medical Negligence* (2nd edn., London, Butterworths, 1994), 512–13.

150 Sect. 3.1 of the decision, as numbered by the Sup. Ct.

151 Sect. 3.71.

market share liability[152] and imposed liability for all injuries caused by DES on every DES producer notwithstanding the fact that each producer could not have caused all the injury for which it was made liable.[153] In support, the plaintiffs used Article 99 of Book 6 of the New Dutch Civil Code 1992, known as the "alternative causation" rule, similar to joint and several liability and, regarding the burden of proof, *res ipsa loquitur*. This stated:

> "If the damage may have been caused by two or more events for each of which a different person is liable, and if it has been established that the damage is caused by at least one of these events, . . . each of these persons has the duty to compensate the damages, unless he proves that they were not caused by an event for which he himself is liable."[154]

The Dutch Supreme Court held that the damages for the DES daughters came under the alternative causation rule.[155] Notwithstanding the fact that Article 99 did not exist during the pertinent years in question (1950s), its wording reflected the legal views obtaining in the Netherlands at the time.[156] The Supreme Court stated, rejecting the view of the Amsterdam Court of Appeal, that the alternative causation rule did not require a concrete act of the defendants in relation to the plaintiffs.[157] Article 99 was regarded as designed to alleviate the unfairness of denying compensation to the plaintiffs for their damages through the inability of the plaintiffs to prove whose acts caused the injuries.[158] The Court said that Article 99's legislative history was silent on the DES-type situation when it was drafted, though such silence was not a rejection of the application of the alternative causation rule to the case.[159]

152 Sect. 3.8.

153 Sect. 3.7.3.

154 Bergkamp, n. 149 above, p2.

155 Sect. 3.7.1., unlike *Sindell* and *Hymowitz* which rejected the alternative causation theory. See *Sindell* 607 P 2d 924 at 930, 931 (1980); *Hymowitz* 541 NYS 2d 941 at 946 (1989). But see *Abel* v. *Eli Lilly & Co.*, 343 NW 2d 164 (holding that plaintiffs' allegations were sufficient to support the theories of alternative liability and concerted action), cert. denied, 469 US 833 (1984). The court thus established the "Dutch equivalent" of the alternative liability doctrine in *Summers* v. *Tice*: 199 P 2d 1 (Cal. 1948), which is authority for the proposition that where two or more defendants have committed negligent acts in a situation where the plaintiff is unable to identify which of them caused the injury, the burden of proof shifts to the defendants to show that they were not responsible for the harm. Direct market share was supported by the AG but this was regarded as "unsatisfactory" by the court, since it let the risk of the manufacturers' insolvency or untraceability fall on the plaintiffs, together with the need for the plaintiff to bring as many producers before the court, coupled with the already noted problems in defining market share: Sect. 3.8; Teulings, n. 149 above, 230.

156 Sect. 3.4.

157 Sect. 3.7.1.

158 *Ibid.*

159 *Ibid.* It is, however, arguable that on a strict interpretation of the rule it would appear that there was no proof, in terms of Art. 99, that the damage was caused by at least one event of a defendant. This accords with the views of the District Court of Amsterdam (*Van Ballegooijen* v. *Bayer Nederland BV* (B 1.0840 EG 57), sects. 3, 5 and 8 of the official judgment) and the Amsterdam CA (*Van Ballegooijen* v. *Bayer Nederland BV* (1197/88), sect. 3 of the official judgment) that it had not been established that the six mothers had taken DES which originated from one of the defendants, let alone which defendant: see Ekering, "The European Approach to Product Liability as Practised in the Netherlands", 24th Biennial Conference of the International Bar Association, Cannes, 20–25 Sept. 1992, 9. I wish to acknowledge the assistance of translations of these judgments by Loeff Claeys Verbeke, on file with Cameron McKenna, Solicitors, London.

The Supreme Court concluded that the appellate court's decision would generate the "unacceptable result" that, even if the drug companies committed a tort by the marketing of DES and the daughters suffered injuries as a result of ingestion of the drug by their mothers, they would be entitled to no compensation since they were unable to prove who produced the DES tablets used by their mothers.[160]

The court examined two options which could give the plaintiffs the right to compensation, *viz.* market share liability[161] and alternative causation. The court rejected market share liability as this assigns the risk to the victims of producers being insolvent or ceasing to exist or being untraceable. Further, the plaintiffs would be required to sue as many producers as they could, establishing the market shares of each. The court concluded that market share liability was unnecessary if each of the producers was entirely, i.e. jointly and severally, liable for all the plaintiffs' damages.[162] In the market share DES cases, the share of liability would be the distinct market share of one of the liable defendants so the liability of one of several defendants could not be 100 per cent. The court, however, said that it was not required to be decided whether market share may play a role in defining each of the producers' proportional contributions,[163] which seems apologetically to reintroduce the tenuous possibility of a more equitable apportionment of damages. The court accepted the alternative causation rule in the context of the DES-type case arguing that the number of plaintiffs was irrelevant, each plaintiff having an action in her own right against each of the defendant companies. The liable producer would have a right to contributions from other producers,[164] though it would seem logical that that contribution would be assessed in terms of market share, i.e. their share in the damages. The Supreme Court merely required the plaintiffs to state (and prove, if required) that: (a) the company put DES on the market and was at fault in so doing; (b) other companies put DES on the market and were also at fault; (c) the damages were caused by using DES but it was no longer possible to determine which company produced the DES taken by a mother. *Prima facie*, the burden of proving those facts is on the plaintiff, but if the plaintiff proves the above facts a defendant company, to avoid liability, must show in relation to each of the plaintiffs that her injuries were not caused by using DES that it put onto the market.[165] The potentially liable parties could also be liable for damage which may have been caused by DES put on the market from producers *not* at fault if

[160] Sect. 3.7.2.

[161] The Sup. Ct. also expressly rejected the concert of action theory, concluding that the pharmaceutical companies did not act as a group: sect. 3.9.

[162] Sect. 3.8. Joint and several liability is liability imposed on each of several parties, jointly and severally, so that someone can claim against all or one for all the damages (100%), leaving it to that one to work out relief from his co-defendants. Several liability is individually separate or distinct liability: see Walker, *The Oxford Companion to Law* (Oxford, Clarendon Press, 1980), 667.

[163] Sect. 3.8.

[164] Sect. 3.7.3.

[165] Sect. 3.7.5.

such DES was put on the market at the relevant period, unless such liability would be unacceptable according to reasonableness and equity criteria.[166]

Of notable importance was the court's failure to resolve the issue whether the alternative causation rule would be applicable in cases of strict product liability as based on the EC Directive (85/374/EEC), the court concluding that the Directive did not apply to products put on the market before 1985.[167] It has been said that the court emphasised that the new rule did not extend to claims resulting from the Directive[168] but the court did not rule out the possibility of such a rule being *used* in the Netherlands in a future case involving the Directive and its implementing legislation. Both the US market share liability[169] and the Dutch alternative causation law[170] allow a defendant manufacturer to escape liability if it proves that it has not manufactured the product that caused an individual's injury. However, as discussed in *Hymowitz* v. *Eli Lilly*,[171] it has been held that showing that a company had not manufactured the product that caused the plaintiff's injury was insufficient. It had to be shown that the company did not participate in the marketing of DES for pregnancy use.

It has been considered that there exists an equitable basis for apportioning damages in the DES cases according to the market share of each defendant by virtue of the fact that the injury is divisible.[172] Joint and several liability, although the choice of the Supreme Court of the Netherlands, operates only when damages are truly indivisible. Bergkamp gives unqualified support to market share liability, particularly in terms of deterrence and risk spreading.[173]

[166] Sect. 3.7.6. It has been suggested that the presence of such non-liable producers would bar the application of Art. 99 since it states "for each of which a different person *is* liable" (author's italics), but if a mother ingested the tablets of a non-liable producer, it is thought that this would fail to release the other manufacturers of liability for the whole of the loss unless liability would be unacceptable according to the reasonable and fair standard: Teulings, n. 149 above, 232. The denial of exculpation in *Hymowitz* would not operate under Dutch law so that appropriate defendants could avail themselves of such a defence but this would not preclude the liability of the other defendants in terms of Art. 99: *ibid.*

[167] Sect. 3.5. It seems more rational to take into account the fact that the Dir. required implementing legislation in each Member State and that the implementing legislation for the Netherlands came into force on 1 Nov. 1990. The correct approach thus seems to be that the law does not apply to products before *that* date in respect of the Netherlands. Indeed, the court stated that Art. 17, which says that the Dir. shall not apply to products put into circulation before the date on which the implementing legislation came into force, i.e. Nov. 1990 (in terms of Art. 19) would apply to remove the Dir.'s application to the case: *ibid.*

[168] Stapleton, *Product Liability* (London, Butterworths, 1994), 288.

[169] *Sindell* v. *Abbott Laboratories*, 607 P 2d 924, 937 (1980).

[170] Sect. 3.7.5.

[171] 541 NYS 2d 941 at 950.

[172] Bergkamp, n. 149 above, 6.

[173] *Ibid.* It would seem, however, that market share liability could not be inserted into the Dutch or English tort systems, since it would conflict with Art. 13 of the EC Product Liability Dir. (85/374/EEC) which preserves contractual, non-contractual or special liability system rules which existed on 30 July 1985. This rule has been understood to forbid the adoption by Member States of new product liability rules that impose a heavier burden on producers than the Dir. does, although it is felt that adoption would be possible if the stricter rules were not confined to product liability but resulted from a more general change in tort law. However, market share liability was unknown before *Sindell* in 1980, not debated in the Netherlands before 1987, and is more

Under the rule of alternative causation the drug company can be liable for damages *not* caused by it because each company marketing an injury-producing drug is jointly and severally liable for all the damages of all the injured plaintiffs. So even though a pharmaceutical company can establish that it cannot have caused more than a proportion of aggregate damages, it will be held liable for the remainder caused by the other companies in the suit. However, similar problems emerge with market share liability where it may be speculative whether any defendants in an action actually caused a plaintiff's injuries.[174] It has already been noted that the relevance of the alternative causation rule in the Netherlands to discussions on strict product liability based on the EC Product Liability Directive (85/374/EEC) is uncertain since the court did not decide the issue. Article 4 of the Directive states that the injured person must "prove the damage, the defect and the causal relationship between the defect and the damage", and it is unclear whether the Article would permit reversal of the burden of proof as to causation. Bergkamp notes that although the Directive was not aimed at harmonising causation requirements, the EC legislature had in mind a "standstill" in the strict product liability sector which would be inconsistent with an expansion of liability by "stretching causation".[175] It has been stated by the Department of Trade and Industry[176] and by the EC[177] that such matters will be determined by each Member State's laws and procedures which suggests that the new Dutch Civil Code 1992, incorporating alternative causation liability, would have the implementing legislation grafted on it.[178] It should be noted that the strongest criticism of the Dutch case is that it fails to heed the experience of *Sindell* v. *Abbott Laboratories*,[179] which rejected the operation in the DES scenario of the alternative liability theory of *Summers* v. *Tice*[180] on the ground that in *Summers* all the parties who were or could be responsible were joined as defendants. In *Sindell*, since one of 200 companies made the product which harmed the plaintiff, the possibility that none of the five defendants joined had made the DES which caused the injury was substantial.[181] In the

directly connected with product liability than alternative causation liability: Ekering, n. 159 above, 13.

174 See Richardson J's dissent in *Sindell* at 938–43.

175 Bergkamp, n. 149 above, 7.

176 *Implementation of EC Directive on Product Liability. An Explanatory and Consultative Note* (London: Department of Trade and Industry, 1985), para. 48.

177 Explanatory Memorandum of Sept. 1976 *EC Bull.*, Supp. 11/76 13, para. 30; Whittaker, "The EEC Directive on Product Liability" (1985) 5 *Ybk. Eur. Law* 233, 234.

178 Indeed, the new product liability legislation is that present in Book 6, Arts. 185–193 of the new Civil Code, having been first incorporated into Arts. 1407a–1407i of the old Civil Code. Ordinary tort law is present in Arts. 162–183 of Book 6 of the new Civil Code, requiring proof of negligence in principle and the joint and several liability provision of Art. 99 is also in Book 6 of the new Civil Code. This seems to be compatible with Art. 13 of the EC Product Liability Dir., which does not affect any rights that an injured person may have according to the rules of law of contractual or non-contractual liability or a special liability system existing on 30 July 1985.

179 607 P 2d 924 (1980).

180 199 P 2d 1 (Cal. 1948).

181 607 P 2d 924 at 930, 931. The odds that any given producer could be responsible could be less than one in 300: Robinson, n. 32 above, 724.

Dutch case it was clear from the decisions of the District Court of Amsterdam and the Amsterdam Court of Appeal[182] that none of the ten may have made the DES which caused the injuries to the plaintiffs.[183] Moreover, and most importantly, the imposition of joint and several liability upon all tortfeasors was an inequitable way to apportion liability since the defendants that manufactured a considerable amount of DES and those that manufactured a small amount were liable equally.[184]

(f) Consumer Protection Act 1987 and Market Share or Alternative Causation Liability

The application of market share liability or alternative causation liability in the context of section 2(1) of the Consumer Protection Act 1987 (which requires the establishment of a causal link between the defective product and the plaintiff's injury) appears to be an unlikely scenario, since the UK courts are most probably likely to follow the law of negligence. *Sindell* v. *Abbott Laboratories* was decided on the basis of an exception to the rule that liability depends on causation. Under traditional tort principles this would be unacceptable.[185]

In addition, the identification of someone liable for damage caused by a defective product will not be so much of a difficulty as it was under the previous law. From the point of view of medicinal products, persons liable would be those who manufactured the drug (deemed producers), those who imported the drug into the EC or those who held themselves out to be producers of the drug by putting their own label on it.[186] Suppliers of the product (contingent producers) are treated as producers unless and until they can inform the injured person within a reasonable time, on request, of the producer's identity, or at least who supplied them with the drug.[187] Problems seem to suggest themselves with generic drugs, the prescription of which is encouraged by the Department of

[182] See above. It was not disputed that there were, remarkably, 200 manufacturers of DES in the Netherlands. (See sect. 3 of District Court of Amsterdam's judgment.)

[183] Because alternative liability conflicts with the basic principle that the plaintiff needs to prove his case on the balance of probabilities, the scope of alternative liability may be restricted to situations where joint tortfeasers act in concert or where vicarious liability applies: Teff, n. 28 above, 841. Vicarious liability and concert of action as explanations of cause-in-fact are both based on fiction, since vicarious liability is necessarily a fiction and the "but for" definition of cause-in-fact is fictional as to the liability of some of the participants for the concerted action. Only when the cause-in-fact is defined in terms of material contribution to a plaintiff's injury does the fiction become eliminated in a concerted action as all of the participants in a concerted action contribute to the injury: see Sheiner, n. 13 above, 979–80.

[184] Note, "Market Share Liability: An Answer to the DES Causation Problem" (1981) 94 *Harv. L Rev*. 668, 672. For a favourable reception to the Sup. Ct.'s decision see Hondius, "A Dutch DES Case: Pharmaceutical Producers Jointly and Severally Liable" [1994] *Consum. LJ* 40, 42.

[185] 607 P 2d 924 at 942 (Richardson J Dissenting).

[186] 85/374/EEC on the approximation of the laws, regs. and administrative provisions of the Member States concerning liability for defective products [1985] OJ L 210/29, Art. 3.1 and 3.2; Consumer Protection Act 1987, ss. 1(2) and 2(2).

[187] 85/374/EEC, n. 186 above, Art. 3.3; Consumer Protection Act 1987, s. 2(3).

Health. Their source is not easy to identify[188] and the supplier would be the health authority in that situation.[189] The opportunity for use of a market share liability approach would thus arise only at the stage where, for example, a chemist seeks indemnity from those who supplied it with a generic drug, such action being decided by domestic law.[190]

It should be noted that it has been submitted[191] that the lack of clarity in the operation of causation in this context could result in a greater obstacle in the obtaining of compensation under the 1987 Act than even the inclusion of the Act's development risk defence.[192]

(ii) Scenario 2: Second Generation Physical Abnormalities of Reproductive Organs and Third Generation Physical Disabilities, Including Cerebral Palsy

(a) Introduction

The question of third-generation lawsuits has also been the focus of judicial determination. In the second scenario, DES administered to pregnant women has allegedly caused damage to the fœtus *in utero*, resulting in physical abnormalities of the child's reproductive organs. It is claimed that by virtue of such abnormalities third-generation children have been born prematurely, leading to several physical disabilities, including cerebral palsy. Such alleged cases of third-generation injury and DES appear to be illustrative of pre-conception torts, occurring when tortious acts of the defendant prior to conception cause resultant harm to the child.[193]

A case of action for a pre-natal tort exists in English and Scots law, thus covering cases of second-generation injury and DES.[194]

[188] See Finch and Ranson, *Product Liability in Europe. What the New EEC Directive Will Mean for Pharmaceutical Companies* (Richmond, PJB Publications, 1986), 25.

[189] *Implementation of EC Directive on Product Liability : An Explanatory and Consultative Note* (London, Department of Trade and Industry, 1985), para. 46; Clark, "The Consumer Protection Act 1987" (1987) 50 *MLR* 614, 616.

[190] Stapleton, n. 168 above, 233. But see, in respect of DES, the problem of extinction of a right of action to obtain indemnity ten years from the date the product was put into circulation: s. 11A(3) of the Limitation Act 1980, and the fact that DES was not supplied after 1 Mar. 1988, the commencement date of the Consumer Protection Act 1987. See below.

[191] B. S. Markesinis and Deakin, *Tort Law* (3rd edn., Oxford, Clarendon Press, 1994), 558.

[192] See Newdick, "The Development Risk Defence of the Consumer Protection Act 1987" (1988) 47 *Camb. LJ* 455; cf R. Goldberg, "The Development Risk Defence and Medicinal Products" (1991) 36 *JLSS* 376.

[193] Mascaro, n. 7 above, 436–7.

[194] *B* v. *Islington Health Authority* [1991] 2 Med. LR 133; *de Martell* v. *Merton & Sutton HA* [1991] 2 Med. LR 209; *Burton* v. *Islington Health Authority, de Martell v. Merton & Sutton Health Authority* [1993] 4 Med. LR 8; *Hamilton* v. *Fife Health Board (Ex Div)*, 1993 SLT 624. All these cases have held it a good cause of action in negligence if a child be born suffering from disabilities caused as a result of medical negligence at the time when the plaintiff was *en ventre sa mère* and unborn. Litigation on the merits of the action, in respect of whether the disabilities were in fact caused by the medical negligence, is a separate legal issue. There would also be a need for the

Third-generation injury remains the problem. However, it has been concluded that in English law, notwithstanding the absence of common law authority, there will be liability for harm caused prior to conception,[195] since pre-conception claims are legally indistinguishable from the pre-natal tort situation.[196] The New South Wales case of *X and Y* v. *Pal*[197] holds that there may be liability to a child as a result of negligent acts or omissions which took place prior to its conception, the existence of a duty depending on the existence of a relevant relationship between the careless person and the class of persons of which the child is a member.[198] It seems that English law would follow the logic of this position, but this still leaves the difficult problem of establishing a causal link between the occurrence and the injury. Lovell and Griffith-Jones have asserted[199] that "[w]e have clearly come a long way from *Walker* v. *Gt. Northern Ry. of Ireland*"[200] and the view of O'Brien J,[201] that extravagant testimony would become the norm, together with difficulties of proof if there was recovery by a child suffering ante-natal injuries.[202] To a large extent this has been vindicated by Dillon LJ's judgment in the Court of Appeal case of *Burton* v. *Islington Health Authority, de Martell* v. *Merton and Sutton Health Authority*,[203] where he disapproved of *Walker* and cited Fraser J's view in *Duval et al.* v. *Seguin et al.*[204] that such proof difficulties have been ameliorated with scientific advances of knowledge. But what this does not address is the fact that evidence and proof difficulties remain current problems in drug product liabil-

plaintiff to identify the manufacturer responsible for the injury which is, as has already been discovered, a thankless task: see Bridgeman, "Diethylstilbestrol: A Case in English Common Law?" [1994] *Consum. LJ* 44, 45–6. Note also that it has been recently reaffirmed that Scots law does not confer on a fœtus a right to exist independently in a mother's womb. Therefore, no person could invoke the power of the court to vindicate such a right: *Kelly* v. *Kelly*, *The Times*, 5 June 1997 (Court of Session). In *Kelly*, the Lord Justice-Clerk observed that if such a right did exist, it could be used as the basis for a father to take action to restrain the mother from a form of activity which was claimed to be harmful to the fœtus, e.g. "smoking and certain sports and occupations".

195 Whitfield, "Common Law Duties to Unborn Children" (1993) 1 *Med. L Rev*. 28, 43–45.

196 *Ibid*., 43–4.

197 (1991) 23 NSWLR 26.

198 (1991) 23 NSWLR 26 at 41, *per* Clarke JA. See also 37, 40, 42.

199 Lovell and Griffith-Jones, " 'The sins of the Fathers'—Tort Liability for Pre-Natal Injuries" (1974) 90 *LQR* 531, 538.

200 (1890) 28 LR Ir. 69.

201 *Ibid*., at 82.

202 It has been noted that difficulty in establishing a connection between the defendant's conduct and the plaintiff's injury is not a sufficient reason for denying an action, but that on the state of medical knowledge at the time of the *Walker* decision, such difficulties in establishing a causal nexus would have proved insurmountable. This difficulty often appears to increase as the time lag between the wrongful act and the accrual of the cause of action increases: Pace, "Civil Liability for Pre-Natal Injuries" (1977) 40 *MLR* 141. Such a time lag is present with DES. In this context, see also the comments of Teff and Munro that difficulties of proof of causation do not justify denying a cause of action in principle for cases of ante-natal injuries: Teff and Munro, *Thalidomide: The Legal Aftermath* (Farnborough, Saxon House, 1976), 40.

203 [1993] 4 Med. LR 8.

204 (1972) 26 DLR (3d) 418 at 434.

ity litigation.[205] Witness the uncertainty as to causation of some of the more frequently alleged side-effects of the drug Opren,[206] and also the Benzodiazepines.[207] *A fortiori*, the practicalities of failing to establish a causal link in law will be the collapse of an action,[208] notwithstanding the court's theoretical recognition of a cause of action in the first place.[209]

In the United States, recognition of pre-conception tort liability emerged with the case of *Jorgensen* v. *Meade Johnson Laboratories*,[210] where the US Court of Appeals, Tenth Circuit, held that a strict liability and negligence liability cause of action was recognisable on behalf of one deceased and one living mongoloid child in respect of damage allegedly caused prior to conception to the mother's chromosomal structure by her Oracon birth-control pills.[211] The court said that the decision would depend on medical evidence of a cause-and-effect relationship, though no opinion was expressed on the merits of the claim.[212] It has been noted[213] that the issue was ultimately not settled in court, but that the action had been brought a number of years before scientific evidence in literature turned against the idea of pre-conceptual causation of the VACTERL syndrome.[214] It is clear that there has never been evidence of any drug, let alone birth-control pills, which has caused or induced mongolism.

The case of *Jorgensen* establishes pre-conception tort liability in respect of strict liability and negligence. However, Mascaro[215] cites the case as one of pre-conception strict liability, and considers[216] that the first case to accept pre-conception negligence liability was *Renslow* v. *Mennonite Hospital*.[217] In that case, the Supreme Court of Illinois found that logic and sound policy required a

[205] Note the "gloomy prognostication" of Baroness Hooper in the House of Lords as cited by Lord Ackner: "[a]lthough advances in medical science have clarified some causal links—for example, the damage to the brain during delivery, is rarely the cause of cerebral palsy—the introduction of innovative techniques and new drugs and the increasingly complex interaction between these and the patient to whom they are applied, heighten rather than diminish the problems of proving causation in the individual case": Lord Ackner, "The Doctor in Court—Victim or Protected Species?" (1992) 8 *PN* 54, 57.

[206] See Hurst J in *Randall* v. *Eli Lilly & Co.*, *The Independent*, 4 Feb. 1988 (QBD).

[207] In *AB and Others* v. *John Wyeth & Brother Ltd and Others (No 2)* [1994] 5 Med. LR, 149, 153, Stuart-Smith LJ noted the "very considerable problems on causation".

[208] *Pinchin* v. *Santam Insurance Co Ltd* [1963] 2 SA 254 (child has an action to recover damages for pre-natal injuries but failure to extablish causation will result in a loss of the case on the facts. See Hiemstra J at 260, 263).

[209] *Hornbuckle* v. *Plantation Pipe Line Co.*, 93 SE 2d 727, 728 (1956).

[210] 483 F 2d 237 (1973).

[211] See Holloway, CJ at 240.

[212] *Ibid.*, 240.

[213] Dukes and Swartz, *Responsibility for Drug-Induced Injury* (Amsterdam, New York, Oxford, Elsevier, 1989), 271.

[214] A term used to describe adverse effects on certain organs of offspring, namely vertebrae, anus, cardiac, trachea, œsophagus, renal, limbs: *ibid.*, 263.

[215] Mascaro, n. 7 above, 442.

[216] *Ibid.*

[217] 367 NE 2d 1250 (1977).

finding of legal duty, and it followed the line of the Scottish Law Commission in recognising liability prior to conception.[218]

The reluctance to accept the scenario of a cause of action involving a drug such as DES causing defects in third or successive generations was implicit in the dissent of Ryan J in *Renslow*.[219] He referred to the possibility of a modern drug causing a genetically transferable defect passed on to successive generations, resulting in the impossibility of determining a potential claim against a pharmaceutical company. All of the dissenters in *Renslow* argued the unacceptability of future generations of plaintiffs suing for genetic injury allegedly caused by a tortfeasor's conduct 50 or 60 years after supply of the drug.[220]

What has created the difficulty in the establishment of a third-generation DES cause of action has been the rejection of pre-conception negligence liability in *Albala* v. *City of New York*,[221] where the New York Court of Appeals concluded that a cause of action for pre-conception negligence liability on behalf of a child was not recognisable[222] because such recognition "would require the extension of traditional tort concepts beyond manageable grounds".[223]

The Court in *Albala* rejected the application of *Jorgensen* by distinguishing it as representing strict liability, whereas *Albala* involved medical malpractice.[224] *Jorgensen* involved a strict liability cause of action where the manufacturer's liability "is extended to the entire class of persons thereby affected regardless of privity, foreseeability or due care".[225] However, in what appears to be a contradiction of *Albala,* the case of *Catherwood* v. *American Sterilizer Company*[226]

[218] 367 NE 2d 1250 (1977), at 1255. See also 1258–9. The Law Commission, like its Scottish counterpart, concluded that there could be liability for harm caused prior to conception, i.e. a child born disabled because of some tortious injury inflicted upon its parent before conception: Report on Injuries to Unborn Children, Law Com., No. 60, Cmnd. 5709/1974, para 78. The Scottish Law Commission concluded "in principle" that there could be liability for acts causing injury prior to conception, saying "in principle" since it was clear that a child relying on a pre-conception act of negligence would face the formidable problem of proving a direct causal connection between the negligence and the injury: *Liability for Antenatal Injury*, Scot. Law Com. No. 30, Cmnd. 5371/1973, para. 21.

[219] *Ibid.*, at 1264, *per* Ryan J (dissenting).

[220] *Ibid., per* Ward, CJ (dissenting) at 1261; *per* Underwood J (dissenting) at 1262; *per* Ryan J (dissenting) at 1262 and arguing that the majority had abandoned the fault concept of liability based on duty and foreseeability and had embraced causation instead.

[221] 445 NYS 2d 108 (1981).

[222] *Ibid.*, at 108.

[223] 445 NYS 2d at 109. *Albala* is described by Prosser as a "thinly reasoned case": Keeton, Dobbs, Keeton and Owen (eds), *Prosser and Keeton on The Law of Torts* (5th edn., St. Paul, Minn., West Publishing Co., 1984), 369, the reasons given for denying such an action being "problems of proof and proximate causation arising, for example, from the imposition of liability upon a chemical, drug or other company for future generations of mutated children resulting from toxic chemicals or radioactive waste": *ibid.* Prosser states that such "staggering problems" will have to be dealt with carefully in future toxic tort contexts but he does not require that a blanket no-duty rule be applied in pre-conception injury cases in the absence of such problems. Perhaps this might infer that in drug-induced injury cases, where causation problems are the norm, that the blanket no-duty rule would reign paramount?

[224] 445 NYS 2d 108 at 110.

[225] *Ibid.*

[226] 498 NYS 2d 703 (NY Sup. Ct. 1986).

has rejected a cause of action for pre-conception strict liability.[227] The decision was upheld by the Appellate Division of the Supreme Court of New York.[228]

If the federal decision of *Albala* is accepted, along with the lower state trial decision of *Catherwood*, then these cases suggest that uncertainty surrounds the whole basis of preconception tort liability. However, the inconsistency between *Albala* and *Catherwood* infers that the issue of pre-conception strict liability remains open to further questioning. Whatever the conclusion of these courts, it will be submitted that the true bar to the establishment of a cause of action for third-generation cases of pre-conception injury may be the fact that establishment of a causal link in these cases would be difficult, if not impossible.

(b) Determining the Causal Link

In respect of the physical abnormalities of reproductive organs in the second generation, an initial problem exists in determining a causal link between the DES and the physical abnormalities, unlike the establishment of a general causal link between DES and vaginal clear cell adenocarcinoma in the second generation. Although examination of the reproductive capability and labour problems of women exposed to DES while fœtuses *in utero* has shown that such women have, *inter alia*, incompetent cervixes, ectopic pregnancies, spontaneous abortions and premature labour to a greater degree than controls, such statistics are confused by the fact that the mothers who took the drug had previously poor obstetric histories.[229] Thus it seems that second-generation daughters may well have genetically acquired the abnormality of their reproductive organs from their mothers, who were a subgroup that was using the drug because of the possibility of miscarriage. Such a subgroup may have had a higher level of infertility than average, opening up the possible range of causes of the second-generation reproductive organ abnormalities together with the problem of the cause of the third-generation disabilities, including cerebral palsy. A cursory glance at this area shows that there are a range of possible causes of the effects in the second and third generation, and that on a traditional factual causation analysis in English law it would be difficult to show the operative cause of the second- and third-generation injuries.[230]

227 *Ibid.*, at 706. The court noted (at 705) that *Albala* v. *City of New York*, CA, 445 NYS 2d 108 (1981) had preserved the issue of whether a pre-conception strict liability cause of action was cognisable "for future decision". The court was "neither controlled by *Albala* nor [was] foreclosed from extending *Albala*". The issue presented was one "of first impression".

228 *Catherwood* v. *American Sterilizer Co.*, 511 NYS 2nd 805 (NY App. Div. 1987), 806. One justice (Callahan J, Green J dissenting) argued that in a product liability action like the case in question, once a causal relationship was established, liability of the manufacturer should automatically extend to the "entire class of persons thereby affected regardless of privity, foreseeability or due care": *ibid.*

229 Mangan, Borow, Burtnett-Rubin, Egan, Giuntoli and Mikuta, "Pregnancy Outcome in 98 Women Exposed to Diethylstilboestrol In Utero, Their Mothers and Unexposed Siblings" (1982) 59 *Obstetrics & Gynæcology* 315 at 315, 318–19.

230 *Wilsher* v. *Essex AHA* [1988] 1 AC 1074.

These scenarios seem potentially to reflect the reverse situation to that in previous market share liability actions involving indeterminate defendants, such as *Sindell* v. *Abbott Laboratories*.[231] Here the situation is one of indeterminate plaintiffs in biological causation cases in which disease manifests itself years after exposure.[232] In an indeterminate plaintiffs situation, the plaintiffs suffer injuries that can result from natural or man-made causes without a synergistic relationship between them,[233] and the injuries are causally indeterminate (not assignable to culpable man-made causes or non-culpable natural ones).[234] If in that situation the plaintiffs establish a *prima facie* case by showing that they have suffered injuries that could result from either natural or man-made causes acting separately and without synergy, and that the injuries are causally indeterminate, that the defendant is the only possible human cause and that the population mode of risk and other variables are stable enough to allow an epidemiological calculation of the increased number of victims, it has been proposed that the burden of proof can shift to the defendant to prove non-causation with respect to each injury. If the defendant fails, liability will be imposed *pro rata* for the number of unproved victims. The defendant can overcome the burden of proof by showing that the plaintiff's number of humanly caused cases is exaggerated or that another human defendant has injured some of the victims. The solution is advocated on fairness grounds[235] though its author concedes that with biological causation cases with long latency periods it will be unlikely to achieve deterrence and economic efficiency if the manufacturer is sued many years later. The draconian nature of the delayed penalty is mitigated by the requirement that the actor's conduct be known to cause an increase in the rate of injury.[236] However, the question is one of how often this will be known at the time of supply. It is arguable in the DES cases that an increase in the prevalence of injury should have been known at the time, and perhaps knowledge of harm of the kind which subsequently transpired should also have been foreseen.[237] Criticisms of this view include the fact that compensation is provided for plaintiffs who have not been demonstrably injured by the actions of the defendant and these remain unanswered. Further, over-compensation and under-compensation seems to be present as well,[238] but this is arguably a better scenario than leaving all potential victims uncompensated. Also, it is generalised probabilistic evidence that will be used to provide compensation, not statistics

[231] 607 P 2d 924 (1980).

[232] Delgado, "Beyond *Sindell*: Relaxation of Cause-In-Fact Rules for Indeterminate Plaintiffs" (1982) 70 *Cal. L Rev*. 881, 883.

[233] However, it is conceded that one can never rule out the possibility of synergism with medicinal products and natural causes or reactions with other medicinal products. Nonetheless, synergism's challenge to legal concepts is fettered by the problems in identifying such interactions: Stapleton, *Disease and the Compensation Debate* (Oxford, Clarendon Press, 1986), 58–9.

[234] Delgado, n. 232 above, 881, 884–6, 906 n. 121.

[235] *Ibid*., 899–902.

[236] *Ibid*., 894 n. 73.

[237] See below.

[238] Delgado, n. 232 above, 903–4.

showing a specific connection between the conduct of the defendant and his injury.[239]

Such an indeterminate plaintiff situation, where a naturally occurring act produces the same kind of harm as a negligent act, was ruled out in the Canadian vaccine damage decision of *Rothwell* v. *Raes*.[240] In that case, the argument that pre-natal injury caused brain damage was rejected by the Ontario Court of Appeal, which accepted the trial judge's conclusion that the plaintiff's neurological damage was idiopathic in origin.[241] However, the possibility of an indeterminate plaintiffs doctrine combining with an indeterminate defendants doctrine in a suit by a class of indeterminate plaintiffs against a class of indeterminate defendants has been mooted, resulting in a massive lawsuit with complex problems of proof and the need for a substantial number of judicial resources.[242] This would seem plausible in the medical product liability field in circumstances where a number of manufacturers produce a substance causing an adverse drug reaction which can occur naturally, e.g. a synthetic hormone or a live vaccine which aggravates or creates the disease it was designed to treat or prevent.[243] *A fortiori*, there is clearly the possibility of second- and third-generation DES cases, since DES may cause reproductive damage in DES daughters, going on to cause cerebral palsy in granddaughters, but all such adverse reactions could occur naturally. The plaintiffs would therefore be indeterminate and, if they were unable to identify the defendants, they also would be indeterminate, producing the possible combination of the two.

In respect of the second scenario, the leading case on this kind of third-generation lawsuit has concerned the right of action for a pre-conception tort in a third-generation strict products liability case in the United States. Since the right of action was rejected, a discussion of the causal issues involved did not take place, yet the case appears to gravitate towards a feeling, certainly alluded to in the dissenting opinion of Hancock J in *Enright* v. *Eli Lilly & Co.*,[244] that the majority may well have dismissed the action with their minds conscious of the possibility of additional difficulties in establishing causation at trial.

In *Enright* v. *Eli Lilly & Co.*,[245] the plaintiff alleged that her grandmother ingested DES during her pregnancy, giving birth to her mother with abnormalities and deformities in her reproductive system. The plaintiff was prematurely born suffering from cerebral palsy and other severe disabilities which were attributed to her premature birth and ultimately to her grandmother's ingestion

239 *Ibid.*, 905.

240 (1991) 76 DLR (4th) 280.

241 *Ibid.*, 282, 283.

242 Delgado, n. 232 above, 907–8.

243 Peppin, "Drug Vaccine Risks: Patient Decision Making and Harm Reduction in the Pharmaceutical Company Duty to Warn" (1991) 70 *Can. Bar Rev.* 473, 500.

244 568 NYS 2d 550 (CA 1991), *per* Hancock J (dissenting) at 557.

245 568 NYS 2d 550 (CA 1991); see Brahms, "Diethylstilbestrol: Third Generation Injury Claims" (1991) 59 *Med. LJ* 126.

of DES.[246] The issue before the court was whether the third-generation plaintiff had a strict product liability cause of action for a pre-conception tort.[247] The Court of Appeals of New York dismissed the third-generation claim, saying that the distinctions between the case and *Albala* v. *City of New York*[248] provided no basis for a departure from the rule that an injury to a mother resulting in injuries to a later conceived child did not establish the child's cause of action against the original tortfeasor.[249] The Court held that policy considerations in respect of limitation of actions (where the limitation period in exposure cases runs now on discovery of an injury and not exposure of a substance)[250] and policy decisions in respect of the adoption of market share liability (to correspond to the overall culpability of each defendant)[251] were responses to procedural barriers and problems of proof. They were no support for the recognition of a new multigenerational cause of action. The fact that the case was a DES case did not justify departure from *Albala*, which failed to recognise pre-conception negligence liability.[252] Secondly, the policy considerations in the negligence liability action of *Albala*, *viz*. cost-shifting, risk-spreading and deterrence, were the same as in a strict product liability action; thus there was no basis for reaching a different conclusion from *Albala*.[253] Thirdly, the Court of Appeals held that the same considerations as applied in *Albala* applied in *Enright* with the same "staggering implications". A cause of action could not be confined without the drawing of artificial boundaries and the "rippling effects" of DES exposure might extend for generations. The court considered that it was its duty to confine liability within manageable limits; limiting liability to the people who had ingested the drug or who were exposed to it served this purpose.[254] The court finally held that the FDA's primary responsibility for encouraging prescription drug safety reduced the need for the tort system to promote such safety. Delivering the opinion, Wachtler J dismissed the idea that the case involved the application of straightforward strict products liability. He said that "[i]n neither this case nor *Albala* was the infant plaintiff exposed to the defendants' dangerous product or negligent conduct; rather, both were injured as a consequence of injuries to the reproductive systems of their mothers".[255] However, it could clearly be argued, as Hancock J did,[256] that the exposure could be *indirect* since the plaintiff's mother was exposed to DES ingestion.

The dissenting Hancock J said that there was no basis in "law or social policy" or any "principled reason in justice and fairness" for holding that the

[246] 568 NYS 2d 550, 551.
[247] *Ibid.*, 552, 553.
[248] 54 NY 2d 269, 429 NE 2d 786, 445 NYS 2d 108 (1981).
[249] 568 NYS 2d 550, 556.
[250] NY Civ. Prac. L & R. 214–c (Consol. 1990).
[251] *Hymowitz* v. *Eli Lilly & Co.*, 541 NYS 2d 941 (CA 1989) at 950.
[252] 568 NYS 2d 550 at 553, 554.
[253] *Ibid.*, 554–5.
[254] *Ibid.*, 555.
[255] *Ibid.*, 556.
[256] *Ibid.*, at 558, Hancock J (dissenting).

plaintiff, unlike other members of the DES class of victims, should not be permitted to prove her case.[257]

The suggestion that causation difficulties were part of the reason behind the majority dismissing the cause of action is provided by Hancock J, who said that the possibility of additional difficulties in establishing causation at trial was no reason for dismissal of a strict products liability action.[258] This perhaps accords with Fraser J's view in *Duval et al.* v. *Seguin et al.*[259] that difficulties with proof of causation and problems of perjury and speculation, once regarded as reasons for dismissing a cause of action by a child suffering antenatal injuries,[260] had been ameliorated with scientific advances of knowledge. As has been submitted, however, such a view fails to address the fact that evidence and proof difficulties remain problems in current drug product liability litigation, and if that is understood as a statement of fact, it could be argued that the difficulties of proof of causation may be reason for the refusal of recognising an action on behalf of third-generation victims of DES. But a rejoinder to this argument might be that the right of a cause of action should have no bearing on the question of the quality of the merits of the case.[261] It seems, however, that at the very least policy reasons were probably the basis for the court's rejection of a cause of action, "not least of which is the indeterminant nature of the potential liability to future generations".[262] Any morality reflected in the law here is thus the product of judicial policy (the "legal policy" view of causation).[263]

A pre-conception cause of action for DES grandchildren has also been rejected in *Grower* v. *Eli Lilly & Co.*[264] A grandmother ingested DES when pregnant. Her daughter, the petitioner, was exposed to DES *in utero* and was born with injuries to her reproductive organs, which included the inability to carry a fœtus to full term. The daughter's son was delivered 11 weeks before term. The petitioners alleged that as a result of the child's premature birth he

257 *Ibid.*, at 554, Hancock J (dissenting).

258 *Ibid.*, at 557, Hancock J (dissenting). In *Woods* v. *Lancet*, 102 NE 2d 691 (1951), the CA of New York held that a complaint alleging prenatal injuries negligently inflicted during the ninth month of a mother's pregnancy on a fœtus which was viable at the time and later born stated a good cause of action: *ibid.*, at 692, 695. The court observed: "[e]very day in our trial courts . . . such issues are disposed of and it is an inadmissible concept that uncertainty of proof can ever destroy a legal right. The questions of causation, reasonable certainty . . . etc., which will arise in these cases are not different, in kind, from the ones which have arisen in thousands of other negligence cases decided in this State, in the past": *ibid.*, 695. See also Keeton, Dobbs, Keeton and Owens (eds.), n. 223 above, 368: "[a]s far as causation is concerned, there will certainly be cases in which there will be difficulties of proof, but they should be no more frequent, nor the difficulties any greater, than as to many other medical problems".

259 (1972) 26 DLR (3d) 418 at 434.

260 See O'Brien J in *Walker* v. *Gt. Northern Ry. of Ireland* (1890) 28 LR Ir. 69 at 82.

261 E.g., Teff and Munro have argued that difficulties of proof of causation do not justify denying a cause of action in principle: Teff and Munro, n. 202 above, 40.

262 Kennedy and Grubb, *Medical Law: Text with Materials* (2nd edn., London, Dublin, Edinburgh, Butterworths, 1994), 947.

263 See P. Cane, *Atiyah's Accidents Compensation and the Law* (5th edn., London, Butterworths, 1993), 105.

264 591 NE 2d 696 (Ohio 1992).

suffered from cerebral palsy and other serious injuries.[265] The Supreme Court of Ohio held that because of remoteness in time and causation the child did not have an independent cause of action and that a pharmaceutical company's liability for the distribution or manufacture of a defective prescription drug did not extend to persons who were never exposed to the drug, either directly or *in utero*.[266]

The court assumed in the case that the grandchild was able to prove that his injuries were proximately caused by his mother's exposure to DES, and stated that it was not evaluating the facts of the case but determining, as a matter of law, whether a grandchild had a legally cognisable cause of action.[267] *Grower* declined to adopt the absolute rule of *Albala* v. *City of New York*,[268] which held that a plaintiff did not have a cause of action for *any* pre-conception tort, regardless of the facts, but rejected the plaintiff's cause of action on the basis that it was far more tenuous than that raised in *Albala*. It was unlikely that a pharmaceutical company in the 1940s–1960s could have foreseen the effect that a drug would have not only on the patient's unborn child but also on that child's children.[269] The court found *Albala's* reasoning persuasive and accepted that knowledge of a propensity to harm reproductive organs would be sufficient to impose liability for different injuries to organs but would not accept that such generalised knowledge would be sufficient to impose liability for injuries to a third party 28 years later. It concluded that a pharmaceutical company that prescribes drugs to a woman does not ordinarily owe a duty to her daughter's child who would be conceived 28 years later.[270]

In a vigorous dissent, criticism was made of the superficial treatment of the issue in the light of its complexity.[271] The majority holding was regarded as unclear, since the court stated that it was required to assume that the plaintiff could prove that his injuries were proximately caused by his mother's exposure to DES, but then finally held that because of the remoteness in time and *causation*, the plaintiff did not have an independent cause of action.[272] The dissenting judge concluded, having analysed the plaintiff's allegations as if they were accurate (since the court stated that it was not evaluating the facts of the case), that DES manufacturers knew or should have known that DES injured the female reproductive system. It was thus foreseeable that a female would at some point seek to use the defective reproductive system. Thus the DES grandchildren were foreseeable, and so the pharmaceutical companies owed them a duty of care; the DES grandchildren were within the actor's range of apprehension. The dissent concluded that the plaintiff had a cause of action. This evidently did not

[265] 591 NE 2d 696 (Ohio 1992), at 697.
[266] *Ibid.*, 700–1.
[267] *Ibid.*, 697–8.
[268] 445 NYS 2d 108 (1981).
[269] 591 NE 2d 696 at 698 n. 1.
[270] *Ibid.*, 699–700.
[271] *Ibid.*, 701 Resnick J (dissenting).
[272] *Ibid.*, 701–2 Resnick J (dissenting) (her emphasis).

open the floodgates since litigation could be concluded with the plaintiff's generation.[273] However, the court added that the petitioners still bore the burden of proving cause.[274]

This case has been subject to trenchant criticism,[275] suggesting that the court relied on "unsound reasoning and questionable policy concerns" to impose its decision.[276] The court should have focused on whether pharmaceutical companies should have foreseen that DES could cause reproductive abnormalities in the fœtus. If such abnormalities were found foreseeable, the court should have questioned whether the drug companies should have foreseen that a fœtus trying to develop within the reproductive tract could suffer abnormalities through injury. In doing so, it is claimed that the court should have concluded that, had the pharmaceutical companies properly tested DES, it would have foreseen that DES could cause reproductive tract abnormalities in exposed mothers' offspring.[277] It is thus concluded that because the injury to the DES grandchild was foreseeable, the child was within the drug company's range of apprehension and it therefore owed a duty of care to the plaintiff.[278] It is argued that policy considerations support the existence of a legal duty.[279] A strong argument against this is the possibility of perpetual liability.[280] However, it is posited that no such threat exists with DES grandchildren since, because there was no evidence that DES could affect the reproductive tract of DES grandchildren, the pharmaceutical companies reasonably could not have foreseen that DES could injure generations after DES grandchildren. Nonetheless, an important rejoinder to that view would be the argument that any evidence of mutated genes, such as with vaginal adenocarcinoma in DES-exposed daughters, might possibly suggest an effect on future generations of DES offspring beyond grandchildren. It is also argued[281] that policy considerations would not bar a cause of action since, in particular, fears of rippling effects of DES exposure would be fixed by traditional notions of the burden of proving cause in fact. This issue will be dependent on how easy it will become to establish causal link in pre-natal and perinatal injuries as technology, and in particular pharmacoepidemiology, genetic scanning and chromosomal analysis, develops.[282]

[273] *Ibid.*, 702–3 Resnick J (dissenting). No explanation was given why the litigation would so conclude.

[274] *Ibid.*, 703.

[275] Myers, "Ohio Rejects Preconception Cause of Action for DES Grandchildren: *Grower v. Eli Lilly & Co.*, 591 N.E. 2d 696 (Ohio 1992)" (1993) 62 *U Cincinnati LR* 283.

[276] *Ibid.*, at 319.

[277] *Ibid.*, at 304–5.

[278] *Ibid.*, at 308.

[279] *Ibid.*, at 309–14.

[280] See, e.g., Kennedy and Grubb, n. 262 above, 943.

[281] Myers, n. 275 above, at 314–19.

[282] See below.

(iii) Scenario 3: Second Generation Chromosomal Damages to Sperm Germ Cells Allegedly Resulting in Female Offspring with Clear Cell Vaginal Adenocarcinoma

(a) Introduction

In addition to a study which notes that the administration of DES to women can result in damage to the male fœtus *in utero*, causing a variety of male genital tract abnormalities including epididymal cysts,[283] the third main scenario is that a grandmother's ingestion of DES has evidently caused genetic damage in the second-generation male fœtus *in utero* in the form of chromosomal damages to germ cells in its sperm, allegedly causing female offspring to have clear cell vaginal adenocarcinoma.[284]

In one of the first cases to claim that DES causes genetic mutation leading to third-generation adenocarcinoma, a male plaintiff in March 1990 filed a lawsuit in the federal district court in Washington against Eli Lilly & Co., alleging that his exposure to DES as a fœtus caused his daughter's death through clear cell adenocarcinoma.[285]

(b) Difficulty of Proving Causation

It has been noted that if a cause of action is sustained in such a case, it will be particularly difficult for a plaintiff to prove causation.[286] At present, mutagenic effects have only been induced by drugs in laboratory studies with animals, and the risk in man is unknown. Clearly evident is the problem of impossibility of human controlled studies and the problem of detecting effects unless they are very gross.[287] Since the disease does not strike until adolescence, a few more years may have to pass before significant numbers of DES grandchildren can be expected to contract clear cell adenocarcinoma and the necessary epidemiological studies can be conducted, although it has been suggested that the plaintiff could rely on a DES animal study of Dr Bruce Walker showing that a higher incidence of uterine adenocarcinomas and ovarian cystadenocarcinomas occur in third generations of mice administered DES.[288] However, it should be noted

[283] Conley, Sant, Ucci and Mitcheson, "Seminoma and Epididymal Cysts in a Young Man with Known Diethylstilbestrol Exposure in Utero" (1983) 249 *JAMA* 1325, 1325 (case of seminoma (cancer of testicle) and epididymal cysts in 28-year old man exposed to DES *in utero*, suggesting possibility of association with DES and development of testicular malignant neoplasms in humans). See Figure 1 in Chap. 2.

[284] This appears to be the mirror image of hæmophilia where a genetic defect occurs naturally in the female and is expressed in the male offspring.

[285] Marcotte, "DES Legacy: Suit Claims Grandchild of Woman Who Took Drug Was Harmed", *ABAJ*, June 1990, at 14.

[286] *Ibid.*

[287] Dukes and Swartz, n. 30 above, 265.

[288] Marcotte, n. 285 above, 14; cf the position in the early 1970s: "[a]s far as I am aware there is no clear evidence, even in animals, to show that specific damage to gametic cells before conception

that the rodent is more prone to cancer from carcinogenic chemicals than the human. Nevertheless, the fact that this scenario reflects the human condition is of very great interest.

The first case to come before a British court alleging genetic damage being passed on from a father's sperm has predictably floundered on the causation issue. In *Reay* v. *British Nuclear Fuels*; *Hope* v. *BNFL*[289] Dorothy Reay died, aged 10 months, of leukæmia in 1962. Vivian Hope, born in 1965, developed non-Hodgkin's Lymphoma (nhl) in 1988 and became partially disabled. Both lived in villages close to BNFL's Sellafield plant where leukæmia among children was higher than the local and national average. In a 1990 report by Professor Martin Gardner, four out of five leukæmia patients in the village of Seascale, two miles from the plant, had fathers employed there who received high doses of radiation while working there. His report suggested a link between paternal pre-conception irradiation (ppi) and leukæmia in the children, in that irradiation mutated the father's sperm resulting in a predisposition to leukæmia in the offspring. Both the families of the two females relied on the Gardner report alleging that the connection with Sellafield was the cause of the diseases. The defendants relied on an A-bomb study of the effects of irradiation in 1945 on atom bomb victims in Hiroshima and Nagasaki which found no excess of leukæmia in the offspring of irradiated fathers.

French J opined that the Gardner Report was virtually unsupported by other studies and had shortcomings which reduced the confidence which could be placed in it.[290] The evidence of genetics experts indicated that the Gardner theory of ppi could not be excluded on "purely mechanistic grounds" but that such biological mechanisms proposed to explain ppi were, in the present state of scientific knowledge, "speculative".[291]

In conclusion, French J held that the plaintiffs had failed to establish, on a balance of probabilities, that ppi was a material contributory cause of childhood leukæmia of Dorothy Reay or nhl of Vivien Hope.[292]

Two things of import emerge in respect of the *Reay* decision. First, it is clear that scientific knowledge may well develop over the next few years to the extent that a causal link between ppi and leukæmia will be demonstrated. Secondly,

can induce anomaly manifest after birth, with the possible exception of chromosomal imbalance and rare genetic changes. With respect to teratogens, the available evidence shows that eggs and embryos are highly resistant to induced malformation shortly before and after fertilisation": Edwards, "The Problem of Compensation for Antenatal Injuries" (1973) 246 *Nature* 54, at 55.

289 [1994] 5 Med. LR 1; *The Guardian*, 15 Oct. 1993. See also Horsnell, "Sellafield Cancer Families Lose Battle for Damages", *The Times*, 9 Oct. 1993.

290 [1994] 5 Med. LR 1, 49.

291 *Ibid.*, 52.

292 *Ibid.*, 53. French J emphasised the difference between epidemiological and legal approaches to causation. He stated that the idea of cause to an epidemiologist was a probabilistic one, through the assembling of evidence from many different angles, whilst his task as a judge was to decide each of the cases on a balance of probabilities: *ibid.*, 10. It thus seems incorrect to say that French J avoided any statement of principle on the legal significance of statistical tests: cf Hedley, "Group Personal Injury Litigation and Public Opinion" (1994) 14 *LS* 70, 85.

the *Reay* decision does not rule out the possibility of another case coming before the courts alleging genetic damage being passed on to offspring by a father's sperm as a result of the ingestion of, say, a medicinal product such as DES by that father's mother. However, it should be noted that disputes may occur in respect of the role of other competing causes such as other drugs, mutagens, the validity of animal and epidemiological data, the dose of the drug and whether the substance is capable of causing the diseases in question. There is also the added basic problem in genetic damage cases of establishing both transmission of mutagen-induced damage in parents to children and also mutagen exposure of an individual with an inherited predisposition to the mutagen in question.[293]

4. THE UK POSITION

Causation appears to remain a problem under the law of negligence, the Congenital Disabilities (Civil Liability) Act 1976 or the Consumer Protection Act 1987. This concluding section of the chapter looks at the current stance of the law in England and Scotland in this area.

(i) Negligence

With respect to negligence, establishing a general causal link in a case brought by a second-generation plaintiff suffering from vaginal clear cell adenocarcinoma would be *prima facie* not so difficult, but the difficulty would emerge in establishing the particular causal link between the drug used and the disease, where the manufacturer of it is unknown. No equivalent to United States market share liability or alternative causation liability in the Netherlands exists in the UK, and cases would be decided on a traditional ground of establishing proof of causation on a balance of probabilities, which would be almost impossible in the context of DES. Logically, if the manufacturer was known proof of cause would not be as difficult, although the burden of proof remains on the plaintiff.[294] Of greater difficulty in negligence would be proving a causal link between the administration of the DES and damage in the second-generation female uterus causing physical abnormalities of her reproductive organs. As has already been noted, the question of reproductive abnormalities may in fact be due to the subgroup of women who took the drug, many of whom had fertility problems anyway. *A fortiori*, of considerable difficulty in respect of proof of causation would be whether the administration of DES in these cases to the first-generation grandmother was causally connected to severe physical injuries in the third-generation grandchild, including cerebral palsy.

[293] See Meeran, "Genetic Damage: Attaining Scientific Proof" (1992) 89 *LSG* 17, 17, 23.
[294] See *Wilsher* v. *Essex AHA* [1988] 1 AC 1074.

The three-stage test of establishing a duty of care, requiring the plaintiff to show foreseeability of damage, proximity or neighbourhood between the plaintiff and the defendant and a situation in which the court considers it "fair, just and reasonable" to impose a duty on one party for the benefit of the other[295] makes it much easier to argue the case of restricting liability by drawing lines than dealing with difficult problems of causation. Thus the three-stage test, though inadequate in defining the exact boundaries of negligence liability,[296] will often restrict the court's need to deal with the thorny issue of causation by disposing of cases at the duty stage. At the very least, in terms of a duty of care in negligence, it could be argued that the occurrence of affected children in the third generation was unforeseeable at the time the DES was put into circulation and that no close and direct relationship of proximity would exist between the affected grandchildren and the manufacturer of DES.[297] Policy, though now playing a subsidiary role of limiting duty of care in exceptional circumstances,[298] may operate to exclude liability in third-generation DES cases, though this remains to be seen.

Clearly, of the greatest difficulty in negligence would be the establishment of a causal link between the administration of DES in the grandmother and chromosomal damage to germ cells in sperm and also the subsequent causal link to female offspring with clear cell vaginal adenocarcinoma. In these circumstances, and in the present state of knowledge, causation would be unlikely to be proved.

(ii) Congenital Disabilities (Civil Liability) Act 1976

In respect of children born on and after 22 July 1976, the Congenital Disabilities (Civil Liability) Act 1976 will apply in England but does not extend to Scotland.[299] The Law Commission, in its *Report on Injuries to Unborn Children*,[300] envisaged the possibility of mutagenesis of the kind illustrated in

[295] See *Governors of the Peabody Fund* v. *Sir Lindsay Parkinson & Co, Ltd* [1985] AC 210, 240–1, *per* Lord Keith; *Yuen Kun Yeu* v. *Attorney General of Hong Kong* [1988] 1 AC 175, 191–4 *per* Lord Keith; *Davis* v. *Radcliffe* [1990] 1 WLR 821, 826, *per* Lord Goff; *Caparo* v. *Dickman* [1990] 2 WLR 358, 365, 379, *per* Lords Bridge and Oliver.

[296] Markesinis and Deakin, n. 191 above, 82.

[297] See *Grower* v. *Eli Lilly & Co.*, 591 NE 2d 696, 700–701 (Ohio 1992) for the US position; cf Myers, n. 275 above, 304–5. The occurrence could also be regarded as too remote at the damage stage in terms of *Overseas Tankship (UK) Ltd* v. *Morts Dock & Engineering Co. Ltd., The Wagon Mound* [1961] AC 388, 426, *per* Viscount Simonds.

[298] E.g., the public interest in granting the police immunity from negligence liability resulting from performing or failing to perform their statutory duties: *Hill* v. *Chief Constable of West Yorkshire* [1989] 1 AC 53, 63; see Markesinis and Deakin, n. 191 above, 81. See now also the reasoning against imposing a duty of case on the Crown Prosecution Service by the CA: *Elguzouli-Daf* v. *Commissioner of Police of the Metropolis and Another*; *McBrearty* v. *Ministry of Defence and Others* [1995] QB 335 at 349–50, *per* Steyn LJ.

[299] S. 6(2) of the Congenital Disabilities (Civil Liability) Act 1976. The Act fails to address the central issue of causation: Brazier, n. 30 above, 235.

[300] Law Com. No. 60, n. 218 above.

the third-generation DES cases involving chromosomal damage to the germ cells of the sperm in the male fœtuses of mothers administered DES, causing disease in the child's child.[301] It discussed the possibility of "something happening to a person which is transmitted to a child in whom the condition is dormant but capable of transmission to the child's child", saying that in that situation a duty ought not to be owed to anyone other than the immediate children of a parent.[302] In conclusion, it recommended that no claim should be available for pre-natal injury otherwise than at the suit of the first generation.[303] Section 1 of the 1976 Act states that a person responsible for an occurrence which affected either parent of the child in his or her ability to have a normal healthy child (pre-conception injury) or which affected the mother during her pregnancy (ante-natal injury) or the mother or child in the course of its birth (perinatal injury) and which causes a child to be born disabled as a result of such an occurrence, will be answerable to the child if he was liable in tort to the parent. The answerability to the child through liability in tort to the parent has been suggested as being designed to rule out third-generation claims, but if looked at literally would appear not to rule out a claim for third-generation injury if the second-generation child is regarded as the parent. Nevertheless, if the Law Commission is correct, such claims would not be compensated for. It has been argued that the 1976 Act will apply "to a more remote descendant than the child of a person originally affected", since the "accident affects the reproductive ability in the ultimate parent of the injured individual however many generations removed from the occurrence",[304] and, it is submitted, this could well be the correct interpretation of the legislation. It is conceded, however, that this would be inconsistent with the view of the Law Commission. Notwithstanding such uncertainty, it is submitted that the 1976 Act will certainly not apply to *second-generation* claims of victims of DES, i.e. those claims from girls who have suffered vaginal clear cell adenocarcinoma, those of girls who have suffered physical abnormalities of reproductive organs, those of boys who have suffered abnormalities of the male genital tract and those of boys who have suffered chromosomal damage to germ cells in sperm, since none of these children were born on or after 22 July 1976, the date of commencement of the legislation, as the product was removed from the market in 1971. These claims would be decided under the law of negligence.

If we assume, for the sake of argument, that the Law Commission is wrong regarding third-generation claims, there will still be two problematic qualifications to liability for third-generation children born after 22 July 1976. First, the

[301] Both the Scottish and English Law Commissions concluded that there could be liability for harm caused prior to conception, i.e. a child born disabled because of some tortious injury inflicted upon its parent before conception: Law Com. No. 60, n. 218 above, para. 78: Scot Law Com. No. 30, Cmnd. 5371/1973, para. 21.

[302] Law Com. No. 60, n. 218 above, para. 79.

[303] *Ibid.*, para. 80; i.e. second generation, if the grandmother taking DES is considered first generation.

[304] Whitfield, n. 195 above, 45.

right of action will be available, according to section 4(3), only if the personal injuries are sustained by the child *immediately after* birth, which means that the court would have to interpret such injuries as including *latent* personal injuries that children were born with, e.g. vaginal clear cell adenocarcinoma sustained immediately *after* birth but latent. The usual third-generation injury is cerebral palsy, which is sustained during and immediately *after* birth and seems to be covered by the legislation. Secondly, in the cases of cerebral palsy and vaginal adenocarcinoma in the third generation, liability would clearly depend on causation, which would be extremely difficult to establish.

Section 1(4) states that the claim of the child will collapse if the parents or either of them knew or ought to have known at the time of conception that, through something happening to one of them previously, there was a risk that a child born of them would be disabled.[305] The Law Commission regarded this as consistent with the general principles of causation,[306] the knowledge of the parents being a *nova causa interveniens* breaking the causal chain between the act or omission (e.g. the manufacture of a defective drug) upon the parent and the injury. It is submitted that it would be possible for knowledge to break the causal chain only if the parents were aware, for example, of abnormalities in their reproductive organs before they conceived the third-generation child.[307]

It has been assumed that when the Act referred to the parents knowing of a risk of a child becoming disabled the Act presumably meant knew and *accepted* the risk.[308] This question of acceptance of risk by the parents has been interpreted as the common law defence of *volenti non fit injuria*,[309] but it operates in the uncomfortable situation where it is not the plaintiff, i.e. the *child*, who has freely and voluntarily assumed the risk, but his *parents*. However, as has been noted, the Law Commission did not explain the rationale of this section in terms of *volenti*, but in terms of the knowledge of the parents breaking the chain of causation between the defendant's act or omission, e.g. the manufacture of the drug, and the injury.

The common law in Scotland is theoretically not the same as that in England on this issue. As Forte[310] has noted, if the parents voluntarily accept the risk of injury the law could apply the maxim *volenti* and deny them a claim. However,

305 S. 1(4) is subject to the fact that this defence will not apply if the father knew of the risk and the mother did not.

306 Law Com No. 60, n. 218 above, para. 78.

307 In the American decision of *Albala* v. *City of New York*, 445 NYS 2d 108 (CA), the infant plaintiff was conceived *after* her mother's uterus had been perforated and *after* she had had an abortion and also *after* a malpractice claim for the perforated uterus had been commenced by her mother. The CA of New York, Wachtler J held that no cause of action for the pre-conception tort was cognisable: *ibid.*, at 108. The mother was thus in the best position to avoid the damage to her child: see also Myers, n. 275 above, at 312–13.

308 Though the Act is silent on this, unlike the Law Commission which refers to knowing and accepting the risk: Law Com No. 60, n. 218 above, Explanatory note 10; Freeman, Congenital Disabilities (Civil Liability) Act 1976 [1976] *Current Law Statutes Annotated*, 28/1.

309 *Ibid.*, 28/1.

310 Forte, "Medical Products Liability" in S. A. M. McLean (ed.), *Legal Issues in Medicine* (Aldershot, Gower, 1981), 80.

the manufacturer could not aver the parents' acceptance of the risk against the child in a claim by him when the child had not accepted any such risk,[311] since *volenti*, in Scots law, although amounting to a waiver of a duty otherwise incumbent on a defender to take care for a pursuer, has been restricted and "now only applies if the pursuer freely and voluntarily assumed the risk" of the harm he suffered.[312] In reality, the confusion lies in the analysis of the Scots law position in terms of *volenti*. If we return to the Law Commission's rationale of explaining the issue in terms of a *nova causa interveniens*, it is submitted that a claim by a child in Scots law against the manufacturer for pre-conception injury, although not failing on the grounds of *volenti*, might fail on the ground that effectively the parents' act amounts to a *nova causa interveniens*, since the parents' knowledge and acceptance of the risk were so unreasonable as to "eclipse" the original wrongdoing of the defender (the pharmaceutical company).[313] Such an intervention, in this case of a third party (the parents), will not operate as a *nova causa* if that intervention was the very kind of thing that the defender was supposed to take reasonable care to prevent, since the intervention was "highly probable or very likely".[314] However, since such an intervention by the parents was not very likely and a duty of care would probably not exist to prevent the intervention of the parents, the case could be regarded as a *nova causa interveniens*, denying the child a claim. At the very least it could be argued that the parents' act of having intercourse with knowledge of the risk that they could produce a handicapped child contributed to the causation of the cerebral palsy, of which the immediate cause was the breach of duty of care in the manufacture of the defective drug.[315] However, this would only operate in circumstances where the cerebral palsy would not have occurred but for the parents' intercourse.[316] This would be the case with third-generation grandchildren suffering

[311] Forte, "Medical Products Liability" in S. A. M. McLean (ed.), *Legal Issues in Medicine* (Aldershot, Gower, 1981), 80.

[312] Stewart, *Delict* (2nd edn., Edinburgh, W. Green/Sweet & Maxwell, 1993), 211.

[313] *The Oropesa* [1943] P 32, *per* Lord Wright, at 39; *McKew* v. *Holland and Hannen and Cubitts* (Scotland) Ltd [1969] 3 All ER 162, applied in *Sabri-Tabrizi* v. *Lothian Health Board*, 1998 SLT 607, 610–11 (pursuer's decision to have sexual intercourse in the knowledge that she was not sterile constituted a *novus actus interveniens*, breaking the chain of causation); cf *Wieland* v. *Cyril Lord Carpets* [1969] 3 All ER 1006; *Emeh* v. *Kensington and Chelsea Area Health Authority* [1985] QB 1012. In *Reeves* v. *Commissioner of Police of the Metropolis* [1998] 2 WLR 401, the CA held the defence of *novus actus interveniens* inappropriate because the plaintiff's act of suicide did not obliterate the wrongdoing of the defendant, since the defendant's act of negligence consisted in a failure to take reasonable care to prevent suicide: 409–10, *per* Buxton LJ; cf Morritt LJ (dissenting) at 418.

[314] *Per* Lord MacKay in *Maloco (Smith)* v. *Littlewoods* [1987] 1 AC 241 at 261; cf Lord Goff at 270–1 who inclined towards a duty-based approach in English law and would argue that no duty of care was owed by the defendant to the plaintiff. See, however, Lord Reid in *McKew* v. *Holland and Hannen and Cubitts (Scotland) Ltd* [1969] 3 All ER 1621 at 1623, who argued that a test of reasonable foreseeability would produce an unsatisfactory result in that case because an unreasonable action might well be foreseeable, though it could be distinguished on the grounds that there was an unreasonable act of a plaintiff and not a third party in that case.

[315] See *Rouse* v. *Squires* [1973] QB 889.

[316] *Ibid.*, *per* MacKenna J at 899, 900.

cerebral palsy due to reproductive abnormalities in their mothers caused by DES ingested by their grandmothers.

Since in Scots law a child's claim is not ordinarily affected by contributory negligence of a parent,[317] in such circumstances the drug company may end up jointly and severally liable to the child, and it may then recover the appropriate portion of damages from the parents reflecting their contribution to the child's cerebral palsy. However, it must be reiterated that the Law Commission's view is that such third-generation claims could not be brought under the 1976 Act. If this is true, then the Congenital Disabilities Act 1976 does not assist at all with DES-induced injury.[318]

Even if third-generation actions were available, the causal chain would almost certainly remain uninterrupted by the parents in the second generation anyway, because they would seldom know of their physical abnormalities or damage to their germ cells before conception.

(iii) Consumer Protection Act 1987

In the context of DES, the problem of proving a causal relationship between the damage and the defect under section 2(1) of the 1987 Act would not emerge for two reasons. Firstly, DES was not supplied after 1 March 1988.[319] Secondly, even if it was so supplied, the obligation to provide indemnity for a defective product (in terms of Scots law) or right of action to obtain such indemnity (in terms of English law) is extinguished ten years from the date the product was put into circulation.[320]

5. CONCLUSION

The spectrum of adverse effects of DES, potentially spanning three or more generations, illustrates the range of levels of difficulty in proving a causal link between an adverse drug reaction and the drug. Compounded with that problem lies the difficulty in identifying the particular manufacturer of the product which caused the injury. There are no English or Scottish equivalents to the

[317] *Taylor* v. *Dumbarton Tramways Co.*, 1918 SC (HL) 96.

[318] See Bridgeman, "Diethylstilbestrol: A Case in English Common Law?" [1994] *Consum. LJ* 44, 44. In that article, however, the author fails to consider the possibility of third-generation injuries being compensatable under the 1976 Act.

[319] See s. 50(7). It should be noted that s. 6(3) of the Consumer Protection Act 1987 applies s. 1 (other than subs. (6)) of the Congenital Disabilities (Civil Liability) Act 1976 in England to cases of congenital disabilities covered by the 1987 Act in respect of damage caused by a defective product to a parent. The application of the 1976 Act does not, however, apply to Scotland: Stewart, n. 312 above, 189.

[320] See for Scotland s. 22A(1) Prescription and Limitation (Scotland) Act 1973 as inserted by Sch. 1 Part II A, Consumer Protection Act 1987; for England s. 11A(3) of the Limitation Act 1980 as inserted by Sch. 1 Part 1, Consumer Protection Act 1987.

solutions of market share and alternative causation liability which, while admirable in their pursuit of compensation and deterrence objectives, are ultimately blighted by operational and definitional problems.

The difficulty of establishing causation seems inherently to be related to the difficulty in establishing pre-conception tort liability since third-generation DES injuries seem to be beyond the contemplation of the courts as being actionable in the United States and possibly in the United Kingdom on policy grounds, and they are probably in causation terms the most difficult to prove.

The law of negligence, the Congenital Disabilities (Civil Liability) Act 1976 and the Consumer Protection Act 1987 continue to present great problems in resolving the DES causation question in the UK.

More generally, it can be stated that other than the clear effects of thalidomide on the fœtus in pregnancy,[321] cases involving pre-natal and perinatal injuries and drugs are more often associated with difficulties of establishing a causal link between the injuries and the drugs. Such dangers of drugs in pregnancy are topical. For example, AZT is an anti-AIDS drug now used in thousands of HIV-positive pregnant women, since it has been shown to diminish the incidence of HIV positivity in the newborn. AZT is a potent drug which could have potential for harm to the fœtus, including its germ cells. The considerations applying to DES could be relevant to AZT and any future drugs which are deemed essential for use in pregnancy.[322] By far the greatest challenge in the future will be the ability to detect by genetic scanning any change in chromosomes which will result in later congenital deformity in future generations. The mapping out of the human genome is being undertaken in many parts of the world, and this will provide a solid base for research of this nature. A pattern of genetic abnormality associated with administration of a drug to a mother could be discovered by such chromosomal analysis, and it could help to prevent pre-natal and perinatal injuries as well as explaining the effects of drugs on future generations with a good deal more accuracy than has hitherto been available. Systems of genetic toxicity testing already exist in the pre-clinical screening of drugs by *in vitro* tests and *in vivo* animal tests to detect gene mutation and chromosomal aberrations;[323] such an approach may provide a prototype for future

[321] It should be noted that the precise mechanism of teratogenic effects of thalidomide remains unclear. Thalidomide defects are largely indistinguishable from similar genetic malformations or malformations of similar sporadic unknown origins. It is suggested that thalidomide's metabolites are the causative agents of its congenital deformities: Sherman and Strauss, "Thalidomide: A Twenty-Five Year Perspective" (1986) 41 *Food Drug & Cosmetic Law Journal* 458, 461–2.

[322] See Connor *et al.*, "Reduction of Maternal Infant Transmission of Human Immunodeficiency Virus Type 1 With Zidovudine Treatment" (1994) 331 *N Eng. J Med.* 1173 (showing that zidovudine (AZT) reduces the risk of maternal infant HIV transmission by approximately two thirds). This seminal study will almost certainly result in continued use of the drug throughout the world. The authors, however, have not addressed themselves to the long-term effects of AZT, bearing in mind that AZT could affect the nucleic acid in genes. Long-term surveillance of the mother's children and of any possible progeny of these children will be necessary.

[323] See Griffin, O'Grady and Wells (eds.), *The Textbook of Pharmaceutical Medicine* (Belfast, Queens University of Belfast, 1993), 71.

genetic scanning of newborn children. Until such tests have been developed and become uniform it is conceded that the task of proving causation in such injuries will be immense, since the effects of a drug, as may well be the case in DES, could extend to future generations.

3

Scientific Evidence, Causation and the Law: Lessons of Bendectin (Debendox) Litigation

1. INTRODUCTION

This chapter[1] attempts to examine the thorny problem of scientific evidence relating to causation and antenatal injury alleged to result from the use of medicinal products. As a paradigm it examines Bendectin, the anti-nausea drug used in pregnancy. In contrast to thalidomide, where many lines of evidence showed that the drug caused phocomelia malformations,[2] no causal link has ever been scientifically established between Bendectin and birth defects.

To understand the legal, scientific and medical issues in this area, it is axiomatic that there be an awareness of both the historical and scientific background of the drug, together with how the regulatory authorities and the manufacturer responded to the question of malformations which were allegedly associated with it.

The starting point in respect of Bendectin's development was in 1953, when the director of medical research at Merrell had the idea that use of pyridoxine hydrochloride (Vitamin B-6) could produce an anti-nausea medicine for the

[1] This chap. is an expanded version of an article published by the author: R. Goldberg, "Scientific Evidence, Causation and the Law—Lessons of Bendectin (Debendox) Litigation" (1996) 4 *Med. Law Rev*. 32.

[2] See Sjöström and Nilsson, *Thalidomide and the Power of Drug Companies* (Harmondsworth, Penguin, 1972), 156–9 and Chap. 1, above. Liability, however, was never established in the thalidomide case: *S* v. *Distillers Co. (Biochemicals) Ltd* [1970] 1 WLR 114. As previously noted in Chap. 1, a compromise was approved by the court of the defendants paying 40% of the damages decided by the court in return for the plaintiffs unreservedly withdrawing all allegations of negligence: see *per* Hinchcliffe J at 117. See also *Distillers Co. (Biochemicals) Ltd* v. *Thompson* [1971] AC 458 (plaintiff's cause of action arose within jurisdiction of New South Wales). A settlement was reached, but not every child was compensated due to disagreement about whether the injuries were due to the administration of the drug: Brazier, *Medicine, Patients and the Law* (2nd edn.,Harmondsworth: Penguin, 1992), 233. Criminal proceedings, however, were brought against 9 persons at Chemie Grunenthal, the initial developers of thalidomide, and they lasted two and a half years. The trial was eventually suspended, but the German court made a declaration with the prosecution that a causal connection had been established between thalidomide and nerve damage and also thalidomide and malformation in the human fœtus: Sjöström and Nilsson, *above*, 207–70, in particular 260. However, it should be noted that the mechanism of teratogenic effects of thalidomide remains unclear: Sherman and Strauss, "Thalidomide: A Twenty-Five Year Perspective" (1986) 41 *Food Drug Cosm. LJ* 458, 461.

treatment of morning sickness in pregnant women.[3] A drug was proposed made of three ingredients, each of which had been separately marketed without any adverse effects, *viz.* dicyclomine hydrochloride (an antispasmodic and anticholinergic), doxylamine succinate (an antihistamine acting as an antinauseant and antiemetic) and pyridoxine hydrochloride (Vitamin B-6 acting as an antinauseant and antiemetic).[4] The drug was named Bendectin in the United States and was introduced by what became Merrell Dow Pharmaceuticals in 1957.[5] Over 33 million women subsequently used it throughout the world,[6] and in the United Kingdom the product was marketed as Debendox. Debendox was first licensed in the UK in 1972. However, suspicion arose between 1972 and 1976 that the drug could produce a spectrum of slight non-specific malformations in offspring, resulting in litigation in the UK and USA and consequent withdrawal of the drug in both countries.[7] This was in spite of the fact that in the USA the Food and Drug Administration's (FDA's) Fertility and Maternal Health Drugs Advisory Committee had concluded that there had been no increased incidence of birth defects among Bendectin exposed infants.[8] More than 2,100 Bendectin claims have so far been made against Merrell Dow in the USA.[9] The manufacturer claimed that the legal costs of litigation had become unbearable[10] and another defendant pharmaceutical company, E. R. Squibb & Sons Inc., claimed that Bendectin was withdrawn in 1983 since the cost of insurance was almost equal to the entire income from sale of the drug, suggesting that insurance and litigation costs may increase the price and diminish the availability of drugs.[11] Indeed, it has been posited that since each state has a childhood disability provision in its statute of limitations, resulting in a "long tail" period between the time of distribution of a product and the time after which a suit cannot be brought, new litigation may yet go into the next century.[12]

[3] Sanders, "The Bendectin Litigation: A Case Study in the Life Cycle of Mass Torts" (1992) 43 *Hastings LJ* 301, 317. Prior to Bendectin, Merrell had been preparing to market thalidomide in the USA when its teratogenic effects were uncovered by European Scientists: Lasagna and Shulman, "Bendectin and the Language of Causation" in Foster, Bernstein and Huber (eds.), *Phantom Risk: Scientific Inference and the Law* (Cambridge, Mass., MIT Press, 1993), 101.

[4] Sanders, n. 3 above, 317; *Richardson* v. *Richardson-Merrell, Inc.*, 649 F Supp. 799 at 800 (DDC 1986) aff'd. 857 F 2d 823 (1988), cert. denied, 110 S, Ct 218 (1989).

[5] Foster, Bernstein and Huber (eds.), n. 3 above, 138.

[6] *Ibid.*

[7] Dukes and Swartz, *Responsibility for Drug-Induced Injury* (Amsterdam, New York, Oxford, Elsevier, 1989), 262.

[8] *Richardson* v. *Richardson Merrell*, 649 F Supp 799 at 802–3 (DDC 1986).

[9] Sanders, n. 3 above, n. 2, 319.

[10] Dukes and Swartz, n. 7 above, 262.

[11] Commented on in *Brown* v. *Superior Court*, 751 P 2d 470, 479 (Cal. 1988), which stated that all prescription drugs were unavoidably unsafe products in terms of Comment K of s. 402A of the American Law Institute *Restatement of the Law: Second: Torts 2d* (St. Paul, Minn, West Publishing Co., 1965) and that a drug manufacturer should not be strictly liable for failure to warn of defects in a drug of which it neither knew nor could have known by the application of scientific knowledge available at the time of distribution: see 751 P 2d 470 at 480–2.

[12] Sanders, n. 3 above, 320.

A leading commentator on the Bendectin litigation[13] has examined 39 epidemiological studies and has been able to state that in none of the 39 did the authors categorically conclude that Bendectin had teratogenic effects. Six studies showed at least one correlation between Bendectin and an adverse drug reaction, and they conclude that although their findings are insufficient to support the existence of a causal link, "one may exist". The remaining 33 studies draw no conclusion or conclude that no statistical relationship exists.[14] The major hurdle for the plaintiffs in respect of Bendectin was the determination of scientific evidence proving the existence of a causal link, particularly when the abnormalities were non-specific, the incidence rate was low and the issue was complicated by spontaneous malformations and a suspected link between severe pregnancy nausea and mild malformations in babies, irrespective of the activities of any drug.[15]

The overwhelming weight of scientific data and opinion is that Bendectin is non-teratogenic.[16] No author of an epidemiologic study has concluded that Bendectin is a teratogen. Indeed, every major drug regulatory agency in the developed world, including the UK Committee on Safety of Medicines (CSM), the American Food and Drug Administration (FDA) and the German and Australian authorities, has concluded that there is no acceptable scientific evidence that Bendectin causes birth defects in children.[17]

2. SCIENTIFIC VERSUS LEGAL EVIDENCE OF CAUSATION

While it may be impossible to make a definitive case which exonerates Bendectin completely, it is equally not possible to prove scientifically the existence of a causal link between the drug and birth defects. Science, therefore, fails under its traditional standards of proof to establish a verdict for the plaintiff.[18] As is indicated by Lasagna and Shulman,[19] collective scientific evidence is required to show that Bendectin's use has been associated with an increase over the usual incidence of fœtal abnormalities. Only then are the data compelling. Such evidence, they state, is unavailable. Lasagna and Shulman here apply the criteria of

[13] Sanders, n. 3 above, 320.

[14] *Ibid.*

[15] Dukes and Swartz, n. 7 above, 262–3.

[16] See Grahame-Smith and Aronson, *Oxford Textbook of Clinical Pharmacology and Drug Therapy* (Oxford, Oxford University Press, 1984), 156; Ashton, "Disorders of Fetus and Infant" in Davies (ed.), *Textbook of Adverse Drug Reactions* (3rd edn., Oxford, Oxford University Press, 1985), 85; McCredie *et al.*, "The Innocent Bystander, Doxylamine/Pyridoxine and Congenital Limb Defects" (1984) 140 *Medical Journal of Australia* 525–7 (no risk of congenital limb defects associated with Bendectin).

[17] Minister for Health. Mr Kenneth Clarke MP. HC Deb. vol. 64, cols. 1174–6, 1179, 25 July 1984.

[18] Sanders, "From Science to Evidence: The Testimony on Causation in the Bendectin Cases" (1993) 46 *Stanford LR* 1, 3, 23, 27. "Proving that Bendectin does not cause birth defects is logically impossible": Lasagna and Shulman, n. 3 above, 109.

[19] Lasagna and Shulman, n. 3 above, 102.

Sir Austin Bradford Hill to determine whether a reported association is causal or not genuine, namely strength of association, consistency (which seems particularly to be suggested by the need for "collective evidence" of a causal link for it to be compelling), specificity, temporality, biological gradient, plausibility, coherence, experiment and analogy.[20] Against the small number of studies which reported a positive correlation between Bendectin and congenital malformations are those many prospective and retrospective studies that have failed to find such an association.[21]

There is, however, a great difference between evidence of causation for science and for the law. For the civil law, it is enough to show that the balance of probabilities—meaning more than 50 per cent, or on a preponderance of the evidence—indicates a causal connection. For medical science, there are rules of epidemiology requiring evidential proof (on a balance of probabilities) of at least 95 per cent to establish causation. However, as Lasagna and Shulman correctly point out, and this seems to be the most pertinent issue, "[t]he point at which the 'preponderance of evidence' standard [legal] and the standard for epidemiology [scientific] intersect is unclear".[22] In the cases involving Bendectin this has been a recurring problem.

The total evidence available for the courts in any of the Bendectin cases has never been sufficiently convincing to establish causation on a scientific basis. Equally, in the overwhelming majority of cases the preponderance of evidence standard in law has not been satisfied, but in a small number it has been.

3. THE US JURISPRUDENCE

The US litigation in respect of Bendectin has almost overwhelmingly resulted in findings against the existence of a causal link between the drug and the deformities on both scientific and legal criteria.

[20] See Hill, "The Environment and Disease: Association or Causation?" (1965) 58 *Pro. R Soc. Med.* 295, 295–300. Hill seems to concede that slighter but similar evidence of the effects of thalidomide with another drug would indicate reasonable circumstances in which to judge by analogy: *ibid.*, 299.

[21] Lasagna and Shulman, n. 3 above, 101–3. Lasagna and Shulman attribute Bendectin's demise to five factors: first, the thalidomide experience; secondly, the significant incidence of congenital irregularities, even in the absence of identifiable causal agents, since congenital defects are common, estimates ranging from 1 to 7% of newborn; thirdly, the way the American social system approaches supposed drug-induced injury; fourthly, the popularity of litigation; and fifthly the problems posed by juries and judges' use of statistics: *ibid.*, 102,109.

[22] Lasagna and Shulman, n. 3 above, 112. However, a possible reconciliation between use of standards of significance in epidemiological evidence and the preponderance of evidence standard in law has been suggested by the court of appeals in *Daubert* v. *Merrell Dow Pharmaceuticals, Inc*,, 43 F 3d 1311 (9th Cir 1995), cert. denied, 116 S Ct. 189 (1995) (*Daubert II*). In that case, the CA, on remand from the US Sup. Ct. held that the plaintiffs had to show not merely that Bendectin increased the likelihood of injury but more likely than not caused their injuries. In terms of statistical proof, their mothers' ingestion of Bendectin more than doubled the likelihood of birth defects: *ibid.*, 1320. This was reaffirmed by the Texas Sup. Ct. in *Merrell Dow Pharmaceuticals, Inc.* v. *Havner* 953 SW 2d 706, 716–18 (Tex. 1997). See below.

In *Turpin* v. *Merrell Dow Pharmaceuticals Inc.*[23] the defendant relied on 35 epidemiological studies purporting to show that the incidence of certain birth defects was no higher with women who used Bendectin than with those who did not.[24] Alternatively, the defendant argued that where statistical association showed a possible causal relationship, a reasonable expert would not be led to infer Bendectin caused birth defects.[25] The plaintiff claimed, using *in vivo* and *in vitro* studies of animals, that chemical compounds of Bendectin interfere with cartilage cell formation in animal cells and test animals, and that because of this Bendectin was capable of causing similar limb defects in humans.[26] The US Court of Appeals for the Sixth Circuit flatly rejected the plaintiff's animal studies, saying that the factual and theoretical bases expressed for the scientific opinions did not support a finding that Bendectin more probably than not caused the birth defects in the case.[27]

The plaintiff's experts stopped short of testifying that Bendectin more probably than not caused these birth defects because they had no factual or theoretical basis for a stronger hypothesis. These experts testified that the animal studies showed that Bendectin was "capable of causing, 'could cause' or its effects [were] 'consistent with causing' birth defects, not that it probably causes birth defects in general or that it did in this case".[28] The US Court of Appeals held that the scientific evidence of the plaintiff was insufficient to allow a jury to find that Bendectin more probably than not caused the child plaintiff's birth defects.[29] The evidence showed merely a possibility and not a probability that Bendectin causes birth defects in babies.[30]

In three other Bendectin decisions, appellate courts have either granted or affirmed judgments n o v (judgment notwithstanding the verdict of the jury), reflecting the federal courts' increasing desire to assess independently the quality of scientific data relied on by expert witnesses: *Richardson* v. *Richardson-Merrell Inc.*,[31] *Brock* v. *Merrell Dow Pharmaceuticals Inc.*[32] and *Ealy* v.

23 959 F 2d 1349 (6th Cir. 1992), cert. denied, 113 S Ct. 84 (1992).

24 959 F 2d 1349 at 1350–1 (6th Cir. 1992); see also Pretl and Osborne, "Trends in US Product Liability—The Plaintiff's Perspective", in Howells (ed.), *Product Liability, Insurance and the Pharmaceutical Industry: An Anglo-American Comparison, Fulbright Papers Proceedings of Colloquia Vol 9* (Manchester, Manchester University Press, 1991), 114, who state that epidemiological evidence suggests that Bendectin does not cause a higher incidence of fœtal limb and other deformities than the incidence of birth defects in the newborn population as a whole.

25 959 F 2d 1349 at 1350–1 (6th Cir. 1992).

26 *Ibid.*, 1358.

27 *Ibid.*, 1359.

28 *Ibid.*, 1359–60.

29 *Ibid.*, 1350.

30 *Ibid.*, 1360.

31 857 F 2d 823 (DC Cir. 1988), cert. denied 493 US 822 (1989) (affirming judgment nov).

32 874 F 2d 307 (5th Cir. 1989), modified, 884 F 2d 166 (5th Cir. 1989) cert. denied, 494 US 1046 (1990) (granting judgment nov). *Brock* established the requirement of statistically significant epidemiological proof necessary to establish causation in the Bendectin cases: 874 F 2d 307, 311 (5th Cir. 1989). Such a strictly defined standard of proof has often, though not always, been rigidly adhered to: see Nosacka, "Bendectin, Birth Defects and *Brock*: A Study in Appellate Review" (1991) 13 *Journal of Products Liability* 231, 271–6.

Richardson-Merrell Inc.[33] The courts in these cases based their conclusions in favour of the defendants on the absence of epidemiological evidence establishing a causal link between Bendectin and birth defects in children.[34]

In the case of *Oxendine* v. *Merrell Dow Pharmaceuticals Inc.*,[35] however, the appeal court reversed a judgment n o v ordering a reinstatement of the jury's verdict for the plaintiff. *Oxendine*[36] was, until October 1996,[37] the only case in which a jury verdict in favour of the plaintiff had survived the appellate process. The plaintiff, through her parents, alleged that her birth defects were caused by her mother's ingestion of Bendectin. The jury in the trial court returned a verdict in favour of the plaintiff, awarding $750,000 in compensatory damages.[38]

[33] 897 F 2d 1159 (DC Cir. 1990), cert. denied, 498 US 950 (1990) (granting judgment nov). It should also be noted that as predicted by the academic literature (see Sanders, n. 3 above, n. 2, 356 and Foster, Bernstein and Huber (eds.), n. 3 above, 140), the case of *Raynor* v. *Richardson-Merrell*, 1993 US District LEXIS 7498 (DDC, 13 Apr. 1993) granted judgment nov and overturned a jury verdict. *Raynor* followed *Richardson* and *Ealy* in establishing that no published epidemiological study had concluded that Bendectin was teratogenic, in the face of overwhelming contrary evidence. On appeal, the CA remanded the case to the dist. ct. for further consideration of the admissibility of the plaintiffs' evidence. The dist. ct. confirmed its original judgment. The plaintiffs again appealed. The CA held that the plaintiffs' expert testimony was inadmissible and affirmed the dist. ct.'s decision: *Raynor* v. *Merrell Pharmaceuticals, Inc.*, 104 F 3d 1371, 1375–6 (DC Cir. 1997). The court stated that even if the expert testimony were admissible, it was unlikely a jury could reasonably find it sufficient to show causation: *ibid.*, 1376.

[34] See also *Lynch* v. *Merrell-National Laboratories*, 646 F Supp. 856 (D.Mass. 1986) (granting summary judgment for the defendant), aff'd., 830 F 2d 1190 (1st Cir. 1987).

[35] 506 A. 2d 1100 (D.C.App. 1986).

[36] *Oxendine* v. *Richardson-Merrell*, no. 1245–82 (1983) (DC Super. Ct.), rev'd., *Oxendine* v. *Merrell Dow Pharmaceuticals, Inc.*, *Oxendine* 1, 506 A 2d 1100 (DC App. 1986) (mem. and order), vacated no. 1245–82 (DC Super. Ct., 11 Feb. 1988), rev'd., 563 A 2d 330 (DC App. 1989), cert. denied, 110 S Ct. 1121 (1990), appeal after remand, 593 A 2d 1023 (DC App. 1991).

[37] See below.

[38] Soon after the first round of the *Oxendine* trial, Carl Rubin DCJ consolidated all cases filed in Ohio to try all common issues of liability and set a cut-off date for all plaintiffs to opt in or out of the trial. Before the trial began, Merrell-Dow Pharmaceuticals offered a $120 million settlement of all current and future claims. Most of the plaintiffs agreed, but some objected and the US CA for the Sixth Circuit ruled that Rubin CJ had exceeded his authority by establishing a non-opt out class of present and future Bendectin plaintiffs, i.e. by preventing those who disliked the settlement from opting out of the class. This ruling resulted in the settlement being defeated: *In re Bendectin Products Liability Litigation*, 749 F 2d 300 (6th Cir 1984). Following the order, Rubin CJ held a trial of the common issues in respect of 818 cases, which were consolidated: *In re Richardson-Merrell, Inc. Bendectin Products Liability Litigation*, 624 F Supp. 1212 (SD Ohio 1985). An offer was made by the court for selection of a jury with special qualifications, either a "blue, blue ribbon jury" (a jury of persons knowledgeable in the field) or a "blue ribbon jury" (a jury of persons having the greatest amount of formal education). Neither concept was recognised in the Federal Rules of Civil Procedure. The defendant's counsel expressed interest but the plaintiffs' counsel rejected the offer. The jury that deliberated consisted of five women and one man, with education ranging from a failure to attend high school by one to the possession of a graduate degree by another: *ibid.*, 1217. The trial was trifurcated into issues of liability, damages and causation and in the first round the jury only heard evidence of general causation: *ibid.*, 1221. After hearing the evidence of 19 expert witnesses: *ibid.*, 1218, the jury gave its verdict in favour of Merrell and decided that the plaintiffs had failed to establish on a preponderance of the evidence that ingestion of Bendectin at therapeutic doses during the period of fetal organogenesis was a proximate cause of human birth defects: *ibid.*, at 1228, 1244. The verdict was upheld by the court of appeals: 857 F 2d 290 (6th Cir. 1988). The US Sup. Ct. denied further review: 488 US 1006 (1989).

The Superior Court of the District of Columbia, however, granted Merrell Dow a motion for judgment n o v, declaring that no jury could reasonably have found Merrell Dow responsible for Oxendine's birth defects. Oxendine appealed and the DC Court of Appeals reversed the trial judge's decision and ordered reinstatement of the jury's verdict for the plaintiff.[39] The Court held that the evidence viewed as a whole formed an "evidentiary mosaic",[40] which was a foundation for the plaintiff's expert, Dr Done, that Bendectin caused birth defects.[41]

The court examined the scientific evidence. It stated that the "structure activity information"[42] provided a clue about Bendectin's possible teratogenicity[43] and the *in vivo* studies raised a "suspicion" of the teratogenicity of the drug. The *in vitro* studies clearly indicated a potential for teratogenicity and a reanalysis of an epidemiological study that had faulty methodology demonstrated a relative risk of between 1.3 and 1.8.[44] Taking all of these data together, such information suggested that a reasonable juror *could* reach a verdict in favour of the plaintiff.[45] The court interpreted statistical significance in a manner differently from that in *Brock*, utilising "a more flexible approach" to epidemiological studies.[46] The court noted the view of an expert witness for the plaintiff that the mere fact that number "1" as a measure of relative risk falls within the confidence interval[47] does not invalidate the study. The expert agreed that relative risk was the best estimate of the existence of a true causal association based on study data.[48] The court in *Oxendine* opined that a disagreement about how the epidemiological and other data should be interpreted should be left to the jury,

[39] 506 A 2d 1100, 1114–15 (DC App. 1986).
[40] *Ibid.*, 1110, 1113 n. 9.
[41] *Ibid.*, 1110.
[42] I.e. the information obtained through looking at the structure of a chemical compound in order to predict its activity: *ibid.*, 1104.
[43] *Ibid.*, 1105.
[44] *Ibid.*, 1107–8. The relative risk is the risk of a disease or defect in exposed people divided by the risk of that disease or defect in non-exposed people. If the relative risk is between 1 and 0, this may indicate a negative or protective association between the exposure and the disease or defect. If the relative risk is greater than 1, this may amount to a positive or direct association between the exposure and the disease or defect. If the relative risk is greater than or equal to 2, this will amount to statistically significant evidence of causal link. See, e.g., Howson, Howe and Fineberg (eds.), *Adverse Effects of Pertussis and Rubella Vaccines* (Washington, DC, National Academy Press, 1991), 34 (discussing methodological considerations in dealing with the question whether a vaccine can cause an adverse event).
[45] *Ibid.*, 1111.
[46] Lasagna and Shulman, n. 3 above, 115. In *Brock* the Court stated that if a confidence interval (a range of relative risk within which a study parameter lies 95% of the time (see below)) included 1.0 then the study was said to show no statistically significant association between the factor and the disease. The plaintiffs failed to offer one statistically significant (one whose confidence interval did not include 1.0) study that concluded that Bendectin was a human teratogen: 874 F 2d 307, 312 (5th Cir. 1989). However, Lasagna and Shulman have criticised the fact that such divergent approaches to standards and criteria of epidemiology result in opposite conclusions about the value of data: *ibid.*, 116.
[47] See definition in n. 44, above.
[48] 506 A 2d 1100, 1109. (DC App. 1986).

noting that "relative risk calculated for a particular study was not carved in stone".[49]

Subsequently, Superior Court Judge Wolf granted Merrell Dow's motion for a new trial after Merrell Dow claimed that an expert witness for the plaintiff had testified falsely at trial. The judge found that the expert had "grossly misrepresented" his credentials to such an extent that all his testimony on the plaintiff's behalf had become suspect. The plaintiff successfully appealed Judge Wolf's decision. The DC Court of Appeals held that the judge erred in vacating the judgment and granting a new trial, and the case was remanded with instructions that a judgment be entered on the verdict.[50] Merrell Dow appealed, but the appeal was dismissed for lack of finality, since the question of punitive damages remain to be tried. The case was remanded to the trial court.[51]

In September 1992, following remand, the trial court ruled that the verdict in favour of *Oxendine* would not be reconsidered in the light of post-1983 developments, and thus declined to satisfy the judgment. On appeal, the Court of Appeals held that although the trial court had correctly determined that Merrell Dow had to meet a rigorous standard in order to reopen the issue of causation, it had erred in refusing to consider any of the post-trial developments. The Court of Appeals "reluctantly" decided to remand the case to the trial court for further limited consideration.[52] On remand, the trial court, in a decision by Richard A. Levie, J concluded that Merrell had "established, by clear and convincing evidence, that post-1983 evidence makes it clear that Bendectin is not a human teratogen and that 'all responsible scientific thought' agrees with this conclusion".[53] The trial court decided to reverse the plaintiff's jury verdict of 1983 on the grounds of the inadmissibility of the plaintiff's evidence. In doing so the court stated:

> "The science that existed in 1983 has changed and it would, in these circumstances, be inappropriate to allow the 1983 judgment to stand or to do anything other than enter a judgment mandated by the state of scientific knowledge".[54]

The overwhelming trend of cases establishing that Bendectin had not caused the birth defects alleged had finally culminated in overturning a jury verdict that had been partly responsible for "[t]he herd instinct of the plaintiffs' bar to pursue more Bendectin litigation".[55]

49 *Ibid.*, 1110.

50 563 A 2d 330, 331. (DC App. 1989).

51 *Merrell Dow Pharmaceuticals* v. *Oxendine*, 593 A 2d 1023, 1023–4, 1028 (DC App. 1991).

52 *Merrell Dow Pharmaceuticals, Inc.* v. *Oxendine* 649 A 2d 825, 827, 830 (DC App. 1994). The trial court had to judge the new evidence in the light of the standard which required the probability that a different verdict would result from a new trial: *ibid*, 831–2.

53 *Oxendine* v. *Merrell Dow Pharmaceuticals, Inc.*, No. 82–1245, 1996 WL 680992 (DC Super. 24 Oct. 1996), at *33.

54 1996 WL 680992, at *34.

55 McGovern, "A Judicial Centralization and Devolution in Mass Torts: Green, Bendectin and Birth Defects: The Challenges of Mass Toxic Substances Litigation; Weinstein, Individual Justice in Mass Tort Litigation: The Effect of Class Actions, Consolidations, and Other Multiparty Devices" (1997) 95 *Michigan Law Review* 2077, 2085.

It has been proposed[56] that there were four reasons why the *Oxendine* trial court was able to conclude that the evidence was equally weighted, with epidemiological evidence being given no primacy. First, all scientific evidence was given equal weight. Secondly, the value of individual studies in a particular scientific area was not assessed. Thirdly, the court ignored the fact that none of the plaintiff's primary causation expert's work in respect of Bendectin had been published. Fourthly, the court failed to distinguish between general and specific causation, seemingly assuming that if the plaintiff was able to show that Bendectin caused any defects, this would suffice to support the jury's verdict.[57] However, the *Oxendine* decision in favour of the plaintiff, although now reversed, is not without its supporters. It had been stated, prior to the overturning of the jury verdict, that *Oxendine* exemplified the enlightened approach of a few courts that had come to terms with the presentation and understanding of epidemiological evidence of causation.[58]

In the light of the above discussion, the conclusion remains that the case law before the American courts points to a failure to maintain successfully a judgment in favour of the plaintiffs in respect of causal link.

4. THE UNPREDICTABLE NATURE OF JURY TRIALS CONSIDERING SCIENTIFIC EVIDENCE

Perhaps the most significant distinction between the American and English tort processes is the presence of the jury trial in American negligence cases. Indeed it has been observed[59] that the institution of the jury trial "is a hallmark of the American tort system". Much concern has been expressed about an "insidious jury encroachment on areas of legal policy"[60] in areas such as causation or foreseeability in American tort cases.[61] In England, however, civil jury trials are now "wholly exceptional" and restricted to a handful of cases.[62] Unlike the United

[56] Sanders, "From Science to Evidence: The Testimony on Causation in the Bendectin Cases" (1993) 46 *Stanford Law Review* 1, 29.

[57] 506 A 2d 1100, 1109. (DC App. 1986).

[58] Brennan, "Causal Chains and Statistical Links: The Role of Scientific Uncertainty in Hazardous-Substance Litigation" (1988) 73 *Cornell LR* 469, 494 n. 127.

[59] Fleming, *The American Tort Process* (Oxford, Clarendon Press, 1988), 101.

[60] *Ibid.*, 118.

[61] *Ibid.*, 119. Fleming notes (*ibid.*) the particularly conspicuous pro-plaintiff judicial policy being evidenced in the vaccine liability decision of *Reyes* v. *Wyeth Laboratories*, 498 F 2d 1264 (1974) where the jury returned a verdict in favour of the plaintiff and found, despite the contrary evidence of Wyeth's expert witnesses, that the plaintiff's polio was vaccine-induced. This was despite the presence of epidemiological evidence that the polio was due to an unrelated and "probably wild" virus. The polio outbreak also occurred in the area and at the time when the plaintiff fell ill. The court stated that it was forbidden to usurp the jury's function by weighing conflicting evidence and reaching its own decision, where the jury's decision had been reached by reasonable and fair-minded men: *ibid.*, 1288.

[62] Bailey and Gunn, *Smith and Bailey on the Modern English Legal System* (London, Sweet & Maxwell, 1991), 703.

States, where the institution of the civil jury has been enshrined in the federal constitution[63] and most state constitutions,[64] the Supreme Court Act 1981 in England severely restricts the use of jury trials. By section 69(1) of that Act, a qualified right to a jury trial is established in cases of fraud, libel, slander, malicious prosecution or false imprisonment. Section 69(3) of the Act gives the judge a discretion to order a jury trial in other cases. The last reported jury trial in a personal injuries action established that the court would use its discretion to order a jury trial in only exceptional cases.[65] This approach was quickly upheld and underlined by the Court of Appeal a year later.[66] Recent case law has, however, indicated that such exceptional circumstances as to merit a trial by jury might emerge in a case where punitive or exemplary damages are demanded to compensate for personal injuries resulting from conduct on the part of those who were deliberately abusing their authority.[67] However, the Court of Appeal has held that a claim in negligence cannot found a claim for exemplary damages.[68] Moreover, it has also been noted that complex issues of fact and complex evidence may be inappropriate for jury trial.[69] It therefore seems that jury trials in cases involving medicinal products, scientific evidence and causation would be extremely rare in England. However, if there were a jury, the judge would instruct the jury about causation and the jury would then make its own decision on causation, based on the evidence.[70]

In Scotland, the Court of Session Act 1988 confines the civil jury trial to the Court of Session in four types of action, including an action for damages for personal injuries.[71] The civil jury trial is almost invariably used in personal injury actions where no special difficulties of law or fact are involved and where the pleadings have no questions of relevancy[72] outstanding.[73] Whether such matters

63 US Constitution, 7th Amendment: "[i]n suits of common law, where the value in controversy shall exceed $20, the right of trial by jury shall be preserved, and no fact tried by a jury shall be otherwise reexamined in any court of the United States than according to the rules of the common law".

64 Fleming, n. 59 above, 101.

65 *Hodges* v. *Harland & Wolff* [1965] 1 WLR 523 at 525–6.

66 *Ward* v. *James* [1966] 1 QB 273, in particular *per* Lord Denning MR at 303. The additional issues of fairness and economic feasibility were reflected in the decision of *Williams* v. *Beesley* [1973] 1 WLR 1295 where the House of Lords concluded that there was a duty on the court, when deciding whether a civil action was to be tried by judge and jury, to act fairly to all parties to an action. They also indicated that if a trial by judge alone would involve a shorter and less expensive hearing and would be more likely to achieve a just result than trial by jury, the court should order trial by judge alone: *ibid.*, 299.

67 *H* v. *Ministry of Defence* [1991] 2 QB 103, 112.

68 See *AB* v. *South West Water Services Ltd* [1993] QB 507 at 530 H.

69 *Singh* v. *London Underground*, *The Independent*, 25 April 1990.

70 Brazier (general ed.), *Clerk & Lindsell on Torts* (17th edn., London, Sweet & Maxwell, 1995), 219, n. 14. In such a situation "attributability or causation is regarded as a point of law": *Pickles* v. *NCB (Intended Action)* [1968] 1 WLR 997, *per* Lord Denning MR at 1000.

71 Court of Session Act 1988, s. 11.

72 A legal claim is relevant when it can be said that were the party's statements in his pleadings accepted as proved, he/she would be entitled to the remedy sought: Walker, *The Oxford Companion to Law* (Oxford, Clarendon Press, 1980), 1055.

73 *Stair Memorial Encyclopædia, The Laws of Scotland*, Black (ed.), vol. 17, "Civil Procedure" (Edinburgh, The Law Society of Scotland, Butterworths, 1989), 1412; Maxwell, *The Practice of the*

exist is a matter for the Lord Ordinary's discretion, although it should be noted that there has been a revival in pursuers pressing for jury trials in recent times.[74]

It seems, therefore, that cases involving questions of causation and medicinal products would rarely come before a jury in the English courts, and would only do so in the Scottish courts at the damages stage. The pervasive use of juries is therefore present mainly in the United States. This being so, there is potentially a greater need there than in England for a "clear, firm and simple" law of negligence, including causation to ease the judge's task of instructing the jury on issues in a consistent and predictable manner.[75]

It appears that such a lack of clarity in negligence law in the USA has been reflected in the outcomes of the Bendectin litigation. Sanders has studied Bendectin trials before American juries, and his results indicate a 40 per cent plaintiff success rate, which makes favourable comparison with corresponding success rates of plaintiffs in product liability suits.[76] He is able to suggest why the jury verdicts diverge from scientific and legal opinion by an analysis of the trials. His conclusion[77] is that a combination of three factors inhibit the jury from assessing the quality of the experts and the importance of the evidence in respect of Bendectin: namely who gives evidence,[78] the content of their evidence[79] and the nature of their cross-examinations.[80] In addition, an analysis by Sanders based on what is called the "story model of decision making",[81] i.e. the parties' ability to construct a persuasive story by "commingling" weak scientific evidence on causation with stronger evidence on breach of duty and damages,[82] shows that a defence entirely based on general causation is a disadvantaged one.[83]

Sanders' analysis has been subsequently vindicated since publication of his article in 1993. He refers to the most recent jury trial verdict in *Havner* v.

Court of Session (Edinburgh, Scottish Courts Administration, 1980), 297. It is not a ground for not having a jury trial that highly technical expert evidence will be given, though this element, in combination with other considerations, may amount to such a ground: Maxwell, above, 299.

[74] *Stair Memorial Encyclopædia*, n. 79 above, 1412.

[75] Robertson, "An American Perspective", in Markesinis and Deakin, *Tort Law* (3rd edn., Oxford, Clarendon Press, 1994), 194.

[76] Sanders, n. 56 above, 5.

[77] *Ibid.*, 27–8.

[78] There was a declining use by Merrell of its own employees and by both sides of primary experts who had written articles on Bendectin; this may have acted contrary to the interests of the defendants, together with the problem of juries discounting defendants' experts as "hired guns": *ibid.*, 32–41.

[79] The trial procedures make lay understanding of the scientific issues impossible and epidemiological evidence, the largest category of evidence, is more difficult for jurors to understand and for lawyers to convey, resulting in the jurors being "one-eyed fact finders" who can see everything: *ibid.*, 41–7.

[80] Juries failed to learn about scientific knowledge through cross-examination since the lawyers were focusing on undermining the witnesses' credibility: *ibid.*, 47.

[81] *Ibid.*, 28.

[82] *Ibid.*, 53.

[83] *Ibid.*, 28, 58.

Merrell Dow Pharmaceuticals Inc.[84] where the jury awarded $3.75 million to the plaintiffs, together with a punitive damages award of $30 million[85] against Merrell Dow, the jury concluding that the child's birth defects were caused by Bendectin. Predictably, this trial judgment was reversed and judgment entered for Merrell Dow in the decision of *Merrell Dow Pharmaceuticals Inc.* v. *Havner*.[86] What is of real interest, however, in this case is the degree to which the court attacked the absence of any scientific proof from the plaintiffs' experts of any causal link between the drug and the child's defects.

The plaintiffs sued Merrell Dow Pharmaceuticals on behalf of their minor daughter. They alleged, and the jury found, that her birth defects were caused by Mrs Havner having taken Bendectin.[87] Merrell appealed the trial court's award of compensatory and exemplary damages and its denial of the defendant's motions both for judgment n o v and for a new trial.[88] Merrell asserted that no evidence of probative value existed on the crucial issue of causation, since there was no scientific evidence of a causal link between Bendectin and birth defects, in general, or limb reduction defects, in particular, nor was there evidence of specific causation, i.e. no evidence that Mrs Havner's ingestion of Bendectin was the actual cause of her daughter's malformations.[89]

The appeal court stated that causation had to be proved by scientific expert testimony on the reasonable probability of that causal link. Lay testimony was legally insufficient to establish causation in this sort of case.[90] The court confined its review to a consideration of the scientific evidence and inferences which tended to support the jury's finding of causation. Such supporting evidence had to have some probative force.[91] The plaintiffs presented testimony of five experts to show that causation existed,[92] but the experts were unable to offer any demonstrable scientific data available to Merrell in 1981, or even available at the time of the decision, which would show that a theoretical causal relationship exists between human birth defects and Bendectin administered at the normal human therapeutic dose. The plaintiffs' experts merely tried to rebut the methodology employed and conclusions reached in the live animal and human epidemiologic studies used by Merrell. They inferred the existence of causation by asserting that proof of the contrary—i.e., that Bendectin did not cause defects—did not exist.

[84] No. 88–3915–F (D. Tex 1991) as cited in Sanders, n. 56 above, 2, n. 1.

[85] This was reduced by the trial court to $15 million: *Merrell Dow Pharmaceuticals, Inc.* v. *Havner* 953 SW 2d 706, 709 (Tex. 1997).

[86] CA 13th Dist. of Texas, Corpus Christi: No. 13–92–540–CV, 17 March 1994.

[87] *Ibid.*, 1–2 of official transcript.

[88] *Ibid.*, 3 of official transcript.

[89] *Ibid.*, 4 of official transcript.

[90] *Ibid.*, 7–8 of official transcript.

[91] *Ibid.*, 10 of official transcript.

[92] *Ibid.*

The Texas Court of Appeals stated, in a manner that puts all plaintiffs' advisers in such cases on notice for the future[93], that:

> "Indulging the Havners' experts to the outer limits of inference in their claim that all the animal studies and all the human epidemiologic studies are wrong, the most we can conclude is that Merrell has no conclusive evidence that Bendectin never causes birth defects in humans. . . . *However, absence of evidence of a fact, standing alone, does not amount to some evidence of its converse. Absence of absolute proof that Bendectin does not cause birth defects in humans is not some evidence that it does.*"[94]

The court further held that, despite the use of the magic words "reasonable probability" by the plaintiffs' experts, there was no evidence that Bendectin more likely than not caused birth defects and, in particular, this child's defect.[95] In essence, the plaintiffs had failed to bring forward anything more than suspicion on the essential element of causation.[96] The court referred to one expert's attempt to piece the suspicions together into a "mosaic"[97] amounting to something more than suspicion, but stated that some suspicion linked to other suspicion produces only more suspicion, which is not the same as some probative evidence.[98] Hence, the court reversed the trial court judgment and entered judgment for Merrell Dow.[99]

However, it was at this point that the Texas Court of Appeals began to show some of the inconsistencies marked by the *Oxendine* litigation.[100] The Havners appealed the reversal of the jury verdict and the Court of Appeals held that the trial court did not abuse its discretion in deciding to admit the testimony of the Havners' experts[101] and that, having reweighed the evidence to the jury to determine whether its verdict was manifestly unjust, held that the trial court's verdict

[93] Despite this strong warning of the court's future intent, the Havners filed a motion for a rehearing and Robert C. Hilliard, the Havners' attorney, filed two documents with the court of appeals which it considered to be "insulting, disrespectful and unprofessional": *Merrell Dow Pharmaceuticals, Inc.* v. *Havner* 907 SW 2d 565, 566 (Tex. App. Corpus Christi 1995) (*en banc*) (*per curiam*). The motion for a rehearing was struck from the court records. In addition, the documents were forwarded by the court to the Office of the General Counsel of the State Bar of Texas, on the ground that the documents evidenced a violation of the Texas Disciplinary Rules of Professional Conduct that raised a substantial question of the lawyer's honesty, trustworthiness, or fitness: *ibid.*

[94] *Ibid.*, 13 of official transcript (my italics). This scenario appears to support the view that shifting the burden of proof in such cases is unrealistic since defendants are usually in no better position to disprove causation than the plaintiffs are to prove it: see Teff, "'Market-Share' Liability—A Novel Approach to Causation" (1982) 31 *ICLQ* 840 842–3; H. L. Hart and A. Honoré, *Causation in the Law* (2nd edn., Oxford, Clarendon Press, 1985) pp. liv, 102, 424; Dodds-Smith, "Product Liability Issues Arising out of the Introduction of Strict Liability Procedures for Dealing with Multi-claimant Cases" in Goldberg and Dodds-Smith (eds.), *Pharmaceutical Medicine and the Law* (London, Royal College of Physicians, 1991), 61–2.

[95] No. 13–92–540–CV, 17 March 1994, at 14 of official transcript.

[96] *Ibid.*, 29 of official transcript.

[97] Cf. *Oxendine* 506 A 2d 1100 at 1110, 1113, n. 9 (DC App. 1986).

[98] No. 13–92–540–CV, 17 March 1994, at 29 of official transcript.

[99] *Ibid.*, 30 of official transcript.

[100] See above.

[101] *Merrell Dow Pharmaceuticals, Inc.* v. *Havner*, 907 SW 2d 535, 554 (Tex.App. Corpus Christi 1995).

on causation was supported by sufficient evidence.[102] The Court of Appeals affirmed the trial court's award of actual damages, but reversed the award of punitive damages.[103] The court betrayed its lack of understanding of the standards of epidemiological evidence by stating that if the relative risk was greater than one, there was an association between the agent studied and the result.[104] Sense prevailed on appeal to the Supreme Court of Texas, which held that the evidence offered to prove that Bendectin caused the plaintiff to be born with a birth defect was legally insufficient to establish causation.[105] Significantly, the court approved of the use of properly designed and executed epidemiological studies supporting causation in a toxic tort case. It held that there was a rational basis for relating the requirement that the risk of an injury or condition in the exposed population be more than double the risk in the unexposed or control population to the more likely than not burden of proof.[106]

5. REMEDYING THE DISTORTION OF SCIENTIFIC EVIDENCE IN TRIALS

Cases such as *Havner* indicate the degree to which scientific evidence has been distorted in its presentation at trials. Sanders has proposed a means of remedying this distortion at three stages in a trial; first, at the "input stage" by *restricting the evidential content*; secondly at the "processing stage" by *changing the mode of presenting evidence*; and thirdly, at the "output stage" by *either changing the actual factfinder or introducing science panels*.[107] This structure seems an appropriate way of responding to this legal conundrum. Indeed, although this response has been geared to the American jury trial system, it would also appear to be relevant in trials by judges alone in which all the scientific evidence is presented. The difficulty of attributing injury causation in drugs cases remains a problem in England and Scotland irrespective of the presence of a jury. Hence this difficult issue is of common concern to US, English and Scottish courts.

[102] *Ibid.*, 559.
[103] *Ibid.*, 564.
[104] *Ibid.*, 555.
[105] *Merrell Dow Pharmaceuticals, Inc.* v. *Havner* 953 SW 2d 706, 708 (Tex. 1997).
[106] *Ibid.*, 716–17. The court stated that "[t]he use of scientifically reliable epidemiological studies and the requirement of more than a doubling of the risk strikes a balance between the needs of our legal system and the limits of science": *ibid.*, 718. In doing so, it echoed the views of the court of appeals in *Daubert* v. *Merrell Dow Pharmaceuticals, Inc.*, 43 F 3d 1311, 1320 (9th Cir. 1995) (*Daubert II*).
[107] Sanders, n. 56 above, 60, 80.

(i) Restricting the Evidential Content

(a) The US Supreme Court decision in Daubert *v.* Merrell-Dow Pharmaceuticals Inc.

In respect of the restriction of the content of evidence, trial court judges have been given "wide leeway"[108] in terms of their ability to admit evidence as a result of the recent US Supreme Court decision in *Daubert* v. *Merrell-Dow Pharmaceuticals Inc.*[109] The petitioners, two minor children through their parents, sued the respondents, alleging that the children's serious birth defects had been caused by the mother's ingestion of Bendectin. The testimony of the petitioners' eight experts concluded that Bendectin could cause birth defects, relying on *in vitro* and *in vivo* animal studies, chemical structure analyses and unpublished reanalyses of previously published epidemiologic studies. However, the District Court concluded that this evidence did not meet the standard of general acceptance in the field to which it belongs.[110] In view of the vast body of epidemiological data relating to Bendectin, the District Court held that expert opinion which is not based on epidemiological evidence is not admissible to establish causation, and granted summary judgment in favour of the defendants. The petitioners' reanalyses were rejected as inadmissible because they were not published or subject to peer review.[111]

The United States Court of Appeals for the Ninth Circuit[112] agreed and affirmed the District Court's decision, citing *Frye* v. *United States*[113] for the rule that expert opinion based on scientific technique is inadmissible unless the technique is "generally accepted" as reliable in the relevant scientific community. The court concluded that the petitioners' evidence provided an insufficient foundation to allow admission of expert testimony that Bendectin caused their injuries, and therefore that the petitioners could not satisfy their burden of proving causation at trial.[114]

On appeal to the US Supreme Court, the Court held[115] that *Frye*'s "general acceptance" test was superseded by the Federal Rules of Evidence, which assigned to the trial judge the task of ensuring that an expert's testimony both rested on a "reliable foundation" and was "relevant to the task at hand".[116] This was in line with the "liberal thrust" of the Federal Rules and their general

[108] Sanders, n. 56 above, 64.

[109] 125 L Ed. 2d 469 (1993) (*Daubert I*).

[110] 727 F Supp. 570 at 572 (SD Cal. 1989), as adumbrated in *Frye* v. *United States*, 293 F 1013, 1014 (DC Cir. 1923).

[111] *Ibid.*, 575.

[112] 951 F 2d 1128, 1129 (9th Cir. 1991).

[113] 293 F 1013, 1014 (D.C.Cir. 1923).

[114] 951 F 2d 1128, 1131 (9th Cir. 1991).

[115] 125 L Ed. 2d 469, 479 (1993).

[116] *Ibid.*, 485, 480.

approach of relaxing the traditional barriers to opinion testimony.[117] Pertinent evidence based on scientifically valid principles would satisfy those demands.[118] Since the judgments of the District Court and Court of Appeals focused almost exclusively on "general acceptance" as gauged by publication and the decisions of other courts, the Supreme Court remanded the case for further proceedings.[119]

Blackmun J gave the opinion of the court and sought to outline a pragmatic approach to whether a witness should be permitted to present to a jury scientific evidence that is inconsistent with the mainstream of science.[120]

The main rule of evidence at the centre of the contested issue was Rule 702 of the Federal Rules of Procedure, which provides that:

> "if scientific, technical, or other specialised knowledge will assist the trier of fact to understand the evidence or to determine a fact in issue, [an expert witness] . . . may testify thereto."

Blackmun J stated that nothing in the rules established "general acceptance" as an absolute prerequisite to admissibility of scientific evidence, since this would be at odds with the "liberal thrust" of the Federal Rules.[121] It is here that the heart of the decision in *Daubert* lies. Admittedly, in order to establish the "gate-keeping role" of the judge,[122] the Rules, especially Rule 702, place limits on the admissibility of purportedly scientific evidence. Blackmun J stated that the trial judge must ensure that all scientific evidence is "not only relevant but reliable".[123] Reliability is established by Rule 702's requirement that an expert's testimony has reference to "scientific knowledge".[124] Relevance is established by a demand for a valid scientific connection to the pertinent inquiry as a precondition to admissibility.[125]

The trial judge's responsibility, therefore, is to make a "preliminary assessment of whether the reasoning or methodology underlying the testimony is scientifically valid" and whether it can be applied to the facts in issue. Blackmun J sanguinely declared that the court was "confident that federal judges [possessed] the capacity to undertake this review".[126] In essence, the trial judge was required to determine whether the expert was proposing to testify to scientific knowledge that would assist the trier of fact to understand or determine a fact in issue.[127] He acknowledged certain criteria were relevant in determining whether a theory or technique amounted to scientific knowledge that would assist a trier of fact.

117 *Ibid.*, 480.
118 *Ibid.*, 485.
119 *Ibid.*
120 See Lasagna and Shulman, "A legal Perspective" in Foster, Bernstein and Huber, n. 3 above, 38.
121 125 L Ed. 2d 469, 480 (1993).
122 *Ibid.*, 485.
123 *Ibid.*, 480.
124 *Ibid.*, 481.
125 *Ibid.*, 482.
126 *Ibid.*
127 *Ibid.*

These criteria were:

(1) whether the theory or technique can be and has been tested;
(2) whether it has been subject to peer review and publication (publication, however, was not a *sine qua non* of admissibility—it was a relevant but not dispositive consideration of scientific validity);
(3) the known or potential rate of error (the statistical significance of the truth);
(4) the existence of standards controlling the technique's operation; and finally,
(5) its widespread acceptance (which can have a bearing on the inquiry).[128]

However, Blackmun J stressed the importance of focusing on principles and methodology and not on the conclusions that they generate.[129]

To respond to the fear of the respondents that abandonment of the "general acceptance" requirement for admission of evidence would result in a scientific "free-for-all", resulting in the juries (or arguably, in the UK, the judiciary) being confounded by absurd pseudoscientific assertions, Blackmun J stressed the importance of vigorous cross-examination, presentation of contrary evidence and careful instruction on the burden of proof as being the appropriate means of attacking questionable but admissible evidence.[130] The rules of evidence were designed, Blackmun J held, not for an "exhaustive search for cosmic understanding" (science's quest for the truth) but for the "particularised resolution of legal disputes" (law's desire to resolve disputes finally and quickly).[131]

Rehnquist CJ's opinion (with which Stevens J agreed) concurred in part but dissented in part from the court's judgment. Rehnquist CJ concurred by agreeing that the *Frye* rule was superseded by the Federal Rules of Evidence, but dissented from the court's "abstract" and "generalised observations" on the construction of the Rules, particularly Rule 702. He questioned whether validity in respect of Rule 702 applied not just to scientific knowledge but also to "technical or other specialised knowledge" or whether the "general observations" were limited only to "scientific knowledge".[132] Rehnquist CJ criticised the statement quoted by the majority that "the criterion of the scientific status of a theory is its falsifiability or refutability or testability"[133] by stating that "he was at a loss to know what was meant by saying that the scientific status of a theory depends on its 'falsifiability'". He suspected that some federal judges would be at a loss too.[134] However, it is arguably a well-known scientific tech-

128 125 L Ed. 2d 469, 483 (1993).

129 *Ibid.*, 484. But this leaves the question of how one addresses the "methodologically legitimate expert who reaches illogical conclusions": Green, *Bendectin and Birth Defects: The Challenges of Mass Toxic Substances Litigation* (Philadelphia, Penn., University of Pennsylvania Press, 1996), 310.

130 *Ibid.*, 484. In addition, it was noted that the trial court could conclude that the evidence was insufficient to allow a reasonable jury to reach a conclusion and there the court may direct a judgment, in terms of Fed. Rule Civ. Proc. 50(a) or grant summary judgment under Fed. Rule Civ. Proc. 56: *ibid.*

131 *Ibid.*, 485.

132 *Ibid.*, 487. It seems that they must refer to both.

133 *Ibid.*, 483.

134 *Ibid.*, 487.

nique to put up a hypothesis and attempt to challenge it on the basis of whether it is false or true. It would seem that Blackmun J's five key criteria attempt to do just that.

The *Daubert* decision has been subject to differing criticisms.[135] One report concluded, as it transpired correctly, that while the decision reinstating the suit was technically a victory for the plaintiffs, the Supreme Court's ruling was likely to prove ultimately more favourable to the defendants.[136] However, it has also been regarded as a decision which introduces a simplified system for admission of scientific testimony for both sides but which may ultimately prove to be more pro-plaintiff due to a lack of clear-cut guidelines to the lower courts in respect of ascertaining the validity of the evidence, and resulting in another decade of appeals over the validity and reliability of scientific theories, particularly in respect of Bendectin.[137] Encapsulating the fears of critics is the belief that "rather than contesting the merits of a particular hypothesis, litigants will be contesting general claims about the nature of scientific knowledge".[138] It is submitted, however, that the latter is surely a precondition of the former's reliability. All in all, it is arguable that the new "relevant and reliable" test is more pragmatic and realistic than its "general acceptance" predecessor. Critics of *Daubert* should note the true weakness of the *Frye* test, namely that not all scientific opinions, especially in medicine, are "generally accepted" in the *Frye* sense of these words.[139] Although there are many generally accepted scientific opinions, the increasing pace of scientific advance has generated controversies on a great number of scientific, especially medical subjects.

Upon remand, and applying the new standard of admissibility of scientific evidence of *Daubert* in the Supreme Court, the Court of Appeals held that the

[135] *Daubert* "buried" *Frye* as the standard for determining the admissibility of expert evidence but left much to be resolved. It seemed to provide "something for everyone", by rejecting *Frye* (as was desired by the plaintiffs) but also stressing the judge's gatekeeping role (as desired by the defendants): Green, n. 129 above, 310.

[136] Greenhouse, "Justices Put Judges in Charge of Deciding Reliability of Scientific Testimony", *The New York Times*, 29 June 1993. See *Daubert* v. *Merrell Dow Pharmaceuticals, Inc.*, 43 F 3d 1311 (9th Cir. 1995), cert. denied, 116 S Ct. 189 (1995) (*Daubert II*), below.

[137] Coyle, "Supreme Court Eases Admissibility of Experts", *The National Law Journal*, 12 July 1993, 12. It has been argued that the majority opinion fails to provide objective standards by which federal judges can resolve the admissibility problems of expert evidence. How and whether state courts will adhere to *Daubert* has yet to be seen, though it is hoped that in states like New Jersey, which have recently adopted the Federal Rules of Evidence, the *Daubert* decision will be of precedential importance: Cohen and DePhillips, "The Challenge Posed by the U.S. Supreme Court Decision in *Daubert* v. *Merrell Dow Pharmaceuticals*: A Commentary" (1994) 15 *Journal of Products & Toxics Liability* 279, 282, 286. The current pattern seems to show an adherence to *Daubert*. See above.

[138] Parascandola, Book Review of Foster, Bernstein and Huber, n. 3 above, *The Times Higher Education Supplement*, 13 May 1994, 24.

[139] In some areas of medicine there has been general acceptance, for example the use of penicillin in the treatment of infection and as a life saver. But in other areas of medicine there has been controversy, and not all scientific opinions could be generally accepted. E.g., the question of how to treat arthritis has resulted in much controversy and extreme views held by eminent people in the field. The same has been said to be true for the treatment of epilepsy and various aspects of psychiatric disease and also asthma.

expert scientific testimony was inadmissible to prove Bendectin caused the plaintiffs' birth defects and thus affirmed the District Court's grant of summary judgment.[140] The Court of Appeals held that the plaintiffs had failed to show that the scientific testimony that they proffered was derived by scientific method, i.e. that it was reliable. In *Daubert*, none of the experts had based his testimony on pre-existing or independent research, none of the plaintiffs' scientists claimed to have studied the effect of Bendectin on limb reduction defects before being hired to testify in this or related cases and none of the plaintiffs' experts had published his work on Bendectin in a scientific journal or had solicited any peer review by his colleagues.[141] In respect of the requirement that the evidence be relevant, the Court of Appeals held that the plaintiffs had failed to show that the experts' scientific testimony would assist the jury on the causation issue, governed by Californian law.[142] Of much significance was the Court of Appeals' establishment of the requirement that the Bendectin plaintiffs show that their mothers' ingestion of the drug more than doubled the likelihood of birth defects.[143] This appears to be the clearest possible attempt as yet to reconcile the use of standards of significance in epidemiological evidence and the preponderance of evidence standard in law. Under Californian tort law, the court held that the plaintiffs had to show not merely that Bendectin increased the likelihood of injury but that it more likely than not caused their injuries. In terms of statistical proof, this meant that the plaintiffs had to establish that their mothers' ingestion of Bendectin more than doubled the likelihood of birth defects.[144] Since none of the plaintiffs' proffered evidence had claimed that ingestion of Bendectin during pregnancy more than doubled the risk of birth defects, the testimony was therefore inadmissible as being irrelevant, by failing to provide a valid scientific connection to the pertinent inquiry of causation.[145]

A subsequent decision reflects the desire of the US Supreme Court in *Daubert* to leave the decision on admissibility of the scientific evidence to the trial courts. In *Wilson* v. *Merrell Dow Pharmaceuticals Inc.*[146] a motion for a summary judgment by Merrell Dow Pharmaceuticals was denied, the District Court having found that substantial scientific evidence existed to support the conflicting arguments of the parties in respect of causation and the birth defects of the plaintiff

[140] *Daubert* v. *Merrell Dow Pharmaceuticals, Inc.*, 43 F 3d 1311 (9th Cir. 1995), cert. denied, 116 S Ct. 189 (1995) (*Daubert II*).

[141] *Ibid.*, 1317–18.

[142] *Ibid.*, 1320.

[143] *Ibid.*

[144] *Ibid.* However, in *Merrell Dow Pharmaceuticals, Inc.* v. *Havner*, 953 SW 2d 706 (Tex. 1997), having stated that the balance between the needs of the legal system and the limits of science could be shown by the use of scientifically reliable epidemiological studies and the requirement of more than doubling the risk, the Sup. Ct. of Texas issued a caveat. It cautioned that: "[w]e do not hold, however that a relative risk of more than 2.0 is a litmus test or that a single epidemiological test is legally sufficient evidence of causation. Other factors must be considered. As already noted, epidemiological studies only show an association. There may in fact be no causal relationship even if the relative risk is high.": *ibid.*, 718.

[145] *Daubert* v. *Merrell Dow Pharmaceuticals, Inc.*, 43 F 3d 1311, 1320–1 (9th Cir. 1995).

[146] No. 90–5257 (DC No. 82–C–710–E) (ND Okla. ,10 March 1994; corrected 14 March 1994).

child. The court permitted Merrell to make an interlocutory appeal with respect to denial of its motion.[147] The United States Court of Appeals for the Tenth Circuit held that Merrell's motion for summary judgment should be denied[148] and remanded the case to the District Court for further proceedings in the light of *Daubert*.[149]

On 28 September 1994, the District Court denied Merrell Dow's motion for summary judgment, directing the parties to submit a suggested form of certified question for an interlocutory appeal to the Tenth Circuit on the issue of the admissibility of the plaintiffs' evidence concerning causation. The parties failed to comply with the 28 September order. The case was subsequently transferred to another District Court judge on 10 November 1994 and was transferred again on 7 March 1995. The court held a status conference on 22 January 1996 and granted Merrell Dow's request to move for summary judgment again under *Daubert II*.

The District Court reviewed the standards set out in *Daubert I* and the Ninth Circuit application of that standard in *Daubert II*, and concluded that the Ninth Circuit had properly applied the new standard governing admissibility of scientific expert testimony in a federal court. Since there was no material question of fact remaining to be determined by a factfinder and the defendant was entitled to judgment as a matter of law, the District Court granted Merrell Dow's motion for summary judgment.[150]

Finally, in *Raynor* v. *Merrell Dow Pharmaceuticals, Inc.*, on remand from the Court of Appeals, the District Court held that the plaintiffs' evidence was inadmissible using the *Daubert* factors, and this was affirmed on appeal.[151]

Thus it seems that, to date, the Bendectin cases have strongly confirmed the inadmissibility of expert testimony in the light of the *Daubert* decision of the Supreme Court.

(b) Parallels in England and Scotland

The American position relating to the restriction of evidential content seems now to be similar to that in England and Scotland. In both England and Scotland, an expert can fortify his opinion by reference to learned articles, publications, letters, etc. which form part of the general corpus of medical knowledge falling within the expertise of an expert in the field in question.[152] What is

147 *Ibid.*, 2 of official transcript.

148 The decision as printed on 10 March 1994 stated that the Dist. Ct.'s order denying motion for summary judgment should be vacated but it was corrected on 14 March 1994.

149 No. 90–5257, at 3 of official transcript.

150 *Wilson* v. *Merrell Dow Pharmaceuticals, Inc.*, 1996 US Dist., LEXIS 13568.

151 104 F 3d 1371, 1375–6 (DC Cir. 1997).

152 *Davie* v. *Magistrates of Edinburgh* 1953 SC 34, *per* Lord President Cooper at 410; *Seyfang* v. *Searle & Co.* [1973] 1 QB 148 *per* Cooke J at 151; *H* v. *Schering Chemicals Ltd* [1983] 1 WLR 143, *per* Bingham J at 148. It is also possible for an expert to rely on the statistics of others to form the basis of opinions in reaching their conclusions: *R.* v. *Abadom* [1983] 1 W.LR 126 (CA).

of interest is the similarity of approach between the pragmatic observations of both Lord President Cooper in *Davie* v. *Magistrates of Edinburgh*[153] and Blackmun J in *Daubert*[154] in relation to the value to be given to expert evidence. Lord President Cooper observed:

> "The value of such evidence depends upon the authority, experience and qualifications of the expert and above all upon the extent to which his evidence carries conviction, and not upon the possibility of producing a second person to echo the sentiments of the first, usually by a formal concurrence."[155]

Thus, it seems that in respect of the value given to expert evidence, the need for an authoritative expert whose evidence carries conviction is paramount.

From an English law perspective, for expert evidence to be admissible it must have both relevance and probative value in relation to the matter in issue.[156] The only statutory requirement in respect of admissibility of expert evidence is section 3(1) of the Civil Evidence Act 1972, which states that where a person is called as a witness in any civil proceedings, his opinion on any relevant matter on which he is qualified to give expert evidence shall be admissible in evidence. This seems to point to both relevance of the evidence (self-evident where the expert evidence concerns a matter in issue) and the competence of the expert to give it, an approach which "begs more questions than it answers".[157] The common law position suggests that in respect of admissibility of expert evidence, particularly that surrounding what may be termed "novel sciences", it is necessary for such evidence to have probative value.[158] This requirement of probative value emerges when an expert lends the proceedings an expertise through knowledge which the triers of fact are unable to provide themselves.[159] The requirement of probative value in respect of scientific evidence appeared at the early stages of the development of expert evidence. In *Buckley* v. *Rice Thomas*,[160] Saunders J observed that "[i]f matters arise in our law which concern other sciences or faculties, we commonly apply for the aid of that science or faculty which it concerns".[161] Likewise, in *Folkes* v. *Chadd*,[162] long regarded as being the leading precedent establishing the acceptability of expert evidence in matters of opinion, Lord Mansfield stated that "[i]n matters of science no other witnesses can be called".[163] This position was later developed in *R.* v. *Turner*,[164]

[153] 1953 SC 34.
[154] 125 L Ed. 2d 469 (1993).
[155] 1953 SC 34, 40.
[156] See Hodgkinson, *Expert Evidence: Law and Practice* (London: Sweet & Maxwell, 1990), 4–5, 121–2.
[157] *Ibid.*, 121.
[158] *Ibid.*, 121–2, 133.
[159] *Ibid.*, 122.
[160] (1554) 1 Plowd. 118.
[161] *Ibid.*, 124.
[162] (1782) 3 Doug. KB 157.
[163] *Ibid.*, 159. He continued: "I cannot believe that whether the question is, whether a defect arises from a natural or an artificial cause, the opinions of men of science are not to be received": *ibid.*
[164] [1975] 1 QB 834.

where Lawton LJ held that an expert's opinion was admissible in respect of scientific information which was "likely to be outside the experience and knowledge of a judge or jury", i.e. outside "ordinary human experience".[165] However, the tendency of the English courts is not to conduct a rigorous inquiry into whether evidence is admissible as expert evidence at the admissibility stage.[166] The inquiry takes place at the adjudication stage of assessing the evidence's weight. The issue of probative value at the admissibility stage (prior to admitting evidence) involves a similar approach to assessment as does the question of weight at the adjudication stage, although the hurdle at the former stage appears to be lower than that at the latter.[167] It therefore appears that the *Daubert* criteria, for ascertaining the existence of scientific knowledge that would assist a trier of fact at the admissibility stage, amount to the English equivalent of a stricter test of probative value than exists under English law. However, these criteria may well reflect the English legal position at the adjudication stage (i.e. when the weight of the evidence is assessed), which is illustrated by *Davie*, a case concerning weight and sufficiency of evidence.[168] It has recently been argued that the test for expert hearsay evidence has shifted from admissibility to issues of weight and probative value.[169] The heart of the confusion in this view is the regarding of probative value (which is an admissibility issue) as a question of weight (which it technically is not). The tests of probative value and weight are, in fact, very similar. It seems, though, that English law would appear to require some clarification on this difficult issue.[170]

It has also been suggested that the "general acceptance" criteria of admissibility in *Frye* are inferentially supported by English law,[171] but minority views in a profession have also been accepted in English courts. In *R.* v. *Robb*[172] auditory techniques in the absence of acoustic analysis were accepted as evidence from a phonetician despite "representing a minority view in his

[165] *Ibid.*, 841.

[166] Hodgkinson, n. 156 above, 13.

[167] *Ibid.*, 4–5.

[168] The case of *Davie* v. *Magistrates of Edinburgh*, 1953 SC 34 has persuasive force in England and has been applied in English law. (See *R.* v. *Benthum* (1989) 153 JP 538, 541 (CA).)

[169] Jones, *Expert Witnesses: Science, Medicine and the Practice of Law* (Oxford, Clarendon Press, 1994), 108.

[170] Note also that as in the USA, experts may testify on the ultimate issue (Civil Evidence Act 1972, s. 53(1) and (3)), but the trier of fact retains the power of decision: *Phipson on Evidence*, Howard, Crane and Hochberg (eds.) (London, Sweet & Maxwell, 1990), at 807. Expert evidence is governed by the Civil Evidence Act 1972 and the rules of court under it. It has, however, recently been recommended by the CA that the Rules of the Supreme Court be amended to enable judges to refuse to allow expert evidence to be given at the trial of an action: *Rawlinson* v. *Westbrook and Another*, *The Times*, 25 Jan. 1995. It has also been announced in a Practice Direction handed down by the late Lord Taylor of Gosforth CJ, that it is the duty of practitioners to reduce or eliminate the expert issues in cases to speed up civil litigation and cut costs: *Practice Direction (Civil Litigation: Case Management)* [1995] 1 WLR 262; [1995] 1 WLR 508.

[171] See Hodgkinson, n. 156 above, 133, citing *DPP* v. *A and BC Chewing Gum Ltd* [1968] 1 QB 159, where Lord Parker CJ stated, at 164, "that with the advance of science more and more inroads have been made into the old common law principles".

[172] (1991) 93 Cr. App. Rep. 161.

profession"[173] and such methods being unsupported by peer publication or review.[174] Thus the English law seems closer to the post-*Daubert* American position than might previously have been expected.

Could the authoritative nature of expert evidence be fostered in another way? The exclusion of evidence through the US Federal Rules of Evidence has been noted as being too limited and unreliable an answer to the factfinder's problem of an inability to assess the balance of opinion on a scientific issue,[175] the suggestion being that court-appointed experts under Federal Rule 706 would provide "a moderating influence on the litigation process".[176] It is stated that an impartial scientist would give a judge (and jury) a less partisan assessment than that of the parties' experts, providing more and perhaps better information for the court and jury, as opposed to the adversarial system which may create a fear on the part of one expert that presenting moderate expert opinion will sway the jury in favour of the other party.[177]

Experts have long been criticised for partiality and bias, and the critics have emphasised the need to provide safeguards against such conduct.[178] The English position is buttressed by the Rules of the Supreme Court, where provision is made for a court expert on the application of one of the parties. The court has no power to appoint an expert of its own volition.[179] Contrary to some beliefs, it is thought that the apparent partiality of some experts' testimony or reports is not due to consultation between the expert and legal advisers, but to a phenomenon of witnesses, particularly expert ones, unconsciously tailoring evidence to support their "own side". It is said that solicitors and counsel tend to persuade expert witnesses to express their views in less argumentative and more objective terms, since legal advisors are well aware that partiality (whether real or merely apparent) may be counterproductive.[180] Scholars have argued that the

[173] (1991) 93 Cr. App. Rep. 161 *per* Bingham LJ at 166.

[174] *Ibid.*, at 165.

[175] Sanders, n. 56 above, 67.

[176] American Law Institute Reporters' Study, *Enterprise Responsibility for Personal Injury Vol. II: Approaches to Legal and Institutional Change* (Philadelphia, Penn., American Law Institute, 1991), 333; Sanders, n. 56 above, 67.

[177] American Law Institute Reporters' Study, n. 176 above, 333–4.

[178] See Hammelmann, "Expert Evidence" (1947) 10 MLR 32, 2,34.

[179] Rules of the Supreme Court 1965 (SI 1965 No.1776), Od. 40. O. 40 r.l(1) states that in any case to be tried without a jury and in which any question for an expert witness arises, the court may on application appoint an independent expert (a "court expert") to inquire and report upon any question of fact or opinion not involving questions of law or construction. An expert is defined in r.l(4) as "any person who has such knowledge or experience of or in connection with [any question arising in a cause or matter] that his opinion on it would be admissible in evidence". Such an expert may be cross-examined: O. 40 r.4. A court expert should be distinguished from an assessor appointed under RSC Od. 33, r.6 who occupies a quasi-judicial position and who should not be sworn or examined as a witness; nor should he examine or cross-examine the witnesses: See *Phipson on Evidence*, n. 170 above, 32–3.

[180] *Phipson on Evidence*, n. 170 above, 816. Cf. American Law Institute Reporters' Study, n. 176 above, 333 which suggests that it is the adversarial nature of the proceedings that creates fear on the part of one party that presenting moderate expert opinion will sway the jury in favour of the other party. In England, expert witnesses have a duty to provide independent, objective, unbiased opinion

adversarial system creates the danger of partiality and that the solution is to take expert evidence "as far as possible out of the adversarial context", with the court calling an expert, and not the parties doing so.[181] Notwithstanding such phenomena, the argument that court experts should be used in more cases rather than experts being called on the part of the parties to litigation is regarded by the editors of *Phipson on Evidence* as merely superficially attractive but not worthy of adoption. There seems to be no incentive to be critical[182] if court-appointed experts merely testify to the scientific community's position on views of the parties' experts rather than delivering a personal judgement about the issues in the immediate case. Certainly in the USA, this would appear to amount to a *Frye* approach to the use of expert evidence, which, although given an inferential nod by the American Law Institute,[183] is seemingly outdated after *Daubert*.[184] However, in England Lord Woolf's interim and final reports on the review of the civil justice system in England and Wales have recommended that the court should have a discretion to appoint a court expert, with or without the parties' agreement.[185] The interim report suggests that although experts should not always be used, there are cases in which it may be appropriate to use an independent expert, and that the court can decide this.[186] It is submitted, therefore, that cases of scientific uncertainty, particularly in relation to causation, may well present situations where court-appointed experts could profitably be used for the purpose of assessing the authoritative nature of scientific evidence in a more cost-effective and equitable manner to both plaintiffs and defendants.

Lord Woolf's final report has called for a wider use of "single" or "neutral" experts, jointly selected and instructed by parties or, if parties cannot agree, for the use of a single expert appointed by the court.[187] It is Lord Woolf's "detailed proposals on experts which have provoked more opposition than any of [his] other recommendations".[188]

Lord Woolf supports the use of single "neutral" experts in resolution of issues, chosen where possible by agreement between the parties, and not

in respect of matters within their expertise: *National Justice Compania Naviera SA* v. *Prudential Assurance Company Ltd (Ikarian Reefer)* [1993] 2 Lloyd's Rep. 69, 81.

181 See Kenny, "The Expert in Court" (1983) 99 LQR 197, 214–15.

182 *Phipson on Evidence*, n. 170 above, 32–40.

183 American Law Institute Reporters' Study, n. 176 above, 334.

184 The editors of *Phipson on Evidence* also cite as a disadvantage of the use of court experts the point that evidence is not cross-examined, thus acquiring a spurious authority: n. 170 above, at 832, although it is submitted that a court expert *can* be cross-examined on his report either at trial or before an examiner: RSC Od. 40, r.4; see now also Rt. Hon. Lord Woolf, *Access to Justice: Interim Report to the Lord Chancellor on the Civil Justice System in England and Wales* (London, Woolf Inquiry Team, 1995), chap. 23 at para. 23, hereafter, Lord Woolf. However, no substantive evidence is actually given by the editors of *Phipson on Evidence* of the incisiveness and fairness of the adversarial system.

185 Lord Woolf, n. 184 above, chap. 23 at para. 39. Recommendation 102; Rt. Hon. Lord Woolf MR, *Access to Justice: Final Report* (London, The Stationery Office, 1996), Recommendation 157.

186 Lord Woolf, n. 184 above, chap. 23 at paras. 22, 23.

187 Lord Woolf, *Final Report*, n. 185 above, 157.

188 Lord Woolf, n. 184 above, chap. 23, para. 5.

imposed by the court.[189] However, the problem remains concerning the types of cases in which a single expert could be utilised. Lord Woolf was unwilling to specify the areas of litigation where a single expert should or should not be used, but observed that single experts seem inappropriate in "some large, complex and strongly contested cases where the full adversarial system, including oral cross-examination of opposing experts on particular issues is the best way of producing a just result".[190] A single expert would be particularly inappropriate where the issues involved were "several tenable schools of thought, or where the boundaries of knowledge are being extended".[191] On the other hand, single experts should be used where the issue is concerned with a "substantially established area of knowledge and where it is not necessary for the court directly to sample a range of opinion".[192]

Lord Woolf has applied this general approach to expert evidence and single experts in the context of medical negligence litigation.[193] He has conceded that in some medical negligence cases the issue of causation may be too complex to be decided on the basis of one expert's evidence.[194] However, he distinguishes between cases where medical issues are "straightforward" or "uncontroversial", where one jointly instructed expert should deal with the case/issue,[195] and those which are "exceptionally complex" or "where the treatment given was at the 'cutting edge' of medical science", when even two opposing experts may be insufficient to represent the whole spectrum of medical professional opinion.[196]

It therefore seems that single experts will be appropriate in uncontroversial cases where scientific evidence is not in issue. However, where there is controversy regarding scientific evidence, particularly with the "novel sciences", even more than two experts may well be necessary. This seems to be the case in highly controversial matters surrounding causation of medicinal products, such as Bendectin and the use of drugs in the treatment of AIDS.

Socio-legal commentary has argued that it is too easy to blame the "built in partisanship" of experts on the adversarial system,[197] and that historically the American support for court experts between 1880–1920 declined as it dawned on people that court experts were as likely to be partial as expert witnesses.[198] Indeed, English Victorian judges explained dissent amongst experts with the view that all experts were partisan.[199] It seems that those judges who voiced such a view expected consensus, despite the fact that recent sociological analy-

[189] Lord Woolf, n. 184 above, chap. 23, para. 17.
[190] *Ibid.*, para. 19.
[191] *Ibid.*
[192] *Ibid.*, para.19; Recommendation 152.
[193] Lord Woolf, *Final Report*, n. 185 above, chap. 15, para.70.
[194] *Ibid.*, para. 72.
[195] *Ibid.*, paras. 72, 73.
[196] *Ibid.*, para. 72.
[197] Jones, n. 169 above, 13.
[198] *Ibid.*, 50.
[199] *Ibid.*, 99.

ses of science have shown that disagreement amongst scientists is natural.[200] As long as dissensus is part of scientific discussion, it is feared that accusations of partiality will always be used as a "stick to beat the scientist with",[201] particularly by lawyers who believe in the consensus approach to scientific opinion. However, it is arguable that Jones is correct in saying that the scientists themselves are partly to blame since they have encouraged this false belief in consensus through faith in an "unambiguous truth".[202] Nonetheless, it is arguable that scientific dissensus is becoming more accepted by a sceptical public who have grown wary of being told the consensus line.

(ii) Changing the Mode of Presenting Evidence

Reverting to Sanders' second proposal for remedying the distortion of scientific evidence in trials by changing the mode of presenting evidence, it has been suggested in the USA that if the jurors' ability to assess scientific evidence is being affected by evidence relevant to other matters such as fault, the party with the strongest case should as far as possible use experts uniquely distinguished in the problem under consideration.[203] It seems, however, that the real change which would potentially be the most effective in respect of the presentation of evidence would be the bifurcation of trials to deal with the issues of causation and other elements separately, allowing the other elements to be tried, but only on condition that the plaintiff was successful on causation. This would conceivably reduce the apparent prejudice resultant from the failure of juries to give enough weight to the causation issue.[204] This corroborates the views of defendant practitioners in the medical product liability area,[205] although no doubt plaintiffs' lawyers would be resistant to such a move. In the UK, in the general absence of jury trials, bifurcation may still be of assistance in a trial by judge alone through separating the causation issue. Indeed, under the Rules of the Supreme Court, provision is made for a "split" trial.[206] Under these rules, the court can order the separate trial of preliminary issues or questions, such as general and specific causation.[207]

200 *Ibid.*, 99, 102.

201 *Ibid.*, 272.

202 *Ibid.*

203 Sanders, n. 56 above, 72.

204 *Ibid.*, at 73–4. "Bifurcated trials are now widely authorized, but their primary purpose is to save court congestion rather than to obviate prejudice": Fleming, n. 59 above, 139. The advantages of enhanced accuracy and a reduction of costs as a consequence of separating the causal issue have been stressed by Green: Green, n. 129 above, 344.

205 Personal communication from Richard Kingham, Covington and Burling, Nov. 1994.

206 See RSC Od. 33 rr. 3, 4(2) and 4(2A).

207 See, e.g., *Loveday* v. *Renton* [1990] 1 Med. LR 117, 122.

(iii) Changing the Factfinder or Introducing Science Panels

Turning now to the third proposal, the controversial question of the elimination of the use of juries in the USA is ultimately eschewed by Sanders,[208] who instead supports the use of expert panels to assess causation. A coherent argument for the introduction of such panels, particularly in respect of cases such as the Bendectin litigation, has been suggested by the American Law Institute.[209] It has attempted to classify hazardous substance litigation according to the kind of uncertainty that accompanies causal attribution and the mode of scientific claim made (mass tort/non-mass tort). Four kinds of uncertainty exist in respect of hazardous substance causation. The first kind of uncertainty is classified as *trans-scientific uncertainty*, occurring when scientific issues are cast in scientific terms but are not amenable to scientific proof. For example, the acceptance that animal carcinogens are human carcinogens is such a form of uncertainty, since such a proposition is unprovable in the light of present knowledge of carcinogenesis. The second form of uncertainty is termed *confidence interval uncertainty*. A confidence interval is a range within which a study parameter lies 95 per cent of the time. This definition derives from the use of probability values (p) which measure the frequency with which an exposure is associated with a disease process as a matter of chance, the threshold of statistical significance being 0.05. This is because a study is statistically significant if p is less than 0.05 (i.e. an association is observed as a matter of chance only five in 100 times). Confidence intervals can then be calculated on the basis of such statistical information. If there are only a few subjects in the study, confidence intervals can be wide, resulting in an uncertainty associated with the causal attribution. The third form of uncertainty is termed *individual attribution uncertainty*. Since statistics deal with groups of subjects, generalisations from such statistics relate to the effects on groups and not individuals; attribution of causation to individuals is thus indeterminate and uncertain. The fourth form of uncertainty is termed *multiple causation uncertainty*. Individual attribution uncertainty is in many ways a subset of multiple causation uncertainty, which occurs when an illness has multifactorial causes which are difficult to attribute to a single cause in the case of a single individual.[210] Bendectin is classified as a mass tort that involves trans-scientific, confidence interval, individual attribution and multiple causation uncertainty, presenting the most difficulty for courts.[211]

This classificatory framework has provided the basis of alternatives for the presentation of scientific evidence in the courts,[212] most particularly with the

208 Sanders, n. 56 above, 80, 85.
209 American Law Institute Reporters' Study, n. 176 above, 339–44.
210 *Ibid.*, 324–8. See also Brennan, n. 58 above,509–12.
211 *Ibid.*, 328–9.
212 *Ibid.*, 330.

American Law Institute's proposal of the creation of a Federal Science Board,[213] identifying a list of approved experts and introducing science panels of widely respected experts in toxicology for mass tort cases with either trans-scientific/ confidence interval uncertainty or individual attribution uncertainty (for example Bendectin, which in fact contains all of the forms of uncertainty together). In a non-mass tort case with individual attribution uncertainty or trans-scientific/ confidence interval uncertainty, a court-appointed expert, as opposed to a panel, is suggested as a means of serving the court.[214] For mass torts, such panels appear to be cost-effective. In respect of Bendectin, any such panel would be unable to focus on attributable fractions (i.e. the portions of a risk of contracting a disease that can be attributed to an exposure) since the required epidemiological evidence is non-existent.[215] It has been suggested that recommendations of the panels would have the status of rebuttable presumptions.[216]

In the general absence of a jury in UK personal injury cases, court-appointed experts and scientific panels would help to assist judges in their assessments of causation involving scientific evidence. In the past, English courts have demonstrated a reluctance to appoint expert assessors. In *Loveday* v. *Renton*,[217] Professor David Miller of the Middlesex Hospital, London, and director of the National Child Encephalopathy Study showed willingness to be called by the court as an expert assessor to give evidence about whether pertussis vaccine could cause permanent brain damage in young children. However, Stuart-Smith LJ told Professor Miller that the only way he could assist the court was to give evidence on the plaintiff's behalf, and so he eventually agreed to do so.[218] Arguably, however, the use of scientific panels and court-appointed experts would help to reduce the pressure on clinical and scientific experts to be partial in such circumstances.

Although expensive to operate,[219] it seems that court-appointed experts, expert panels and the use of bifurcated trials have a role in remedying the

[213] See also Brennan, n. 58 above, 525–7, exploring the role of a Federal Hazardous Substance Science Panel in reviewing epidemiological evidence and establishing fractions of proportionate causation caused by a toxic substance.

[214] American Law Institute Reporters' Study, n. 176 above, 339–44.

[215] *Ibid.*, 347–8.

[216] *Ibid.*, 348, 349, 351. The Swedish pharmaceutical insurance scheme accepts statistical causal relationships in order to satisfy a more lenient evidentiary requirement that an injury was probably caused by the drug: Oldertz, "Security Insurance, Patient Insurance, and Pharmaceutical Insurance in Sweden" (1986) 34 *The American Journal of Comparative Law* 635, 648–9; Oldertz, "The Swedish Pharmaceutical Insurance—Construction and Rules", Skandia International Symposia, Stockholm, 1984, 259, 261. However, traditional strict proof is assumed to apply in the German strict liability statute for dangerous pharmaceuticals: Fleming, "Probabilistic Causation in Tort Law" (1989) 68 *Can. Bar Rev.* 661, 663, citing Sander, Arzneimittelrecht. Erl. para. 84 AMG 15 (1977–89); Kullmann and Pfister, Produzentenhaftung 1, 34–38 (1988); Wolter, Haftregelung des Neuen Arzneimittelgesetzes", (1976) 29 *Betrieb* 2001, 2003.

[217] [1990] 1 Med. LR 117.

[218] *Ibid.*, at 181. Professor Miller's desire to have given evidence solely as a court-appointed expert has been confirmed in an interview with the author at the Academic Department of Public Health, St Mary's Hospital Medical School on 20 June 1995.

[219] Sanders, n. 56 above, 81.

distortion of scientific evidence in trials, whether by judge and jury or judge alone. It is also hoped that in the USA the pragmatic gate-keeping role assigned to judges in *Daubert* will operate to filter out scientific opinion which is neither reliable nor relevant to the suit in question. The interim and final Woolf Reports' recommendation that the courts in England and Wales will have the power to appoint their own independent court experts may help to reduce the polarisation of views in such contentious cases as those which have been reviewed.[220] However, as Lord Woolf suggests, there will be a need for such experts to appreciate that when giving evidence in court, their primary responsibility will be to the court and not to the client.[221]

6. CONCLUSION

This chapter has tried to depict Bendectin, both by science and case law, as an example of a medicinal product which has repeatedly failed to show incontrovertible evidence of teratogenicity. With only one verdict against Merrell that had not been overturned by either a trial or appeal court, until its final overturning by the trial court in 1996,[222] it appears in retrospect that the fundamental lesson of the Bendectin litigation has been the vulnerability of effective drugs of this nature and their possible exclusion from the therapeutic armamentarium on the basis of tenuous and inadequate scientific evidence of causation.[223]

The chapter has also tried to show the extent to which American jury trials in favour of plaintiffs in this area have been forcibly reversed by the use of a plurality of American procedural responses, and has suggested ways of attempting to overcome the distortion of scientific evidence through the use of science panels, court experts and the bifurcation of trials. It has been argued that such procedural responses are equally applicable to a trial by judge alone in the UK. The pragmatic response of *Daubert* to the role of expert testimony in causation cases is welcomed, subject to the price of an eternally vigilant eye on the jurisprudence which emerges from it. Indeed, it seems that this decision should result in easier

[220] Lord Woolf, n. 184 above, chap. 23 at para. 39, Recommendation 102; Lord Woolf, n. 185 above, Recommendation 157.

[221] Lord Woolf, n. 184 above, chap. 23, at para. 39, Recommendation 104; Lord Woolf, n. 185 above, chap. 13 at para. 29; Recommendation 159. See also Opinion, "A Civil Crusade: The Citizen has Reason to be Grateful to Lord Woolf", *The Times*, 24 Oct. 1994.

[222] See *Oxendine* v. *Richardson-Merrell*, n. 39 above, at n. 37. The trial court overturned the verdict against Merrell in the light of the "clear and convincing" post-1983 evidence that Bendectin was not a human teratogen: *Oxendine* v. *Merrell Dow Pharmaceuticals, Inc.*, No. 82–1245, 1996 WL 680992 (DC Super. 24 Oct. 1996), at *33. It should be noted, however, that this case is as yet not resolved. The plaintiffs filed their appeal against Merrell's judgment on 21 Sept. 1998 (personal communication from Richard Meier, Senior Paralegal, Hoechst Marion Roussel, Inc, Cincinnati, 19 Oct. 1998).

[223] See Jackson, "Pharmaceutical Product Liability May be Hazardous to Your Health: A No-Fault Alternative to Concurrent Regulation", (1992) 42 *The American University Law Review* 199, 207, citing Bendectin as the main example of access to individual drugs suffering through product liability.

acceptance of expert evidence from both sides by the court, particularly in the light of the fact that not all scientific opinions, especially in medicine, are generally accepted in the *Frye* sense.

Daubert II's attempt to reconcile the use of standards of significance in epidemiological evidence and the balance of probabilities standard in law should help bridge the gap between law and science in satisfying standards of proof using statistical evidence. On remand, it appears that, to date, the Bendectin cases have strongly confirmed the inadmissibility of expert testimony in the light of the *Daubert* decision of the Supreme Court.

The debate for and against expert panels and court-appointed experts continues, but there is no doubt that a pressing need exists to improve on the archetypal multimillion dollar jury verdict, which is later reversed by the more sober deliberations of the judiciary or even a further trial. *Havner* acts as a timely reminder to experts and their legal advisers of the problems that may ensue as a result of the evidence of partisan experts and unconvincing evidence in such cases. In the long run, such testimony tends to emerge as being prejudicial both to the cases in question and to the very experts themselves. It is, perhaps, a lesson for English courts that they should continue to exercise discretion against jury trials in personal injury cases. It also seems evident that Scottish courts should not seek to have the types of action heard by civil juries extended to embrace questions of liability and causation in personal injury cases.

Both lawyers and scientists must not lose sight of the principal aim of providing to the trier of fact as true a picture of the state of scientific evidence as is possible,[224] not only for the efficient resolution of legal controversies but also for the advancement of therapeutics and pharmacovigilance generally. The more that is known about a drug's adverse reaction potential, the more chance that doctors and patients will have of enjoying the relative safety of therapeutically beneficial products as pharmaceutical medicine advances.

224 It is important to remember that it is not the trier of fact's role to ascertain the truth of all the facts, decide what the law is and apply the law to the facts. The judge or jury must deliver a decision on the basis of evidence presented over which it has no responsibility: Eggleston, *Evidence, Proof and Probability* (2nd edn., London, Weidenfeld and Nicolson, 1983), 1–2. Michael Green supports the legal system's eventual resolution of the Bendectin litigation. However, he still believes that it can improve on its job in the resolution of toxic tort cases, and that increased education in the sciences of human toxicology and statistical methods, or large expenditures for scientific advisory boards, may be necessary to make a significant difference: Green, n. 129 above, 22. Nevertheless he cautions against overreacting to the Bendectin litigation. To him this is a greater danger than ignoring its lessons: *ibid.*, 345. However, the primacy of genuine scientific evidence has been emphasised in the CA by Posner CJ in *Rosen* v. *Ciba-Geigy Corporation*, 78 F 3d 316 (7th Cir. 1996) where, in applying *Daubert* and holding that scientific evidence of causation of a heart attack by a nicotine patch was not real science and was therefore inadmissible, he stated that "the court room is not the place for scientific guesswork, even of the inspired sort. Law lags science; it does not lead it": *ibid.*, 319.

4

Vaccine Damage and Causation: A Comparative Perspective[1]

1. BACKGROUND

Vaccines have played an important part in advancing medical treatment in the twentieth century. But associated with such scientific and medical advancement has been the problem of vaccine damage and its effect, primarily on the injured patient but also on the inhibition of technological innovation in the development of new vaccines through expensive tort litigation and rising insurance premiums.[2] The relevance of vaccine damage to product liability litigation involving drugs is enormous. As Forte has observed:

> "In many ways the whooping cough vaccine issue highlights the dilemmas facing the drug industry, the medical profession and the public affected by immunisation. The vaccine may be properly prepared, the Health Authority may offer adequate advice to doctors on precautions and contra-indications, and the statistics may demonstrate the overall beneficial effects of vaccination. Yet in some cases the consequences for an individual child may be terrible."[3]

The difficulties in establishing causation in vaccine damage are considerable. Active immunisation has classically been produced by vaccines prepared in three ways:

(1) from live attenuated micro-organisms or pathogens,[4] e.g. oral sabin polio vaccine;
(2) from killed inactivated micro-organisms, e.g. inactivated salk killed vaccine;
(3) from purified fractions of micro-organisms.[5]

Recent work in molecular biology, particularly genetic engineering, has greatly extended knowledge in this area; but the composition of the main conventional vaccines in groups (1) and (2) is generally undefined. The live attenuated vaccine can cause the disease it was intended to prevent; for example, the

[1] This chap. is an expanded version of an article published by the author: R. Goldberg, "Vaccine Damage and Causation—Social and Legal Implications" (1996) 3 *JSSL* 100.

[2] See, e.g., Earley, "Can Biotechnology Immunise Vaccine Manufacturers from the Products Liability Crisis?" (1990) 30 *Jurimetrics Journal of Law, Science and Technology* 351, 351–3.

[3] Forte, "Medical Products Liability", in McLean (ed.), *Legal Issues in Medicine* (Aldershot, Gower, 1981), 72.

[4] A pathogen is a microbe or other material capable of causing disease.

[5] Earley, n. 2 above, 355.

most recent cases of polio in the USA have been traced to the live attenuated sabin polio vaccine. It is conceivable also that different pathogens can contaminate vaccine stock.[6]

In other cases, atypical clinical syndromes are associated with the administration of vaccines of undefined constitution. All these considerations add to the difficulties in establishing causation of vaccine damage.[7] In the case of vaccines developed by modern biotechnology, the patient is never exposed to the complete pathogen against which the vaccine is designed to protect, making it impossible to transfer the disease; this is in contrast to conventional attenuated or killed vaccines where isolation of the virus from human cells brings into play the possibility of contamination by undetected pathogens inhabiting the cell. Such "biotech" vaccines are theoretically incapable of transferring a disease, but may "enhance" infection or "fail to prevent infection" by a wild pathogen, so that in respect of causation biotechnological vaccines may result in arbitrary conditions similar to conventional vaccines regarding causation.[8] These problems of proof of causation can result in plaintiffs being denied compensation and, though a non-existent issue as yet in the United Kingdom but an issue in the United States, the possibility of manufacturers being held responsible for harm that they did not cause.[9] For example, the controversy surrounding whether pertussis vaccine can cause brain damage has provoked a hypothesis suggesting that the cause of brain damage attributed to the vaccine may in fact be neurological conditions (e.g. a child with a personal or family history of convulsions) occurring in the particular age group, even without immunisation.[10] However, recent Irish authority has accepted that pertussis vaccine can in rare cases cause encephalopathy.[11] The trial judge found this as a fact.[12] On appeal Wellcome served a notice to vary the judgment on this point, but this was not pursued at the court hearing.[13] The Irish Supreme Court held that, having established the time of the first convulsion in close proximity to the injection, the plaintiff was entitled to a finding against the defendants of negligence causing personal injuries arising from the encephalopathy.[14] Such controversy has also underlined the possibility of an AIDS vaccine being incorrectly linked with adverse side effects.[15] The fear has been expressed that when a plaintiff has been administered an AIDS vaccine he may be unable to satisfy the burden of proof of

6 *Ibid.*

7 *Ibid.*, 355, 356.

8 Earley, n. 2 above, 365–7.

9 Smith, "Vaccinating AIDS Vaccine Manufacturers Against Product Liability" (1992) 42 *Case Western Reserve LR* 207, 232.

10 Golden, "Pertussis Vaccine and Injury to the Brain" (1980) 116 *J Pædiatrics* 854 (epidemiological studies fail to show a clear causal relationship between administration of pertussis vaccine and the onset of serious acute neurologic disorders followed by permanent residua: *ibid.*, 856–7).

11 *Best* v. *Wellcome Foundation Ltd* [1994] 5 Med. L.R. 81.

12 *Ibid.*, 88.

13 *Ibid.*, 94–5.

14 *Ibid.*, *per* Finlay J at 98; *per* O'Flaherty J at 104–5. See below.

15 Smith, n. 9 above, 236.

causation and he may have to rely on government assistance programmes as an alternative form of indemnity.[16]

The difficulty of establishing a causal link with brain damage was recognised in the 1977 report of the Joint Committee on Vaccination and Immunisation.[17] The Committee also noted that convulsions symptomatic of, for example, whooping cough vaccine could occur naturally and might be wrongly attributed to the vaccine.[18] Such problems were also recognised by the Pearson Commission, and it was not aware of any other clinical tests that could distinguish the one type of convulsions from the other.[19] It has been noted that some children who have convulsions leading to severe brain damage immediately after being vaccinated may have such convulsions "simply by chance", since such convulsions usually occur first under the age of two, at a time when many vaccines are being administered to children each day.[20] The uncertainty regarding the cause of the adverse drug reaction when administering a vaccine still remains an issue of controversy.[21]

This chapter proposes to consider both the common law and statutory bases of vaccine damage and causation in the UK, Canada, Republic of Ireland and the USA. What seems to emerge from the ensuing case law is a marked contrast between Commonwealth and American approaches to this difficult problem. As we shall see, however, the situation in the USA is complicated by the number of varying decisions in respect of several vaccine types, rendering an overall conclusion on the American case law that bit harder to achieve. In addition, it will be argued that the UK legislation has failed to improve on the difficulties in proving causation at common law.

[16] Smith, n. 9 above, 233, 234.

[17] Department of Health and Social Security, *Whooping Cough Vaccination: Review of the Evidence on Whooping Cough Vaccination by the Joint Committee on Vaccination and Immunisation* (London, HMSO, 1977), para. 38. The Joint Committee supported continued use of pertussis vaccine: *ibid.*, 34.

[18] *Ibid.*, para. 47.

[19] Royal Commission on Civil Liability and Compensation for Personal Injury, Cmnd 7054–1/1978, paras. 1386, 1406, 1411, hereafter Pearson. See also Teff, "Compensating Vaccine Damaged Children" (1977) 127 *NLJ* 904, 904, 905.

[20] Dworkin, "Compensation and Payments for Vaccine Damage" [1978/9] *Journal of Social Welfare Law* 330, 330, 331.

[21] Prof. Ehrengut of Hamburg appeared as a key expert witness in *Best* v. *Wellcome Foundation Ltd* [1994] 5 Med. LR 81, referring to studies he directed in 1970–8 which showed that pertussis vaccination could, in rare cases, cause brain damage (see *The Sunday Times*, 25 Apr. 1993) and it is thought that this research evidence will merit a reopening of the issue in this country. Legal aid funding has been granted to investigate the issue of a causal connection between the vaccine and brain damage. A series of test cases are being selected for a case to begin in the UK: *ibid.*; Dyer, "Man Awarded Damages after Pertussis Vaccination" (1993) 306 *BMJ* 1365; Murray, "Parents to Sue over Vaccines that Led to Brain Damage", *The Times*, 2 June 1997.

2. COMMON LAW

(i) United Kingdom Position

The current common law position in the United Kingdom regarding causation and vaccines has been a bleak history of plaintiffs consistently failing on the grounds of causation. In respect of the general requirements of establishing factual causation in medical negligence law, it is clear from the cases of *Bonnington Castings* v. *Wardlaw*[22] and *Wilsher* v. *Essex Area Health Authority*[23] that the onus of proof is on the plaintiff to show that a breach of duty on a balance of probabilities was the operative cause of a loss.[24] The law in the United Kingdom has yet to recognise the concept of compensating a loss of a chance of achieving a satisfactory outcome or of avoiding loss in a personal injury case,[25] but, even if it did, it seems that the question of a vaccine causing brain damage would be one of past fact, suggesting that compensation for loss of a chance would be an inapplicable approach.[26] Turning specifically to the vaccine cases, the case of *Bonthrone* v. *Millan*[27] was the first decision of importance to go before the courts being heard in the Scottish Court of Session. In *Bonthrone*, five months after birth the child was administered his first DTP[28] vaccine. A report by a health visitor showed the child to be normal but overweight. At the age of seven months the child was given a second dose of DTP; six days later the baby had a spasm and after repeated fits was admitted to hospital. When discharged about one and a half months later the child greatly deteriorated and his brain damage was severe with a mental age of six months. The case was sufficiently persuasive in terms of temporal link, since any reaction which could be linked to the vaccination occurred within six days.[29] The case satisfied the Vaccine Damage Tribunal, which accepted that on a balance of probability the brain damage was caused by the pertussis vaccine. An action in negligence was brought by the parents against the GP and health visitor.[30] Lord Jauncey was satisfied on the weight of evidence that on rare occasions and within certain time limits

[22] [1956] 1 AC 613 at 620.

[23] [1988] 1 AC 1074. In this case, the plaintiff's injury was attributable to a number of potential causes.

[24] *Ibid.*, at 1090–1, *per* Lord Bridge.

[25] See *Hotson* v. *East Berkshire Area Health Authority* [1987] 1 AC 750.

[26] See Hill, "A Lost Chance for Compensation in the Tort of Negligence by the House of Lords" (1991) 54 *MLR* 511, and the recent CA decision of *Allied Maples Group* v. *Simmons & Simmons* [1995] 1 WLR 1602 (CA) at 1609–10, 1614, *per* Stuart-Smith LJ (a case involving causation and professional negligence of solicitors). For further discussion, see Chap. 1.

[27] [1985] 2 The Lancet 1137.

[28] Diphtheria, Tetanus, Pertussis (Whooping Cough).

[29] [1985] 2 The Lancet 1137. See Lee, "Vaccine Damage: Adjudicating Scientific Dispute" in Howells, (ed.), *Product Liability, Insurance and the Pharmaceutical Industry: An Anglo American Comparison, Fulbright Papers Proceedings of Colloquia Vol. 9* (Manchester, New York, Manchester University Press, 1991), 54.

[30] [1985] 2 *The Lancet* 1137, 1137.

pertussis could cause severe and permanent brain damage but a causal link could not be established in this case.[31] Lord Jauncey laid emphasis upon the existence of cryptogenic (unknown) causes to eliminate a possible causal connection between the administration of pertussis vaccine and brain damage and refused to attribute encephalopathy to vaccination on the basis of a temporal association and no other known cause of brain damage in an otherwise healthy baby. He believed that it would be difficult to eliminate rare cases of vaccine-induced injury from childhood encephalopathies with an unknown cause.

Lord Jauncey stated:[32]

> "If a very substantial proportion of infantile spasms and other symptoms of encephalopathy occurring in children at seven months old resulted from known causes, an association in time, together with cryptogenic symptoms and anecdotal evidence might well tip the scales in favour of pertussis vaccine as a cause. But when about 50% of infantile spasms and other encephalopathic symptoms occurring at this stage are cryptogenic it seems to me difficult to say that these symptoms are more likely to be attributable to vaccine than any one of the unknown causes".

Lord Jauncey's analysis eschews the real question in this case which remains unanswered, namely whether pertussis vaccine caused brain damage to the baby in question. The statement that about 50 per cent of encephalopathic symptoms, e.g. infantile spasms, were cryptogenic fails to address the question of specific causation. Such an emphasis on possible cryptogenic mechanisms was regarded as speculative by Stuart Smith LJ in the High Court in *Loveday* v. *Renton*.[33]

At the stage when *Bonthrone* v. *Millan* was decided it was said that the scientific case linking pertussis vaccine with brain damage was slim since the principal source of such an association was a temporal link which "may obviously be merely fortuitous".[34] *Bonthrone* appeared, however, to recognise the possibility of pertussis causing brain damage which was addressed in a subsequent English case, *Kinnear* v. *DHSS and Others*.[35] In *Kinnear* it was alleged that brain damage of a teenager resulted from DTP vaccination at the age of 14 months. Legal aid to pursue the claim against the manufacturers and the DHSS was withdrawn, but Wellcome asked to remain as a "party interested" in the case. However, the case ended in its sixth week when the Law Society discharged the legal aid certificate on the basis that the child's mother's evidence did not match any of the available medical records as she was not telling the truth, and that the

[31] [1985] 2 *The Lancet* 1138.

[32] [1985] 2 *The Lancet* 1137 at 1138.

[33] [1990] 1 Med. LR 117, 184.

[34] Brahms, "Pertussis Vaccine and Brain Damage. Two Claims Before the Courts" [1985] 2 *The Lancet* 1137.

[35] 17 Mar. 1986 to 16 May 1986 (unreported, QBD). See Legal Correspondent, "The Law Tries to Decide whether Whooping Cough Vaccine Causes Brain Damage: Professor Gordon Stewart Gives Evidence" (1986) 292 *BMJ* 1264 (discussing Anthony Machin QC's devastating attack in cross examination on the unreliable reports and interpretations of Prof. Gordon Stewart in *Kinnear*: *ibid.*, 1266) and Stuart-Smith LJ's discussion of the case in *Loveday* v. *Renton* [1990] 1 Med. LR 117, 122.

claim could not succeed. The plaintiff's early evidence was lost, together with the opportunity of 200 other pending claims which were all based on the causation problem.[36]

Before addressing the implications of the leading English case on vaccine damage and causation, *Loveday* v. *Renton*,[37] mention should be made of the principal studies which have addressed the problem whether pertussis vaccine causes brain damage in young children. By far the most important epidemiological study was the National Childhood Encephalopathy Study (NCES), established in 1976 at a time when the safety of pertussis vaccine was being seriously questioned.[38] The NCES's aims were "to assess the relative risk of serious neurological disorders associated with immunization of infants and young children against pertussis and other infectious diseases" and "to identify other factors that may cause or predispose to the development of such disorders in immunized and unimmunized children".[39] A case-control approach was chosen by virtue of its relative simplicity and because of the impossibility of using a cohort study since large numbers of immunised and unimmunised children would be needed to demonstrate significant differences between rates of neurological illnesses.[40] The Report on the NCES concluded that the results "suggest but do not prove that immunization with DTP vaccine does cause the development of serious neurological disorders in a small number of children who were previously apparently neurologically normal" and that "[t]hese disorders occur typically up to seven days after immunization but most often within seventy-two hours".[41] The Report on the NCES also established that the estimated attributable risk[42] of serious neurological disorders occurring within seven days of DTP in previously normal children irrespective of outcome was one in 110,000 injections (95 per cent confidence limits one in 360,000 to one in 44,000)[43] and the estimated attributable risk of previously normal children with neurological disorders persistent one year later was one in 310,000 injections (95 per cent confidence limits, one in 5,310,000 to one in 54,000). It was emphasised

[36] Lee, n. 29 above, 55.

[37] [1990] 1 Med. LR 117.

[38] Alderslade, Bellman, Rawson, Ross and Miller, *The National Childhood Encephalopathy Study. Whooping Cough: Reports from the Committee on Safety of Medicines and the Joint Committee on Vaccination and Immunisation* (London, HMSO, 1981), 79–169.

[39] *Ibid.*, V.(IV).I., 100.

[40] Miller, Ross, Alderslade, Bellman and Rawson, "Pertussis Immunisation and Serious Acute Neurological Illness in Children" (1981) 282 *BMJ* 1595–9.

[41] Alderslade, Bellman, Rawson, Ross and Miller, n. 38 above, V.(VII). 10, 143.

[42] The attributable risk is that part of the incidence of a disease which can be attributed to a particular causal agent. It represents the difference between the incidence of the condition (serious neurological disorders) in exposed (immunised) and non-exposed (unimmunised) subjects: Miller, Ross, Alderslade, Bellman and Rawson, n. 40 above, 1595–9.

[43] A confidence interval or confidence limit is a range within which a study parameter lies 95% of the time: see the discussion on kinds of uncertainty in respect of hazardous substance causation in American Law Institute Reporters' Study, *Enterprise Responsibility for Personal Injury Vol II: Approaches to Legal and Institutional Change* (Philadelphia, Penn., American Law Institute, 1991), 324–8.

as a caveat that because of the broad nature of assumptions and the wide confidence limits these risk figures had to be cautiously interpreted and were not to be regarded as "precise measures of risk".[44] In such circumstances the Joint Committee on Vaccination and Immunisation concluded that routine vaccination of children with DTP should continue to be recommended.[45]

The leading case in England has been that of *Loveday* v. *Renton*,[46] where the sole issue tried was "can or could pertussis vaccine cause permanent brain damage in young children?".[47] The plaintiff sued Dr Renton for damages for permanent brain damage after treatment with whooping cough vaccine. Four suggested biological mechanisms were posited by the plaintiff, namely febrile convulsions, anaphylactic shock, neurotoxic effect and adjuvant effect, to explain the alleged causal link between the vaccine and her brain damage.[48] By far the most significant epidemiological evidence was derived from the National Childhood Encephalopathy Study (NCES), which supported the conclusion that encephalopathy resulting occasionally in permanent brain damage or death does sometimes occur in close temporal proximity to pertussis vaccination.[49] Stuart-Smith LJ held in the High Court that all four suggested biological mechanisms were improbable[50] and that the NCES did not provide evidence that prolonged febrile convulsions following DTP vaccine caused permanent brain damage.[51] He concluded that the results of the NCES, both in the admission tables and the follow-up tables were biased towards overstating the risk.[52] In the follow-up table in respect of previously normal children with evidence of subsequent neurological damage, there were seven cases immunised with DTP within seven days prior to onset of damage and three controls.[53] This produced a high relative risk[54] of 4.67 with a 95 per cent confidence interval of 1.21 to 25.43.[55] The follow-up table was readjusted in court by Stuart-Smith LJ and became five

44 Alderslade, Bellman, Rawson, Ross and Miller, n. 38 above, V.(VII). 12, 143.

45 "Joint Committee on Vaccination and Immunisation, Whooping Cough Vaccination 1981" in *Whooping Cough: Reports from the Committee on Safety of Medicines and the Joint Committee on Vaccination and Immunisation* (London, HMSO, 1981), 76–8.

46 [1990] 1 Med. LR 117.

47 *Ibid.*, 122.

48 *Ibid.*, 182–3.

49 *Ibid.*, 182.

50 *Ibid.*, 184.

51 *Ibid.*, 147, 184.

52 *Ibid.*, 178.

53 Alderslade, Bellman, Rawson, Ross and Miller, n. 38 above, 167.

54 The relative risk is the risk of a disease or defect in exposed people divided by the risk of that disease or defect in non-exposed people. If the relative risk is between one and zero, this may indicate a negative or protective association between the exposure and the disease or defect. If the relative risk is greater than one, this may amount to a positive or direct association between the exposure and the disease or defect. If the relative risk is greater than or equal to two, this will amount to statistically significant evidence of causal link. See, e.g., Howson, Howe and Fineberg (eds.), *Adverse Effects of Pertussis and Rubella Vaccines* (Washington, DC, National Academy Press, 1991), 34 (discussing methodological considerations in dealing with the question whether a vaccine can cause an adverse event).

55 Alderslade, Bellman, Rawson, Ross and Miller, n. 38 above, 167.

cases and four controls producing a relative risk of 2.5 with a confidence interval 0.67 to 10.94.[56] Stuart-Smith LJ concluded this was not statistically significant, although this is debatable since if the relative risk is greater than or equal to two, this will amount to statistically significant evidence of causal link.[57] He consequently concluded that the results of the NCES did not support the plaintiff's case on the preliminary issue.[58]

Although initially impressed by case reports that the vaccine could, albeit rarely, cause permanent brain damage he held, after examining the evidence and arguments, that the plaintiffs had failed to show on the balance of probability that pertussis could cause permanent brain damage in young children.[59] He observed that the *Bolam* test[60] was only concerned with the issue of breach of duty, i.e. if a doctor acts in accordance with the practice and opinion of a respectable and responsible body of medical opinion, he is not guilty of negligence even if another respectable and responsible body holds different views. Such a test could not apply to the causation issue where the question was whether the vaccination caused brain damage.[61]

56 [1990] 1 Med. LR 117, 179, 184.

57 See above.

58 [1990] 1 Med. LR 117, 179, 181.

59 *Ibid.*, 185.

60 *Bolam* v. *Friern Hospital Management Committee* [1957] 1 WLR 582 at 586–7, *per* McNair J.

61 [1990] 1 Med.LR 117, 123, 124, 182; cf the CA decision on causation in *Bolitho* v. *City & Hackney Health Authority* [1993] 4 Med. LR 381, suggesting that *Bolam is* relevant to causation. In that case the majority of the CA held that the plaintiffs had to prove that the doctor would probably have intubated the child suffering from croup, who subsequently suffered cardiac arrest and consequently sustained severe brain damage, and that if the doctor did not do so, it had to be shown that such failure was contrary to accepted medical practice: [1993] 4 Med. LR 381, 386, *per* Farquharson and Dillon LJJ. Cf Simon Brown LJ (dissenting) who applied the "robust and pragmatic approach" of *Wilsher* v. *Essex AHA* [1988] AC 1074, 1090 and assumed causation since an attending doctor "would" probably have intubated the plaintiff: [1993] 4 Med. LR 381, 390–1. It has been suggested that the majority was wrong and that the material issue in that case was "what in fact would on a balance of probability have occurred": Machin, "Preparation for Trial: Leading Counsel and Causation" in Powers and Harris (eds.), *Medical Negligence* (2nd edn., London, Butterworths, 1994), 16.44, 402. See also Kennedy and Grubb, *Medical Law: Cases and Materials* (2nd edn., London, Dublin, Edinburgh, Butterworths, 1994), 491–2, who state that the majority confuses the issue of what *should* have been done (a question of breach of duty) with what *would* probably have been done (a question of causation). However, it seems that Simon Brown LJ also confuses the causation issue (would) with the duty of care issue (should) in the following dictum: "[t]he question surely is: what would an attending doctor probably have done? And given the doctor would probably do that which she or he should do, the question becomes: what *should* a doctor do in such circumstances?": [1993] 4 Med. LR 381, 388. The position is rendered more complex by the CA decision of *Joyce* v. *Wandsworth HA* [1996] 7 Med. LR 1. In *Joyce*, Roch LJ considered *Bolitho* and stated that the plaintiffs had to prove whether a reasonable doctor "would and should have" taken action to prevent an injury: *ibid.*, *per* Roch LJ at 14 (which reflects the majority in *Bolitho*). However, Hobhouse LJ notes the requirement as being that "a plaintiff can discharge the burden of proof on causation by satisfying the court *either* that the relevant person would in fact have taken the requisite action (although she would not have been at fault if she had not) or that the proper discharge of the relevant person's duty towards the plaintiff required that she take action": *ibid.*, *per* Hobhouse LJ at 20 (a "would or should" approach). Since Nourse LJ agreed with both (*ibid.*, *per* Nourse LJ at 20), it remains unclear which is the correct approach. Perhaps the key observation is that the *Bolam* test is only relevant to causation in the context of an *omission* and not an act (see *ibid.*, *per* Hobhouse LJ at 19–20), and that the question whether the vaccine caused brain damage is

A failure to establish a causal link between permanent brain damage and pertussis vaccine was prejudicial to the plaintiff in *Loveday*. The factors relevant to establishing causation in disease[62] were not satisfied by the nature of the adverse drug reaction attributed to the vaccine. No identifiable clinical syndrome existed which was specific to pertussis vaccine. No specific pathology peculiar to cases of death following pertussis vaccination existed, and the injury was not replicated by animal experiments. A close temporal association, established by the case reports and the clinical evidence of certain expert witnesses, including Professor Ehrengut of Germany, was insufficient ("*post hoc* is not *propter hoc*")[63] and none of the four suggested biological mechanisms could be established on the balance of probability.[64] The results of the NCES provided no evidence that convulsions following the vaccine caused permanent brain damage and the results of the study did not support the plaintiff's case.[65]

It has been said that the scientific knowledge of the *Loveday* case, most particularly the NCES, was "deconstructed" by law, and that it is unclear whether such a deconstructionalist approach serves the aims that vaccines and medicinal product liability should seek to achieve.[66]

There is potential justification for this argument since the readjustment of the NCES results, on the basis that they were biased towards overstating the risk, only reflected the position in respect of previously normal children with evidence of neurological damage. It is arguable, when the figures are looked at as a whole, that systematic bias or error is not demonstrated in the NCES and that, given the size of the risk ratios and the levels of statistical significance, it is questionable whether undisclosed bias/error is sufficiently powerful to account for such findings.[67]

In an interview with the author, Professor David Miller (who was director of the original NCES) suggested that the crux of the issue in respect of bias was that

a factual causation issue, i.e. an alleged *act*. This view seems to have been confirmed by the HL in *Bolitho* v. *City & Hackney HA* [1998] AC 232, where their Lordships have held (at 239–40) that *Bolam* in the majority of cases has no application in deciding questions of causation, but in cases where a breach of duty of care consists of an omission to do an act which ought to be done, the question of what would have amounted to a continuing exercise of proper care fell to be judged by the *Bolam* test. The HL also held that in applying the *Bolam* test, the court had to be satisfied that exponents of the body of opinion relied upon could demonstrate that such an opinion had a "logical basis": *ibid*., 242. In particular, in cases involving the weighing of risks against benefits, the judge would need to be satisfied that the experts had directed their minds to the question of comparative risks and benefits and had reached a defensible conclusion on the matter: *ibid*., 241–2. Thus the HL regarded cases involving risk assessment as such as requiring experts to direct their minds to the question of comparative risks and benefits, which reflects a recognition by their Lordships of the increased importance of risk assessment to the courts. For further discussion, see Keown, "Reining in the *Bolam* Test" [1998] *CLJ* 248.

62 [1990] 1 Med. LR 117, 126–7, 182.

63 *Ibid*., 182.

64 *Ibid*.

65 *Ibid*., 184.

66 Lee, n. 29 above, 65.

67 Miller, Wadsworth and Ross, "Severe Neurological Illness: Further Analyses of the British National Childhood Encephalopathy Study" (1988) 13 *Suppl. Tokai J Exp. Clin. Med*. 145, 153–4.

there were 39 cases of vaccine-associated illnesses, seven of which were cases of infantile spasms. These seven were discounted, leaving 32 cases, 26 of which were previously normal. These 26 were crucial cases but only seven of them had evidence of lasting damage. Professor Miller suggested that Anthony Machin QC took the seven cases of lasting damage, the most vulnerable in the study, and alleged bias in respect of these seven. Professor Miller argues that when the whole study is looked at in total, evidence of bias evaporates.[68]

It is arguable that the conclusions of the NCES are consistent with Stuart-Smith LJ's judgment in *Loveday* in that while he was not satisfied on a balance of probabilities that pertussis vaccine caused brain damage, he could not exclude the possibility that the vaccine rarely causes brain damage.[69] In 1986, the US National Childhood Vaccine Injury Act was passed by the US Congress,[70] section 312 of which mandated the review of all medical and scientific literature regarding, *inter alia*, the relationship between pertussis vaccine and adverse events and rubella vaccine and adverse events by the Institute of medicine (IOM). The IOM established the Committee to Review the Adverse Consequences of Pertussis and Rubella Vaccines, which reported in 1991.[71] The Committee concluded that there was evidence consistent with a causal relation between DPT vaccine and acute encephalopathy and that the range of excess risk of acute encephalopathy following DPT immunisation was consistent with the NCES estimate of 0.0 to 10.5 per million immunisations. The Committee also concluded that there was insufficient evidence to indicate a causal connection between DPT vaccine and permanent neurologic damage.[72]

[68] Interview with Prof. David Miller, St Mary's Hospital Medical School, London, 20 June 1995. Cf Griffith, "Permanent Brain Damage and Pertussis Vaccination: Is the End of the Saga in Sight?" (1989) 7 *Vaccine* 199, 207, who states that if the cases of Reye's syndrome and viral origin were excluded from cases involved in the NCES calculation of attributable risk on the basis of evidence that they are not caused by DTP, no cases of permanent brain damage or death can be said to be caused by the vaccine, except for one possible but doubtful case of infantile spasms. In a powerful rejoinder to Griffith (Miller, Wadsworth and Ross, "Pertussis Vaccine and Severe Acute Neurological Illnesses" (1989) 7 *Vaccine* 487), it is explained that the main thrust of Griffith's criticism depends on a reassessment of selected individual NCES cases to "correct" estimates of risk and that this is "scientifically unacceptable" since Griffith's assessments were made in full knowledge of the vaccination status of cases resulting in a risk of serious bias and an offending of a basic epidemiological rule: *ibid.*, 487. The paper reaffirms that no biases were shown to have operated in a manner or to an extent as to have significantly affected the overall results and conclusions of the NCES: *ibid.*, 487–8.

[69] [1990] 1 Med. LR 117, 185; Miller, Wadsworth and Ross, n. 68 above, 489. See, *per contra*, Griffin, Ray, Mortimer, Fenichel and Schaffner, "Risk of Seizures and Encephalopathy After Immunization With the Diphtheria-Tetanus-Pertussis Vaccine" (1990) 263 *JAMA* 1641; Cherry, Editorial, "'Pertussis Vaccine Encephalopathy': It is Time to Recognise It as the Myth That It Is" (1990) 263 *JAMA* 1679 (describing the new American National Vaccine Injury Compensation Programme (see below) as a "new national tragedy" since it has legitimised causation ideas concerned by special interest groups and not epidemiologically trained physicians, resulting in unscientific precedents being set for what is and is not a vaccine related injury: *ibid.*, 1680.

[70] Title III of Public Law 99–660; see below.

[71] Howson, Howe and Fineberg (eds.), *Institute of Medicine: Adverse Effects of Pertussis and Rubella Vaccines* (Washington, DC, National Academy Press, 1991).

[72] *Ibid.*, 118.

However, when Professor Miller undertook a follow-up study of cases and controls of children who had severe acute neurological illness in early childhood associated with pertussis immunisation and who were recruited into the original NCES,[73] the whole issue of pertussis vaccination and its relation with brain damage seemed to be opened up again. The follow-up study concluded that the role of pertussis as a prime or concomitant factor in the ætiology of severe acute neurological illnesses in children remains unclear and cause cannot be attributed in individual cases. The attribution of cause in individual cases remains speculative.[74] Although seized on by Anthony Machin QC as confirmation of Stuart-Smith LJ's judgment,[75] the US Public Health Service was prompted by the follow-up study to convene a Committee to Study New Research on Vaccines, with the remit of studying new data and, if necessary, reevaluating the causal relation between DPT and chronic nervous system dysfunction.[76]

The Committee reported in 1994 and appeared to confirm the original conclusions of the NCES study. Since the NCES did not and probably could not rule out the possibility that only children with underlying brain or metabolic abnormalities react to stimuli like DPT with acute neurological illness, and no other studies could rule out or establish such a possibility, the Committee concluded "that the *evidence is insufficient to indicate* whether or not DPT increases the overall risk in children of chronic nervous system dysfunction".[77]

Significantly, the NCES data were consistent with the possibility that some children *without* underlying brain or metabolic abnormalities might experience serious acute neurologic illness within seven days of receiving DPT and that acute neurologic illness could have chronic nervous system sequelae. The NCES data were also consistent with the possibility that some children *with* underlying brain or metabolic abnormalities (which promote a "triggering" by DPT of an acute neurologic illness) might subsequently develop chronic nervous system dysfunction as a result of a DPT-triggered acute illness. Consequently, the Committee concluded "that the *balance of evidence is consistent with* a causal relation between DPT and the forms of chronic nervous system dysfunction described in the NCES in those children who experience a serious acute neurologic illness within seven days after receiving DPT vaccine".[78]

In conclusion, these results confirm the view of the NCES that DPT vaccine can very rarely cause serious acute neurological illnesses and that as a consequence some children may suffer permanent brain damage. It would also seem that the statement that "[t]he NCES results do not allow the possibility of very rare serious neurological reactions which could lead to brain damage to be dis-

[73] Miller, Madge, Diamond, Wadsworth and Ross, "Pertussis Immunisation and Serious Acute Neurological Illnesses in Children" (1993) 307 *BMJ* 1171.

[74] *Ibid.*, 1175.

[75] Machin, n. 61 above, 16.73 n. 1.

[76] Stratton, Howe and Johnston (eds.), *Institute of Medicine, DPT Vaccine and Chronic Nervous System Dysfunction: A New Analysis* (Washington, DC, National Academy Press, 1994).

[77] *Ibid.*, 2, 15.

[78] *Ibid.*, 2–3, 15.

missed",[79] has been confirmed by the follow-up study and the IOM Reports of both 1991 and 1994. The real question, however, is whether this is enough to establish proof on a balance of probabilities in law. As stated above, the Committee to Study New Research on Vaccines concluded that the balance of evidence *was consistent with a causal relation* between DPT and brain damage in children experiencing a serious acute neurological illness within seven days of receiving the vaccine. They were thus not stating that the evidence "*indicate[d]* a causal relation", the highest category, but were choosing the second highest category.[80] It is arguable that this would be enough to establish causation on a balance of probabilities. It is submitted that this would satisfy the American common law preponderance of evidence standard but the position in the UK remains unclear.

However, even if causation was established on a balance of probabilities, the real problem would occur if there were cases of serious acute neurologic illness within eight or nine days, just outside the IOM range. Although such "borderline" cases would be arguably consistent with causal link, they might well be rejected by an American court. Since it is unclear whether an English court or indeed the United Kingdom Vaccine Damage Payments Tribunal[81] would accept the establishment of causal link within the seven day period, it is quite possible that such cases would be rejected under English law.

(ii) Canadian Position

(a) Rothwell *v.* Raes

In the Canadian case of *Rothwell* v. *Raes*[82] the infant plaintiff received three immunisation doses of "DPTP" vaccine (quadrigen). Just after the third injection a serious developmental abnormality was suspected. After examination by a series of physicians it was concluded that the infant was blind, almost deaf and severely retarded both physically and mentally. A claim was brought against the physician who administered the vaccine for failure to warn of the alleged material risks of vaccination and against the manufacturer for negligence and for failing to bring to the attention of the medical profession the inherent dangers that existed in the use of the vaccine. Osler J held in the Ontario High Court of

79 Miller, Wadsworth and Ross, n. 67 above, 154.

80 Howson, Howe and Fineberg, n. 54 above, 62. The Committee to Study New Research on Vaccines stressed that its conclusion was not the strongest statement regarding causality and that such evidence did not "establish" or "prove" a causal relation: Stratton, Howe and Johnston, (eds.), *Institute of Medicine, DPT Vaccine and Chronic Nervous System Dysfunction: A New Analysis* (Washington, DC, National Academy Press, 1994), 15; Stratton, Howe and Johnston (eds.), *Institute of Medicine: Adverse Events Associated with Childhood Vaccines: Evidence Bearing on Causality* (Washington. DC, National Academy Press, 1994), 32.

81 See below.

82 (1989) 54 DLR (4th) 193.

Justice that the burden was on the plaintiff to establish that the brain damage was caused by the vaccine and that the vaccine did so with respect to the infant plaintiff.[83] The plaintiffs failed to discharge the onus since the evidence persuaded the judge that the vaccine could not cause serious permanent brain damage.[84] Even if he had found that the vaccine could cause serious brain damage, the condition of the child supported the view that the infant suffered neurological deficits from the beginning (i.e. the child was brain damaged before DPTP was given) and that his case of neurological damage was idiopathic in origin[85] (i.e. the specific pathology and cause of the damage was unknown) which, with its emphasis on unknown cause, seems to follow the rationale of Lord Jauncey in *Bonthrone* v. *Millan,*[86] but not that of Stuart-Smith LJ in *Loveday* v. *Renton.*[87] The latter judge regarded possible unknown causes in that case as irrelevant. *Rothwell* has been severely criticised on the basis that (1) the issue whether pertussis vaccine could cause brain damage (general causation) was "conflated" with (2), the issue whether it did so in the infant's case ("specific causation").[88] With regards to the former issue, (1), it has been said that, faced with study after study concluding it could, Osler J concluded it could not, which suggested that having identified (1), he allowed himself to be "swayed" in answering (1) by evidence that the brain damage was not caused by the vaccine in the plaintiff's case.[89] The decision was affirmed by the Ontario Court of Appeal[90] which held that they could find no error, "[l]et alone any palpable and overriding error", in the trial judge's conclusion that the vaccine could not cause brain damage[91] and that the trial judge had applied the correct test in determining the general question whether the vaccine could cause brain damage.[92] The onus of proof was not satisfied by the mere possibility that, in admittedly rare cases, pertussis vaccine might be a cause of brain damage.[93] However, it was noted by Osler J in the Ontario High Court of Justice that a scientific advance in evidence "might easily ensure a different result".[94]

(b) Indeterminate Plaintiffs

Delgado has mooted the possibility of an indeterminate plaintiffs situation. In such a scenario, the plaintiffs suffer injuries that may result from natural or

[83] (1989) 54 DLR (4th) 193 at 201, 219, 250.
[84] *Ibid.*, 251.
[85] *Ibid.*, 335.
[86] [1985] The Lancet 1137 at 1138.
[87] [1990] 1 Med. LR 117, 184.
[88] Hutchinson and Hodgson, "Who's Zoomin' Who? Comments on Liability for Pharmaceutical Products in Canada" in Howells, n. 29 above, 101.
[89] *Ibid.*, 100.
[90] *Rothwell* v. *Raes* (1991) 76 DLR (4th) 280.
[91] *Ibid.*, 282.
[92] *Ibid.*, 283.
[93] *Ibid.*
[94] (1989) 54 DLR (4th) 193 at 354.

man-made causes, in the absence of a synergistic relationship between these two categories and the injuries are causally indeterminate (not assignable to non-culpable natural causes or culpable man-made ones).[95] If these conditions are satisfied, the defendant is the only possible human cause and the population mode of risk and other variables are sufficiently stable to permit an epidemiological calculation of the increased number of victims, Delgado suggests that the burden of proof can shift to the defendant to prove non causation in respect of each injury.[96]

The possibility of such an indeterminate plaintiffs situation arising was ruled out in *Rothwell.* In that case, the argument that pre-natal injury caused the brain damage was rejected by the Ontario Court of Appeal which accepted the trial judge's conclusion that the plaintiff's neurological damage was idiopathic in origin.[97] The possibility, however, of an indeterminate plaintiffs' problem combining with an indeterminate defendants' problem has been mooted[98] when a number of manufacturers produce a substance causing an adverse drug reaction which can occur naturally; for example, a synthetic hormone or a live vaccine which aggravates or creates the disease it was designed to treat or prevent.[99] Such an indeterminate defendants problem emerges where all the defendants caused harm to members of the class to which the plaintiff belongs, but the particular defendant who caused the plaintiff's harm cannot be identified from other defendants.[100] In the United States, the application of market share liability[101] in the context of indeterminate defendants, though accepted in *Sindell* v. *Abbott Laboratories*[102] and *Hymowitz* v. *Eli Lilly*,[103] has not been embraced in the context of vaccines on a public policy basis.[104] In *Shackil* v. *Lederle Laboratories*, the majority stated that collective liability would have a "regressive effect on the social policy of encouraging vaccine production and research".[105] In addition, the majority observed that potential compensatory relief was provided under the National Childhood Vaccine Injury Act of 1986, which was available as an alternative to the tort action.[106]

95 Delgado, "Beyond *Sindell*: Relaxation of Cause-In-Fact Rules for Indeterminate Plaintiffs" (1982) 70 *Cal. L Rev.* 881, 881, 884–6, 906 n. 12.

96 *Ibid.*, 902.

97 (1991) 76 DLR (4th) 280, 282–3.

98 Delgado, n. 95 above, 907–8.

99 Peppin, "Drug Vaccine Risks: Patient Decision-Making and Harm Reduction in the Pharmaceutical Company Duty to Warn" (1991) 70 *Can. Bar Rev.* 473, 500.

100 *Ibid.*, 501.

101 See Chap. 2.

102 607 P 2d 924 (1980).

103 541 NYS 2d 941 (CA 1989).

104 *Shackil* v. *Lederle Laboratories*, 561 A 2d 511, 512, 528–9 (NJ 1989).

105 *Ibid.*, 528.

106 *Ibid.*, 512, 529. The concept of alternative liability, i.e. the shifting of the burden of proof onto two tortious actors where it is proved that harm has been caused to the plaintiff but by only one of them, and it is uncertain which one caused such harm, was rejected in the context of DTP vaccines in *Chapman* v. *American Cyanamid Co.*, 861 F 2d 1515, 1520 (11th Cir. 1988) and in *Senn* v. *Merrell Dow Pharmaceuticals*, 751 P 2d 215, 223 (1988) (on public policy grounds and on the grounds that liability was inconsistent with common law principles of tort liability).

(c) Proximate Causation

In the context of proximate causation, Osler J in *Rothwell* v. *Raes* applied the objective "reasonable person in the patient's position" test of *Reibl* v. *Hughes*[107] to assess causation for the doctors[108] concluding that a reasonable person in the plaintiff's mother's position would not have refused the vaccination if the unexplained risk had been explained to her.[109] Having concluded that Connaught Laboratories had breached their duty to warn by providing insufficient warnings to physicians,[110] Osler J held that it could not be presumed that such doctors would not have discussed those possibilities with the plaintiff's mother,[111] so that the plaintiff would not fail on that ground. Since Osler J had concluded that the plaintiff's mother would have proceeded with the vaccination[112] this case would fail on the grounds of legal causation. However, since factual causation (scientific and particular) was not proved the trial judge did not reach the legal (or proximate) causation issue.[113]

(d) Intervening Causation

Questions of intervening causation have also been decided by the courts. In *Davidson* v. *Connaught Laboratories*[114] it was found by Linden J that a phar-

[107] *Reibl* v. *Hughes* (1980) 114 DLR (3d) 1, 15–17. The objective test of *Reibl* v. *Hughes* was, however, regarded as inappropriate in product liability cases in *Buchan* v. *Ortho Pharmaceutical (Canada) Ltd* (1986) 25 DLR (4th) 658, 685–7. The court stated (at 686): "[w]hen a manufacturer's breach of the duty to warn is found to have influenced a physician's opinion as to the safety of a drug thereby contributing to the physician's non-disclosure of a material risk and the consumer's ingestion of the drug, the *manufacturer is not entitled to require the injured consumer to prove that a reasonable consumer in her position would not have taken the drug if properly warned*". The Court continued, accepting a subjective test, "[w]hether the particular consumer would have taken the drug even with a proper warning is a matter to be decided by the trier of fact on all the relevant evidence": *ibid*. The subjective approach was commended on the grounds of principle and policy because it facilitates meaningful consumer choice and encourages full disclosure: *ibid.*, 687. The subjective test of causation in product liability cases has been upheld by the Sup. Ct. of Canada as appropriate in an action against a breast implant manufacturer when determining whether a breach of duty to warn of risks associated with implants caused the plaintiff's injury: *Hollis* v. *Dow Corning Corp*. (1995) 129 DLR (4th) 609, 632, *per* La Forest J. However, it was also observed that the "modified objective test" of *Reibl* v. *Hughes* should continue to be applied in negligence actions between doctor and patient: *Hollis* v. *Dow Corning Corp* (1995) 129 DLR (4th) 609, 633, *per* La Forest J, and this was upheld by the Sup. Ct. of Canada in *Arndt* v. *Smith* (1997) 148 DLR (4th) 48, 52, 57, i.e. "a test which asks whether a reasonable person in the circumstances of the plaintiff would have consented to the proposed treatment if all the risks had been disclosed": *ibid.*, 57. Use of an objective test of causation in order to counteract an unduly wide duty of disclosure of risks by a doctor has been criticised as resting "on a confusion between substantive law and evidence and an exaggerated view of the impact of the objective test": A. Honoré, "Causation and Disclosure of Medical Risks" (1998) 114 *LQR* 52, 54–5.

[108] *Rothwell* v. *Raes* (1989) 54 DLR (4th) 193 at 276.

[109] *Ibid.*, 280.

[110] *Ibid.*, 341.

[111] *Ibid.*

[112] *Ibid.*, 280.

[113] See Peppin, n. 99 above, 510.

[114] (1980) 14 CCLT 251 (Ont. HCJ).

maceutical company's warnings regarding a rabies vaccine were "inadequate and unreasonable in the circumstances",[115] but that the role of the doctors led to the case failing on the grounds of causation since a proper warning would have made no difference, as it was not the practice of the doctors to discuss neurological side-effects with their patients for fear that the patients might refuse the necessary treatment.[116] It thus appears to be the case that the plaintiff's action failed on the grounds of *nova causa interveniens* since an "independent judgement of the defendant doctors intervened in the chain of causation between the manufacturer and the consumer causing the plaintiff's action to fail on this basis".[117]

Where a manufacturer's duty to supply information about a drug is discharged by providing that information to a responsible intermediary, it is presumed that if the doctor was informed by the manufacturer, the doctor would disclose the risk, acting non-negligently.[118] In *Rothwell*,[119] Osler J followed *Buchan* v. *Ortho Pharmaceutical (Canada) Ltd*,[120] finding that the presumption was not overcome since the doctors would have discussed the possibilities with Mrs Rothwell, or at least mentioned they existed. If a causal relationship had been established in *Rothwell*, Connaught Laboratories would have been negligent.[121]

However, Osler J in *Rothwell* indicated his distress in the resolution of the case by saying that such a litigation process was an "utterly inappropriate procedure for dealing with claims of this nature".[122] He referred to the fact that a number of jurisdictions such as the United Kingdom and the United States have provided statutory provision for compensation to persons who have suffered neurological damage in close temporal association with vaccine administration.[123] He believed that it would be appropriate for Canadian society to agree to compensation "upon proof of prior good health, the administration of vaccine and catastrophic damage within a limited period of time".[124] It thus appears that Osler J's compensation scheme requirements would amount to a standard less than that of traditional causation, which is certainly not that of the UK Vaccine Damage Payments Act 1979, requiring causation to be proved on the balance of probabilities.[125] With the US National Childhood Vaccine Injury Act 1986,[126] an injured party may demonstrate a compensatable injury listed in

115 *Ibid.*, 276.

116 *Ibid.*, 277. The manufacturer also avoided liability since full information of the risks was given to the plaintiff in British Columbia: *ibid.* See also 280.

117 Peppin, n. 99 above, 512.

118 *Buchan* v. *Ortho Pharmaceutical (Canada) Ltd* (1986) 25 DLR (4th) 658 at 681–2.

119 *Rothwell* v. *Raes* (1989) 54 DLR (4th) 193 at 339.

120 (1986) 25 DLR (4th) 658.

121 *Ibid.*, 341, 342.

122 *Ibid.*, 354.

123 *Ibid.*

124 *Ibid.*

125 Vaccine Damage Payments Act 1979, s. 3(5).

126 42 USC 300aa–1 to 34. See below.

the Vaccine Injury Table[127] which lists the injuries allegedly caused by vaccines that are covered under the Act.[128] This must be demonstrated within a specified time laid down by the Vaccine Injury Table[129] for causation to be presumed.[130]

(iii) Republic of Ireland Position

Hope for victims of brain damage allegedly caused by a vaccine has been spurred on by the Irish decision of *Best* v. *Wellcome Foundation*.[131] In *Best* the plaintiff was administered the DTP vaccine on 17 September 1969 and became grossly mentally retarded.[132] The plaintiff alleged that the manufacturer was negligent in releasing a vaccine batch which was excessively high in both potency and toxicity. In the High Court the trial judge held that the manufacturers were negligent in releasing the vaccine batch (which had exceeded the recommended levels of potency and toxicity and had failed to pass a toxicity test for pertussis vaccine, the mouse weight gain test), and that there was a possibility that the pertussis component in the vaccine could in rare cases cause encephalopathy.[133] However, the trial judge concluded that the onset of the symptoms did not occur until late November 1969, which was not sufficient to establish a close temporal association between the vaccination and the onset which was necessary for a relationship between the vaccination and the damage.[134] The Supreme Court held that in the light of the evidence of the vaccine's excessive potency and toxicity and the "undoubted failure of the mouse weight gain test", the trial judge had been correct in concluding that the manufacturers were negligent.[135] In respect of causation, the Supreme Court held that the first convulsion was in close proximity to the injection (occurring on the evening of the injection) which was sufficient to entitle a finding against the defendants of negligence causing the brain damage in the case in question.[136] It was also held that the negligence of the manufacturer in releasing the vaccine could not result in throwing on to Wellcome the burden of proving that the plaintiff's injuries were not caused by the vaccine.[137] A trial of the issue of damages was directed by the Supreme Court to the High Court,[138] resulting in an agreement to pay £2.75 million damages to the plaintiffs. This figure was approved by the Irish

[127] 42 USC 300aa–11(c)(1)(c)(i).
[128] 42 USC 300aa–14(a).
[129] 42 USC 300aa–11(c)(1)(c)(i).
[130] HR Rep. No. 908, 99th Cong., 2d. Sess. at 15. See below.
[131] [1994] 5 Med. LR 81.
[132] *Ibid.*, 83–4.
[133] *Ibid.*, 88.
[134] *Ibid.*, 90.
[135] *Ibid.*, *per* Finlay CJ at 98; *per* O'Flaherty J at 104–5.
[136] *Ibid.*, *per* Finlay CJ at 103; *per* O'Flaherty J at 109.
[137] *Ibid.*, *per* O'Flaherty J at 109.
[138] *Ibid.*, *per* Finlay CJ at 103; *per* O'Flaherty J at 109.

High Court.[139] The reopening of this issue by the *Best* case has now resulted in English test cases being selected for an action against the drug manufacturers.[140]

It seems clear, therefore, that the Irish Supreme Court placed its emphasis upon close temporality between the vaccination and the onset. In the light of the conclusion by the Committee to Study New Research on Vaccines that the balance of evidence is consistent with a causal relation between DPT and brain damage in children who experience serious acute neurologic illness within seven days of receiving DPT vaccine,[141] temporality would appear to be a critical issue in the obtaining of compensation. However, a range of other factors could also affect such a decision,[142] including the fact that *Best* concerned a vaccine that had a potency and toxicity which had exceeded the recommended levels.[143]

(iv) The US Position

In contrast to the strict standard of proof of causation in existence in the United Kingdom, Ireland and Canada, some courts in the United States have moved towards a strict liability standard and the use of "relaxed criteria" in determining causation. This lax standard, coupled with differences between the tort laws of all 50 states, means that it is becoming impossible to determine future liability exposure.[144]

It is submitted, nonetheless, that mixed patterns are emerging in respect of the establishment of causal link, often dependant on the type of vaccine at issue and the court's approach to the specific factual scenario being examined, together with an individual state's approach to dealing with the problem of establishing causal link between vaccines and adverse events.

(a) Polio Vaccine

In contrast to pertussis vaccine, a clear scientific link has been established between live attenuated oral polio vaccine (OPV) and both paralytic and

[139] Dyer, n. 21 above, 1365.

[140] Murray, "Parents to Sue over Vaccines that Led to Brain Damage", *The Times*, 2 June 1997. The test cases will try to prove that batches of vaccines were faulty and caused a higher proportion of children suffering brain damage than those immunised with properly manufactured vaccines. This tactic is being adopted solely because of the difficulty in establishing the cause of brain damage in cases involving vaccines: *ibid.*

[141] Stratton, Howe and Johnston (eds.), n. 76 above, 2–3, 15.

[142] See the criteria of Sir Austin Bradford Hill to determine whether a reported association is causal or non-genuine, *viz.* strength of association, consistency, specificity, temporality, biological gradient, plausibility, coherence, experiment and analogy: Hill, "The Environment and Disease: Association or Causation?" [1965] *Proc. R Soc. Med.* 295, 295–300. Hill's criteria have been recently applied by French J in *Reay* v. *British Nuclear Fuels plc*; *Hope* v. *BNF* [1994] 5 Med. LR 1, 49.

[143] See the observations of O'Flaherty J in *Best* [1994] 5 Med. LR 81, 105.

[144] Earley, n. 2 above, 356.

non-paralytic polio.[145] Indeed, between 1980 and 1994, 133 people contracted polio in the United States and 125 (94 per cent) of cases were attributed to the vaccine derived from the live attenuated polio virus. The US Centers for Disease Control and Prevention has issued new guidelines for the administration of polio vaccine to prevent this.[146] However, it appears, nevertheless, that the courts have even found manufacturers liable when scientific evidence was able to establish that the vaccine was not the source of the infecting virus.[147]

Such lenient treatment of proof of causation is illustrated by *Reyes* v. *Wyeth Laboratories*.[148] In that case, an eight-month-old girl (the plaintiff) contracted poliomyelitis having received a dose of Sabin oral polio vaccine at a county Department of Health clinic.[149] The plaintiff's father alleged that live polio virus in the vaccine had caused the girl's polio and that the defendants had failed to warn her parents of the danger and thus were liable for her injuries. The jury returned a verdict in favour of the plaintiff, despite contrary evidence of Wyeth's expert witnesses that the girl's polio was not vaccine-induced.[150] The Fifth Circuit Court of Appeals held the defendants liable for failing to warn the plaintiff's parents directly of the vaccine's unreasonably dangerous condition and small risk that the vaccine could cause polio[151] despite epidemiological evidence that the polio was due to an unrelated and "probably wild" virus. A polio outbreak also occurred at the time in the area in which the plaintiff fell ill.[152] The court dealt with the issue whether a sufficient causal connection existed between failure to warn of the danger and the child's injury by examining Texas law. It concluded that "[w]here a consumer, whose injury the manufacturer should have reasonably foreseen, is injured by a product sold without a required warning, a rebuttable presumption will arise that the consumer will have read any warning provided by the manufacturer, and acted so as to minimise the risks. In the absence of evidence rebutting the presumption, a jury finding that the defendant's product was the producing cause of the plaintiff's injury would be sufficient to hold him liable".[153]

The court claimed that the test made sense in the case in question and suggested that instead of foregoing vaccination in the light of the warning, the child's parents would have "taken preventive steps" by agreeing to the taking of a Salk killed-virus vaccination as a preliminary.[154]

145 Stratton, Howe and Johnston (eds.), n. 80 above, 194–5; see also Kitch, "The Vaccine Dilemma" (1986) 2 *Issues in Science and Technology* 108, 117.

146 Johnson, "US Changes Polio Vaccination Programme" (1997) 314 *BMJ* 465.

147 Kitch, n. 145 above, 117.

148 498 F 2d 1264 (1974).

149 *Ibid.*, 1269–70.

150 *Ibid.*, 1288.

151 *Ibid.*, 1277–8, 1295

152 *Ibid.*, 1271.

153 *Ibid.*, 1281.

154 *Ibid.*, 1281–2. The court observed: "[b]uttressing the presumption that Mrs Reyes might have taken preventive steps is the testimony of Reyes' expert . . . that some pædiatricians in Hidalgo County, at least by the time of trial, had begun administering killed-virus vaccine to infants in order to build up their level of antibodies before feeding them the live virus drug": *ibid.*, 1282.

However, this presumption that the parent would have "taken preventive steps" by the taking of Salk killed-virus vaccination has been subject to trenchant criticism.[155] It appears that the court's conclusion that the presumption was not rebutted runs counter to expert evidence estimating the child's risk of contracting polio from the wild virus in the community as one in 30,000 and the risk of contracting polio from the vaccine itself as one in 5.88 million, since the "great disparity" between both figures would suggest that a reasonable person would have taken the vaccine even if given a warning.[156]

The case of *Givens* v. *Lederle*[157] extended the liability of vaccine manufacturers to third parties where the mother of a Sabin oral polio-vaccinated child contracted polio, despite having never received a polio vaccination. The plaintiff had apparently contracted polio from her vaccinated daughter[158] although there was no discussion of the issue why the mother contracted polio through contact with the vaccinated child but the child did not.[159] Such decisions arguably run the risk of being biased in favour of plaintiffs.[160] However, failure to establish causal link was demonstrated in *Plummer* v. *Lederle Laboratories*.[161] In *Plummer*, Orimune (an OPV) was prescribed and administered to the plaintiff's infant granddaughter. The doctor did not convey warnings to the granddaughter's mother and the plaintiff thereafter contracted paralytic poliomyelitis. The plaintiff had never been vaccinated and contracted polio through contact with his granddaughter.[162] The Court of Appeals, Second Circuit, held that the plaintiff had failed to prove that the inadequacy of the warnings was the proximate cause of his injury since, although the doctor was aware of information that the plaintiff claimed should have been in the insert (that an unimmunised person should avoid contact with the vaccine for 30

[155] See Franklin and Mais, "Tort Law and Mass Immunization Programs: Lessons from the Polio and Flu Episodes" (1977) 65 *Calif. L Rev.* 754, who state that those who would have chosen Salk vaccine in the light of being warned of the danger of Sabin vaccine would find it difficult to obtain it since it had been discontinued by its manufacturers in the 1960s and that the court failed to note the importance of the fact that the plaintiff was vaccinated during an outbreak of polio in her area. In such circumstances where quick protection is essential, Sabin vaccine is preferred over Salk. They added that even if Salk was available, a warning of Sabin vaccine's risks would not necessarily have caused the plaintiff's parent to chose Salk: *ibid.*, 761–2.

[156] *Ibid.*, 758–9. However, this rebuttable presumption has recently been rejected under Mississippi law in the medicinal product case of *Thomas* v. *Hoffman-La Roche, Inc*, 949 F 2d 808, 812, 814 (5th Cir. 1992) (plaintiff must show that adequate warning would have convinced the prescribing physician not to prescribe the drug for the plaintiff). The plaintiff had to show by a preponderance of the evidence that the inadequate warning caused the plaintiff's injuries: *ibid.*, 808, 814. In *Thomas*, the plaintiff failed to introduce sufficient evidence to show that the allegedly inadequate warning on Accutane had caused her injury: *ibid.*, 811. For further discussion, see Chap. 6.

[157] 556 F 2d 1341 (1977).

[158] *Ibid.*, 1343, 1345. "Testimony showed that a mother changing her baby's diapers would be particularly susceptible to contracting the disease": *ibid.*, 1344.

[159] Earley, n. 2 above, 358.

[160] Institute of Medicine, *Vaccine Supply and Innovation: Report of the Committee on Public–Private Sector Relations in Vaccine Innovation* (Washington, DC,National Academy Press, 1985), 92.

[161] 819 F 2d 349 (2nd Cir. 1987) (judgment nov).

[162] *Ibid.*, 352.

days),[163] he still did not warn the plaintiff's daughter. Thus the plaintiff failed to prove that a proper warning would have altered the doctor's conduct.[164] On the other hand, it has been recently held that breaches of regulations approving polio vaccine were the cause of poliomyelitis suffered by the fathers of vaccinees.[165]

Notwithstanding an established causal link between the vaccine and polio it is perhaps arguable that there should be no automatic right to compensation. Although the ætiology is not well understood it may be that those who receive the vaccine and yet contract polio are especially susceptible to polio virus; it seems therefore to be those susceptible people who may benefit most from the pervasive use of Sabin polio vaccine in so far as it contributes to the production of a polio-free environment.[166]

(b) Swine Flu Vaccine

The most prodigious area of vaccine liability litigation has centred on a series of decisions arising out of the Swine Flu Vaccination programme. The results of a Centers for Disease Control (CDC) study halted the programme after establishing an apparent temporal association between the onset of Guillain-Barré Syndrome (GBS) within ten weeks of vaccination and the vaccination itself, which was sufficient to presume causation.[167] The government limited its liability to cases where a causal link could be shown between GBS and the vaccination.

This was a heavy burden of proof to overcome in the light of the fact that there was at the time (and there remains to this day) no understood causal path between the vaccination and the syndrome.[168] Such liability was encoded in the Swine Flu Act 1976, the legislation transferring the manufacturer's liability for injuries to the US government.[169] An exclusive remedy was provided against the US government "for personal injury or death arising out of the administration of swine flu vaccine under the swine flu program and based upon the act or omission of a program participant".[170] The programme adopted a no-fault approach to the provision of compensation, requiring a determination of

[163] The illness onset of paralytic polio in contacts can occur within 60 days, according to the Institute of Medicine's latest statistics: Stratton, Howe and Johnston (eds.), n. 80 above, 194.

[164] *Ibid.*

[165] *In re Sabin Oral Polio Vaccine Products Liability Litigation*, 984 F 2d 124 (4th Cir. 1993).

[166] Kitch, n. 145 above, 117.

[167] Schonberger *et al.*, "Guillain-Barré Syndrome Following Vaccination in the National Influenza Immunization Program, United States, 1976–1977" (1979) 110 *American Journal of Epidemiology* 105; see also *Institute of Medicine: Vaccine Supply and Innovation: Report of the Committee on Public-Private Sector Relations in Vaccine Innovation* (Washington, DC, National Academy Press, 1985), 98.

[168] *Ibid.*; Strutton, Howe and Johnston (eds.), n. 80 above, 47.

[169] Swine Flu Act (National Swine Flu Immunisation Program), Pub. L. 94–380, 90 Stat. 113, 1976, codified at 42 USC 247b (j)–(l); repealed by Pub. L. 95–626, sec. 202, 92, Stat. 3574, 1978.

[170] Pub. L 94–380 sec. 2(k)(2)(A).

whether the plaintiff's injuries were in fact caused by the vaccine's administration.[171] The swine flu decisions provide the best guide on the likely results of future vaccine liability litigation.[172] Cases in which GBS occurred within ten weeks of the vaccination have all been deemed compensatable,[173] and virtually all other cases where GBS occurred outside the ten-week period have been deemed uncompensatable.[174] However, about eight cases depart from this pattern and raise the spectre of potential liability under the common law of tort in unexpected circumstances.

In *Unthank* v. *United States*[175] the court accepted that, "ruling out other possibilities",[176] the plaintiff had established by a preponderance of evidence that her transverse myelitis was proximately caused by the swine flu vaccine.[177] The court, whose decision was affirmed on appeal,[178] extended the stipulated liability of the USA concluding that GBS was a broad-embracing term, including transverse myelitis. The court stated that transverse myelitis was "a neurological disorder expected to occur following influenza vaccination" and added that "[t]he fact that GBS alone was singled out . . . [did] not justify differing treatment for other 'closely related' disorders *proven* to have been caused by the swine flu vaccine".[179] It would seem, however, that the court's conclusion that a causal link had been proven was made in the complete absence of any supporting epidemiological data, deference being given to the plaintiffs' experts' opinions and to a close temporal relation of 30 days between the vaccination and the onset of neurologic symptoms.[180]

The decision of *Hockett* v. *United States*[181] has been severely criticised as predicating recovery on a "bizarre theory of causation".[182] In *Hockett*, the plaintiff received a swine flu vaccination and was diagnosed six months later as having GBS. The US government contended that a flu-like illness which the plaintiff had suffered several days prior to the onset of GBS, and not the vaccination, had caused GBS.[183] The plaintiff's theory of causation was based on the

[171] *In re Swine Flu Immunization Product Liability Litigation. Unthank* v. *United States*, 533 F Supp. 703, 718 (1982).

[172] Institute of Medicine, n. 160 above, 95.

[173] E.g., *Titchnell* v. *United States*, 681 F 2d 165, 169 (1982); *Benedict* v. *United States*, 822 F 2d 1426, 1430 (6th Cir. 1987).

[174] E.g., *Lima* v. *United States* 708 F 2d 502, 509 (1983); *Gates* v. *United States*, 707 F 2d 141, 1142–3, 1146–7 (1983); *Kennedy* v. *United States*, 815 F Supp. 926, 936 (SDW Va 1993) (note, however, that this case erroneously attributes cause of GBS to an upper respiratory infection when in fact it was the virus *causing* the upper respiratory infection which caused the GBS: *ibid.*).

[175] 533 F Supp. 703 (1982).

[176] *Ibid.*, 710.

[177] *Ibid.*, 714, 729.

[178] 732 F 2d 1517, 1520 (1984).

[179] 533 F Supp. 703, 722.

[180] *Ibid.*, 714.

[181] 730 F 2d 709 (1984).

[182] Kitch and Mortimer, "American Law, Preventive Vaccine Programs and The National Vaccine Injury Compensation Program" in Plotkin and Mortimer, *Vaccines* (2nd edn., Philadelphia, Penn., W. B. Saunders Co., 1994), 935.

[183] 730 F 2d 709, 710.

presence of P_2 in the vaccine and P_2 antibodies in the plaintiff's blood. The plaintiff claimed that antibodies created by the human body in response to foreign chicken P_2 fail adequately to discriminate chicken P_2 protein from human protein in the myelin sheath surrounding the peripheral nerves, so that the antibodies attack the myelin.[184] Summarising the scientific analysis of a Dr Eylar, the court noted:

> "Dr Eylar tested a sample from the same lot of vaccine given to plaintiff and found that it contained chicken P_2 protein. He also tested plaintiff's blood serum and found that it contained antibodies that reacted with chicken P_2. Dr Eylar testified that he found P_2 antibodies in the blood sera of approximately 50% of 30 people who had been vaccinated and had contracted GBS *and that no P_2 antibodies had ever been found in the blood sera of 'conventional' GBS patients (those who had not received a swine flu vaccination)*."

The Institute of Medicine, however, suggests that this summary implies that Dr Eylar did not give evidence that he himself or anyone else had ever looked for P_2 antibodies in the blood of GBS victims who had not received swine flu vaccine.[185] It is submitted, however, that the summary does indeed *infer* that someone has looked for P_2 antibodies in such circumstances.

The US government then attempted to rebut the causation evidence on the basis of the CDC statistical study, suggesting that GBS occurred more than ten weeks after vaccination.[186]

The District Court rejected the study, stating that:

> "[T]he mere fact that the time interval in plaintiff's case was significantly longer is not dispositive. The statistics reveal a skewed bell curve relationship between the vaccinations and the onset of GBS; *that does not rule out the possibility of a causal relationship between the two*. . . . After ten weeks, the incidence of GBS in the vaccinated population does not fall to zero—it drops to the background incidence rate. That background rate reflects unknown causal factors.
> . . . If *cases such as this were to be decided on the bell curve statistics alone, no plaintiff who contracted GBS more than nine weeks after his vaccination would ever be able to recover* [legally]."[187]

The IOM criticises this logic as treating "failure to prove the existence of a relationship as having no bearing on proof of its absence".[188] However, the Institute appears to ignore the court's additional statement that "[w]hile such a result might be justified in a case where there was no other evidence, in this case there is additional evidence which this court must consider"[189] which reflects the

[184] 730 F 2d 709, 711.
[185] Institute of Medicine, n. 160 above, 102.
[186] 730 F 2d 709, 711.
[187] *Ibid*., 712. See above in respect of pertussis borderline cases. If *Hockett* was followed, causation might be established in a borderline case of serious acute neurologic illness occurring just outside 7 days after DPT vaccine administration.
[188] Institute of Medicine, n. 160 above, 103.
[189] 730 F 2d 709, 712.

fact that searching attempts would be required to establish no causal link, whereas the additional evidence in the case was that Dr Eyler had found the plaintiff's blood serum to contain P_2 antibodies. The problem for the defendants was that their experts had *not* tested the plaintiff's blood for antibodies[190] so that they could not argue that such antibodies were not present in the plaintiff's blood serum. The Court of Appeals thus held that the plaintiff's expert's evidence had helped the plaintiff establish a *prima facie* case and had proved causation on a preponderance of evidence. The plaintiff's expert's testimony showed that the P_2 antibodies were present in the plaintiff's blood, that P_2 protein was in the plaintiff's vaccine and that P_2 antibodies were present in animals that had been injected with P_2 protein and that they contracted a similar disease to GBS as a result. In addition, the evidence showed that P_2 antibodies did not appear in control animals or people who had contracted GBS without being given a vaccine. The defendant's testimony did not sufficiently rebut the plaintiff's proof of causation.[191]

In *Sulesky* v. *United States*[192] the onset of the plaintiff's GBS occurred on the 14th week after administration of her swine flu injection. The District Court held, based upon the evidence of the plaintiff's treating physician and the assessment of other testimony and evidence, that the proximate cause of the plaintiff's GBS was the administration of the swine flu injection.[193] The court found that the resolution of the causation issue turned on the evidence of the treating and evaluating physicians and not on the expert epidemiological evidence.[194] The IOM criticised the approach of the court in *Sulesky* on the ground that it was taken notwithstanding the absence of anything in the scientific literature to suggest that there is something about an individual patient's condition or history to allow someone to distinguish between GBS caused by vaccination and GBS caused by something else.[195] The Institute posits the view that a doctor has no expertise to determine the cause of a condition. The notion that he does so "is one that has been discarded in areas such as proving the efficacy of drugs."[196] However, it is submitted that this view fails to appreciate two points of importance. First, although an individual doctor may not know a cause since the doctor is mainly dealing with one case, that patient may suffer a reintroduction of an adverse effect on rechallenge with a drug. The doctor should then have a shrewd idea that the drug caused the effect. Secondly, the report confuses drug efficacy with cause. Efficacy can only be established after the assessment of controlled clinical trials. A doctor, on the other hand, may well be able to assess possible cause in individual cases.

190 *Ibid.*
191 *Ibid.*, 713.
192 545 F Supp. 426 (1982).
193 *Ibid.*, 430–1.
194 *Ibid.*, 430.
195 Institute of Medicine, n. 160 above, 104.
196 *Ibid.*

Another case in which the "speculative theories"[197] of the plaintiff's expert was preferred to that of the defendants was *Spencer* v. *United States*.[198] There, the plaintiff deceased was immunised in late 1976 and went to see the doctor more than 15 weeks later, in early 1977, complaining of numbness of the left side of his face of two weeks' duration. The patient was admitted to hospital on 31 March 1978 in an acutely ill state and died on 30 April 1978.[199] The court followed the views of the plaintiff's expert in preference to the government's expert test witness and held that a common-sense inference of causation between swine flu and GBS was supported by medical expertise of considerable quality.[200] The case was a "smouldering GBS" case.[201] The court found the plaintiffs' expert's evidence "more persuasive" than that of the "less knowledgeable" government witness, the latter appearing "to testify more from knowledge of orthodox theories and materials published in past decades than from current and thorough familiarity with the applicable field".[202]

The court once again appeared to establish that inability to prove causal link did not prove that the vaccine did not cause the adverse event[203] in *Gassman* v. *United States*.[204] The plaintiff received a swine flu inoculation, and within two weeks was diagnosed as suffering from "probable viral encephalitis, probably with secondary transient cerebral ischaemic episodes".[205] The plaintiff contended that the swine flu vaccine caused her to develop inflammatory encephalitis. The District Court held that the plaintiff had proved by a preponderance of evidence that she had developed inflammatory encephalitis and polyradiculitis as a proximate result of the swine flu vaccine.[206] The court found it significant that the plaintiff's expert "not only personally examined the plaintiff but was her treating physician during the onset of her encephalitic symptoms through progressive stages of her recovery".[207] The court appeared erroneously to infer that polyradiculitis is a characteristic of post-vaccinal GBS when it is a feature of all types of GBS,[208] notwithstanding the fact that no causal relation has been established between polyradiculitis and swine flu vaccine, but only an association between GBS and swine flu vaccine.[209]

Again, preference was given to the plaintiff's personal physician's expert evidence in *Petty* v. *United States*.[210] In *Petty*, the plaintiff received a swine flu

[197] Institute of Medicine, n. 160 above, 105.
[198] 569 F Supp. 325 (1983).
[199] *Ibid.*, 326–8.
[200] *Ibid.*, 326, 331.
[201] *Ibid.*, 326.
[202] *Ibid.*, 330.
[203] Institute of Medicine, n. 160 above, 106.
[204] 589 F Supp. 1534 (1984).
[205] *Ibid.*, 1537, 1539.
[206] *Ibid.*, 1543, 1549.
[207] *Ibid.*, 1541.
[208] *Ibid.*
[209] Institute of Medicine, n. 160 above, 106.
[210] 536 F Supp. 860 (1980).

inoculation and was admitted to hospital eight days later. The plaintiff's doctor gave evidence that in his medical opinion the plaintiff's sickness was caused by the vaccination, the sickness being diagnosed as a "serum sickness-like reaction to a foreign protein"[211] The United States District Court, Northern District of Iowa, Western Division, held that the plaintiff had suffered serum sickness and a neurological disorder which was caused by the swine flu inoculation.[212] The plaintiff's expert's theory of causation was that the swine flu injection caused the plaintiff's severe serum sickness, which in turn caused the plaintiff's congestive heart failure. According to the plaintiff's expert, the "[v]accine was a foreign protein which caused an immune complex to form, setting up an antibody-antigen reaction, which created an inflammatory condition throughout the body. [The plaintiff's expert] testified that there was no evidence that plaintiff received any other foreign protein besides the swine flu vaccine".[213] The court regarded the evidence of the plaintiff's expert as more convincing since he was the plaintiff's personal physician and had examined the plaintiff throughout the relevant times of this matter. No contrary medical testimony was presented at trial. The Court of Appeals reversed, but not on causation grounds.[214] However, in *Petty* v. *United States (Petty II)*[215] the Court of Appeals affirmed the District Court's application of a rebuttable presumption which shifted the burden of proving cause onto the defendant,[216] following *Reyes* v. *Wyeth Laboratories*,[217] i.e. had Petty been adequately warned it is presumed he would have acted to minimise the risk.[218] The court justified the rebuttable presumption on the basis of factual distinctions, the fact that the case was a mass-immunisation one, the public policy consideration favouring allocating the risk of loss on manufacturers, not consumers, and the occurrence of a "hard sell" public relations campaign pursued by the government, both encouraging participation and minimising the impact of the warning. The rebuttable presumption of *Petty II*, which presumes that failure to warn is the proximate cause in swine flu vaccination cases, was upheld by the Court of Appeals in *Brazzell* v. *United States*[219] on the grounds of the same public policy concerns and the government's "hard sell" programme, established in *Petty II*. In addition, the District Court's reliance on the plaintiff's doctor's opinions on actual cause[220] was reasonable.

[211] *Ibid.*, 862–3.
[212] *Ibid.*, 864, 871.
[213] *Ibid.*, 871.
[214] *Petty* v. *United States*, 679 F 2d 719, 729 (1982) (court's finding of a causal connection between the swine flu vaccine and the plaintiff's serum sickness not erroneous).
[215] 740 F 2d 1428 (1984).
[216] *Ibid.*, 1438.
[217] 498 F 2d 1264, 1281.
[218] *Ibid.*, 1437.
[219] 788 F 2d 1352, 1360 (8th Cir. 1986).
[220] These opinions were based on observations of the respondent, a three-year study of medical literature on the effects of the vaccine, the temporal proximity of the vaccination and the respondent's symptoms, resulting in the belief to a reasonable degree of medical certainty that the vaccination caused the respondent's myalgia: *ibid.*, 1359.

The final case which has raised the possibility of potential liability in unexpected circumstances is *Manko* v. *United States*,[221] accepting the "smouldering GBS theory". In *Manko*, the plaintiff received swine flu vaccination and was diagnosed as having GBS 13 weeks later. The sole issue was whether the plaintiff's swine flu vaccination caused his GBS.[222] The plaintiff argued three causation theories. First, the plaintiff demonstrated GBS symptoms in the autumn shortly after the plaintiff received the swine flu vaccination, and the symptoms smouldered until early January the next year, when the plaintiff became acutely ill and the diagnosis of GBS was made. Secondly, the causal relationship between the plaintiff's GBS and swine flu vaccination was based on a proper epidemiological analysis of available data. Thirdly, based on cases deemed by the court to be long onset cases of GBS as a sanction for failing to comply with a discovery order imposed by the court, a causal relationship was established between the plaintiff's GBS and swine flu vaccination. The District Court found for the plaintiff on all three theories, particularly the smouldering GBS theory.[223] The Court of Appeals held that the "smouldering" theory (i.e. the first theory) was an adequate and independent ground for the court's finding on the causation issue. The finding in favour of the "smouldering GBS theory" was therefore affirmed.[224] The US government argued that the effect of the District Court's sanctions on it for failing to comply with the discovery order was to preclude the government from contesting the assertions of fact made by the plaintiff, thus crippling its entire factual defence. The court decided that the discovery dispute that led to the sanctions had nothing to do with the smouldering GBS theory of the case, but it observed that the discovery issue would affect the second and third theories based on inferences from long onset cases of GBS. However, the first theory still stood on its own.[225] It is arguable though that the second epidemiological theory was the most important of the three and would indeed be affected by the sanctions. This case therefore appears particularly pro-plaintiff in such circumstances.

It appears, however, that other than the rebuttable presumption of *Petty II*, which presumes that failure to warn is the proximate cause in swine flu vaccination, there is no requirement to shift the burden of proof to the defendant to disprove any causal connection, since it is said that knowledge of causation of GBS is equally inaccessible to both plaintiffs and defendants and that they both have access to the same studies and information.[226] Nevertheless, it is arguable

221 636 F Supp. 1419 (WD Mo. 1986), aff'd. 830 F 2d 831 (8th Cir. 1987).

222 *Ibid.*, 1424.

223 *Ibid.*, 1435, 1437–8.

224 830 F 2d 831, 835.

225 *Ibid.*, 834–5.

226 *Lima* v. *United States*, 708 F 2d 502, 508–9 (1983); followed in *Gundy* v. *United States*, 728 F 2d 484, 488 (1984). In *Gundy*, however, the plaintiff failed to prove a causal link between swine flu vaccination and physical and mental complications. The plaintiff did not contract GBS because none of the symptoms associated with GBS were established: *ibid.*, 487, 489.

that the US government has greater access to information than any plaintiff would.

It should also be noted that other cases have denied liability in the absence of an established causal connection between swine flu vaccine and other conditions, such as juvenile rheumatoid arthritis,[227] adhesive capsulitis[228] and dermatomyositis.[229]

It therefore appears that the uncertainty in respect of proof of causation in specific cases has led to courts in some cases providing compensation irrespective of scientific proof of causal link.[230] Such an arrangement can hardly be satisfactory when others more deserving may go uncompensated.

(c) DPT Vaccine

Although it is arguable that a similar laxity in causation had emerged in respect of DPT vaccine, plaintiffs have not actually been successful against DPT producers in the last seven years.[231]

In *Toner* v. *Lederle Laboratories*,[232] the plaintiff was vaccinated with Tri-Immunol and suffered transverse myelitis, a rare condition of the spine, the cause of which is unknown. The jury found that the pertussis component of the vaccine had caused the plaintiff's paralysis.[233] The main thrust of the respondent's negligence argument at trial concerned Lederle's failure to develop the safer, less toxic fractionated cell pertussis vaccine, rather than a whole cell vaccine.[234] The Court of Appeals held that the plaintiff had shown that Lederle's negligence was an actual or proximate cause of the plaintiff's injury. The court considered that evidence by witnesses regarding the length of time that fractionated cell pertussis vaccine was available, and absence of evidence that the FDA would not have approved it had Lederle submitted the product, were both cogent reasons that the plaintiff's injury could in fact have been avoided by use of the alternative (fractionated cell) vaccine.[235] However, this decision is arguably disputable in the light of the fact that only one previous case of transverse myelitis had been reported prior to this.[236]

[227] *Hasler* v. *United States*, 718 F 2d 202, 205–6 (1983).

[228] *Freeman* v. *United States*, 704 F 2d 154, 159–60 (1983) (plaintiff's adverse reaction to vaccine in the form of adhesive capsulitis was unforeseeable and plaintiff's expert never intimated that swine flu vaccine was more likely or more capable of this result than penicillin or any other vaccine or injection).

[229] *Novak* v. *United States*, 865 F 2d 718, 725 (6th Cir. 1989).

[230] Institute of Medicine, n. 160 above, 117. The authors of one paper concede the possibility of detection signal bias in the vaccinated population in respect of the diagnosis of GBS: Langmuir *et al.*, "An Epidemiologic and Clinical Evaluation of Guillain-Barré Syndrome Reported in Association with the Administration of Swine Influenza Vaccines" (1984) 119 *Am. J Epidemiol.* 841, 865–6.

[231] See Kitch and Mortimer, n. 182 above, 951.

[232] 779 F 2d 1429 (9th Cir. 1986).

[233] *Ibid.*, 1430.

[234] *Ibid.*, 1430–1.

[235] 828 F 2d 510, 514 (9th Cir. 1987).

[236] 779 F 2d 1429, 1431.

Since in *Unthank* the Utah District Court also "proved" that the swine flu vaccine caused transverse myelitis, the courts had therefore concluded that two very different vaccines had "caused" the same disease. It has been argued, in the light of these decisions, that it will be impossible for a manufacturer to reduce the uncertainty of liability since courts are linking vaccines to adverse events in the face of inconsistent and contradictory scientific evidence.[237]

However, further decisions have demonstrated an inability to establish causal link. In *Graham* v. *Wyeth Laboratories*[238] the plaintiff (by her parents) alleged that she had suffered severe and irreversible brain damage after being vaccinated against diphtheria, pertussis and tetanus with a defective vaccine produced by the defendant and that the defendant's DTP vaccine caused brain damage. The jury returned a verdict in favour of the plaintiff for $15,000,000 in compensatory damages. On appeal, the defendant claimed that the plaintiff had suffered a stroke prior to her vaccination and that the pre-vaccination stroke resulted in her disability.[239] The Court of Appeals held that District Court rulings, which prevented the experts' evidence, based on CT scans, of pre-vaccination stroke from reaching the jury, effectively vitiated the causation theory which the defendant was entitled to establish.[240] Secondly, the court held that when newly discovered evidence about the miscalculations of the toxicity of the defendant's vaccine was produced, the District Court failed to exercise its discretion by vacating the plaintiff's judgment and granting the defendant a new trial. In the light of these two holdings the court reversed the judgment and remanded the case to the District Court for a new trial.[241]

The Court of Appeals observed that there were three errors in respect of causation. First, the trial court's exclusion of the evidence of a pædiatric ophthalmologist who gave evidence that the plaintiff had suffered a stroke *before* her vaccination and that therefore the DTP vaccine was not the cause of her disability. In the light of a CT scan made available to him after his initial diagnosis he attributed the plaintiff's eye problem to a "clear manifestation of stroke". This exclusion of evidence deprived the defendant of a primary defence that it was not liable due to an intervening cause (pre-vaccination stroke) and instead left the defendant with merely an "alternative theory that the DTP vaccine *could not*, rather than *did not*, cause a stroke" (court's italics).[242] Secondly, the trial court erred by exclusion of evidence of a specialist in pædiatric radiology who conducted a CT head scan of the plaintiff which, in his opinion, showed that the child suffered a stroke before her DTP vaccination.[243] Thirdly, the trial court erred by failing to observe the evidence of a pædiatrician that an examining pædiatrician would not necessarily be able to reveal symptoms of a stroke, since

237 Earley, n. 2 above, 361.
238 906 F 2d 1399 (10th Cir. 1990).
239 *Ibid.*, 1403–4.
240 *Ibid.*, 1410.
241 *Ibid.*, 1419.
242 *Ibid.*, 1407–8.
243 *Ibid.*, 1409.

loss of functions, slurring of speech and distortions of the face, which manifest themselves when adults have strokes, do not show up in children at that young age.[244] On remand, the defendants brought a motion that the judge "recuse" himself, which he declined to do, finding that his comments failed to denote any bias or hostility and that they demonstrated no partiality on his part.[245] A failure to establish causal link was also demonstrated in *Rohrbough* v. *Wyeth Laboratories Inc.*[246] and also in *Toon* v. *Lederle Laboratories.*[247]

(d) Other Vaccines

In one of the earliest cases involving vaccines and causation, *Harries* v. *United States*,[248] the Ninth Circuit Court of Appeals held that the plaintiff had failed to sustain the burden of proving that a smallpox vaccination was the proximate cause of encephalitis and that it was as probable that the plaintiff's encephalitis was caused by his mumps as by the smallpox vaccination.[249] However, almost 30 years later the District of Columbia Court of Appeals held that expert evidence was sufficient to create a genuine issue of material fact whether the plaintiff's encephalitis was caused by the combined administration of smallpox and yellow fever vaccines in *Mendes-Silva* v. *United States.*[250]

Two cases establish a clear causal link between Quadrigen (DPTP) and brain damage. In *Parke-Davis and Company* v. *Stromsodt*[251] the Court of Appeals held that the evidence of three expert witnesses, *viz.* the family physician, the pædiatrician to whom the child was taken by his family and the neurologist who kept the plaintiff under observation for several days supported the attribution of causation of serious permanent brain damage to an injection of Quadrigen on a balance of probability. The case of *Ezagui* v. *Dow Chemical Corp.*[252] involved an infant being vaccinated against Quadrigen, manufactured by Parke-Davis, or Compligen, manufactured by Dow. Five days later, however, the child was diagnosed as suffering from post-vaccinal encephalopathy ("PVE"), known to cause brain damage, convulsive seizures, blindness, deafness, paralysis, mental retardation and possibly death.[253] The preservative for use in Quadrigen was

244 *Ibid.*, 1410.

245 *Graham* v. *Wyeth Laboratories* 760 F Supp. 1410, 1451 (D Kan. 1991). Although the judgment was intended to reject claims of partiality and hostility to the defendants, it seems to reaffirm such claims: see *ibid.*, 1411 ff. The judge continued to doubt whether the pædiatric ophthalmologist was qualified to recite opinions on causation: *ibid.*, 1441. This case illustrates the idiosyncrasy of the judicial process, in terms of who happens to be judging the case in question, and also the difficult problems of evidence used to prove or disprove causal link.

246 916 F 2d 970, 973, 976 (4th Cir. 1990).

247 603 So.2d 245, 247 (La. App. 3 Cir. 1992) (failure to establish causal connection between DTP vaccine and stroke).

248 350 F 2d 231 (1965).

249 *Ibid.*, 235.

250 980 F 2d 1482, 1488 (DC Cir. 1993).

251 411 F 2d 1390, 1396–7 (1969).

252 598 F 2d 727 (1979).

253 *Ibid.*, 730.

Phemerol, which caused some endotoxins in the pertussis vaccine to leak out from the bacterial cell into the fluid which was injected. One such endotoxin, lipopolysaccharide, was known to cause a fever which could lead to convulsions and brain damage, as occurred in the case.

Parke-Davis research personnel believed that the leakage of endotoxins was responsible for a measured increase in adverse drug reactions associated with Quadrigen, leading to its withdrawal from the market.[254] The Second Circuit Court of Appeals held that although the plaintiff failed to introduce sufficient evidence to convince the jury on the question of proximate cause regarding Compligen,[255] the plaintiff introduced enough evidence to convince the jury on the question of proximate cause regarding Quadrigen.[256] The court observed that the jury could reasonably conclude from the evidence that pertussis vaccine was capable of causing encephalopathy such as that experienced by the child and that Quadrigen's combination of pertussis vaccine with other chemicals materially increased the risk of causation.[257] The court also noted that there was no shifting of the burden of proof of causation, as in *Summers* v. *Tice*,[258] since the plaintiff was unable to show negligence on the part of two defendants.[259]

Finally, a causal link was established between paralysis and rabies vaccine in *Hitchcock* v. *United States*.[260] There the District of Columbia Court of Appeals, upon careful scrutiny of the witnesses' expert evidence, upheld the District Court's decision that the plaintiffs had established by a preponderance of evidence that DEV rabies vaccine injections given to the plaintiff caused her demyelinating disease or, if her transient loss of vision in her right eye 18 years before was an early symptom of multiple sclerosis, triggered an otherwise dormant demyelinating disease or accelerated a very slowly developing one.[261]

(v) Conclusion

Thus the common law position in the United States suggests an inconsistent approach to causation which is resulting in an almost impossible position for the manufacturer in his ability to assess potential liability. The ultimate effects on innovation through this approach are potentially damaging. The United Kingdom, Ireland and Canada are much more traditionally rigid in their approach to causation with the upshot that it is extremely difficult to obtain compensation.

254 598 F 2d 727, 731–2 (1979).
255 *Ibid.*, 736.
256 *Ibid.*, 735–6.
257 *Ibid.*, 735. This appears to mirror the language of Lord Reid in *McGhee* v. *NCB* [1973] 1 WLR 1, *per* Lord Reid at 5.
258 199 P 2d 1 (1948).
259 598 F 2d 727, 736–7.
260 665 F 2d 354 (1981).
261 *Ibid.*, 357–8.

It may be that the *Best* decision in Ireland may open up the possibility of a review of the *Bonthrone* and *Loveday* rulings, but this remains to be seen.

3. THE US NATIONAL CHILDHOOD VACCINE INJURY ACT 1986

(i) General

The US National Vaccine Injury Compensation Programme was enacted as part of the National Childhood Vaccine Injury Act 1986. This Act was passed to help vaccinated persons who suffer vaccine-related injuries after the commencement of the Act, 1 October 1988,[262] although it applies with some limitations retrospectively to those who received the vaccine at any time before 1 October 1988. The Programme establishes in Subpart A of the Act a no-fault compensation system for adverse reactions to vaccines for immunising children in the USA against seven infectious diseases which occur in childhood, i.e. diphtheria, pertussis, tetanus, poliomyelitis, measles, mumps and rubella. Compensation is available only to seriously injured victims with ongoing disabilities[263] where the injury lasted for at least six months after the vaccine was administered or the victim died.[264]

The programme is administered by the US Claims Court[265] and claims for compensation are initiated by a petition.[266] The injured party must have been administered a vaccine listed in the Vaccine Injury Table (see Table 2 on pages 177–8), and have suffered an injury covered by the Act and occurring within a specified time listed in the Vaccine Injury Table.[267] If the petitioner demonstrates a compensatable injury within this time, causation is presumed.[268]

However, in proposed revisions[269] to this situation under the legislation, the burden of proof of causation has shifted to the petitioners, which should make it harder for disorders unrelated to the vaccine to end up being compensated, but at the same time should make hearings that bit more adversarial in nature.[270]

262 See 42 USC 300aa–1to 34.

263 HR Rep. No. 391, 100th Cong., 1st Sess. 697 as cited in Jacquot, "The National Childhood Vaccine Injury Act: Implications for DPT Vaccine Manufacturers and Victims" (1988) 28 *Washburn Law Journal* 274, 280.

264 42 USC 300aa–11 (c)(1)(D)(i), (ii).

265 42 USC 300aa–12(a).

266 *Ibid.*, 300aa–11(a), 11(c).

267 *Ibid.*, s. 300aa–11(c)(1)(C)(i). This is known as a table claim.

268 HR Rep. No. 908; 99th Cong. 2d. Sess. 6 at 15.

269 42 USC 300aa–14(c) provides for revision of the Table, one reason for such revision being scientific evidence linking a condition not on the Table to a vaccine: see Jacquot, n. 263 above, 279.

270 Federal Register: Health Resources and Services Administration. National Vaccine Injury Compensation Program. Revision of the vaccine injury table. Fed. Register 57: 36878–36885, 1992 as cited in Kitch and Mortimer, n. 182 above, 948.

In respect of potential eligibility and compensation generally, the preponderance of evidence standard applies, the burden of proof being on the petitioner. He must show that the illness, disability, injury, condition or death is not due to factors unrelated to the vaccine's administration.[271]

The Vaccine Injury Table[272] lists types of adverse reactions that, on the basis of the existing epidemiological studies, are presumed to be caused by a vaccine within the time frame listed. It is intended to eliminate the most problematic issue of tort litigation with vaccines, *viz.* that of proving causation. It was conceded that using the Table would result in some people being compensated for injuries that were not caused by a vaccine[273] but defendants of the programme argued that savings in time and energy would offset the cost of the few cases in which this would occur.[274] However, the first four years of the programme have established that most of the compensated injuries involve cases which were unrelated to the administered vaccines, particularly with DTP.[275] More than half of the DTP cases dealt with sudden infant death syndrome (SIDS), notwithstanding the IOM's conclusion that the scientific evidence does not show a causal relation between DPT vaccine and SIDS.[276] It appears that some of the millions of dollars expended on the programme may have been wasted as a result.[277]

Particular attention has been drawn to the vagueness of the definition given to encephalopathy in the aids to interpretation of the Table,[278] in that minor reactions to DTP, such as anorexia, fever, excessive crying and lethargy, have been held to represent encephalopathy resulting in SIDS or subsequent neurological disorders.[279] However, encephalopathy has now been strictly defined in the proposed changes to the Aids to Interpretation of the Table, as "any acute or chronic significant acquired abnormality of, or injury to, or impairment of function of, the brain" with detailed definitions provided of both acute

[271] 42 USC 300aa–13(a).

[272] 42 USC 300aa–14(a).

[273] HR Rep. No. 908, 99th Cong. 2d Sess. 6 at 18.

[274] Mariner, "The National Vaccine Injury Compensation Program in the United States: A Preliminary Overview" in Shulman and Lasagna (eds.), *Trends in Product Liability Law and No Fault Compensation For Drug-Induced Injuries* (Boston, Mass., The Centre for the Study of Drug Development, 1990), 42.

[275] Kitch and Mortimer, n. 182 above, 944, 946.

[276] Howson, Howe and Fineberg (eds.), n. 71 above, 4, 140; Kitch and Mortimer, n. 182 above, 946.

[277] Kitch and Mortimer, n. 182 above, 947.

[278] 42 USC 300aa–14(b)(3)(A): "the term 'encephalopathy' means any significant acquired abnormality of, or injury to, or impairment of function of the brain. Among the frequent manifestations of encephalopathy are focal and diffuse neurological signs, increased intracranial pressure or changes lasting at least 6 hours in level of consciousness, with or without convulsions. The neurological signs and symptoms of encephalopathy may be temporary with complete recovery, or may result in various degrees of permanent impairment. Signs and symptoms such as high pitched and unusual screaming, persistent inconsolable crying, and bulging fontanel are compatible with an encephalopathy, but in and of themselves are not conclusive evidence of encephalopathy. Encephalopathy usually can be documented by slow wave activity on an electroencephalogram."

[279] Kitch and Mortimer, n.182 above, 97.

encephalopathy and chronic encephalopathy.[280] Other proposed changes which have emerged particularly in the light of the IOM's report on Adverse Effects of Pertussis and Rubella Vaccines[281] include the introduction of SIDS as an alternative cause of death, the reduction of the interval between one of the vaccines and anaphylaxis reduced from 24 to four hours and the removal from the Table of shock-collapse syndrome, infantile spasms and residual seizure disorder.[282]

There are two exceptions to the Vaccine Damage Table. First, a petitioner whose injury does not fall within the Vaccine Injury Table may be able to show that the injuries were caused by the vaccine,[283] but the burden is on the petitioner to prove the causal link and he must "affirmatively demonstrate" that the injury was caused by the vaccine.[284] Secondly, if the injury is a listed one, but occurred outside the time limit, the petitioner may file for compensation[285] but again must affirmatively prove causation.[286]

In the majority of cases, causation has been disputed, particularly in respect of DPT, the arguments turning on whether the scientific evidence shows a Table injury or one caused by factors unrelated to the vaccine.[287] By 7 September 1994, only 32 per cent of retrospective petitions (i.e. before 1 October 1988) actually decided by the US Court of Federal Claims were compensatable, whereas 44 per cent of prospective petitions were compensatable.[288] The programme, however, is abundantly more successful in terms of favourable claims than is its British counterpart.[289] It is arguable, however, that much of this is due to overcompensation with the American Vaccine Injury Table.

(ii) Reported Cases

Decisions under the US National Childhood Vaccine Injury Act 1986 are reported in the general law reports (the Federal Law Reports, Second Series) if they are appealed from the US Claims Court to the Federal Court of Appeals. This section analyses the principal decisions reported on appeal. The results are a mixed bag of recovery or non-recovery for varying reasons.

280 See Stratton, Howe and Johnston (eds.), n. 80 above, 50, adapted from US Department of Health and Human Services, US Public Health Service, National Vaccine Injury Compensation Program, Revision of the Vaccine Injury Table, Proposed Rule, Federal Register, 42 CFR Part 100, 14 Aug. 1992, 57 (158): 36877–85.

281 Howson, Howe and Fineberg (eds.), n. 71 above.

282 Kitch and Mortimer, n. 182 above, 948 citing Fed. Register 57: 36878–85, 1992.

283 42 USC 300aa–11(c)(1)(C)(ii)(I). This is known as a causation in fact claim.

284 HR Rep. No. 908, 99th Cong. 2nd Sess. 6 at 15.

285 42 USC 300aa–11(c)(1)(C)(ii)(II).

286 HR Rep. No. 908, 99th Cong. 2nd Sess. 6 at 15. In both these cases scientific studies or expert medical evidence is necessary to show causation: *ibid.*

287 Mariner, "HIV Vaccines, Adverse Reactions, Liability and Compensation", *Final Report to the Office of Technology Assessment, Congress of the United States* (Final Draft, 1994), 118.

288 *Ibid.*, 123.

289 See below.

Compensation has been held payable under the Act when the onset of the injury or condition is not within the requisite time period in the Vaccine Injury Table but causation is established between the vaccine and the injury or condition by a preponderance of the evidence as a whole.[290] In *Bunting* v. *Secretary of DHHS*[291] the Court of Appeals upheld the Special Master's decision holding that the preponderance of evidence standard was satisfied by medical records, documentary evidence and other evidence, and that this demonstrated that encephalopathy and seizure disorder was caused by DPT vaccine.[292] The preponderance of evidence standard was also satisfied in respect of Quadrigen vaccine in *Grant* v. *Secretary of DHHS*.[293] In *Grant*, the plaintiff suffered seizures after administration of Quadrigen vaccine and eventually suffered permanent spastic diplegia rendering him fully dependent on his parents. At a new hearing, the Chief Special Master took additional evidence, including depositions from two doctors about the unique dangers of Quadrigen. The Chief Special Master reaffirmed that the plaintiffs had not proved an injury on the Vaccine Injury Table but he determined that the plaintiff's new evidence showed actual causation. In particular, he relied on new evidence showing Quadrigen's propensity to cause myoclonic seizures, encephalopathies and other neurological insults in infants. The Claims Court adopted the Chief Special Master's award.[294] The Court of Appeals held that the Chief Special Master and the Claims Court had correctly determined that the plaintiff had produced a preponderance of evidence to show actual causation, and that there was not a preponderance of evidence that the plaintiff's injury was due to factors unrelated to the vaccine.[295] The court concluded such, despite epidemiologic evidence that children who receive DPT vaccine are less likely to have spasms between seven and 28 days after the vaccine's administration. The Secretary had concluded that because the plaintiff had shown symptoms ten days after the vaccination, the vaccine could not have caused his injuries,[296] but the court distinguished *Richardson* v. *Richardson-Merrell*[297] and its precedence for epidemiological evidence, on the basis that the epidemiological studies cited by the Secretary related to general DPT vaccine, not Quadrigen. The court emphasised the unique nature of Quadrigen and evidence showing that it used preservative agents, increasing the tendency of endotoxins associated with pertussis bacteria in the vaccine to detach themselves from the bacteria's cellular structure, thereby causing neurological damage.[298] The court stressed the importance of "proof of a logical

[290] In terms of 42 USC 300aa 11(c)(1)(C)(ii)(II).

[291] 931 F 2d 867 (Fed. Cir. 1991).

[292] *Ibid.*, 870.

[293] 956 F 2d 1144 (Fed. Cir. 1992).

[294] *Ibid.*, 1145–6.

[295] *Ibid.*, 1150.

[296] *Ibid.*, 1148.

[297] 857 F.2d 823, 830 (DC Cir. 1988), cert. denied, 493 US 882, 110 S Ct. 218, 107 L Ed. 2d 171 (1989).

[298] 956 F 2d 1144, 1149.

sequence of cause and effect" indicating that the vaccination was the reason for the injury.[299]

It is also clear that an idiopathic cause cannot defeat a claim for compensation.[300] In *Koston* v. *Secretary of DHHS*[301] recovery for DPT vaccine-induced injury was allowed, since although the child suffered from a variant of Rett Syndrome, Rett Syndrome was idiopathic and idiopathic conditions do not defeat recovery. In addition, the seizures occurred within three days of the vaccination, the period the Vaccine Injury Table sets for recovery.[302] This position was reiterated in *Whitecotton* v. *Secretary of DHHS*[303] where the Court of Appeals held that a pre-existing idiopathic or unknown cause (microencephalopathy) could not be used to defeat a petition for compensation where the claimant's encephalopathy manifested itself in the form of seizures occurring within the Vaccine Injury Table time period after vaccination, i.e. three days. The Secretary bore the burden of proving the pre-existing encephalopathy.[304] However, it seems that an idiopathic disorder is compensatable where the only clinical signs are those upon which an inference of vaccine causation is also founded. If the clinical signs are other than those upon which an inference of vaccine causation depends, the idiopathic disorder will be uncompensatable.[305]

Two decisions appear above reproach in their denial of recovery for death following DTP and DPT vaccine respectively. In *Hellebrand* v. *Secretary of DHHS*[306] a child was given her first DTP vaccination and found dead the next morning. The precise cause of the child's death was never determined, but the autopsy classified her death as "Sudden Infant Death Syndrome" (SIDS).[307] In terms of the Vaccine Injury Table, compensation is rendered available if shock collapse or hypotonic-hyporesponsive collapse (HHE) occurs within three days of the vaccine's administration,[308] and it is noted in the qualifications and aids to interpretation in the Vaccine Injury Table that "[a] shock-collapse or a hypotonic-hyporesponsive collapse may be evidenced by indicia or symptoms such as . . . cardiovascular or respiratory arrest".[309] The US Claims Court concluded that because the child died of an unknown cause and therefore it was undisputed that she had suffered cardiovascular or respiratory arrest, the Special Master should have held that she had suffered a Table injury.[310] The Federal Court of Appeals held, reversing the Claims Court and remanding the

299 *Ibid.*, 1148.
300 In terms of 42 USC 300aa–13(a)(2)A.
301 974 F 2d 157 (Fed. Cir. 1992).
302 In terms of 42 USC 300aa–14(a)I; 974 F 2d 157, 160–1.
303 17 F 3d 374 (Fed. Cir. 1994).
304 *Ibid.*, 376–8.
305 *Roedl by Roedl* v. *Secretary of DHHS*, Fed. Cl. 1993, 28 Fed. Cl. 740 as cited in USCA 42 300aa–13, Notes of Decisions (1994 Cumulative Annual Pocket Part).
306 999 F 2d 1565 (Fed. Cir. 1993).
307 *Ibid.*, 1566.
308 42 USC 300aa–14(a)I.
309 42 USC 300aa–14(b).
310 999 F 2d 1565, 1569.

case to the Court of Federal Claims, that recovery for a death following a DTP vaccination based on a Table claim is conditional upon the injury or condition in the Table being within the time period in the Table for that injury or condition and upon the petitioner showing that death occurred as a sequela of that injury or condition. In this case, the petitioners had to show that, within 72 hours of receiving DTP vaccine she suffered HHE and that her death was a sequela of HHE. Since the Special Master had found that the petitioners had failed to establish that the child had suffered HHE, the claim based on the Table injury was properly denied.[311] The court observed that while respiratory or cardiovascular arrest may be the most dramatic symptom of HHE, Congress did not intend that there be any circumstance in which respiratory or cardiovascular arrest would automatically serve to establish the presence of HHE.[312] Newman CJ filed an opinion concurring in judgment and supporting the use of statistics in such cases. She stated that it was possible to ascertain where the preponderance of evidence would be by a statistical analysis of relevant data and that this would determine whether it was more likely than not that the child's death was due to the administration of the vaccine.[313] She observed:

> "The probability that an unvaccinated child of [deceased's] age will suffer an unexplained death during any given period can be calculated, as can the probability that a child will die within a given time after inoculation. Applying standard techniques of medical statistics, it can readily be determined whether it is more likely than not the death was caused by the vaccine."[314]

The observations of the role of statistics are interesting and important, since epidemiological studies remain of paramount significance in the ascertainment of drug causality. However, these dicta display a sanguine and potentially overconfident view of the role that statistics can play in vaccine damage, bearing in mind the difficulties associated with epidemiological evidence in cases involving adverse effects allegedly caused by vaccines, which have previously been discussed.

Recovery for death following DPT was also denied in *Hodges* v. *Secretary of DHHS*.[315] In *Hodges*, the plaintiffs petitioned for compensation under the National Childhood Vaccine Injury Act 1986 on behalf of their daughter, who died within hours of receiving DPT vaccination. The petition alleged that the child had suffered hypotonic-hyporesponsive collapse (HHC), a Table injury under 42 USC 300aa–14(a)(I)(c), within 35 hours after DPT vaccination. The Special Master denied compensation, finding that the plaintiffs had not proven a Table injury, since although the child suffered symptoms not unlike HHC as part of death, death *per se* is not a compensatable Table injury. The Special Master also found that the plaintiffs had not proven actual causation and that

311 999 F 2d 1565, 1569–70.
312 *Ibid.*, 1570.
313 *Ibid.*, 1573.
314 *Ibid.*
315 9 F 3d 958 (Fed. Cir. 1993).

the temporal relationship of the child's death to the vaccine administration alone did not establish causation.[316] The Federal Court of Appeals upheld the Special Master and held[317] that the plaintiffs had failed to show that the child's death was a sequela of HHC. Symptoms which are consistent with HHC but which are also part of death did not on these facts independently establish an HHC that was a Table injury. Secondly, the Court of Appeals held that the plaintiffs had failed to show actual causation since they were unable to prove "a logical sequence of cause and effect", following *Grant* v. *Secretary of DHHS*.[318] Newman CJ gave the dissenting judgment and opined that the Special Master had failed to apply the correct standard of proof by confusing the clinical standard of medical certainty with the legal standard of evidentiary preponderance, and that the Special Master had erred in failing to consider epidemiological evidence.[319] Newman concluded that a scientific inability to identify the cause of a child's death did not mean that the preponderance of evidence could not support a causal link to a vaccine in her case. However, it is still arguable that this does not infer that the preponderance of evidence standard necessarily can support the existence of a causal connection in law. As the court stated in the case of *Merrell Dow Pharmaceuticals, Inc.* v. *Havner*:[320]

> "[A]bsence of evidence of a fact, standing alone, does not amount to evidence of its converse. Absence of absolute proof that Bendectin does not cause birth defects in humans is not some evidence that it does".[321]

Indeed although Newman CJ appears to favour the application of statistics in such cases it remains unclear how the medical and legal standards are to intersect.[322]

However, in *Jay* v. *Secretary of DHHS*,[323] recovery for a death following DPT was awarded on appeal from the Claims Court, which had upheld the Special Master's finding that the parents had not shown an encephalopathy by a preponderance of the evidence.[324] The Federal Court of Appeals held that the evidence presented no factual dispute whether the infant suffered encephalopathy, since the child was otherwise healthy and when he received DPT he screamed intermittently over six hours and died 18 hours after receiving it. The preponderance of evidence standard was satisfied.[325]

Four other conditions have demonstrated an inability to establish causal link. The case of *Cucuras* v. *Secretary of DHHS*[326] utilised the IOM's conclusion that

[316] *Ibid.*, 959–60.

[317] *Ibid.*, 960

[318] 956 F 2d 1144, 1148.

[319] 9 F 3d 958, 963 (Fed. Cir. 1993).

[320] CA, 13th Dist. Texas, Corpus Christi: No. 13–92–540–CV, 17 Mar. 1994. See Chap. 3.

[321] No. 13–92–540–CV, 17 Mar. 1994 at 13 of official transcript.

[322] See Lasagna and Shulman, "Bendectin and the Language of Causation" in Foster, Bernstein and Huber (eds.), *Phantom Risk: Scientific Inference and the Law* (Cambridge, Mass., MIT Press, 1993), 12.

[323] 990 F 2d 979 (Fed. Cir. 1993).

[324] *Ibid.*, 982–3.

[325] *Ibid.*, 983.

[326] 993 F 2d 1525 (Fed. Cir. 1993).

the evidence does not indicate a causal relation between DPT vaccine and infantile spasms[327] in deciding to uphold a finding of no causation in fact between DPT and a child's seizure disorder.[328] The case of *Hines* v. *Secretary of DHHS* affirmed a finding by the Special Master that Measles Mumps and Rubella vaccine (MMR) did not cause hearing loss on a preponderance of evidence.[329] Pneumonia has been held to amount to a factor unrelated to the administration of FTP vaccine, precluding legal recovery[330] in *Munn* v. *Secretary of DHHS*.[331] Finally, in *Bradley* v. *Secretary of DHHS*[332] the plaintiff failed to show by a preponderance of evidence that an onset had occurred within the relevant time period in the Vaccine Injury Table in the light of the fact that no medical records showed that the symptoms occurred within 72 hours of the administration of DPT vaccine.[333]

(iii) Conclusion

These decisions seem to reflect the differing of views of the establishment of causation, much of which is dependent on the factual scientific presentation of each case. The particular scientific position at the time each case is decided should not be seen, however, as set in stone. It may well be that a number of these decisions will be decided differently in years to come. Thus it seems that the issue of causation both within and outside the Vaccine Injury Table requirements is still a difficult problem and the controversy surrounding certain vaccines and adverse events remains a contestable issue in the operation of the programme.

4. VACCINE DAMAGE PAYMENTS ACT 1979 (UK)

(i) Pearson Commission

The Pearson Commission made extensive examination of the question of vaccine damage.[334] Such conclusions were ultimately based on the premise that vaccine damage merits special treatment by dint of the difference in social effect between vaccines and other drugs. With most drugs other than vaccines, the risk of taking a drug normally rests with the individual patient since no one else suf-

[327] Howson, Howe and Fineberg (eds.), n. 71 above, 4, 17.
[328] 993 F 2d 1525, 1529.
[329] 940 F 2d 1518, 1528 (Fed. Cir. 1991).
[330] In terms of 42 USC 300aa–13(a)(1)(B).
[331] 970 F 2d 863, 868, 873 (Fed. Cir. 1992).
[332] 991 F 2d 1570 (Fed. Cir. 1993).
[333] *Ibid.*, 1574.
[334] Pearson, n. 19 above, chap. 25.

fers if he does not take the drug and no one else directly benefits if he does. With vaccines, it has been argued that through immunisation not only the child, but also his friends, benefit through eradication of the risk that he will transmit the disease on to them. Hence vaccinations have been actively promoted by the Department of Health.[335] This differentiation between vaccines and drugs provided the basis for the Pearson Commission's recommendations, notwithstanding the fact that the report had stated that the compensation and care of severely handicapped children was based on the principle that they were to be treated alike, without regard to the cause of their condition[336] which would *prima facie* infer that vaccine damaged children would be dealt with within that provision.[337]

With arguments surrounding the differentiation between vaccines and drugs in mind, the Pearson Commission suggested that since vaccination is recommended by the government or a local authority,[338] the government or local authority concerned should be strictly liable in tort/delict for severe damages suffered by anyone (adult or child) as a result of vaccination recommended in the community's interest.[339] Such liability should be subject to matters of cause and fact and without defences. Proof of causation was recognised as a continuing and difficult issue for the resolution of the courts, since convulsions which may be symptomatic of whooping cough vaccine can also occur naturally[340] and it was aware of "no clinical tests which could distinguish the one from the other".[341] In respect of its recommended strict liability scheme, Pearson stated that proof of causation under the scheme "could pose problems for the courts".[342] It was suggested that the standard of proof should be that of the balance of probabilities and that case law would no doubt "develop on this *difficult*

335 Brazier, *Medicine, Patients and the Law* (2nd edn., Harmondsworth, Penguin, 1992), 187. Drugs which are not vaccines which also benefit the community are those used in the treatment of tuberculosis, e.g. strepotomycin.

336 Pearson, n. 19 above, para. 1489; Dworkin, n. 20 above, 332.

337 Dworkin, n. 20 above, 332. As is noted by Cane: "[w]hy do 356 vaccine damaged children have a better claim to financial support than other disabled children?" In the Pearson Report, the following two paragraphs raise more questions than they answer: "1406 . . . We do not think it is right to try to distinguish one severely disabled child from another, and to produce a situation where two children have the same needs, but one is compensated and the other is not. We decided, therefore, that vaccine-damaged children should be considered with other severely disabled children, irrespective of the cause of disablement . . . 1407 . . . For those children who can be shown to have been victims of vaccine damage, we consider that there is a case for an additional remedy in the field of tort": P. Cane, *Atiyah's Accidents Compensation and the Law* (4th edn., London, Weidenfeld and Nicolson, 1987), 149. *A fortiori*, they appear to contradict each other.

338 Pearson, n. 19 above, para. 1408.

339 *Ibid*., para. 1413.

340 "[I]respective of the cause, infants frequently develop convulsions for the first time in the first two years of life. By chance some of these will occur shortly after a child has been vaccinated and will be wrongly attributed to the vaccine": Department of Health and Social Security, *Whooping Cough Vaccine: Review of the Evidence on Whooping Cough Vaccination by the Joint Committee on Vaccination and Immunisation* (London, HMSO, 1977), para. 47.

341 Pearson, n. 19 above, para. 1411.

342 *Ibid*.

matter".[343] This approach should be borne in mind in the light of the fact that Pearson rejected the proposals for no- fault compensation for medical accidents due to difficulties in establishing causation.[344] In practice, the difficulty would be that of "distinguishing medical accident from the natural progression of a disease or injury, and from a foreseeable side effect of treatment".[345]

(ii) Analysis of the 1979 Act

On the recommendations of the Pearson Commission, the Vaccine Damage Payments Act 1979 was passed to establish a no-fault compensation scheme in the United Kingdom for vaccine-damaged persons for death/severe disablement[346] caused on a balance of probabilities[347] by vaccination against diphtheria, tetanus, whooping cough, poliomyelitis, measles, rubella, tuberculosis, smallpox and any other disease specified by the Secretary of State by statutory instrument.[348] The Secretary of State must be satisfied that a person was severely disabled as a result of vaccine damage[349] and that certain conditions of entitlement of section 2 are fulfilled. The claimant must have been vaccinated when he or she was under 18 except in the cases of rubella or poliomyelitis,[350] and the Act applies to protect an unborn child whose mother has been so vaccinated.[351] If a causal link is established and disablement suffered is 80 per cent or more[352] a lump sum of £30,000 is awarded.[353]

(iii) Vaccine Damage Tribunal

Of particular relevance to causation is section 4(2)(b), which provides for review of the question whether the vaccination caused the disablement by reference to an independent tribunal by the Secretary of State. The compensation system of the 1979 Act has been severely criticised as having been the result of a "disturbing ad hoc, politically-motivated approach to compensation issues".[354]

343 Pearson, n. 19 above, para. 1411. Emphasis added.

344 *Ibid.*, paras. 1364–5, 1371.

345 *Ibid.*, para. 1365.

346 Vaccine Damage Payments Act 1979, s. 1(1).

347 S. 3(5).

348 S. 1(2).

349 S. 1(1).

350 S. 2(1),(6).

351 S. 1(3).

352 S. 1(4).

353 The original lump sum was £10,000 but this was raised to £20,000 by The Vaccine Damage Payments Act 1979 Statutory Sum Order 1985 (SI 1985 No. 1249) which came into operation on 16 Aug. 1985. The lump sum was again raised to £30,000 by The Vaccine Damage Payments Act 1979 Statutory Sum Order 1991 (SI 1991 No. 939) which came into operation on 15 Apr. 1991.

354 Cane, n. 337 above, 149. It is erroneously posited by Cane, *Atiyah's Accidents Compensation and the Law* (5th edn., London, Butterworths, 1993), 92, that the main beneficiary of a

Under the Vaccine Damage Payments Act 1979 proof of causation remains necessary and indeed difficult. The onus of showing the causal link is not expressly discussed in the Act but the standard of proof is the balance of probabilities.[355] One of the Act's principal deficiencies is that the onus appears to be on the claimant even when vaccination and disability are not disputed.[356]

The test of a "balance of probability" has several consequences.[357] The Vaccine Damage Payments Tribunal may deny most claimants on the basis of inability to prove causation. Also, if the evidence is accepted in a too relaxed manner the claimants may be satisfied, but this may go beyond the authority of the Act. If separate civil proceedings are brought for full compensation,[358] then if causation has been admitted for one purpose it would appear ridiculous for the Department of Health to deny compensation in the civil proceedings since they would be admitting that the Act was being administered too liberally.[359] Also, the system appears ultimately unfair on the victim's part "[i]f the Vaccine Damage Tribunal . . . says '[o]n the balance of probabilities we are satisfied that there is a claim' and awards £20,000,[360] [and] you then go to a court which, with tremendous care, looks at all the medical evidence again which presumably the Vaccine Damage Tribunal did, and says 'No, it did not cause it . . . ' ".[361] If more

vaccination is not a child himself but other younger children with whom the child comes into contact, since whooping cough is most dangerous when transmitted to very young babies prior to the normal vaccination age. By the time a child is vaccinated, Cane submits, it is normally past the age when the disease could be fatal so that vaccinated children are being used for the benefit of young babies. However, the correct position is in fact that a child is given three injections administered at 1–2 months intervals beginning at the age of 1½ to 3 months. The fourth dose is given when the child is about 1½ years and a booster dose is given before entry to school: Imnemann, "Bordetella", Sect. 5 in Weatherall, Ledingham and Warrell, *Oxford Textbook of Medicine* (2nd edn., Oxford, Oxford Medical Publications, 1987), 241. It is submitted that these injections are not administered to babies past the age when the disease could be fatal since the disease could be fatal at any period up to the age of six months. Moreover, infective complications can emerge right up till the age of two years, e.g. acute bronchopneumonia or chronic ear infections leading to deafness.

355 S. 3(5).

356 Gamble, "Vaccine Damage Payments Act 1979" (1979) 36 *Scolag. Bull.* 136, 138.

357 Dworkin, n. 20 above, 334, 335.

358 The Act permits a separate civil action in respect of disablement to be raised (s. 6(4)), amounting to a *de facto* recognition of the inadequacy of the Act's lump sum. Cf the US legislation, 42 USC 300aa–11(2)(A), *barring* civil actions after 1 Oct. 1988, *unless* a petition is filed for the compensation programme and the US Claims Court has issued a judgment on such a petition, a person elects to file a civil action (under 42 USC 300aa–21(a)) and such a person elects to *withdraw* the compensation programme petition (under 42 USC 300aa–21(b)). If a person elects to receive compensation under a court judgment in respect of the US legislation such a person may *not* bring a civil action for damages against the vaccine manufacturer for a vaccine related injury or death for which the judgment was entered: 42 USC 300aa–21(a).

359 Dworkin, n. 20 above, 335.

360 Now £30,000; see above.

361 See Prof. Gerald Dworkin's comments in Dworkin, "The Impact of the Product Liability Directive upon Medicine and Pharmacy" (1987) 55(1) *Med. Leg. J* 25, 40. In *Kinnear* v. *DHHS* (unreported) (see above), Counsel for the child, Julian Priest QC, stated that it was illogical for Stuart-Smith J (as he then was) to have to try the issue whether the vaccine caused the damage when the Vaccine Damage Tribunal had proceeded on the assumption that it could do so. However, it was clear that the fact that such an award was made could not pre-empt Stuart-Smith J's decision: see Legal Correspondent, "The Law Tries to Decide whether Whooping Cough Vaccine Causes Brain

probably than not the adverse drug reaction was caused by the vaccine, the burden of proof is discharged "but, if the probabilities are equal, it is not".[362] It has been stated that if the convulsions and brain damage occur soon after vaccination then unless there is persuasive evidence of a contrary cause the claim will be accepted.[363] Such a temporal relationship was sufficient for the Vaccine Damage Tribunal to establish a causal link between the vaccine and the brain damage in *Bonthrone* v. *Millan*, but this was rejected in the Court of Session by Lord Jauncey.[364] Lord Wells-Pestell noted that "[a]t the other end of the spectrum there will be cases in which there is strong evidence pointing to a congenital condition or some other cause, or in which the symptoms have first shown themselves a long time after vaccination".[365] Most cases will fall between the strong temporal relationship case and the other case. Thus the proximity of the vaccination to the adverse event is "crucial" in determining causation.[366]

(iv) Tribunal Results

It appears that the "greatest of all problems at tribunal level" has been causation.[367] The failure rates are high. By 1984, only 13 per cent of initial determinations produced successful awards. Of those claims which were rejected, half went to appeal and in 72 per cent of the appeals the appeal was rejected.[368] Success rates seemed to vary from 39 per cent in Manchester to 12 per cent in Belfast.[369] Such variations reflect divisions of medical opinion as to the frequency of the occurrence of vaccine damage, but it indicates that many physicians accepted the phenomenon of vaccine-induced brain damage which they would assess in individual claims relating to such a condition.[370]

Table 1 provides an analysis of the most recent decisions of the Vaccine Damage Tribunals in the years 1989–93.[371] On the basis that:

Damage. Professor Gordon Stewart Gives Evidence" (1986) 292 *BMJ* 1264, 1265–6. Under the US legislation, the Vaccine Injury Table, a finding of fact or conclusion of law of the US Court of Federal Claims or of a Special Master, and the final judgment of the US Court of Federal Claims and subsequent appellate review shall be inadmissible at any stage in any civil proceedings: 42 USC 300aa–23(e).

362 *Per* Denning J (as he then was) in *Miller* v. *Minister of Pensions* [1947] 2 All ER 372, 374.

363 See Lord Wells-Pestell in HL Debs., vol. 399 cols. 306–7 (Second Reading).

364 [1985] The Lancet 1137, 1137–8.

365 HL Debs., vol. 399, cols. 306–7.

366 Jones, "Vaccine Damage Payments Act 1979" [1979] *Current Law Statutes Annotated.*

367 Lee, n. 29 above, 53.

368 Hansard HC, vol. 19, 2 Mar. 1982, col. 123.

369 Newdick, "Strict Liability for Defective Drugs in the Pharmaceutical Industry" (1985) 101 *LQR* 405, 429–30.

370 Lee, n. 29 above, 54.

371 I am grateful to the Fylde Benefits and War Pensions Directorate, Norcross, Blackpool, for use of these figures.

$$\frac{\text{Rate of Reversal}}{\text{at Tribunal}} = \frac{\text{No. of Decisions not to make a payment reversed by tribunal}}{\text{Total no. of decisions at tribunal}}$$

$$= \frac{R}{U + R}$$

$$\text{The rate of reversal at Tribunal} = \frac{15}{92}$$

$$= 16\%$$

Thus in the years 1989–93 the percentage of appeals rejected rose to 84 per cent. Success rates now seem to vary even more widely, from 0 per cent in Liverpool, Wales and Northern Ireland to 50 per cent in Newcastle. However, caution should be used with such figures since the numbers are generally so small. The highest numbers of cases are in London where the success rate is 6/38, i.e. 16 per cent. Scotland's success rate is 2/12, i.e. 17 per cent and these would appear to conform to a general pattern. Liverpool (0/11) seems, however, to be particularly against the tide. The overall success rate (ratio of awards to total

Table 1: Decisions of Vaccine Damage Tribunals, 1989–1993

Year		*1989*	*1990*	*1991*	*1992*	*1993*	*Total*
Region							
Scotland	U	1	2	3	2	2	10
	R	0	0	1	0	1	2
Wales	U	0	1	1	1	2	5
	R	0	0	0	0	0	0
Northern	U	0	1	0	1	0	2
Ireland	R	0	0	0	0	0	0
London	U	3	4	5	12	8	32
	R	0	0	1	2	3	6
Birmingham	U	2	1	1	1	0	5
	R	0	0	2	0	0	2
Liverpool	U	0	5	2	2	2	11
	R	0	0	0	0	0	0
Newcastle	U	1	0	0	1	0	2
	R	1	1	0	0	0	2
Leeds	U	1	1	2	3	3	10
	R	0	0	0	2	1	3
Total	U	8	15	14	23	17	77
	R	1	1	4	4	5	15

N.B.: U = Decision not to make a payment Upheld by tribunal
R = Decision not to make a payment Reversed by tribunal
Source: Fylde Benefits and War Pensions Directorate

claims) runs at 24 per cent, which takes account of decisions made by the Secretary of State and Tribunals.[372] These low compensation levels can be contrasted with the American compensation programme, utilising the Vaccine Injury Table to presume causal link. As has already been noted, by 7 September 1994, 32 per cent of retrospective petitions decided by the Federal Claims Court were compensatable and 44 per cent of prospective petitions were compensatable.[373] The US programme is clearly more successful in terms of favourable claims than the Vaccine Damage Payments Act 1979 but the question arises of the distinctly large levels of over-compensation in the USA. One cannot, however, ignore the potential for regional variations in the UK at the tribunal level, such as between Liverpool (0 per cent success rate) and London (16 per cent success rate) and Newcastle (50 per cent success rate).[374] The number of cases in Newcastle appear, however, to be too small to be of statistical significance.[375] In contrast to the Vaccine Injury Table, the Vaccine Damage Payments Act 1979 has appeared to do nothing to ameliorate difficulties in proving causation. That, and its low level of award, only given to children of severe disability[376] has led to considerable dismay regarding the Tribunal's operation. It may well be the case that if the programme was paid for by taxes on the pharmaceutical companies, as in the USA, that success rates and compensation payments might be higher. This remains to be proved, however. It has been said that the decision in *Loveday* v. *Renton* that pertussis vaccine does not cause brain damage "has plunged the vaccine damage scheme into even greater disarray".[377] To what extent the *Best* v. *Wellcome* decision will help to improve the situation remains a moot point, noting especially that the batch vaccine in *Best* was excessively potent and toxic.[378] *Best* could potentially be distinguished on this point alone.

[372] Lee, n. 29 above, 54. Cf Prof. Harlow's figures for the years 1988–93 which indicate that 282 claims were made, of which 28 (9.93%) were successful and 254 (90.07%) were rejected: Harlow, *Understanding Tort Law* (2nd edn., London, Fontana Press, 1995), 79.

[373] Mariner, n. 287 above, 118.

[374] However, when the Liverpool and London success rates are compared statistically the results are not statistically significant. The figures are:

Chi squared test
P = 0.16

Fisher exact test
P = 0.2 (i.e. a 1 in 5 chance that these results are due to chance,
which is not statistically significant)

I am grateful to Prof. Kenneth McColl, Department of Medicine and Therapeutics, University of Glasgow, for his assistance in obtaining these figures.

[375] 2 out of 4 cases.

[376] See above.

[377] Brazier, n. 335 above, 189.

[378] See above, and the observations of O'Flaherty J in *Best* [1994] 5 Med. LR 81, 105, in which he states that the batch vaccine was what would be termed in the USA as a "hot lot", i.e. one of excess potency and toxicity.

5. CONCLUSION

It appears that both the common law and statutory bases of vaccine damage and causation are beset with severe problems, principally due to the lack of scientific knowledge establishing general causation between a vaccine and an adverse reaction and also due to the lack of proof of a causal connection establishing specific causation in the case in issue. This has resulted in either the strict approach of the UK or Canadian courts, leading to a denial of liability in all cases that have come to trial, on the one hand, or the pragmatic but scientifically flawed casuistry of some American courts, particularly in the face of contrary epidemiological evidence. The significance for English law of the Irish decision in *Best* v. *Wellcome* remains uncertain when viewed in the light of *Loveday* v. *Renton*, although the IOM offers a glimmer of hope to the parents of brain damaged children administered with DPT in its recent report on chronic nervous system dysfunction, but only, it should be stressed, in the most exceptional circumstances.

The US National Childhood Vaccine Injury Act 1986 sails as close to the wind as possible in eliminating causation but, if the Vaccine Injury Table is subject to exceptions (as it must always be), then the legal position surrounding causation becomes contentious again. Also, the allegation that compensation may be awarded under the Act in some cases where there is no real causal link between the vaccine and the injury but where the Act's and the Table's requirements are satisfied remains a valid bone of contention. This is perhaps overshadowed by the Act's potential for providing the majority with an efficient compensation programme. The Vaccine Damage Payments Act 1979 in the UK does nothing, however, to ameliorate the causation problem as is witnessed by the universally poor success rates at Tribunal level.

Table 2: Vaccine Injury Table (USA)

Vaccine	Time Period for First Symptom or Manifestation of Onset or of Significant Aggravation After Vaccine Administration
I. DTP; P; DTP/polio combination or any other vaccine containing whole cell pertussis bacteria, extracted partial cell bacteria, or specific pertussis antigens(s), illness, disability, injury, or condition covered:	
A. Anaphylaxis or anaphylactic shock	24 hours
B. Encephalopathy (or encephalitis)	3 days
C. Shock-collapse or hypotonic-hyporesponsive collapse	3 days
D. Residual seizure disorder in accordance with subsection (b)(2)	3 days

Table 2: cont.

Vaccine	Time Period for First Symptom or Manifestation of Onset or of Significant Aggravation After Vaccine Administration
E. Any acute complication or sequela (including death) of an illness, disability, injury, or condition referred to above which illness, disability, injury, or condition arose within the time period prescribed	Not applicable
II. Measles, mumps, rubella, or any vaccine containing any of the foregoing as a component; DT; TD; or tetanus toxoid	
A. Anaphylaxis or anaphylactic shock	24 hours
B. Encephalopathy (or encephalitis)	15 days (for mumps, rubella, measles, or any vaccine containing any of the foregoing as a component) 3 days (for DT, Td, or tetanus toxoid)
C. Residual seizure disorder in accordance with subsection (b)(2)	15 days (for mumps, rubella, measles, or any vaccine containing any of the foregoing as a component) 3 days (for DT, Td, or tetanus toxoid)
D. Any acute complication or sequela (including death) of an illness, disability, injury, or condition referred to above which illness, disability, injury, or condition arose within the time period prescribed	Not applicable
III. Polio Vaccines (other than inactivated polio vaccine)	
A. Paralytic polio	
– in a non-immunodeficient recipient	30 days
– in an immunodeficient recipient	6 months
– in a vaccine-associated community case	Not applicable
B. Any acute complication or sequela (including death) of an illness, disability, injury, or condition referred to above which illness, disability, injury, or condition arose within the time period prescribed	Not applicable
IV. Inactivated Polio Vaccine	
A. Anaphylaxis or anaphylactic shock	24 hours
B. Any acute complication or sequela (including death) of an illness, disability, injury, or condition referred to above which illness, disability, injury, or condition arose within the time period prescribed	Not applicable

Source: 42 U.S.C. 300aa–14(a)

5

Causation, Medicinal Products and the "Gulf War Syndrome"[1]

1. INTRODUCTION

There has been much controversy surrounding the health consequences resulting from military service in the Persian Gulf War (1991). Nearly 700,000 US troops, (7 per cent of whom were female),[2] were sent to the Persian Gulf theatre for Operation Desert Shield (the build-up of US ground troops sent to the Southwest Asia theatre of operations) and Operation Desert Storm (the coalition air force attacking of Iraqi targets).[3] Of these, approximately 30,000 US veterans have had unexplained health complaints since their return.[4] 51,000 UK service personnel were involved in the Gulf War conflict, and of these 1,228 have complained of health consequences of their service.[5] Not all the Gulf War veterans saw active service, but even those who did not may have been involved through vaccination programmes, taking medicinal products for prevention of damage from nerve gas (NAPS),[6] or possible exposure to organophosphate pesticides. The health complaints of Gulf War veterans have been described as the "Gulf War Syndrome", but a major problem has been the provision of a case definition of this term. The syndrome has been described by the Institute of Medicine in its report, *Health Consequences of Service During the Persian Gulf War. Initial Findings and Recommendations for Immediate Action*[7] as a

[1] This chap. is an expanded version of two articles published by the author: R. Goldberg, "Medicinal Products and the 'Gulf War Syndrome'" (1995) 145 *NLJ* 1443 and R. Goldberg, "The House of Commons Defence Committee Report on the 'Gulf War Syndrome'" [1996] 5 *Expert Evidence* 54.

[2] Abou-Donia *et al.*, "Increased Neurotoxicity Following Concurrent Exposure to Pyridostigmine Bromide, DEET and Chlorpyrfos" (1996) 34 *Fundamental and Applied Toxicology* 201–22, 201.

[3] Institute of Medicine, *Health Consequences of Service During the Persian Gulf War. Initial Findings and Recommendations for Immediate Action* (Washington, DC, National Academy Press, 1995), 3.

[4] Abou-Donia, n. 2 above.

[5] House of Commons Defence Committee, Sixth Report, *Gulf War Illnesses: Latest Developments* (London, The Stationery Office, 1997), para. 73.

[6] *RCP Audit of Gulf War Medical Assessment Programme* (London, Royal College of Physicians, 1995), 1. NAPS is an acronym for nerve agent pre-treatment sets.

[7] Institute of Medicine, n. 3 above, 5. As a result of widespread public concern, two preliminary reports, one American and one British, were commissioned to assess the current situation and to suggest recommendations for further action. Under the US Persian Gulf War Veterans' Health Status Act 1992: PL 102–585, sect. 706 established an agreement between the Secretary of Veterans Affairs and the Secretary of Defence with the National Academy of Sciences for review of the

"complex of ill-defined and often poorly characterised symptoms and signs of illness",[8] such as pain in the muscles and joints, weakness, fatigue, headache, memory loss and other mental impairment.[9] Congenital defects have also been noted in the offspring of Gulf War veterans, ranging from Goldenhar Syndrome (oculo-auricular-vertebral dysplasia) to Down's Syndrome, to miscarriage to failure to thrive.

It is arguable that this so-called "Gulf War Syndrome" is clinically amorphous and not distinct. A case definition is hampered by the lack of any generally recognised probative physical signs or laboratory findings and by uncertainty whether the syndrome exists and, in the event of its existence, its incidence in Gulf War veterans.[10] In 1997, however, an attempt was made to analyse these symptoms by Haley and his colleagues. Of 249 Gulf War veterans in the USA, 175 (70 per cent) reported having had serious health problems which were analysed as six separate syndromes identified in 63 veterans (25 per cent).[11] The syndromes differed from post-traumatic stress, depression and malingering and appeared to reflect a spectrum of neurological injury involving central, peripheral and autonomic nervous systems. It seems that the Gulf War syndrome litigation has emerged as a direct result of health consequences suffered by troops in that war, with much emphasis on the possibility that it was the medical measures against chemical and biological warfare, possibly combined with vaccines, that caused the illnesses.

As previously noted, of the 51,000 UK service personnel who served in the Gulf, 1,228 Gulf War veterans have served notice of their intention to pursue a claim against the Ministry of Defence in respect of their illnesses.[12] Two firms of solicitors were awarded the legal aid contract to manage the generic work in respect of the claims by the Legal Aid Multi-Party Actions Committee.[13] However, an application for judicial review of the Committee's decision to award the contract has been recently allowed in the case of *Regina* v. *Legal Aid Board, ex parte Donne & Co. (a firm)*,[14] Ognall J stating that the public dimen-

existing scientific, medical and other information on the consequences of military service during the Persian Gulf War. An agreement was made requiring the National Academy of Sciences to submit a report on the results of the review carried out under the agreement, the report containing recommendations on whether there was a "sound scientific basis" for epidemiological studies on the health consequences of such military service and, if the recommendation was that such a sound scientific basis for such studies existed, the nature of such studies. The Report was published in mid-1995 and was entitled "Health Consequences of Service During the Persian Gulf War: Initial Findings and Recommendations for Immediate Action": *ibid.* Meanwhile, in the UK a Royal College of Physicians report, entitled *RCP Audit of Gulf War Medical Assessment Programme* was published: n. 6 above.

[8] *Ibid.*, 5.

[9] *Ibid.*, 24.

[10] *Ibid.*, 26.

[11] Haley, Kurt and Hom, "Is there a Gulf War Syndrome?: Searching for Syndromes by Factor Analysis of Symptoms" (1997) 277 *JAMA* 215–22.

[12] House of Commons Defence Committee,n. 5 above, para. 73.

[13] See Morton, "Gulf War Claims" (1995) 145 *NLJ* 1154.

[14] [1996] 3 All ER 1.

sions of the matter were of a quality which made it justiciable in public law. This decision has now resulted in a declaration that the contract is ineffectual and has raised concern about the length of time required to launch this litigation against the Ministry of Defence. The key issue, however, for the Gulf War veterans is compensation. The reason causation is the central problem in such cases is that a causal link between the illness and service in the Gulf War is necessary to establish liability in negligence against the Ministry of Defence.

2. POSSIBLE CAUSES

Possible agents of the so-called mystery illness, the "Gulf War Syndrome" have been identified, including organophosphate pesticides,[15] the exposure of personnel to chemical/biological weapons,[16] the vaccination programmes used, the medication taken for the prevention of damage caused by nerve gas (NAPS), e.g. pyridostigmine bromide, and insect repellants (e.g. DEET).[17] In addition, there was the problem of the stress and psychological trauma associated with all such conflicts.[18] What has become abundantly clear, however, is that the scope and nature of the health problems of servicemen in the Gulf is as yet not completely ascertained.[19] Indeed, the then Surgeon General, Vice-Admiral Revel, has even declared that no evidence has emerged that any organic disorder has been more prevalent in Gulf War veterans than in any similar population, over a period of four years:[20] but this now appears to have been possibly outdated in the light of more recent evidence of human epidemiological studies and human and experimental animal data, which are presented in the Appendix.[21]

In October 1995, the House of Commons Defence Committee produced a report on the Gulf War Syndrome[22] (the Eleventh Report 1995), which was particularly critical of the Ministry of Defence. It first reviewed the possible causes, ruling out burning oil wells, uranium and chemical/biological weapons. The focus, however, was on medical counter-biological and chemical warfare measures, particularly when combined with vaccines.[23]

[15] See below.

[16] E.g. Sarin. See below.

[17] N. 6 above, 1.

[18] *Ibid.*

[19] Institute of Medicine, n. 3 above, 1.

[20] Revell, "The Gulf War Syndrome" (1995) 310 *BMJ* 1073. It has also been noted that although 2,000 Gulf War veterans died, since 700,000 US troops served in the Gulf the expected numbers of deaths for that age and sex group would be in fact 3,000. Thus it would seem, says Wessely, that the Gulf War veterans are actually healthier than the average citizen: Wessely, "What is this Mystery Illness which We Call Gulf War Syndrome?" *The Times*, 27 July 1995. However, it is submitted that this is an illogical conclusion, since mortality rate over such a short period is not a total indicator of health or non-health.

[21] See below.

[22] House of Commons Defence Committee, Eleventh Report, *Gulf War Syndrome* (London, HMSO, 1995).

[23] *Ibid.*, paras. 3, 7.

(i) Vaccines

The reason for the administration of vaccines in the Gulf War was the fear of anthrax and botulism.[24] The problem associated with vaccines was the fact that there was thought to be no restriction on the number of vaccines administered, and that they were often given in multiple combinations.[25] The effects associated with such vaccines were and remain unclear. Although the Institute of Medicine ("IOM") concluded that there was no evidence that vaccines caused non-specific complaints associated with service during the Gulf War,[26] the House of Commons Defence Committee observed that it was impossible to rule out with certainty whether the "cocktail" of drugs given to service personnel was the cause of the Gulf Veterans chronic symptoms.[27] In addition, the Eleventh Report stated that the problem was exacerbated by the Ministry of Defence's failure to consider the staggering of antibiological warfare vaccinations to reduce the incidence of side-effects and the fact that there was a failure to record vaccinations in the Gulf and then to transfer them onto the veterans' individual medical records.[28]

Importantly, the House of Commons Eleventh Report indicates that the French armed forces received no vaccinations against chemical/biological agents both before or during the Gulf conflict and there are no reported cases among French Gulf War veterans of Gulf War Syndrome.[29] The question emerges how statistically significant that information is when viewed in the light of other coalition forces, particularly the UK and US, which both demonstrate symptoms of the Gulf War Syndrome.

Anthrax vaccine was given involuntarily and no chronic sequelae have been reported.[30] A botulinum toxoid vaccine was taken by the US Marine Corps, the US Army VII Corps and the First Marine Division. This vaccine was given on voluntary basis with informed consent and had the status of an investigational new drug (IND) by the US Food and Drug Administration (FDA). Again, no chronic sequelae have been reported in respect of this vaccine.[31] It is clear that British soldiers were also given these vaccines and it may also be the case that British soldiers were attached to the American units which were administered the botulinum toxoid vaccine, and may have received the latter vaccine.

[24] Institute of Medicine, n. 3 above, 54.

[25] Minutes of Evidence taken before the Defence Committee, 1 Feb. 1995, Q705, in House of Commons Defence Committee, Eleventh Report, *Gulf War Syndrome*, n. 22 above.

[26] Institute of Medicine, n. 3 above, 56.

[27] House of Commons Defence Committee, Eleventh Report, n. 22 above, para. 53.

[28] *Ibid.*, paras. 48, 58.

[29] *Ibid.*, para. 36.

[30] Although UK soldiers who were given anthrax injections were also given pertussis vaccine as research indicated that it enhanced the effectiveness of the anthrax vaccine: Evans, "Minister Promises Fresh Start in Effort to Uncover the Truth," *The Times*, 13 May 1997.

[31] Institute of Medicine, n. 3 above, 54–5.

What also seems to be of major import is the number of *other* vaccines administered to military personnel and their possible effect on the soldiers in combination with the two vaccines already cited. Seven vaccines were administered during basic training to army recruits and all active duty personnel received one other vaccine, amounting to eight vaccines, together with boosters to two of the basic training immunisations. In addition, seven other vaccines were given for deployment to high-risk areas and to alert forces (as required by the host country or as directed by the Surgeon General). Thus potentially 17 different vaccines may well have been given to service members and this "antigenic load" has been described as "considerable".[32] However, the IOM noted the larger number of antigens given to employees (up to 75 cc) at Fort Detrick, Maryland. These people were studied over 15 years and no evidence appeared of immune-associated illness.[33] The IOM Committee concluded that there was "no evidence that vaccines in general cause[d] non-specific complaints associated with service during Operation Desert Storm".[34]

However, doubts remain whether the vaccines are causally linked to the veterans' illnesses. The Royal College of Physicians audit sharply criticised both the paucity and quality of the vaccination records that it had seen and recommended an expert immunological assessment of long-term damage to immune systems following vaccination.[35]

(ii) Pyridostigmine Bromide, Organophosphate Pesticides and Insect Repellants

Individual troops were given pyridostigmine bromide (PB) pills as a prophylactic to the threat of nerve agent exposure. The IOM has noted that there has been no documented long-term side-effects, but other frequent side-effects have been present such as nausea, vomiting, diarrhoea, abdominal cramps, increased peristalsis (bowel activity), increased salivation, bronchial secretions, miosis, and diaphoresis.[36]

However, questions still remain surrounding the role of PB as a possible causal agent. It seems that it is possible that the dose (30 mg, three times a day) was not adequately tested in some cases, and that there is also the chance of drug interactions occurring in women on birth control pills.[37] There is also the role

[32] *Ibid.*, 55.

[33] *Ibid.*

[34] *Ibid.*, 56. There is no evidence, it appears, linking vaccines with long-term problems such as chronic fatigue syndrome: Wessely, n. 20 above.

[35] N. 6 above, 4. The Royal College of Physicians also noted (*ibid.*) that it provided no investigation of reports of pregnancy failures and birth defects in children of Gulf War veterans because it was outside its remit and competence, although it is arguable that such remit should be extended to address these important issues.

[36] Institute of Medicine, n. 3 above, 57.

[37] *Ibid.*, 57–8.

of possible conditions contraindicated to PB such as asthma, peptic ulcer disease, liver disease, kidney disease or hypersensitivity to PB, although it can be assumed that other than hypersensitivity, few of these conditions would be present in troops on active duty. There is, in addition, the possibility of a synergistic reaction between PB, organophosphate pesticides and insect repellant DEET applied to the skin or impregnated on clothing. Each of these chemicals, PB, organophosphate pesticides and DEET insect repellant is a acetylcholinesterase inhibitor, which has been shown to produce neuropathological changes in hens and rats. Human epidemiological studies and experimental human and animal studies have implicated these drugs and chemicals in possible nerve damage of Gulf War veterans (see Appendix). Other medicinal products conceivably may increase the risk of side-effects of PB. For example, the use of beta blockers could cause further reduction in cardiac output and blood pressure, medication causing vasodilation may be responsible for lightheaded feelings or syncope and the use of antimalarial medications along with PB could result in diarrhoea.[38] There has been no uniformly accepted evidence of a causal link between the use of PB and the illnesses in the Gulf War, but the Eleventh Report severely criticised the fact that it took 12 years to license PB finally in August 1993.[39]

Dr Graham Pearson, Director General of the Chemical Biological Defence Establishment, when questioned by the Defence Committee, suggested that no evidence existed in the USA or UK to propose the need to carry out further work into possible side-effects from PB.[40] However, this seems to ignore the possibility of a synergistic reaction between the concurrent exposure to PB, pesticides and insect repellant-impregnated clothing and other drugs, increasing the risk of PB side-effects.[41]

3. EPIDEMIOLOGICAL EVIDENCE

The Eleventh Report is unambiguous in its support for an epidemiological study of the health of Gulf War veterans, in which they would be compared to a matched group of military personnel who did not serve in the Gulf.[42] It indicated that the Medical Assessment Programme established by the Ministry of Defence had not been publicised, which had the effect of reducing the possible numbers needed for establishing reliable epidemiological evidence.[43] The fact that not much more than half of the veterans involved in the litigation at the time of the Eleventh Report had undergone a medical assessment emphasised the lack of data on which to base epidemiological studies.[44]

[38] Institute of Medicine, n. 3 above, 58–9.

[39] House of Commons Defence Committee, Eleventh Report, n. 22 above, para. 39.

[40] Minutes of Evidence taken before the Defence Committee, 1 Feb. 1995, Q752 in House of Commons Defence Committee, Eleventh Report, n. 22 above.

[41] Institute of Medicine, n. 3 above, 58–9.

[42] House of Commons Defence Committee, Eleventh Report, n. 22 above, para. 26.

[43] *Ibid.*, para. 11.

[44] *Ibid.*, para. 20.

The Eleventh Report severely criticised the Ministry of Defence for the time delay (four years) before it even contemplated compiling the data necessary to help establish an epidemiological study.[45] It also emphasised the need for sufficient resources to be placed in the proposed epidemiological study.[46] It will be undertaken by the Defence Medical Services Directorate (DMSD) and the Defence Analytical Services Agency (DASA). Significantly, the Defence Committee has also recommended the need for a follow-up study to be performed by an independent body. The Defence Committee recommended that information on the health of children be collected as part of the above epidemiological study. Clearly there will be a need to compare the information on children of military personnel who did not serve in the Gulf with those children of military personnel who did.[47]

The IOM has emphasised the need for epidemiological studies to provide a broader view of the collection of studies to date[48] recommending research on specific exposures likely to adversely affect the reproductive health of men/women both at the time of exposure and after such time of exposure.[49] The need for control studies in this area has also been suggested[50] since the issue of reproductive health outcomes has received limited scientific attention and has not shown any incidences of birth defects greater than that expected.[51] This is of particular importance, bearing in mind the fact that 7 per cent of the 700,000 US force were women.[52]

[45] *Ibid.*, para. 28.

[46] *Ibid.*

[47] House of Commons Defence Committee, Eleventh Report, n. 22 above, paras. 28, 31.

[48] Institute of Medicine, n. 3 above, 11–12.

[49] *Ibid.*, 14.

[50] *Ibid.*, 14–15.

[51] *Ibid.*, 37. Two studies were discussed in the IOM report. First, the Mississippi cluster study, evaluating 54 birth outcomes of the Army Reserve Unit of Waynesboro, Miss., and those of the Army Surgeon General regarding major and minor birth defects of active duty personnel in all army hospitals between 1985–93. Both sets of incidences of major and minor defects appeared unelevated from expected rates but two qualifications were noted by the IOM. First, only births in the army hospitals to active duty women or the spouses of active duty service members were included, and the data only reflect the birth defects recognised at the time of discharge after birth (2–3 days). Thus the data fail to record minor malformations and conditions detected later in infancy. Secondly, the Department of Defence study reviews have noted that births to active duty personnel outside the Department of Defence hospitals were not included in the Department of Defence database. In addition, infertility and miscarriages were not included in the database, leaving the present figures open to doubt: *ibid.*, 37–8.

[52] Abou-Donia *et al.*, n. 2 above. "Gulf War Babies", a BBC Panorama programmme, 25 Sept. 1995, considered the causation of congenital defects in Gulf War veteran children. 151 birth defects in such children were found by Betty Mecdeci, who had made a similar study of children of Vietnam veterans. She found 10 cases of Goldenhaar Syndrome, three times the expected prevalence. Excessive atmospheric lead after the Iraquis set fire to the Kuwaiti oil fields was suggested as a possible cause by Ellen Silbergeld, University of Maryland, an expert in lead intoxication. Mustard gas contamination, a potent chromosomal toxin, was also suggested as another potential cause.

4. HOUSE OF COMMONS DEFENCE COMMITTEE: SIXTH REPORT (1997), GULF WAR ILLNESSES: LATEST DEVELOPMENTS

In March 1997, the House of Commons Defence Committee reported on the latest developments concerning Gulf War Illnesses (the Sixth Report (1997)),[53] which reveals the increasing importance being attached to the role of epidemiological studies in attempting to throw light on the illnesses suffered by over 1,000 UK Gulf War veterans, around 200 of whom have hitherto eluded diagnosis.[54] The Committee welcomed the establishment of such studies. It believed that causal research deserved a higher priority. Such research was regarded as "worthwhile in its own right"[55] and the Committee noted that American research indicated the high toxicity of the combination of nerve agent pretreatment sets (NAPS) (containing pyridostigmine bromide) and organophosphate pesticides, work which has now been replicated in a number of other countries. It observed evidence of neurological damage, resulting from exposure to organophosphate pesticides found in the UK and USA and recommended further research in the fields of neurology and immunology.[56] It affirmed the importance of recent studies in the University of Texas, which have identified six different illness syndromes which "appear to reflect a spectrum of neurological injury involving the central, peripheral and autonomic nervous systems".[57] Epidemiological evidence was reckoned to support the hypothesis that wartime exposure to combinations of organophosphates (acetylcholinesterase inhibitors),[58] other acetylcholinesterase inhibiting chemicals (e.g. PB) and DEET (an insect repellant rubbed on skin of Gulf War service personnel), produced such variants of chronic conditions in Gulf War veterans.[59]

However, David, Ferry and Wessely have criticised the Texas research, claiming that it is "hypothesis generating, rather than hypothesis testing".[60] In addition, this view of the possible causal link between these chemicals and Gulf War illnesses was not supported by the US Presidential Advisory Committee, which

[53] House of Commons Defence Committee, Sixth Report, n. 5 above.

[54] *Ibid.*, para. 11.

[55] *Ibid.*

[56] *Ibid.*, para. 11.

[57] Haley, Kurt and Hom, "Is there a Gulf War Syndrome? Searching for Syndromes by Factor Analysis of Symptoms" (1997) 277 *JAMA* 215, as cited in House of Commons Defence Committee, Sixth Report, n. 5 above, para. 14.

[58] *Acetyl choline* is a very important nerve transmitter across junctions of nerves (at ganglions) or across the junction between nerve and muscle. *Acetylcholinesterase* is an enzyme which inactivates acetyl choline, thus controlling the action. *Acetylcholinesterase inhibitors* inhibit the effect of acetyl-cholinesterase, thus prolonging the effect of acetyl choline. Organophosphates, pyridostigmine bromide (PB), DEET (insect repellant) are all acetylcholinesterase inhibitors.

[59] Haley and Kurt, "Self-reported Exposure to Neurotoxic Chemical Combinations in the Gulf War" (1997) 277 *JAMA* 231, 236, as cited in House of Commons Defence Committee, Sixth Report, n. 5 above, para. 14.

[60] David, Ferry and Wessely, Editorial, "Gulf War Illnesses: New American Research Provides Leads but not Firm Conclusions" (1997) 314 *BMJ* 239, 240.

has suggested the need for further research.[61] Attributing causal link between organophosphate pesticides and current illnesses has been obfuscated by the passage of six years since the Gulf War, and the fact that the services did not apparently know the quantities of pesticides taken to the Gulf "let alone used there".[62]

The contrast between French forces serving in the Gulf and those of the US and UK revealed that the French somehow avoided any after-effects. It was noted that this could provide a useful control for the epidemiological studies.[63]

In respect of the award of compensation, the Defence Committee was sympathetic to Gulf War veterans.[64] Mr Edgar Buckley, the Assistant Under-Secretary of State (Home and Overseas), giving evidence before the Defence Committee, stated in relation to war disability pensions that "British veterans do not have to prove that any disability from which they are suffering is attributable to their military service".[65] The burden of proof is on the government to disprove that it is attributable to their military service. This burden remains with the government for seven years after the end of service. Veterans can also sue for damages where causation and negligence can be shown.[66]

The Defence Committee observed that the 1,228 notices of intention would be likely to be "settled in the courts".[67] The Committee considered other suggestions for compensation, including a no-fault compensation approach, *ex gratia* payments by the Department of Social Security and the Inland Revenue and the establishment of a special fund, similar to that set up for hæmophiliac HIV victims. However, the Committee concluded that the lack of evidence of causation in Gulf War veterans and the varieties of their illnesses, which was not a problem in the HIV litigation, meant that the special fund approach was inappropriate.[68]

The Committee was concerned about the lack of a definite link between the exposure to chemicals and the illnesses, and the time that it would take to establish such definite causation. Because of the widespread use of organophosphate pesticides and the appreciation of their potential dangers to health, it suggested that Gulf War veterans who can establish that they were exposed to

[61] House of Commons Defence Committee, Sixth Report, n. 5 above, Written Evidence, 50; *ibid.*, para. 14.

[62] *Ibid.*, para. 41.

[63] *Ibid.*, para. 16. Dr Goram Jamal has confirmed in discussions on 23 Apr. 1997 that he was assured that the French contingent was not exposed to organophosphates, pesticides, pyridostigmine bromide tablets and DEET insect repellant, which could explain the difference. Further, it was situated further west on the battlefront, which made it less likely to be exposed to SARIN (another organophosphate) in Iraqui bunkers and released after US bombardment: personal communication from Dr Goram Jamal.

[64] *Ibid.*, para. 73.

[65] Minutes of Evidence, Q1242, in House of Commons Defence Committee, Sixth Report, n. 5 above.

[66] *Ibid.*, Q1243.

[67] House of Commons Defence Committee, Sixth Report, n. 5 above, para. 73.

[68] *Ibid.*, para. 73; Minutes of Evidence, Q1243, in House of Commons Defence Committee, Sixth Report, n. 5 above.

organophosphate pesticides and for whom there is no other explanation of current illnesses, have a strong case for *ex gratia* compensation. It recommended that the government make such payments.[69] However, it is arguable that any such *ex gratia* payment could also relate to those administered PB tablets and insect repellant DEET, since they all share the same common mechanism, i.e. that of acetylcholinesterase inhibitors.

5. CONCLUSION

Lack of epidemiological evidence remains a considerable problem for plaintiffs in establishing causal link in the Gulf War Syndrome cases. New evidence, *viz.* human and experimental animal studies, may change this blurred picture.

This new evidence, coupled with the American evidence of such neurological damage resulting from exposure to organophosphate pesticides and the related epidemiological evidence, may add strength to the legal arguments of Gulf War veterans in their attempt to establish factual causation. The Ministry of Defence has accepted that it will carry out the recommendation of the House of Commons Defence Committee that further epidemiological follow-up studies by an independent body will take place.[70]

The Defence Committee's view that the difficulties of proof of causation and widespread use of organophosphate pesticides in the Gulf merited *ex gratia* compensation for those exposed to organophosphates may help to resolve some of the inequities of the current situation.

This case study is still unfinished,[71] but the problems involved in it are illustrative of the central importance of causation in cases involving medicinal products and litigation.

APPENDIX: HUMAN AND ANIMAL STUDIES RELEVANT TO CAUSATION IN GULF WAR SYNDROME (GWS)

Human Studies

1. 14 Gulf War veterans (UK), randomly selected from a list of 40, each with GWS, were compared with a group of 13 healthy civilian control subjects matched for age, gender, handedness (right or left) and physical activity. The

[69] *Ibid.*, para. 77.

[70] House of Commons Defence Committee, Sixth Report, n. 5 above, Annex, p. xxix.

[71] The incoming Labour government has now committed itself to "substantial . . . resources" for additional research into the possible damaging combination of multiple vaccines and NAPS. This will be in the form of an internal Ministry of Defence project: McGrory, "Ministers Order an MoD About-turn on Gulf War Syndrome", *The Times*, 12 May 1997; Evans, "Minister Promises Fresh Start in Effort to Uncover the Truth", *The Times*, 13 May 1997.

GWS group showed significant abnormalities in peripheral nerve function when compared to the control group.[72]

2. Of 249 Gulf War veterans of the USA, 175 (70 per cent) reported having had serious health problems which were analysed as six separate syndromes identified in 63 veterans (25 per cent). The syndromes differed from post-traumatic stress, depression and malingering, and appeared to reflect "a spectrum of neurological injury, involving the central, peripheral and autonomic nervous systems".[73]
3. The authors Haley and Kurt, in a further epidemiological study,[74] were able to correlate three of these syndromes with self-responsed (by memory recall) exposure to neurotoxic chemical combinations of anticholinesterase inhibitors, such as pyridostigmine bromide and the insect repellant DEET (Diethyl-toluamide).

Animal Studies

1. Friedman *et al.*[75] reported that simulated stress in mice (by forced swim protocol) caused enhancement of pyridostigmine passage through the blood-brain barrier, as tested by reduced activity of mouse brain acetylcholinesterase activity. Such stress could be relevant to Gulf War veterans.
2. Abou-Donia *et al.*[76] treated hens with pyridostigmine bromide, DEET insect repellant and the organophosphate insecticide chlorpyrifos. The chemicals were administered either singly or in combination. There were increases of inhibition of brain acetylcholinesterase, neurological dysfunction and neuropathological lesions in the combined treatment groups compared to those given single chemicals.
3. Hubert and Lison[77] compared the effect of pyridostigmine bromide on resting and exercising[78] rats. Exercise significantly increased biochemical changes associated with muscle damage in these rats. Such exercise-induced differences may be relevant to Gulf War veterans.

[72] Jamal, Hansen, Apartopoulos and Pede, "The 'Gulf War Syndrome', Is there Evidence of Dysfunction in the Nervous System?" (1996) 60 *J Neurology, Neurosurgery and Psychiatry* 449–51.

[73] Haley, Kurt and Hom, n. 57 above, in particular 215.

[74] Haley and Kurt, n. 59 above, 231–7.

[75] Friedman, Kaufer, Shemer, Hendler, Soreq, and Tur-Kaspa, "Pyridostigmine Brain Penetration under Stress Enhances Neuronal Excitability and Induces Early Immediate Transcriptional Response" (1996) 2 *Nature Medicine* 1382–5.

[76] Abou-Donia, n. 2 above.

[77] Hubert and Lison, "Study of Muscular Effects of Short-Term, Pyridostigmine Treatment in Resting and Exercising Rats" (1995) 14 *Human and Experimental Toxicology* 49–54.

[78] Through rotating a drum.

6

Causation and Medicinal Products: An Economic Analysis[1]

1. INTRODUCTION

In view of the economic importance of the pharmaceutical industry and the increasing occurrence of medicinal product liability litigation, this chapter attempts to address the hypothesis that a probabilistic approach to causation and medicinal products promotes economic efficiency. This hypothesis will be matched with other economic and non-economic theories to determine which of those are consistent with its approach. The hypothesis will then be considered as a solution to the practical problems of inefficiency in product liability and pharmaceuticals stemming from the uncertainties of determining injury causation.

2. THEORETICAL ANALYSIS

(i) The Importance of Efficiency

It is my submission that the use of statistical methods of establishing causal link in cases involving alleged adverse effects surrounding medicinal products would promote economic efficiency. An attempt will be made to show that this approach is consistent with an economic analysis of causation.

Posner in his *Economic Analysis of Law*[2] submits that the traditional rules of tort law can be explained and justified on economic grounds.

The task of economics, according to Posner, is to explore the implications "of man as a rational maximizer of his self-interest".[3] There are three fundamental principles of economics that arise from this proposition. First, the inverse relation between the price charged and the quantity demanded (law of demand);[4] secondly, the fact that economics is not about money but is about

[1] This chap. is an expanded version of elements of R. Goldberg, "The Role of Scientific Evidence in the Assessment of Causation in Medicinal Product Liability Litigation: A Probabilistic and Economic Analysis" (1998) 1 *Current Legal Issues* 55.

[2] Posner, *Economic Analysis of Law* (4th edn., Boston, Toronto, London, Little, Brown and Company, 1992).

[3] *Ibid.*, 4.

[4] *Ibid.*, 4.

resource use;[5] a distinction is made between (a) transactions that affect the use of resources, whether or not money changes hands, and (b) purely pecuniary transactions (transfer payments);[6] thirdly, the fact that resources tend to gravitate toward their most valuable uses if voluntary exchange, in the form of a market, is allowed. When resources are used if their value is highest we say that they are employed *efficiently*.[7]

It seems clear, from an early stage in the development of law and economics, that causation was inherently linked to efficiency through the internalisation of costs. Calabresi submitted, in one of the seminal articles on law and economics, that "tort costs should be borne by the activity which causes them".[8] It is submitted that this proposition remains entirely true today when looked at in the context of the pharmaceutical industry. However, it is also arguable that the efficiency theory can be criticised on the ground that it champions wealth maximisation over other goals, including compensation and the protection of the poor.[9]

Landes and Posner's economic analysis of causation in tort law stresses the importance of economic efficiency in determining the cause of an injury. They state:

> "If the basic purpose of tort law is to promote economic efficiency, a defendant's conduct will be deemed the cause of an injury, when making him liable for the consequences of the injury would promote an efficient allocation of resources to safety and care; and when it would not promote efficiency for the defendant to behave differently, then the cause of the accident will be ascribed to an 'act of God' or some other force on which liability cannot rest. In this view, the injurer 'causes' the injury when he is the cheaper cost avoider; not otherwise."[10]

Wright has submitted that the efficiency theory is inconsistent with the requirement of causation and that any attempt to reconcile the two is both "unscientific and unrealistic".[11] The basis of this criticism is that the use of "probabilistic cause"[12] is regarded as flawed since it is not proof that it was the cause of the actual result in question. It is merely "proof that it increased the risk or probability of the result's occurring".[13] Legal economists are thus criticised for "assum[ing] a functional relationship, but . . . never fill[ing] it out with a

[5] *Ibid.*, 7.

[6] *Ibid.*

[7] *Ibid.*, 10–11.

[8] Calabresi, "Some Thoughts on Risk Distribution and the Law of Torts" (1961) 70 *Yale LJ* 499, 533.

[9] Stapleton, *Product Liability* (London, Butterworths, 1994), 159–60.

[10] Landes and Posner, "Causation in Tort Law: An Economic Approach"(1983) 12 *J Legal Stud.* 109, 110; Landes and Posner, "Causation" in Landes and Posner, *The Economic Structure of Tort Law* (Cambridge, Mass., London, Harvard University Press, 1987), 229.

[11] Wright, "The Efficiency Theory of Causation and Responsibility: Unscientific Formalism and False Semantics" (1987) *Chicago-Kent LR* 553, 553, 557.

[12] I.e. causation inferred by statistical probability.

[13] Wright, n. 11 above, 560.

mathematical description of any *specific* causal generalization".[14] Wright continues:

> "[I]dentification of *actual* instances of causation . . . is missing from the efficiency theory."[15]

However, an important observation left unnoticed by Wright is the fact that probabilistic methods of causation can refine statistics into those specific to a particular situation, using the Bayes' Theorem.[16] The Bayes' Theorem is one approach which can "mathematically manipulat[e] . . . causal generalizations"[17] by the refinement of statistics to produce specific causal generalisations. The Bayes' Theorem also appears to be a response to Wright's criticism that legal economists are unable to reconcile the *ex post*[18] focus of causation with the *ex ante*[19] focus of efficiency theory, since Bayes' Theorem can operate using statistics *ex ante*, on a futuristic basis, or *ex post*, after the principal data have been obtained.[20]

(ii) The Cheapest Cost Avoider and its Relation to Causation

Economic theory necessitates that any market deterrence approach to liability places injury costs on the party who is best able to assess whether avoidance of risks is cheaper than bearing costs. That party is termed the " 'cheapest cost avoider' of an accident who would be held responsible for the accident costs under the market deterrence standard".[21] It is apparent that causal link is generally required to establish the cheapest cost avoider since, "[t]o put it another way, how can a person be the cheapest cost avoider of an injury if his actions do not increase [or decrease] the chances that the injury will occur?"[22] It is submit-

[14] *Ibid.*, 561. My emphasis.

[15] *Ibid.*, 562. Again my emphasis.

[16] See Chap. 1.

[17] Wright, n. 11 above, 561.

[18] I.e. viewed after the event.

[19] I.e. viewed before the event into the future.

[20] Wright indicates his support for a traditional corrective justice approach through the court recognising a new type of injury, *viz.* risk exposure *per se* or risk exposure which possibly led to the subsequent injury: *ibid.*, 576. However, this merely appears to be redefining the gist of an action from injury into exposure to a risk of injury; this approach is similar to probabilistic causation and one that inevitably brings in statistics for its quantification. If it does not use statistics, it appears to be similar to the court's approach in *McGhee* v. *NCB* [1973] 1 WLR 1 (HL), and open to the criticism that the defendant may have to pay for injuries which he has not been shown to have caused on a balance of probabilities: see Stapleton, "The Gist of Negligence Part II: The Relationship Between Damage and Causation" (1988) 104 *LQR* 389, 401–2. Wright also suggests that with risk exposure as the new injury, the duplicative or synergistic portion of the risk could be allocated to all parties contributing to the duplicative or synergistic portion under joint and several liability, holding each tortious defendant responsible for the risk they created: Wright, n. 11 above, 577–8. However, this fails to explain how these portions of risk are to be quantified.

[21] Calabresi, "Concerning Cause and the Law of Torts: An Essay for Harry Kalven, Jr" (1975) *U. Chi. LR* 69, 84.

[22] *Ibid.*

ted that the reconciliation of the requirements of the efficiency theory with the traditional requirements of causation can only transpire when probabilistic causation and statistics are used to show that on a balance of probabilities a *particular* product (say a medicinal product) caused a *particular* loss complained of by the plaintiff.[23] I support Calabresi's view that "causal linkage", i.e. "a prediction of future risk" is required to ascertain the identity of the cheapest cost avoider.[24] Stapleton attacks Calabresi's attempt to render the traditional causation requirement as an "acceptable vehicle for achieving efficiency"[25] as being an approach predicated upon a "centrally flawed"[26] reliance on probabilistic linkage. Stapleton states that such an approach is wrong, since it required the identification of those but—for factors which "increase the probability of the event occurring" and that because all such factors are necessary for an outcome, "relative to what can one factor be said to have increased the chance of harm once it has occurred".[27] It is arguable, however, that Stapleton gives an unduly harsh interpretation of Calabresi in this context. It is true that Calabresi states that market deterrence[28] relies heavily on "causal linkage" to identify the cheapest cost avoider. This element is "crucial", according to Calabresi, but this is not the case in respect of the "but for" relationship. But-for cause is relied on by market deterrence as a way of determining on an *ad hoc* basis the burden to be placed on the cheapest cost avoider. It has a "limited significance".[29] The but-for test is not to be regarded "as an absolute requirement in case by case determinations".[30] *A fortiori*, Calabresi continues:

> "[W]here it is difficult to prove a *but-for* relationship or where either of two independent defendants was a sufficient cause of the harm and hence neither was a necessary (*but-for*) cause, it is, at the very least, doubtful whether blind adherence to the requirement that the victim prove a *but-for* relationship serves the purposes of market deterrence."[31]

It is submitted that Calabresi correctly states that causal link is relevant to selecting the cheapest cost avoider since causal link is the "predictability as to how much the recurrence of one activity, relative to others, increased the risk of injury".[32]

Stapleton's criticism is that because all factors are necessary for an outcome, "relative to what can one factor be said to have increased the chance of harm once it has occurred?".[33] The weakness in this argument is that Stapleton is referring to "but-for" factors, when Calabresi is in fact referring to *probabilistic* measures

23 Cf Stapleton, *Product Liability*, n. 9 above, 120.
24 Calabresi, n. 21 above, 85.
25 Stapleton, n. 9 above, 120.
26 *Ibid.*, 121.
27 *Ibid.*
28 I.e. deterring economically inefficient conduct through the market.
29 Calabresi, n. 21 above, 8.
30 *Ibid.*, 86.
31 *Ibid.*, 86–7.
32 *Ibid.*, 89.
33 Stapleton, n. 9 above, 121.

of incidence. Stapleton's problem of "relative to what can one factor be said to have increased the chance of harm once it has occurred"[34] can only be addressed by *probabilistic* approaches which embrace statistical significance, and yet she rejects Calabresi's use of probabilistic causation as "confusing".[35]

Stapleton considers that it is generally the manufacturer rather than the victim who is the cheapest cost avoider and that therefore internalisation of costs to the cheapest cost avoider is appropriate.[36] This appears to be appropriate in pharmaceutical product liability cases since it will most often be the manufacturer who is deemed the cheapest cost avoider. For example, Stapleton gives the example of a cough syrup sold by Sainsbury's and concludes that the relevant party is the independent producer of the cough syrup who is able to check most cheaply the product's quality.[37] Nevertheless, the greatest challenge to the cheapest cost avoider concept is the extent to which traditional causal theory approximates to the cheapest cost avoider.[38] Stapleton regards the cheapest cost avoider as an *ex ante* concept, since it is the cheapest cost avoider whose behaviour *in future* "most cheaply makes a difference to the incidence of the relevant losses".[39] By contrast, cause explains the occurrence of loss in the past.[40] Stapleton provides an example to demonstrate that the concept of cause does not always identify the cheapest cost avoider in the context of medicinal products. A drug is found to cause adverse drug reactions in some of those who are administered it which are unforeseeable before their first manifestation. However, further investigation reveals that such adverse drug reactions are suffered by a precisely identifiable group of users, e.g. red-haired males. Stapleton argues that although the past victims of such reactions will never be regarded as their cause we may regard red-haired males as the cheapest cost avoiders in the future.[41] It is submitted, however, that this is incorrect since the cheapest cost avoider remains the manufacturer and is not red-haired males in the future *until* the manufacturer puts a warning on a product. This action is the cheapest way to avoid cost and therefore the cheapest cost avoider is still the manufacturer and the manufacturer remains the cause of the adverse reactions. Then and only then, if a red-haired male takes the product in spite of the warning, is the cheapest cost avoider now the red-haired male. Moreover, the red-haired male is probably also now the cause under the traditional causation test since his act of taking the drug is now a voluntary one and one that would break the chain of causation.[42] Cause still seems to approximate to the cheapest cost avoider in the

[34] Stapleton, n. 9 above, 121.
[35] *Ibid.*, 121.
[36] *Ibid.*, 125.
[37] *Ibid.*, 103.
[38] *Ibid.*, 125.
[39] *Ibid.*, 125–6.
[40] *Ibid.*, 126.
[41] *Ibid.*
[42] Alternatively, it may be a doctor who becomes the cheapest cost avoider at the same time as being a learned intermediary in the context of certain medicinal products, his act amounting to a break in the chain of liability and thus causation.

context of medicinal products, suggesting that there is consistency between the efficiency theory and traditional causal rules in the context of drugs. Stapleton considers that cases in which the future cheapest cost avoider is not reconciled with the traditional causation requirement will be rare and that the traditional causal requirement is an "acceptable vehicle" to ascertain the cheapest cost avoider.[43] Stapleton appears correct in noting that the Product Liability Directive[44] is difficult to justify in efficiency terms since "liability is not even directed to the party causally responsible for the condition of the product which injured the victim".[45] In the Product Liability Directive, there is merely a sub-set of potentially relevant causes, *viz.* the manufacturer of the product, the component manufacturer, the importer and the own-brand supplier, the latter two having little causal relevance and being unlikely to be the cheapest cost avoider.[46] Nevertheless, in most cases involving pharmaceuticals under the Directive, the cheapest cost avoider and the cause of the condition of a defective product will be the manufacturer; hence, the Directive will not result in a dilution of economic incentives, as it may for other products.

The identity of the cheapest cost avoider cannot be readily provided in latent damage cases involving multiple possible causes, including medicinal products, and where epidemiological data produce less than even statistics, rendering proof of causation, on a balance of probabilities under the traditional test, impossible. Moreover, imposing liability 20 years after supply may not have any deterrent effect since the product may no longer be marketed.[47] It is submitted that the cheapest cost avoider could only be identified in such cases where the epidemiological data are statistically refined by probabilistic methods, such as the Bayes' Theorem,[48] to identify the *probability* that a product caused an adverse event. The solution would then be considered in terms of *probabilities* of cause and not in terms of traditional causation. It would also mean that the manufacturer could be proportionately liable as a cheapest cost avoider for a loss, reducing the possibility of over-deterrence in such cases.

(iii) Landes and Posner's Economic Model of Causation

(a) The Basis of the Economic Model—the Learned Hand Formula

Economic theorists like Posner say that their approach to tort problems is compatible with the law of negligence, at least in respect of the Learned Hand

43 *Ibid.*

44 Dir. 85/374/EEC on the approximation of the laws, regulations and administrative provisions of the Member States concerning liability for defective products [1985] OJ L210/29.

45 Stapleton, n. 9 above, 126.

46 *Ibid.*

47 *Ibid.*, 149.

48 See Chap. 1.

formula in *United States* v. *Carroll Towing Co.*[49] In that case, Learned Hand J established that "if the probability of harm be called P; the injury L and the burden [of adequate precautions] B; liability depends upon whether B is less than L multiplied by P: i.e., whether B < PL".[50] The Learned Hand formula could be relevant to the problems of escalating costs of drug innovation in the pharmaceutical industry. The experience in the past 30 years of clinical injury directly caused by the introduction of new drugs, e.g. thalidomide, practolol, Opren and other non-steroidal anti-inflammatory drugs, has necessitated increasingly complicated and costly safety requirements by the drug regulatory authorities. These have involved more pre-clinical and clinical trials before new drugs have been able to obtain product licences, thus extending the pre-marketing phase by years and increasing costs by millions of pounds. It could be argued that this is inherent in the development of more powerful drugs, with greater potential for therapeutic benefit but, on the other side of the coin, more liable to cause potentially graver injury (increasing L), more frequently (increasing P). Thus B (the burden of adequate precautions) must inevitably rise. This whole consideration has led to understandable pressure by the drug industry to extend effective patent life of new drugs as compensation to prevent the inhibition of new drug development.[51]

However, expected accident costs must be compared at the margin by measuring the costs and benefits of small increments in safety and ceasing investing in more safety where another £1 spent would yield a £1 or less in extra safety. Negligence-based liability facilitates a marginal approach since it is difficult in practice to get information on more than small changes in the manufacturer's safety precautions.[52]

(b) The Learned Hand Formula and Causation

Posner examines the scenario where the defendant's conduct is clearly causally unrelated to the plaintiff's harm. In *Blyth* v. *Birmingham Water Works*[53] the court addressed the question whether a water company was negligent in failing to keep its water pipes and the apparatus connected with them in proper order to prevent them bursting due to frost and damaging the plaintiff's home. The court stressed, holding the company not negligent, that the frost that caused the damage had been of unprecedented severity, i.e. the probability of the loss had been low and any reasonable precautions would have been to no

49 159 F 2d 169 (2d Cir. 1947).

50 *Ibid.*, 173 per Learned Hand, CJ.

51 See resulting Council Reg. (EEC) No. 1768/92, which came into force on 2 Jan. 1993 in the UK and all other Member States except Greece, Portugal and Spain introducing a supplementary protection certificate ("SPC") for medicinal products: Reg. 1768/92 concerning the creation of a supplementary protection certificate for medicinal products [1992] OJ L182/1. See Chap. 8.

52 Posner, n. 2 above, 148, 149, 164.

53 (1856) 11 Exch. 781.

54 See Alderson B at 784–5.

avail.[54] Applying the Learned Hand Formula, the probability of damage (P) was not so great as to make the expected cost of the accident (PL) greater than the cost of the prevention (B).[55] Posner posits a variant of *Blyth* where the city failed to take precautions against a normal frost but the frost that took place was unprecedented. *Ex hypothesi*, if the defendant had not been negligent it would have made no difference. Since the unprecedented damage caused by the abnormal frost is not part of L (since L relates to *probable* loss) and L is the precedented damages the defendant must pay if he fails to take precautions that would have prevented the accident and an accident occurs, the effect of liability for unprecedented damages would make the defendant's expected damages for negligence greater than L, which would be akin to imposing punitive damages.[56] For drug-induced injuries which are unprecedented and causally unrelated to all of the defendants' conduct, i.e. the conduct of all pharmaceutical manufacturers in a case such as diethylstilbestrol, liability would be imposed again akin to imposing punitive damages, but Posner argues that in these specific circumstances it would be an "economic mistake" not to receive compensation.[57]

Posner further illustrates his argument by the example of two hunters (A and B) who carefully mistake someone (C) for a deer; both hit him and each shot is fatal, i.e. a case of "additional causation" in Hart and Honoré terminology.[58] Viewed separately, neither of the hunters has caused C's death. This scenario has already been illustrated in the context of medicinal products by *Basco* v. *Sterling Drug Co.*[59] where the plaintiff took two drugs, Avalen and Triquin, which were each sufficient to damage his retina. The US Court of Appeals, Second Circuit, held that where it was assumed that the plaintiff's blindness could have been caused by either of the two drugs and where the jury could have found a breach of duty by the defendant in respect of Triquin but no breach in respect of Avalen, the defendant's negligence would be found, if the assumption was correct, to be a substantial factor in bringing the blindness about.[60] To let both A and B escape liability "would be an economic mistake" according to Posner, thus C's estate should be permitted to get damages from A and B.[61] The analysis is the same even if only one bullet hits C and it is not known whether A or B fired it as long as both A and B were negligent. This was the case in *Summers* v. *Tice*,[62] where both defendants were held jointly and severally liable for the whole of the damages. Growing support exists for

[55] Posner, n. 2 above, 166.

[56] *Ibid.*, 182–3.

[57] *Ibid.*, 183.

[58] Hart and Honoré, *Causation in the Law* (2nd edn., Oxford, Clarendon Press, 1985), 205, 235–6.

[59] 416 F 2d 417 (1969).

[60] *Ibid.*, 430.

[61] Posner, n. 2 above, 183.

[62] 199 P 2d 1 (1948).

liability in this situation, e.g. *Sindell* v. *Abbott Laboratories*,[63] which accepted the concept of market share liability as the most realistic alternative to tort liability.

Posner submits that such cases involving market share liability and medicinal products seem to owe little to notions of causation and much to considerations of economic policy.[64] Thus it seems that in cases in which it is difficult to apply traditional notions of causation but where it would be an "economic mistake" for plaintiffs to receive no indemnity, traditional causal rules are replaced by economic policy principles in order to assist the victims of medicinal product-induced injury. To what extent such an approach emanating from the USA could be applicable in the UK is unclear. It is clear, however, that under traditional tort principles this would be unacceptable.[65]

(c) Landes and Posner's Economic Model Analysed—its Reconciliation with a Probabilistic Approach to Causation

Landes and Posner attempt to produce a refinement of the Learned Hand formula ($B < PL$) to take account of factors which affect the probability of an accident.[66] They express the Learned Hand formula in marginal terms as:

$-\text{Ø}_z\,(p/v - p/nv)\,D = B_z$

where Ø = probability of violating the standard of care.

$-\text{Ø}_z$ = marginal reduction in the probability of violating the applicable standard of care.

z = additional inputs of care to reduce Ø.

p/v = probability of an accident in the event an injurer violates the standard of care.

p/nv = probability of an accident if an injurer does not violate the standard of care.

D = victim's damages if accident occurs.

B_z = marginal cost of additional inputs of care.[67]

[63] Cal. 607 P 2d 924 (1980). Landes and Posner note the danger that the joint liability of *Summers* v. *Tice* will result in misallocative effects in terms of each company's avoidance of costs where there is a large number of tortfeasors and a use of an average rather than an individual case to determine negligence: Landes and Posner, "Joint and Multiple Torts" in Landes and Posner, n. 10 above, 213. However, Landes and Posner do not answer the "very difficult question" whether the above danger is greater than the danger that non-use of *Summers* v. *Tice* in DES cases will result in none of the DES manufacturers, however negligent, bearing any tort liability: *ibid*. Strictly speaking, *Summers* v. *Tice* is inapplicable in DES cases since it is market share liability that applies and not the alternative causation liability of *Summers*. Alternative liability was rejected in the DES case of *Sindell*, Cal. 607 P 2d 924, 930–1. However, alternative liability was accepted in the Dutch decision of *Van Rallegooijen* v. *Bayer Nederland BV* (Rvdw 1992, No. 219) (sect. 3.71 of the decision as numbered by the Sup. Ct.). See Chap. 2.

[64] Posner, n. 2 above, 184.

[65] See *Sindell* Cal. 607 P 2d 924, 937, per Mosk J.

[66] Landes and Posner, "Causation in Tort Law", n. 10 above, 111–14.

[67] *Ibid*., 112–14.

They conclude that an efficient level of care depends on the difference between p/v and p/nv. If p/v − p/nv is 0, the optimal level of care z^* is 0, and the defendant's failure to take care should not be deemed actionable negligence or the *cause* of the accident. However, if p/v − p/nv is positive, z^* is also positive, provided the cost of the first unit of z is less than the expected reduction in damages resulting from the first unit. An injurer is deemed to be negligent or to have caused the injury if the optimal level of care is such that the benefits from the additional efforts to comply with the standard of care (left hand side of the equation) are greater than (>) B_z, the marginal costs of efforts, i.e. benefits > costs.[68]

Although Landes and Posner are correct in saying that the refinement of the Learned Hand formula allows us to analyse cases without invoking causal concepts,[69] it replaces the idea of causal concepts with the need to utilise *probabilistic* concepts, since the probability that the defendant's failure to take care has caused the accident is determined by the difference between p/v and p/nv. It now appears to be necessary, in complex cases, to invoke statistical constructs such as the Bayes' Theorem[70] to ascertain the probability that an accident will occur if care is not taken (p/v) and the probability it will occur even if care is taken (p/nv).

(d) Landes and Posner's Economic Model Applied to Cases Involving Causation and Medicinal Products

Bendectin

In the overwhelming majority of cases no statistically significant association has been shown between the administration of Bendectin and childhood defects. Indeed, proof of causation is compounded by the fact that congenital abnormalities manifest themselves in 1 to 7 per cent of newborn children, even in the absence of exposure to known teratogens.[71] In terms of Landes and Posner's economic model, p/v − p/nv (i.e. the probability that a child would suffer congenital abnormalities as a result of, say, failure to warn of an adverse effect of Bendectin administered, minus the probability of a possible adverse effect given the proper warning and non-administration of Bendectin to pregnant women) is near 0. In such cases, the cost of legal proceedings, the deterrence of socially valuable conduct in administering the drug and the rendering of the potential injurer to use excessive care are the factors suggesting that liability is unwarranted.[72]

[68] *Ibid.*, 114.

[69] *Ibid.*

[70] See Chap. 1.

[71] Lasagna, "The Chilling Effect of Product Liability on New Drug Development" in Huber and Litan (eds), *The Liability Maze: The Impact of Liability Law on Safety and Innovation* (Washington, DC, The Brookings Institution, 1991), 339.

[72] Landes and Posner, n. 10 above, 122. Landes and Posner illustrate the comparable situation, where it was unclear whether an accident would have occurred if the defendant had not been

Thalidomide

In terms of the Landes and Posner economic model, it is more probable than not that phocomelia in the children of pregnant women administered thalidomide would not have occurred if before clinical testing the manufacturer had subjected the drug to teratogenicity tests, and then had warned pregnant women in the light of such tests against using the drug (i.e. p/v − p/nv is substantial).[73] However, this presupposes that such preclinical teratogenicity tests were routine procedures at that time for drugs used in pregnancy. Sadly, although thalidomide was recommended for use in pregnancy, such teratogenicity tests were not then routine requirements.[74]

Pertussis Vaccine

The administration of pertussis vaccine has occasionally been associated with the problem of encephalopathy. In *Bonthrone* v. *Millan*[75] Lord Jauncey emphasised unknown causes to eliminate a possible causal link between pertussis vaccine and brain damage.[76] In terms of the Landes and Posner economic model, it was impossible to ascertain whether p/v − p/nv was positive or zero.[77]

Diethylstilbestrol (DES)

In the DES cases, the identity of the injurer was unclear, since there were numerous manufacturers of the drug. In such circumstances, a strict application of the Landes and Posner economic model is infeasible. There was the added complication that, although a subsequent direct link was shown between DES and vaginal cancer in the daughters of the women who were administered the drug, this effect manifested itself many years after initial exposure. However, market share liability should theoretically be consistent with the economics of Landes and Posner's modification of the Learned Hand formula,[78] in that it creates incentives for companies to take care and to show that their act did not cause the plaintiff's injury. If this can be shown, the defendant can escape liability for

negligent, with the case of *New York Cent. R Co.* v. *Grimstad* 264 F 334 (2d Cir. 1920). In that case, the Circuit CA, Second Circuit, held that the death of a captain of a barge was not due to the failure to provide a barge with life preservers or buoys, in the absence of evidence to show that the presence of such appliances would have saved the deceased: *ibid.*, 335.

[73] See Landes and Posner's (Landes and Posner, n. 10 above, 122) reference to the traumatic cancer case of *McGrath* v. *Irving*, 265 NYS 2d 376 (1965), at 377–8. In that case, the plaintiff received an injury to her throat as a result of hitting the side of the car in which she was a passenger, and swallowed glass which the court held on a preponderance of evidence had caused an epidermoid carcinoma of the larynx.

[74] See Chap. 7.

[75] [1985] 2 *The Lancet* 1137.

[76] *Ibid.*, 1138.

[77] See Landes and Posner's reference (Landes and Posner, n. 10 above, 123) to the parallel decision of *Doumitt* v. *Diemer*, 23 P 2d 918, 920 (1933) (where it was considered impossible to tell whether a scar was caused by tuberculosis or by use of X-rays).

[78] Landes and Posner, n. 10 above, 124–5. Here, Landes and Posner address the problem of "cases where the identity of the injurer is unclear".

its market share of the product,[79] thus creating incentives for care. However, the DES decision of *Hymowitz* v. *Eli Lilly*[80] seems economically incorrect since it recognises a manufacturer's liability for damage despite his showing that his product had not caused the plaintiff's injury, since it had not been used.[81]

(iv) Shavell, the Efficiency Theory and Causation

The idea that manufacturers should only be liable for the accidents that they cause is supported by Shavell, on the basis that restricting the scope of liability on causation grounds prevents the discouragement from engaging in a socially worthwhile activity.[82] This is of particular importance in the area of causation and medicinal products, since in the absence of an effective ability to establish no liability on causation grounds, many pharmaceutical companies will be discouraged from engaging in the production of innovative treatments, particularly in respect of high-risk patient groups. Nevertheless, despite the causation requirement, it seems apparent that the difficulty in establishing causation accurately has resulted in uncertainties in product liability litigation and withdrawal of treatment in the areas of pregnancy drugs, vaccines, orphan drugs, contraceptives and medical devices.[83] The issue of restricting liability on the grounds of causation is of increasing relevance where there is a greater probability that an accident involving an alleged injurer was not caused by that "injurer", e.g. cancer in the context of multifactorial causes including a defective medicinal product and a patient susceptible to carcinogenesis.[84]

(v) The Problem of Overlapping Enterprises and Multifactorial Causes

Stapleton considers that normative economic theories of product liability collapse in the context of overlapping enterprises.[85] The rules of the Consumer Protection Act 1987 and the Product Liability Directive differentiate "products-related factors" (which are given preferential treatment) from a "complex interaction of causal factors". Nevertheless, Stapleton concedes that Posner's approach is less problematic than strict liability since Posner's standard is one

79 See *Sindell* v. *Abbott Laboratories*, 607 P 2d 924, 930 (1980). Cf Schwartz, who states that *Sindell* has turned out to be not economically feasible in that eventual awards are not sufficiently large to justify the delays, uncertainties and costs in the legal process: Schwartz, "The Beginning and the Possible End of the Rise of Modern American Tort Law", (1992) 26 *Georgia Law Review* 601, 688.

80 541 NYS 2d 941 (CA 1989).

81 *Ibid.*, 950.

82 Shavell, *Economic Analysis of Accident Law* (Cambridge, Mass., London, Harvard University Press, 1987), 108.

83 Lasagna, n. 71 above, 334–5.

84 Shavell, n. 82 above, 109.

85 Stapleton, n. 9 above, 146, 341.

of negligence, giving the plaintiffs as much an opportunity to sue those parties not covered by the "separate products rule".[86] It is Stapleton's view that the efficiency theory may support the separate products rule (i.e. the rule requiring the separate legal treatment of products-related injuries), where a pool of potential cheapest cost avoiders consists of only the victim and those in the chain of supply.[87] This appears to contemplate the situation with medicinal products since the manufacturer and supplier are the main protagonists in the causal chain, who should be identifiable, the other potential protagonists being the patient and, possibly, the doctor. However, this may not necessarily be the case, particularly where a drug is alleged to have caused cancer, and there are a series of other potential causes, including environmental ones, that may be culpable. Nevertheless, it is submitted that Landes and Posner's use of their economic model in the context of causal uncertainty could promote economic efficiency. They contemplate the most complicated problems of causal uncertainty where there is considerable delay between an accident and an injury creating "an opportunity for all sorts of other causal factors to come into play".[88] In such circumstances, they suggest the compensating of all people whom the defendant's negligence exposes to risk. They state that, assuming a reduction in the life expectancy is compensatable, the victim will be entitled to a sum of damages (discounted to present values) that the victim's estate would have received annually in future if the victim had died, multiplied by an incremental probability of death (i.e. incremental from the norm) in respect of the accident.[89] This approach will depend, Landes and Posner assert, on a "sophisticated statistical analyses of large groups of people over long periods of time".[90] Although criticised by Stapleton,[91] it is submitted that this probabilistic approach is entirely appropriate and consistent with the efficiency theory. The refining of statistics by a Bayesian approach could reduce any feared overdeterrence when the statistics are looked at *ex ante*,[92] though it is conceded that there are limits to the amount of scientific data available for such a futuristic assessment.[93]

[86] Stapleton, n. 9 above, 146, 341.

[87] *Ibid.*, 147.

[88] Landes and Posner, "Catastrophic Personal Injuries" in Landes and Posner, n. 10 above, 264–5. Also relevant is the fact that causation appears to be affected by the state of the art, and has a temporal dimension to it, even under a standard of strict liability: Stapleton, n. 9 above, 123.

[89] Landes and Posner, n. 10 above, 267.

[90] *Ibid.*, 268.

[91] Stapleton argues that there are no social costs in the mere exposure to the risk of future losses, that damages for social losses should not be distributed on those merely exposed to risk, and that nearly all cases of latent injuries are deleterious outcomes which were unforeseen or poorly perceived at exposure: Stapleton, n. 9 above, 150.

[92] See Chap. 1.

[93] Viscusi is supportive of a proportional liability approach to mass toxic torts but also provides a criticism: "Although this approach is attractive in instances in which relative contribution to causality can be ascertained, the fine-tuning this approach requires may be infeasible when complex scientific information and dimly understood scientific relationships are involved": Viscusi, *Reforming Products Liability* (Cambridge, Mass., London, Harvard University Press, 1991), 170. However, it is arguable that statistical "fine-tuning" may be performed by utilising the Bayes' Theorem, but this would depend on the acquisition of sufficient prior probability in each case. See

(vi) Non-Economic Theories of Causation as Applied to Medicinal Products

(a) Epstein's Theory of Strict Liability

Epstein regards causation as the basis for assignment of responsibility in tort liability.[94] In the words of Hart and Honoré, Epstein is a causal maximalist and one who believes that "causing harm is a necessary and sufficient condition of tort liability".[95] Epstein lays down four causal paradigms to show that the concept of causation in respect of physical injury can be analysed in a way that makes it "internally coherent and relevant to the ultimate question [of] who shall bear the loss".[96] Those four causal paradigms are: *force*, *fright*, *compulsion*, and *dangerous conditions*.[97] The latter is most relevant to medicinal products in that "dangerous conditions" includes the creation of a dangerous product because it is defective.[98] Here, Epstein refers to the person who made the product creating "a dangerous condition that causes harm when subjected to the stress that it was designed to receive when used in its intended manner".[99] However, Stapleton is particularly critical of these paradigms on the basis that they are justified by easy examples, are incomplete and ignore difficult cases.[100] In respect of the causal paradigm, the creation of a dangerous product, Stapleton notes that the creating of "a dangerous condition that causes harm when subjected to the stress that it was designed to receive when used in its intended manner"[101] ignores the issue of what *was* the "intended manner" of the product's use. Perhaps "intended manner" is clearer in cases involving medicinal products by virtue of compulsory data sheets and patient package inserts, which detail instructions for drug use. There could, however, be borderline cases, e.g. the injection of a vaccine at an incorrect time or when a patient is being administered an additional medication, the combined use of which has aroused initial suspicions of a possible drug interaction but which has not yet been contra-indicated with the vaccine in the data sheet. Difficulties in the use of the causal paradigms arguably forced Epstein into conceding the fact that the "basic intuition against causing harm" had to be changed into the "limited prohibition against the use of force[102] against the person or property of

Chap. 1. It is also Viscusi's belief that risks not understood at the time of the original exposure to the risk would mean that the proportional liability approach would not work effectively. As noted above, the limitations to an *ex ante* assessment of statistics are conceded but nevertheless they could be used, as Landes and Posner appreciate.

[94] Epstein, "A Theory of Strict Liability"(1973) 2 *J Legal Stud*. 151, 160.

[95] Hart and Honoré, n. 58 above, p. lxxiv.

[96] Epstein, n. 94 above, 165–6.

[97] *Ibid*., 166.

[98] *Ibid*., 168.

[99] *Ibid*., 178.

[100] Stapleton, n. 9 above, 167.

[101] Epstein, n. 94 above, 178.

[102] See the first causal paradigm.

another".[103] The fundamental weakness in Epstein's theory is identified by Stapleton, namely the absence of a theoretical justification for "why causing harm" should produce compensation. As Stapleton notes:

> "To say, as Epstein did initially, that causing harm should result in compensation is simply an assertion that this is the appropriate limit of liability. It gives no independent theory of rights, specifically of why rights should be limited in this way."[104]

What now follows is an examination of Stapleton's approach, which is supportive of causation in the form of a limited causal-based strict liability regime with its perimeters based on moral principles.[105]

(b) Stapleton's Moral Enterprise Liability Theory

The theoretical justification for such liability is noted by Stapleton as follows:

> "[I]f, in seeking to secure financial profit an enterprise causes certain types of loss, it should be legally obliged to pay compensation to the victim."[106]

It will be instantly noted that *causation* is still a requirement under the Stapleton approach, despite her stated opposition to probabilistic approaches in ascertaining causal link. In trying to justify this form of liability, Stapleton is left with the need to defend the morality of making the pursuit of profit susceptible to liability. She explains that moral enterprise liability is supported by the resentment and special discredit caused when a bad outcome is *perceived* as due to commercial operations.[107] The difficulty with that approach is that the uncertainties of causation and the problem of development risks may render such a perception a false one. It is conceded that this is an ongoing difficulty with causation, but her rejection of probabilistic approaches to causal link makes such uncertainties more likely. This ultimately weakens the argument for imposition of liability in such circumstances and suggests that the Calabresi and Landes and Posner approaches are more amenable as an explanation for efficient decision-making in courts.

Stapleton regards her moral enterprise liability as potentially illustrated by market share liability in the context of the DES cases, in that abandoning the causation requirement in tort is "a radical strategy for fixing liability on an enterprise".[108] It is submitted, however, that there is difficulty reconciling market share liability with an "enterprise caus[ing] certain types of loss",[109] as

[103] Epstein, "Causation and Corrective Justice: A Reply to Two Critics" (1979) 8 *J Legal Stud.* 477, 481. This is regarded by Stapleton as an abandonment of reliance on causal language: Stapleton, n. 9 above, 167.

[104] Stapleton, n. 9 above, 170.

[105] *Ibid.*, 173.

[106] *Ibid.*, 186. My emphasis.

[107] Stapleton, n. 9 above, 187.

[108] *Ibid.*, 190.

[109] *Ibid.*, 186.

adumbrated in Stapleton's justification for moral enterprise liability. Nevertheless, even if it is conceded that there is a possibility of reconciling the two on the ground that it is the DES generic industry enterprise which is pursuing the profit,[110] it is unclear how Stapleton's moral enterprise liability would handle the DES decision of *Hymowitz* v. *Eli Lilly*,[111] imposing liability despite a manufacturer's positive showing that his product did not cause the plaintiff's injury since it had not been used.[112] Stapleton correctly notes that the plaintiff need not show that the defendant caused a defect under the Product Liability Directive, since the profit idea of defendants acting "in the course of a business" warrants absence of a causal requirement;[113] yet causation is still a requirement, in that the defect must cause damage under Article 4 of the Directive. It now seems that the defect has replaced the defendant in the shift to strict liability from negligence. So the requirement of factual causation between the medicinal product and the damage will be just as hard to prove as a breach of duty causing the damage. Causation perhaps might be interpreted even more restrictively on a policy basis, since there is no duty of care requirement to restrict liability.[114] The justifying principle of moral enterprise liability cannot divorce itself from causal link and enterprises are deemed liable by Stapleton through financially creating the opportunity for a product to cause loss in the pursuit of profit.[115] Scholars have shown a healthy scepticism of this basis of liability.[116] Stapleton talks of a "developing moral consensus concerning the special status of losses generated by the pursuit of financial profits".[117] It would nevertheless appear that there is a limit to "moral consensus" in the product liability area, particularly in respect of pharmaceuticals, where the primary function of the product is to do good and treat or prevent disease. It is also arguable, in respect of medicinal products but unlike other products, that there are perhaps moral, and certainly economic, justifications for the boundaries that presently exist in this area.[118]

(c) Causal Determinism and Indeterminism and Lost Chance Cases

Reece has recently described the significance of the distinction between "deterministic" and "indeterministic" events whilst discussing the development of the law of lost chances and causation.[119] She states that with a deterministic event,

110 *Ibid.*, 190.

111 541 NYS 2d 941 (CA 1989).

112 *Ibid.*, 950.

113 Stapleton, n. 9 above, 192.

114 Arguably, however, the development risk defence is as close to a "standard of care" defence of *Roe* v. *Minister of Health* [1954] 2 QB 66, *per* Denning L.J at 84, 86. See Chap. 7.

115 Stapleton, n. 9 above, 193.

116 See Fleming, "Product Liability De-Constructed" (1996) 16 *OJLS* 185, 186.

117 Stapleton, n.9 above, 196 (discussing statutory examples of moral enterprise liability).

118 Cf *ibid.*, 199.

119 Reece, "Losses of Chances in the Law" (1996) 59 *MLR* 188, 192.

probability is purely "epistemological",[120] whereas an indeterministic event results in "objective" interpretations of probability.[121] Reece defines an event as indeterministic "if and only if it could not have been predicted at any point in the past, it cannot be predicted in the present even given unlimited time, resources and evidence, and we cannot imagine how it would become predictable in the future even given the success of present research programmes".[122] It is asserted that although we cannot know that it is an indeterministic event, "it is treated as such" since "it is not humanly possible to predict the event", referring to such an event as a "quasi-indeterministic event" and the associated chance as a "quasi-objective chance".[123] Reece considers that lost chance cases are "quasi-indeterministic"[124] and that *Hotson* v. *East Berkshire AHA*[125] was a deterministic case,[126] since the bone necrosis of *Hotson* was fully determined by the events which occurred.[127] It is submitted that although it is correct to regard *Hotson* as deterministic, many cases involving medical causation (particularly causation and drugs) would be regarded as deterministic since they could not be regarded as indeterministic according to Reece's definition. An example of this potential paradox is put forward. A child of six years has cancer within the abdomen. A preliminary biopsy is taken which defines the cancer as one with a 40 per cent chance of cure. Sadly the child dies during this procedure and the cause of death is identified as due to a negligently administered anaesthetic. Reece might well reject the scenario as being worthy of assistance by a loss of a chance analysis on the ground that it is possible to use statistical analyses to predict the likelihood or the probability of the event (i.e. cure). It is submitted, however, that in such cases it is not a question of the prediction of an event, but the prediction of the *chance* that an event has happened; this is entirely probabilistic. This example would be *deterministic* under her terminology but yet it would still be a *loss of a chance case*, and one that could be compensatable if the scenario was regarded as an *unresolved future hypothetical question*, as opposed to being a past fact,[128] an approach which she rejects.[129]

Even if she regarded this as a quasi-indeterministic situation, her theory that only *objective* chances and not epistemological probabilities can be the basis of claims for loss of a chance[130] eschews the fact that an objective chance cannot be personal to an individual and needs refinement from a statistical chance into

[120] Reece, "Losses of Chances in the Law" (1996) 59 *MLR* 188, 193. This is because "probability is purely a means of managing our lack of knowledge": *ibid.*

[121] *Ibid.*

[122] *Ibid.*, 194.

[123] *Ibid.*

[124] *Ibid.*, 197.

[125] [1987] AC 750.

[126] Reece, n. 119 above, 195–7.

[127] *Ibid.*, 197. See *Hotson* v. *East Berkshire AHA* [1987] AC 750, 782, *per* Lord Bridge.

[128] See Hill, "A Lost Chance for Compensation in the Tort of Negligence by the House of Lords" (1991) 54 *MLR* 511, 511, 523.

[129] Reece, n. 119 above, 197, n. 40.

[130] *Ibid.*, 197.

a personal chance. The only way that this refinement can take place is through a Bayesian approach to legal decision-making, which is necessarily *subjective*,[131] since in calculating the likelihood ratio, observed frequences presented through expert evidence are not necessarily adopted by factfinders. This emphasises the subjective view of the likelihood ratio as being an essential element in Bayesian probability.[132] In Reece's conclusion to her paper she somewhat relents from her rigid hypothesis that "[r]ecovery for loss of a chance is permitted only if the situation is quasi-indeterministic".[133] She suggests that "[a] continuum between determinism and indeterminism is more plausible than a clear division . . . [for which] we could not expect to divide legal cases into two categories".[134] This approach seems a more rational one in the context of causation and medicinal products.

(d) Problems of Corrective, Distributive and Individualised Justice

Corrective Justice and Distributive Justice

Some scholars have supported the non-economic corrective justice theory as being one which "explains, justifies and illuminates the general structure, content and institutions of tort law".[135] Corrective justice has been defined as "the justice that rectifies or remedies inequalities which arise in dealings . . . between individuals",[136] and can be distinguished from distributive justice, which deals with the problems relating to the allocation of divisible common stock,[137] i.e. responses to the problems of distributing the "common stock and the incidents of communal enterprise", which cannot serve the common good until they are distributed to particular individuals.[138] What is clear from distributive justice is that no causal connection is necessary to support valid distributive justice,[139] whereas corrective justice "presupposes that the defendant has caused harm to

131 See Fienberg and Schervish, "The Relevance of Bayesian Inference for the Presentation of Statistical Evidence and for Legal Decisionmaking" (1986) 66 *BUL Rev*. 771, 794.

132 *Ibid*., 776. In addition, Reece's approach runs up against her own criticism that recovery for loss of chance seems to fail the necessary standard of proof on a balance of probabilities: Reece, n. 19 above, 204. The problem with her approach is that it ignores the fact that Stapleton's reformulation of the damage into a lost chance *becomes* the gist of the action, and that damages can be obtained for proof on a balance of probabilities that the defendant's fault had caused the new reformulated damage: see above and Stapleton, "The Gist of Negligence—Part II" (1988) 104 *LQR* 389, 391–2.

133 Reece, n. 119 above, 204.

134 *Ibid*.

135 Wright, "Right, Justice and Tort Law" in D. G. Owen (ed.), *Philosophical Foundations of Tort Law* (Oxford, Clarendon Press, 1995), 168, 182. See also A. Honoré, "The Morality of Tort Law—Questions and Answers" in Owen (ed.), above, 80–94; Coleman, "The Practice of Corrective Justice" in Owen (ed.), above, 56.

136 Finnis, *Natural Law and Natural Rights* (Oxford, Clarendon Press, 1980), 177.

137 Stapleton, n. 9 above, 174. Indeed, Aristotle provided such a distinction between corrective and distributive justice: *ibid*.

138 Finnis, n. 136 above, 166.

139 Wright, n. 135 above, 169; Finnis, n. 136 above, 180.

the plaintiff".[140] Causation is thus a necessary condition of corrective justice.[141] Yet, paradoxically, it has also been convincingly argued that corrective justice does not require causation but instead requires liability based on tortious creation of risk of the occurrence of harm, irrespective of whether it actually does or does not occur.[142]

It is arguable that, since corrective justice sees a rule in tort law in terms of correcting a wrong done by an individual defendant to an individual plaintiff,[143] the approach of refining causal link to the particular individuals in question by use of the Bayes' Theorem is essentially a corrective justice construct. However the deficiency here lies in the distinction between both corrective and distributive justice. The theoretical debate concerning the distinction between the two has been criticised by Stapleton on the grounds of the loose way in which terms such as corrective and distributive justice have been used.[144] She argues that "[t]erms such as 'corrective' (or 'commutative')[145] and 'distributive justice' are often used in opposition to each other even though arguably they are more plausibly seen as merely different perspectives of a broader issue".[146] The distinction has been downplayed as "no more than an analytical convenience, an aid to orderly consideration of problems".[147]

The shift in strict product liability has been from a corrective justice perspective to a distributive justice perspective, since distributive justice does not rely (unlike corrective justice) on the requirement that wrong necessitates fault.[148] It is argued that the wider the distributional effects of civil liability that are considered, the less likely a coherent distributional rationale will emerge for burdening the increasingly disparate parties involved.[149] This seems to show the weakness of the distributive justice paradigm. The rationale for market share liability, as exemplified in *Sindell* v. *Abbott Laboratories*,[150] though reflecting a strong distributive justice approach to the problem of compensating the victims

140 Honoré, n. 135 above, 80.

141 As Tony Honoré has observed: "there must be a causal link between the defendant's conduct and the plaintiff's loss. The conduct need not be *the* cause of the harm. It is enough that it is *a* cause, and there can be more than one human cause of the harm in question, in which case both (or all) harm-doers can be responsible. The existence of the causal link is a *necessary* condition of corrective justice and of the duty to compensate in a tort action": *ibid.*, 80.

142 Schroeder, "Corrective Justice and Liability for Increasing Risks" (1990) 37 *UCLA LRev.* 439, 469.

143 Stapleton, n. 9 above, 201.

144 *Ibid.*, 6.

145 Commutative justice is Thomas Aquinas' wider term than corrective justice, which deals with "what dealings are proper between persons": Finnis, n. 9 above, 179; Stapleton, n. 9 above, 175.

146 Stapleton, n. 9 above, 6.

147 Finnis, n. 136 above, 179.

148 Stapleton, n. 9 above, 202. However, on a wider view, based on what is termed "outcome responsibility", corrective justice requires those who have without justification harmed others, to put the matter right even in the absence of fault: Honoré, n. 135 above, 81–2, 94. This suggests that the corrective justice approach can be used to justify a strict product liability regime.

149 Stapleton, n. 9 above, 204.

150 607 P 2d 924 (1980).

of DES, is weakened by the lack of accuracy in the individual cases of the market share approach.

However, it has been argued that the use of aggregative devices to consolidate and manage tort cases presents a distributively just needs-based approach, which supports lower settlement figures than full compensation on the basis that requiring a corporate defendant to pay full compensation to victims of a mass tort is an unjust imposition of liability, disproportionate to the nature of a defendant's wrongdoing.[151] But such an approach does not address the problem of assessing or quantifying the extent to which full reparations are diminished. Weinstein and Hershenov have noted the problem of the unavailability, most particularly at the early stages of mass torts, of reliable scientific causation evidence.[152] Nevertheless, it is submitted that increasing epidemiological evidence in respect of medicinal products is becoming available for early use in litigation.

Although the corrective justice model can accommodate multiple potential defendants in a mass tort claim,[153] it is submitted that a moral defence of corrective justice may well be insufficient in mass tort cases involving indeterminate causation and drugs; perhaps the Bayes' Theorem approach in refining statistics to the individual particularly strengthens an *economic* defence of a corrective justice model.[154]

However, it has been submitted by Strudler that the Aristotelian conception of corrective justice is served through tort law in the context of indeterminate causation cases, by the forging of a *moral* link between tortfeasor and victim.[155] Strudler argues that only the person who *causes* the injury can provide aid and that assists in the function of expressing *regret*, and that *regret* can be expressed in indeterminate causation cases, thus indirectly satisfying corrective justice in such situations. This satisfaction of corrective justice would be achieved through a tort pool scheme, where the tortfeasor satisfied his corrective justice duties by paying into the pool.[156] A "fractional award", reflecting, e.g., the epidemiological evidence available, may express suitable regret.[157] It is arguable, therefore, that if this evidence was sufficiently refined then it would strongly reinforce the corrective conception of mass torts, including a moral defence of such a conception.

[151] See Goldberg, "Misconduct, Misfortune and Just Compensation: Weinstein on Torts" (1997) 97 *Colom. L Rev*. 2034, 2051, 2054–5.

[152] Weinstein and Hershenov, "The Effect of Equity in Mass Tort Law" (1991) *U.Ill.L.Rev*. 269, 312. See also Weinstein, *Individual Justice in Mass Tort Litigation: The Effect of Class Actions, Consolidations, and Other Multiparty Devices* (Evanston, Illinois, Northwestern University Press, 1996), 151–2.

[153] Stapleton, n. 9 above, 345; Wright, n. 135 above, 177.

[154] Cf Wright, who would say that corrective justice here promotes equal freedom, and who rejects the utilitarian efficiency theory: Wright, n. 135 above, 181. Owen has posited that Aristotle believed that corrective justice required a "mathematical" rather than a proportional (cf distributive justice) form of equality, and this seems to be consistent with the numerical Bayesian approach: D. G. Owen, "Philosophical Foundations of Fault in Tort Law" in Owen (ed.), n. 135 above, 212.

[155] Strudler, "Mass Tort and Moral Principles" (1992) 11 *Law and Philosophy* 297, 315–16.

[156] *Ibid*., 326.

[157] *Ibid*., 330.

The Inherent Tension Between Individualised Justice and Collective/Distributive Justice

There has been much discussion in the American literature of the inherent tension between individualised justice ("the tailored application of governing norms to the circumstances and interests of the particular parties",[158] or "party autonomy in an adversary system")[159] and collective justice ("the aggregated handling of legal claims")[160] in the context of mass torts. Both Weinstein and Hershenov have conceded the inherent tension between individualised justice and distributive justice and that, in attempting to do mass justice, individual rights are being destroyed, including the right to focus on causation in the individual, which may leave individual tort claimants with a lower recovery than they might otherwise have received.[161] Much support for collective justice came from Rosenberg's idea that despite the inability to show causal link between tortfeasor and victim in many mass torts, "public law" remedies in mass tort cases, particularly in the form of class actions, have helped to re-emphasise the protection of individual entitlements to personal security and autonomy.[162] This process has been achieved by his support for the "public law" proposal of proportional liability, to resolve causal connection in mass exposure cases.[163] Indeed, Rosenberg stressed that with proportional liability the incentive would be to offer additional particularistic evidence,[164] which seems entirely consistent with the writer's encouragement of statistical refining in ascertaining causal link. Rosenberg has continued to argue the use of individualised justice through this "public law" approach in several important papers,[165] most recently in the context of *ex ante* risk-based claims, i.e. claims based on an exposure to a tortiously imposed risk, as opposed to being based on actual harm and loss, in order to support greater collectivisation,[166] even where, in the process of compulsory aggregation, all particularising and personalised approaches are denied.[167] Nevertheless, it is submitted that particularisation is still needed for the pursuit of individualised justice, if and when that particularisation is helpful

[158] Rosenberg, "Class Actions for Mass Torts: Doing Individual Justice by Collective Means" (1987) 62 *Ind. LJ* 561, 586.

[159] Cramton, "Individualized Justice, Mass Torts, and 'Settlement Class Actions': An Introduction" (1995) 80 *Cornell L Rev.* 811, 811 (1995).

[160] *Ibid.*

[161] Weinstein and Hershenov, n. 152 above, 324; Weinstein, n. 152 above, 160. But they also argue that the individual clients' position is not very different from and may be considerably worse without aggregation: Weinstein and Hershenov, above, 325; Weinstein, above, 160.

[162] Rosenberg, "The Causal Connection in Mass Exposure Cases: A 'Public Law' Vision of the Tort System" (1984) 97 *Harv. L Rev.* 851, 851, 860, 881, 907. Class actions seem to provide more opportunity for individualisation than the case-by-case process.

[163] *Ibid.*, 859.

[164] *Ibid.*, 869–70.

[165] See, e.g., Rosenberg, n. 158 above, 566–7.

[166] Rosenberg, "Individual Justice and Collectivising Risk-Based Claims in Mass-Exposure Cases" (1996) 71 *NYUL Rev.* 210.

[167] *Ibid.*, 326.

and possible. Without particularisation, it is arguable that over-deterrence and under-deterrence would still remain a problem in mass tort cases.[168]

Perhaps, as has been argued by Rabin, this dominant tension between individual justice and a more compensation-driven conception of collective justice is "inevitable".[169] But it is clear that problems of causation are not unique to mass torts and the multiple plaintiff context. As has been observed by Siliciano:

> "Rather, such causation problems typically stem from the inherent difficulty of reconstructing events in the distant past, the perennial problem of separating multiple causal influences, and the general limits of scientific knowledge. These same difficulties in proof can present themselves in single-plaintiff, one-of-a-kind cases as well."[170]

It may well be the case that the use of epidemiological approaches in both single-plaintiff and mass tort cases will reduce the inherent tension between individualised and collective justice/distributive justice paradigms, and such a use in both situations should result in a reduction in overdeterrence and underdeterrence for *ex post* and *ex ante* measures of probabilistic risk.

Cost Implications

Whatever approach is taken to ascertaining causation, and whether such an approach is supportive of either individualised or collective/distributive justice, determining causation will be inherently costly.[171] Much can be said for Schuck's view that the mass tort litigation system is evolving to reduce uncertainty, and he notes the use of statistical models to make claim values more predictable.[172] But this move appears to be directed more towards averaging awards and not towards the tailoring of causation to individual circumstances.[173] It is submitted that the Bayesian approach to refining statistics to the individual is perhaps a better form of evolutionism in both single plaintiff and mass tort law to reduce uncertainty.[174] This process could be encouraged

[168] Cf Rosenberg, n. 158 above, 579–81, 586. Rosenberg states that it is not a ground for objection that class actions can only be given access by averaging causation and damages to remove the expense of individualised determinations and a series of trials after resolution of common questions: *ibid.*, 580. However, this comment could well be interpreted as encouraging the fettering of an individual's right to have causation accurately determined.

[169] Rabin, "Continuing Tensions in the Resolution of Mass Toxic Harm Cases: A Comment" (1995) 80 *Cornell L Rev*. 1037, 1041. He observes that: "[s]o long as there is one discrete common law system for non-mass claimants and a collective hybrid system for mass claimants, a tension between the two perspectives is virtually inevitable": *ibid.*

[170] Siliciano, "Mass Torts and the Rhetoric of Crisis" (1995) 80 *Cornell L Rev*. 990, 993.

[171] *Ibid.*, 998.

[172] Schuck, "Mass Torts: An Institutional Evolutionist Perspective" (1995) 80 *Cornell L Rev*. 941, 959.

[173] *Ibid.*, 960.

[174] In McGovern's commentary on Schuck's above paper, she observes a possible future evolution in the mass tort process by the use of statistics in resolving causation problems. She gives the example of alternative approaches to the resolution of causation, including statistics, by the UN Compensation Commission to resolve claims for reparation arising from the Iraq–Kuwait conflict in 1990: McGovern, "Looking to the Future of Mass Torts: A Comment on Schuck and Siliciano" (1995) 80 *Cornell L Rev*. 1022, 1027–32.

through the reduction of costs as a result of a more rigorous case selection, using the epidemiological approach. The cost of adjudicating proportional liability could be higher than under the traditional rules of causation, since it requires more precision. Yet it is likely that, through the filtering of weak cases using a refined statistical approach to proportional liability, a decrease in the volume of mass tort litigation would result.[175] We shall return to the economic implications of the application of probabilistic and epidemiological approaches to establishing causation in Chapter 8.

Conclusion

It is clear that the requirement of causation, albeit reinforced by a probabilistic approach, where non-numerical solutions prove elusive, will remain an essential core element in the resolution of medicinal product liability controversaries. Although a marginal academic element supports the elimination of the requirement of causation,[176] and it is conceded that causation dramatically draws attention to the inherent tension between individualised and collective/distributive justice paradigms, it is submitted that epidemiological approaches to causation reduce that inherent tension and both overdeterrence and underdeterrence, for *ex post* and *ex ante* assessments of probabilistic risk.

[175] For discussion of costs see Rosenberg, n. 162 above, 898. McGovern's second vision of the future is a more rigorous case selection in mass torts. She observes that this may result in a return to more traditional tort litigation: McGovern, n. 174 above, 1033. See above in respect of the Woolf Report's recommendations in respect of reducing the cost of undeserving cases in multi-plaintiff litigation.

[176] See Berger, "Eliminating General Causation: Notes Towards a New Theory of Justice and Toxic Torts" (1997) 97 *Colum. L Rev*. 2117. Berger's theory is that proof of causation should be abolished since the causation model "is blind to the realities of scientific uncertainty and corporate behaviour, and is inconsistent with notions of moral responsibility in tort law". Berger suggests a model which imposes liability for failure to develop and disclose information which is required to assess serious latent risks: *ibid*., 2117, 2140, 2143. She suggests the move towards the "development of a meaningful legal standard governing a corporation's obligation to pursue and provide information without requiring proof that the missing information caused the plaintiffs adverse health conditions": *ibid*., 2140. However, no indication is given of how this legal standard will be assessed in determing liability, and this is arguably more uncertain than the problems relating to scientific knowledge and ascertainment of causation. Under her model, the burden of proof of causation is reversed on to the defendant to prove in general that certain adverse reactions could not arise from exposure to the defendants product: *ibid*., 2144–5. This merely reverses the burden of proof of causation and relaunches the problem back into the realms of causal uncertainty in circumstances where the defendant must prove a negative, namely that their drug did not cause a particular plaintiff's defect: *ibid*., 2148. Cf *Merrell Dow Pharmaceuticals, Inc*. v. *Havner*, CA 13th District of Texas, Corpus Christi: No 13–92–540–CV, 17 March 1994, 13 of official transcript.

3. THE PROBLEM IN PRACTICE

(i) The Cost of Product Liability in Medicinal Product Litigation—its Relation to Uncertainty in Proving Injury Causation

Costs are an economic issue of considerable importance in the pharmaceutical industry, particularly in the context of product liability. The best way to conceptualise costs is in the form of a mathematical equation. It is clearly established that:[177]

Economic performance (industry's contribution to living standards, i.e. economic efficiency)	=	social benefits (desirable consequences)	minus	social costs (undesirable consequences)

Social costs are defined as either resource costs (labour, buildings, machines and materials) or injury costs (the suffering of injuries from medicinal products and devices).[178] We are concerned with injury costs, and to what extent difficulties in proof of causation increase injury costs and hence reduce economic efficiency. The RAND Corporation, in its report *Product Liability and the Economics of Pharmaceuticals and Medical Devices* observed evidence for costs and benefits in four kinds of industry outcomes, namely *product availability*, *pricing*, *product safety and effectiveness*, and *innovation*. Each relevant industry outcome is now examined from the point of view of difficulties in proving causation to ascertain the nature and extent of the injury costs in this sphere. In respect of *availability*, uncertainty regarding injury causation has resulted in economically inefficient withdrawals of drugs, which previously had wide medical support, e.g. childhood vaccines, some intra-uterine devices and Bendectin.[179] It is important that vaccines, products for conditions specific to pregnancy and contraceptives are all high risk products and that "unusually large liability costs" have been associated with these products. Large awards have been made where causation has been disputed by experts resulting in a misperception in liability costs.[180] A recent US Congress report has observed the

177 Garber, *Product Liability and the Economics of Pharmaceuticals and Medical Devices* (Santa Monica, Cal., RAND, 1993), pp. xxii–xxiii.

178 *Ibid.*

179 *Ibid.*, p. xxvii. Indeed, in the case of Bendectin the number of lawsuits decreased as the plaintiffs failed to establish causal link between Bendectin and birth defects: *ibid.*, 84–5. See also 88–9. Lasagna has observed in respect of the legacy of Bendectin's withdrawal and the litigation surrounding it that "[i]t seems safe to predict that never again will a manufacturer petition the FDA to approve for marketing a new prescription drug for the nausea and vomiting of pregnancy": Lasagna, n. 71 above, 341.

180 Garber, n. 177 above, 60, 73. It is arguable that a "bias" already exists against high risk products through government risk regulation, and that associated with such products is the danger that innovation of high risk medicinal products will be hindered by both regulation and product liability: Viscusi and Moore, "An Industrial Profile of the Links between Product Liability and Innovation" in Huber and Litan, n. 71 above, 82.

reduction in R & D in the areas of contraceptives, pregnancy drugs and vaccines against the AIDS virus.[181] With all of these products there is considerable uncertainty in proving injury causation.

In respect of *pricing*, the inability of prices to signal relative risks of products is related to the difficulty of proving injury causation.[182] The prices of drugs, incorporating insurance premiums, do not directly correlate with the safety risks of medicinal products because of the lack of a link between these safety risks and the cost of injuries for which companies are held liable. Costs may ensue from injuries not caused by medicinal products and some adverse drug reactions caused by products do not result in injury costs.[183] In the case of childhood vaccines, a rapid price increase took place in the mid-1980s due to the perceived association of brain damage with pertussis vaccine. Since the commencement of the US National Childhood Vaccine Injury Act of 1988, which presumes causal link in certain circumstances but not others according to the terms of a vaccine injury table,[184] the real prices of DTP vaccine have fallen.[185]

"Confusing signals" have been generated surrounding the *safety* of medicinal products due to the uncertainty over the cause of an adverse effect; for example, despite the support given by the Food and Drug Administration (FDA) to Bendectin and vaccines, witness the negative effect of the legal system as a result of causal uncertainty.[186]

Innovation, however, remains the most important of the four industry outcomes. It appears that, despite a paucity of data to assess the effects of product liability on innovation in respect of medicinal products[187] and the fact that such information is largely "anecdotal",[188] there has been a clear discouragement of high risk medicinal products, particularly products for pregnancy conditions such as DES and Bendectin.[189] This is particularly relevant to the problem of establishing injury causation since the companies are not developing the products, as many birth defects are of unknown cause.[190] Expected liability costs

[181] US Congress, Office of Technology Assessment, *Pharmaceutical R & D: Costs, Risks and Rewards* (Washington, DC, US Government Printing Office, 1993), 179, 182.

[182] Stapleton, n. 9 above, 109, 111.

[183] Garber, n. 177 above, 121–2.

[184] 42 USC 300aa–11(c)(1)(C)(i). See Chap. 4.

[185] Garber, n. 177 above, 106–7. Nevertheless, some commentators have alleged that most of the compensated cases are causally unrelated to the administered vaccines: Kitch and Mortimer, "American Law, Preventative Vaccine Programs and The National Vaccine Injury Compensation Program" in Plotkin and Mortimer, *Vaccines* (2nd edn., Philadelphia, Penn., W. B. Saunders Co., 1994), 944, 946.

[186] Huber and Litan, "Overview" in Huber and Litan (eds.), *The Liability Maze: The Impact of Liability Law on Safety and Innovation* (Washington, DC, The Brookings Institution, 1991), 14.

[187] US Congress, Office of Technology Assessment, *Pharmaceutical R & D: Costs, Risks and Rewards* (Washington, DC, US Government Printing Office, 1993), 173.

[188] Viscusi and Moore, "An Industrial Profile of the Links between Product Liability and Innovation" in Huber and Litan, n. 71 above, 81.

[189] Garber, n. 177 above, pp. xxix, 147, 174.

[190] Proof that a drug is teratogenic is difficult because congenital abnormalities are found in 1 to 7% of newborn children, even in the absence of exposure to human teratogens: Lasagna, n. 71 above, 339.

may reduce incentives to innovate but it is the uncertainty of liability and risk that is having a greater deleterious effect.[191] Again this reaffirms the generation of uncertainty through the problem of determining injury causation. Nevertheless, there are difficulties in establishing links between product liability and innovation.[192] Distinctions exist between the legal systems of the UK and USA in terms of America's greater number of cases and higher *per capita* costs than the UK and other countries.[193]Indeed, in respect of the different international legal regimes in the area of medicinal products and product liability it has been conceded that "little comparative data on the development or marketing of innovative drugs under the different regimes" has emerged.[194]

What emerges from this assessment is that liability has become inefficient as a result of both inappropriate incentives and a misperception of incentives by companies. In respect of inappropriate incentives, companies are sometimes held liable when they ought not to be, when an injury is not caused by their medicinal product; but are sometimes not held liable when they should be, i.e. when an injury has been caused by their product. Also, decision-makers may misinterpret risk because of common psychological biases, rendering them likely to overestimate the possible risk of their products being blamed for injuries attributable to other causes and to underestimate the chance of liability where particular products have not experienced publicised problems.[195] It is submitted that one way to reduce the inefficiency of inappropriate incentives and misperception of incentives is through the use of probabilistic statistics that are refined to particular circumstances in order to determine injury causation and risk. It is only then that liability will become more efficient, and this is true both in theory and in practice.

(ii) The Case Law

Increasing judicial discretion has been observed in the determination of liability through scientific uncertainty in respect of injury causation. However, it is not

191 Garber, n. 177 above, 174.

192 Viscusi and Moore demonstrate that a link between an innovative environment and liability costs is "theoretically ambiguous" and that it is largely dependent on the nature of what is innovated. A safer new product may emerge from less risky innovative industries, whereas a riskier product may emerge from more innovative industries with high insurance levels: Viscusi and Moore, "An Industrial Profile of the Link between Product Liability and Innovation", n. 188 above, 107.

193 Schwartz, "Product Liability and Medical Malpractice in Comparative Context" in Huber and Litan, n. 71 above, 46–7, 64–6,76. Schwartz argues that compliance with the EC Product Liability Dir. will not increase liability since, when Germany's implementing statute came into effect on 1 Jan. 1990, product liability in Germany did not increase premiums: *ibid.*, 49.

194 Huber and Litan, "Overview", n. 186 above, 19.

195 Garber, n. 177 above, pp. xxx–xxxi. That uneasiness over the ability to determine injury causation has extended to concern over the jury's role in cases involving expert evidence, causation and medicinal products. This concern is due to the complexity of causation and drugs and the questionable ability of jurors to understand technical evidence surrounding causation: Cecil, Hans and Wiggins, "Citizen Comprehension of Difficult Issues: lessons from Civil Jury Trials" (1991) 40 *The American University Law Review* 727, 740.

possible to say whether the plaintiff or the defendant is favoured on balance by difficulties in establishing injury causation.[196] By far the most controversial decision in respect of the uncertainty in proving injury causation, other than *Oxendine* v. *Merrell Dow Pharmaceutials Inc.*,[197] is that of *Wells* v. *Ortho Pharmaceutical Corp.*[198] Indeed, it has been noted that this case "has come to symbolize the possibility of major financial liabilities based on findings of causation in the absence of scientific evidence".[199] In *Wells*, the plaintiffs, on behalf of their daughter, brought an action against the defendant alleging that a spermicide manufactured and marketed by the defendants and allegedly used by the plaintiff several months before and after the child's conception had caused birth defects.[200] The medical and scientific studies were in direct conflict and failed to show conclusively whether or not the spermicide had caused any or all of the birth defects.[201] The District Court emphasised that the plaintiffs' burden was "not to produce an unassailable scientific study" proving the spermicides caused the birth defects, but rather to show from all the evidence presented, to a reasonable degree of medical certainty, that the spermicide had caused some or all of the child's birth defects.[202] The District Court's decision turned on the oral evidence of the expert witnesses, the court paying attention to the "demeanour and tone" of each expert and attempting to ascertain "motives, biases, and interests that might have influenced each expert's opinion".[203] The District Court found the plaintiffs' expert evidence more credible[204] holding to a reasonable degree of medical probability, in the light of competent and credible evidence, that the spermicide had caused the birth defects of the child's left shoulder and arm and right hand.[205] On appeal, the Court of Appeals affirmed the District Court's finding that the plaintiffs had proved to a reasonable degree of certainty that the spermicide had caused the child's defects.[206]

The Court observed, in a clear digression from other settled decisions:

> "A cause–effect relationship need not be clearly established by animal or epidemiological studies before a doctor can testify that, in his opinion, such a relationship exists. As long as the basic methodology employed to reach such a conclusion is sound, such as use of tissue samples, standard tests, and patient examination, products liability law does not preclude recovery until a 'statistically significant' number of people have been injured or until science has had the time and resources to complete sophisticated laboratory studies of the chemical."[207]

[196] Garber, n. 177 above, 47.
[197] 506 A 2d 1100 (DC App. 1986). See Chap. 3.
[198] 615 F Supp. 262 (DC Ga. 1985), aff'd. in part, modif'd. in part, 788 F. 2d 741 (11th Cir. 1986), reh'g. denied en banc, 795 F 2d 89 (11th Cir. 1986), 615 F Supp. 262 (DC Ga. 1985).
[199] Garber, n. 177 above, 47.
[200] 615 F Supp 262, 266 (DC Ga. 1985).
[201] *Ibid.*, 266, 292.
[202] *Ibid.*, 266.
[203] *Ibid.*, 267.
[204] *Ibid.*
[205] *Ibid.*, 294–5.
[206] 788 F 2d 741, 744–5 (11th Cir. 1986).
[207] *Ibid.*, 744–5.

However, it is arguable that in this case there was insufficient evidence to show any association between spermicides and birth defects. It would seem that uncertainty in respect of injury causation creates the opportunity for inconsistent judicial decisions such as *Wells*. Judicial discretion in the determination of such cases may not be unwelcome, but the lack of consistency surrounding the way in which evidence is utilised by judges in assessing injury causation is something that can only generate economic inefficiency in the long term. In the light of subsequent scientific data, and a reassessment of a key evidentiary study in the *Wells* litigation, the same federal district, albeit in a case with factual differences, held that the epidemiological studies and genetic data relied on by the plaintiffs' experts on the issue whether the vaginal spermicide caused a child's birth defects were not the type of data reasonably relied on by experts in determining the cause of such defects. Thus the expert evidence was ruled inadmissible.[208] On this occasion, the court placed its emphasis upon the epidemiological studies relied on by the plaintiff which were insufficient to establish causal link. It is submitted that it was the court's failure in *Wells* properly to assess the probative value of the epidemiological evidence that led to the incongruous decision in that case. A greater use of probabilistic statistics, refined to address the particular instances of each case, could reduce the possibility of abuse of judicial discretion in such circumstances.[209]

Nevertheless, recent authorities have suggested that courts have become harder on plaintiffs on their need to show through epidemiological studies that a defective medicinal product caused the plaintiff's injuries.[210] Indeed, the rebuttable presumption in favour of causation in *Reyes* v. *Wyeth Laboratories*,[211] i.e. that a consumer would have read any warning provided by a manufacturer and acted so as to minimise the risks,[212] has recently been rejected under Mississippi law in *Thomas* v. *Hoffmann-La Roche, Inc.*[213] It also

[208] *Smith* v. *Ortho Pharmaceutical Corp.*, 770 F Supp. 1561, 1581 (ND Ga. 1991).

[209] See Chap. 1.

[210] See *Turpin* v. *Merrell Dow Pharmaceuticals Inc.*, 959 F 2d 1349 (6th Cir. 1992), cert. denied, 113 S Ct. 84 (1992); *Richardson* v. *Richardson-Merrell Inc.*, 857 F 2d 823 (1988), cert. denied, 493 US 822 (1989) (affirming judgment nov); *Brock* v. *Merrell Dow Pharmaceuticals Inc.* 874 F 2d 307, 311 (5th Cir. 1989), modified, 884 F 2d 166 (5th Cir. 1989), cert. denied, 494 US 1046 (1990) (granting judgment nov) and *Ealy* v. *Richardson-Merrell Inc.*, 897 F 2d 1159 (1990), cert. denied, 498 US 950 (1990) (granting judgment nov); Henderson and Eisenberg, "The Quiet Revolution in Products Liability: An Empirical Study of Legal Change" (1990) 37 *UCLA L Rev.* 479, 489, 491. Although Henderson and Eisenberg have suggested that medicinal product liability cases were promising in the late 1970s and early 1980s when based solely on epidemiological evidence of causal links between the medicinal products and the injuries (*ibid.*, 486), it is submitted that it was not so much the *sole* use of epidemiological evidence but the use of it, as in *Oxendine*, in a more flexible manner than might be expected with such evidence.

[211] 498 F 2d 1264 (5th Cir.), cert. denied 419 US 1096 (1974).

[212] 498 F 2d 1264, 1281 (5th Cir.).

[213] 949 F 2d 806, 808, 812, 814 (5th Cir. 1992) (plaintiff must show that adequate warning would have convinced the prescribing physician not to prescribe the drug for the plaintiff). The plaintiff had to show by a preponderance of the evidence that the inadequate warning caused the plaintiff's injuries: *ibid.*, 808, 814. In that case, the plaintiff failed to introduce sufficient evidence to show that the allegedly inadequate warning on Accutane had caused her injury: *ibid.*, 811. This so-called

seems that mechanisms to adjudge liability on the basis of market share in the DES cases have attracted criticism. *Sindell* v. *Abbott Laboratories*,[214] the doyen of the market share liability decisions, has been criticised as being economically unfeasible on the ground that the size of the awards have not been sufficiently large to justify the delays, uncertainties and costs in the legal process.[215] It may be, however, that a refinement of the market share approach through a reassessment of the statistical evidence available may reduce the uncertainties of such cases.[216]

(iii) Quantification of Effect of Product Liability on Incentives

There has been a dearth of information on the quantitative effects of product liability on innovation in the pharmaceutical industry. General statistics relating to product liability and innovation have been assembled using the ratemaking files of the US Insurance Services Office (ISO) in respect of product liability coverage for 1980–4.[217] Nevertheless, the results are subject to certain caveats. First, the results are by no means exhaustive and pharmaceutical companies are not well represented in the ratemaking files. Secondly, the statistics do not explain the move to self-insurance by pharmaceutical companies in the 1980s, which may have skewed some of the figures. Thirdly, the majority of decisions involving product liability and pharmaceuticals occurred after the survey.[218] Nevertheless, the results show that the loss ratios (the ratios of losses to premiums for insurance policies) for pharmaceuticals are well above the national average, and that there have been dramatic declines in premiums and ratios of premiums to sales. This may, however, be partly explained by the drug industry's move to self-insurance.[219]

The most recent qualitative assessment on the effects of product liability on company incentives in the pharmaceutical industry has been produced by the RAND Corporation in their report *Product Liability and the Economics of*

"heeding presumption" in favour of causation has also been rejected in the context of prescription drugs and medical devices by §6 of the new Restatement (Third) of Torts: American Law Institute, *Restatement of the Law Third, Torts: Products Liability* (Philadelphia, Penn., American Law Institute, 1998). See also Schwartz, "The Impact of the New Products Liability Restatement on Prescription Products" (1995)50 *Food and Drug Law Journal* 399, 404. Schwartz suggests that the new Restatement will probably "accelerate" the already existing pro-defendant trends of the US courts in product liability: *ibid.*, 413.

214 607 P 2d 924 (1980).

215 Schwartz, "The Beginning and the Possible End of the Rise of Modern American Tort Law" (1992) 26 *Georgia LR* 601, 688.

216 It has already been noted that a slavish adherence to market share liability is not always consistent with an analysis of such cases in terms of reformulation of the gist of an action into loss of a chance of avoiding a physical injury: see above, cf Stapleton, *Product Liability*, n. 9 above, 287–8.

217 Viscusi and Moore, "An Industrial Profile of the Links between Product Liability and Innovation", n. 188 above, 84.

218 See US Congress, Office of Technology Assessment, *Pharmaceutical R & D: Costs, Risks and Rewards*, n. 181 above, 178 and Viscusi and Moore, n. 188 above, 85.

219 Viscusi and Moore, n. 188 above, 94–6.

Pharmaceuticals and Medical Devices.[220] They have shown that the incentive to introduce an already developed product "is sensitive to unusual liability risks".[221] Liability risks of a 1 per cent annual probability of product failure reduce the incentive by about 10 per cent. Liability risks of 4 per cent reduce the incentive by about 33⅓ per cent. The incentive to invest in clinical trials is even more sensitive to liability risks than incentives to introduce a developed product. Liability risks of a 1 per cent annual probability of product failure reduce the incentive by approximately 15 per cent. Liability risks of 4 per cent reduce the incentive to invest in clinical trials by about 50 per cent. This greater sensitivity to liability risk can be explained by the longer delay between the decision to invest in clinical trials and the time profits might accrue, in comparison with introducing an already developed product.[222] Although these figures are those of the United States, they remain a cause for concern in their relevance to the UK, which has no equivalent quantitative figures. Of great importance is the fact that the RAND Corporation has shown that an unusual liability risk (particularly present with high risk products associated with difficulty in proving injury causation) is a greater problem for incentives than the delay in the FDA approval process. RAND have calculated that liability risks of a 1 per cent annual probability of product failure may reduce the incentive to invest in clinical trials by more than an extra year of expected delay in the FDA approval process.[223]

As already indicated, no equivalent quantitative figures exist for the UK. It has been submitted that extrapolation from the US experience to predicting the long-term impact of the EC Product Liability Directive has been rendered unlikely by the institutional differences between the USA and the UK.[224] However, both systems share uncertainty in the assessment of risk and the difficulties of proof of injury causation.

Without a systematic study of the effect of product liability on innovation in the pharmaceutical industry, with particular emphasis on difficulties associated with medicinal products of high risk areas, such as pregnancy drugs and vaccines, these issues will remain unanswered. The fact also that the US market is the dominant market in the world pharmaceutical industry will have an effect on the innovation decisions made by pharmaceutical companies in Europe.

[220] Garber, n. 177 above, 159, 162, 163.

[221] *Ibid.*, 159.

[222] *Ibid.*

[223] Nevertheless, RAND has concluded that liability has a lesser effect on innovation than patent policy: *ibid.*, 187.

[224] Stapleton, n. 9 above, 85. What is certainly clear is that no more money has been spent on research and development as a result of the EC Product Liability Dir.: Hodges, *Report for the Commission of the European Communities on the Application of Directive 85/374/EEC on Liability for Defective Products* (London, McKenna & Co., 1994), para. 83, 28. In the Commissioner's First Report on the application of the Product Liability Dir., the Commission has considered it unnecessary to submit any proposals for the Dir.'s amendment: Commission of the European Communities First Report on the Application of Council Dir. on the Approximation of Laws, Regulations and Administrative provisions of the Member States Concerning Liability for Defective Products (85/374/EEC) Brussels, 13 Dec. 1995, COM (95) 617 final, 2.

(iv) The Solution—Reform of How Science is Used in Court to Determine Injury Causation

It has been argued that the current liability system promotes inefficient incentives through their distortion by factors such as the difficulty of proving injury causation.[225]

In respect of high risk products, such as contraceptives, vaccines and products for pregnancy-related illnesses, misperceptions of liability are generated by "decisions reflecting controversial science",[226] highlighting the establishment of liability in the absence of concrete epidemiological evidence. As a result, liability in respect of some products is overestimated and, in relation to others, underestimated. The unpredictability of the eventual liability costs with such products results in deterring companies from producing socially valuable medicinal products.[227] The RAND report argues that the means of improving the quality of scientific evidence to determine injury causation are the key to reform in this area.[228] The report recognises the need to "promote economic efficiency" by a new approach. Such reforms would need to "strengthen the beliefs of company decision-makers that injuries caused by their products will be recognised as such [whilst allaying] concerns that companies will be held liable for injuries not caused by their products".[229] The report concludes:

> "Improving the scientific basis for legal determination of liability is a policy initiative that could strengthen efficient deterrence while attenuating inefficient deterrence."[230]

It is submitted that the use of probabilistic statistical methods, such as the Bayes' Theorem,[231] may improve the scientific basis for the determination of injury causation, together with the use of court-appointed experts to interpret such evidence for the assistance of the courts.[232] This has already been recognised by Lasagna, who notes the need for assistance in dealing with the evaluation of epidemiologic evidence through court experts or "adopt[ing] a more discrete evidentiary standard that would reflect more accurately the realities of causation".[233]

225 Garber, n. 177 above, 180–181.
226 *Ibid.*, 184.
227 *Ibid.*, 184–5.
228 *Ibid.*, 194.
229 *Ibid.*, p. xxiv. See also 194.
230 *Ibid.*, 194.
231 See Chap. 1.
232 See Chap. 3.
233 Lasagna, n. 71 above, 356. Cf support for traditional causation, except "in unusual circumstances", but not where identification of the defendant is possible: Henderson and Twerski, "A Proposed Revision of Section 402A of the Restatement (Second) of Torts" (1992) 77 *Cornell LR* 1512, 1518, 1535.

The courts have shown a tendency to be uncomfortable with probabilistic assessments and multiple causation.[234] In a recent criminal case, *Regina* v. *Adams*,[235] Rose LJ expressed the view, in a reserved judgment, that evidence of the Bayes' Theorem was inadmissible in a criminal case since "it trespassed on an area peculiarly and exclusively within the jury's province, namely the way in which they evaluated the relationship between one piece of evidence and another"[236]. He observed that the Bayes' Theorem might be an appropriate and useful tool for statisticians, but that it was not appropriate for use in jury trials or as a means to assist the jury. In the first place, the theorem's methodology required items of evidence to be assessed separately according to their bearing on the guilt of the accused before being combined in the overall formula. Secondly, and more fundamentally, the attempt to determine the guilt or innocence on the basis of a mathematical formula applied to each separate piece of evidence was an approach, inappropriate to the jury's task.[237]

In *Regina* v. *Adams (No. 2)*,[238] Lord Bingham CJ, giving judgment for the Court of Appeal, held that reliance on the evidence of the Bayes' Theorem in respect of non-scientific evidence was "a recipe for confusion, misunderstanding and misjudgment, possibily even among counsel, . . . very probably among judges and . . . almost certainly among jurors",[239] and that in the absence of "special features", expert evidence should not be admitted to induce juries to attach mathematical values to probabilities arising from non-scientific evidence adduced at the trial.[240] Lord Bingham CJ opined that the jury would not be assisted "by reference to a very complex approach which they are unlikely to apply accurately, which the [court judged] to be likely to confuse them and distract them from their consideration of the real questions on which they should seek to reach a unanimous conclusion".[241]

Two points should be noted. First, the Bayes' Theorem is not evaluating the guilt or innocence of the accused in such a case. It is merely a method of evaluating evidence that can be used by judge and jury in making the decision on the guilt or innocence of the accused. Secondly, despite the criticisms and reservations of Rose LJ and Lord Bingham CJ, it is submitted that it would be a useful tool to assist the judge in deliberating on whether a drug caused damage in a civil medicinal product liability case, where the standard of proof is the balance of probabilities and where the "special features" of scientific epidemiological evidence are present. The judge could use the theorem and court experts/panels to aid him in his deliberations. Such experts would include those with statistical

[234] Grabowski, "Product Liability in Pharmaceuticals: Comments on Chapters Eight and Nine" in Huber and Litan, n. 71 above, 363.

[235] [1996] 2 Cr. App. Rep. 467.

[236] *Ibid.*, 481.

[237] *Ibid.*

[238] [1998] 1 Cr. App. Rep. 377.

[239] *Ibid.*, 384.

[240] *Ibid.*, 385.

[241] *Ibid.*

experience in the area at issue. In this way, economic efficiency would be promoted in practice. A corresponding reduction in Legal Aid resources wasted on frivolous litigation could also transpire so that such resources could be redirected to more deserving cases. The Legal Aid Fund would be alerted to the use of such evidence and would be able to make its own decisions on the basis of it.

4. CONCLUSION—THE RECONCILIATION OF THE ECONOMIC ANALYSIS IN THEORY AND IN PRACTICE

A theoretical analysis has attempted to show that the use of statistical approaches to the ascertainment of causal link in cases involving medicinal products promotes the efficiency theory of law and economics. The analysis appears to show that, in the majority of cases, cause seems to approximate the Calabresian concept of the cheapest cost avoider in the context of causation and medicinal products. The Landes and Posner economic model of causation, derived as a refinement of the Learned Hand formula, has been found to be consistent with a probabilistic approach to causality and illustrations of the model's application to cases involving causation and medicinal products have been shown. It is conceded, however, that difficulties in the case of overlapping enterprises exist but that Landes and Posner's use of their economic model in the context of causal uncertainty could promote economic efficiency, even in such difficult cases, using a probabilistic approach. The idea that manufacturers of medicinal products should only be liable for the accidents that they cause in *probabilistic* terms is consistent with Shavell's interpretation of the efficiency theory and causation.

A criticism has been provided of non-economic theories of liability, i.e. Epstein's theory of strict liability, Stapleton's moral enterprise liability theory and Reece's causal determinism and indeterminism and their relation to lost chance cases, concluding with the view that a probabilistic approach to ascertaining cause is the most efficient one to promote accurate decision-making in courts in the medicinal product area and that this has been eschewed by these non-economic theorists. None of their solutions addresses the difficult problem of ascertaining specific instances of causal link in individual cases and none promotes efficient decision-making from an economic perspective. Although this writer concedes that the requirement of causation dramatically draws attention to the inherent tension between individualised and collective/distributive justice paradigms, it is submitted that a probabilistic approach to causation will help promote efficiency in practice. It has been demonstrated that there is considerable support for the need for efficient decision-making and resolution of causal problems in practice. Such an approach is necessary to counter the problem of inefficient product liability, resulting from both inappropriate and misperceived incentives by companies, creating inconsistent and incongruous judicial decisions.

Incentives to introduce developed medicinal products or to invest in clinical trials have been shown to be sensitive to unusual product liability risks. In the light of such problems, theories of economic efficiency have been presented as consistent with probabilistic methods of ascertaining cause in cases involving causation and medicinal products.

7

The Development Risk Defence and Medicinal Products[1]

1. THE DISTINCTION BETWEEN "PROBABILISTIC RISK" AND "DEVELOPMENT RISK"

In the previous chapters, emphasis has been placed upon an epidemiological approach to resolving problems involving causation and medicinal products. When encountering the term "risk", the thesis has so far focused on "*probabilistic* risk", namely the probability of a drug causing an adverse effect to an individual patient. It has been previously argued in Chapter 1 that such risk should take into consideration the circumstances which are personal to an individual, and the Bayes' Theorem has been proposed as a suggested means of achieving such an objective.

Closely related to the economics issues of the previous chapter is the issue of liability for undiscoverable defects. It is here that a distinction should be made between "*probabilistic* risk" and another form of risk, "development risk", which is the inherent risk of a defective product being undiscoverable at the time of supply by a manufacturer.

2. THE NATURE OF THE DEVELOPMENT RISK DEFENCE

The development risk defence (the defence) is defined in section 4(1)(e) of the Consumer Protection Act 1987 (the Act). It is a term preferable to "state of the art defence", since "development risk" refers to undiscoverable defects[2] whereas "state of the art" is associated with the most up-to-date technology and safety standards in a particular industry, the latter term (state of art) being relevant to ascertaining defective products.[3]

[1] This chap. is an expanded version of R. Goldberg, "The Development Risk Defence and Medicinal Products" (1991) 36 *JLSS* 376.

[2] "Development risks" have been defined as "risks present in production sectors in which an advance in technological and scientific knowledge may make a product appear defective *ex post*, whereas it was not regarded as such at the time when it was manufactured": Case C–300/95 *EC Commission* v. *United Kingdom of Great Britain* [1997] ECR I–2649, *per* Tesauro AG, para. 18.

[3] Clark, *Product Liability* (London, Sweet & Maxwell, 1989), 151; Newdick, "The Development Risk Defence of the Consumer Protection Act 1987" (1988) 47 *Camb. LJ* 455. Indeed, Tesauro AG seemed aware of this distinction when he said that since Art. 7(e) referred "solely to the scientific and technical knowledge at the time when the product was marketed, it [was] not concerned with the practices and safety standards in use in the industrial sector in which the producer [was]

Section 4(1)(e) of the Act states that there will be a defence to the person proceeded against to show that the state of scientific and technical knowledge at the relevant time was not such that a producer of products of the same description as the product in question might be expected to have discovered the defect if it had existed in his products while they were under his control. Article 7(e) of the EC Directive on Product Liability[4] states that the defence will arise if "the state of scientific and technical knowledge at the time when [the producer] put the product into circulation was not such as to enable the existence of the defect to be discovered". The alleged distinction between the two versions of the defence led to infringement proceedings being brought by the Commission against the UK under Article 169 of the EC Treaty for failure to fulfil the obligation of implementing the Directive correctly in this respect. The UK made a formal reply to the Commission's formal notice regarding incorrect implementation of the Directive, saying it considered that it had implemented it in the only way possible in the UK. A reasoned opinion for failure to implement the Directive on Product Liability was sent by the Commission to the UK,[5] to which the UK replied. The Commission considered that the complaint relating to section 4(1)(e) of the Act was justified and brought an action for a declaration that the UK did not correctly implement Article 7(e). An oral hearing took place on 7 November 1996.[6] Advocate General Tesauro delivered his opinion on 23 January 1997 and proposed that the Court should dismiss the application and order the Commission to pay the costs.[7]

The Advocate General attempted to describe in his opinion what the concept of the state of scientific knowledge actually was. He observed:

> "[T]he state of scientific knowledge cannot be identified with the views expressed by the majority of learned opinion, but with the most advanced level of research which has been carried out at a given time."[8]

Prima facie, this appears to give clear guidance to researchers in the pharmaceutical industry. However, it is at this point that his observations appear to become unclear. He observes that "one isolated opinion" which might eventually become the generally accepted view of the potentially defective nature of a product is outside the scope of liability.[9] It seems, however, that the word "isolated" could have two possible connotations, namely isolated in terms of the

operating": Case C–300/95 *EC Commission* v. *United Kingdom* [1997] ECR I–2649, *per* Tesauro AG, para. 20. This position was affirmed by the ECJ's judgment: *ibid.*, para. 26.

[4] 85/374/EEC, on the approximation of the laws, regulations and administrative provisions of the Member States concerning liability for defective products [1985] OJ L210/29, 7.8.85, hereinafter referred to as "the Directive".

[5] Searles and Scott-Larson, "European Update" (Oct. 1990), *Product Liability International* 155.

[6] Mildred, "Class Actions", in Miller, *Product Liability and Safety Encyclopædia* (London, Butterworths, 1997), Division IIIA, para. 131.

[7] Case C–300/95 *EC Commission* v. *United Kingdom* [1997] ECR I–2649, *per* Tesauro AG, para. 31.

[8] *Ibid.*, *per* Tesauro AG, para. 21.

[9] *Ibid.*, para. 22.

accessibility of scientific and technical knowledge and isolated in terms of general acceptance of such knowledge.[10] Although Advocate General Tesauro closely links isolation with availability and accessibility of such knowledge,[11] his choice of the word "isolated" creates an uncertainty whether there is a link between an isolated opinion and one which might be regarded as a maverick opinion and lacking general acceptance. If there is such a link, then it would have been useful for the Advocate General to have made this clear from his opinion.

The Advocate General defined the state of knowledge as including "all data in the information circuit of the scientific community as a whole, bearing in mind, however on the basis of a reasonableness test, the actual opportunities for the information to circulate".[12] However, there is obviously a need to take into account the instantaneous nature of modern scientific knowledge on CD Rom, the Internet and other data retrieval systems for scientific and medical research.[13] The opinion lacks discussion of the impact of the information superhighway on scientific and technical knowledge, and this is to be regretted.

The Advocate General reaffirmed the settled legal position of the European Court of Justice that the scope of national laws, regulations and administrative provisions had to be assessed in the light of their interpretation by national courts,[14] and that the failure of the Commission to wait until the Act was applied by the national courts before bringing an action against the UK for incorrectly implementing the Directive was "over-hasty".[15]

In the light of these observations, the Advocate General opined that the Commission had failed to show that section 4(1)(e) of the Act had not correctly implemented Article 7(e) of the Directive.[16]

The European Court of Justice, in its judgment of 29 May 1997, followed the opinion of the Advocate General in dismissing the application and ordering the Commission to pay the costs on five grounds.[17]

First, section 4(1)(e) placed the burden of proof on the producer, as required by Article 7. Nevertheless, it seems that the defence itself has been constructed

[10] Case C–300/95 *EC Commission* v. *United Kingdom* [1997] ECR I–2649, *per* Tesauro AG, para. 22.

[11] *Ibid.*, para. 23.

[12] *Ibid.*, para. 24.

[13] It has been argued that powerful computerised databases are available without regard to the industrial sector within which a producer works, and that there is therefore no reason to confine discoverability by accessibility to a particular sector: Mildred and Howells, "Comment on 'Development Risks: Unanswered Questions'" (1998) 61 *MLR* 570, 572. However, since the knowledge content of databases is great, it is arguably impossible and unjust for a producer to be aware of all knowledge in respect of a defect in *every* sector.

[14] Case C–382/92 *EC Commission* v. *United Kingdom* [1994] ECR I–2435, para. 36; Joined Cases C–732/91, C–138/91 and C–139/91 *Katsikas and Others* [1992] ECR I–6577, para. 39.

[15] Case C–300/95 *EC Commission* v. *United Kingdom* [1997] ECR I–2649, *per* Tesauro AG, para. 29.

[16] *Ibid.*

[17] Case C–300/95 *EC Commission* v. *United Kingdom* [1997] ECR I–2649, paras. 34–40.

in a manner which reflects the requirements of negligence, in that it stresses the conduct of producers and whether they might be expected to discover the defect.

Secondly, the Court held that section 4(1)(e) placed no restriction on the state and degree of scientific and technical knowledge at the material time which was to be taken into account. The Court had held that Article 7(e) was unreservedly directed at "the most advanced level of such knowledge, at the time when the product in question was put into circulation".[18] Arguably, however, the discoverability and accessibility of such knowledge is more restrictive than the European Court of Justice has held. Indeed, Advocate General Tesauro had already stated that although Article 7(e) was not concerned with the practices and safety standards in use in the industrial sector in which the producer was operating, it was assessing the producer's conduct by the "yardstick" of the "knowledge of an expert in the sector".[19] In addition, the state of knowledge "included all data in the information circuit of the scientific community as a whole, *bearing in mind, however, on the basis of a reasonableness test the actual opportunities for the information to circulate*".[20] There is clearly therefore *some* restriction on the discoverability and accessibility of scientific and technical knowledge.[21]

Thirdly, the Court held that the wording of section 4(1)(e) did not suggest that the defence's availability depended on the subjective knowledge of a producer taking reasonable care in the light of the standard precautions of the relevant industrial sector. The producer's ability to discover the defect was formulated as an objective test by Advocate General Tesauro[22] on the basis that reference to the producer's ability is an "objectively verifiable assessable parameter, which is in no way influenced by consideration of the actual subjective knowledge of the producer or by his organizational and economic requirements".[23] But even if one were to concede that the test was objective, there seems to be a subjective element in the sense that the judge is left to decide in the circumstances of the particular case whether a reasonable producer might have been expected to discover the defect. This is in line with Lord MacMillan's description of the standard of foresight of the reasonable man in negligence, when assessing whether a breach of duty of care has occurred, in *Glasgow Corporation* v. *Muir*.[24]

[18] *Ibid.*, para. 26.

[19] *Ibid.*, *per* Tesauro AG, para. 20.

[20] *Ibid.*, para. 24. Emphasis added.

[21] Cf. Hodges, Note, "Development Risks: Unanswered Questions" (1998) 61 *MLR* 560, 565, 567 who considers that the ECJ's approach of the most advanced level of scientific and technical knowledge does not accord with the *reality* of scientific and technical knowledge, and is so high a standard that it could arguably never succeed in practice.

[22] N. 17 above, para. 26.

[23] *Ibid.* However, the pharmaceutical industry has consistently argued that discoverability should be linked to economic feasibility. See below.

[24] [1943] AC 448.

He observed:[25]

> "The standard of foresight of the reasonable man is in one sense an impersonal test. It eliminates the personal equation and is independent of the idiosyncrasies of the particular person whose conduct is in question . . . The reasonable man is presumed to be free both from over-apprehension and from over-confidence, but there is a sense in which the standard of care of the reasonable man involves in its application a *subjective*[26] element. It is still left to the judge to decide what, in the circumstances of the particular case, the reasonable man would have had in contemplation and what, accordingly, the party sought to be made liable ought to have foreseen."

Fourthly, having reaffirmed the rule that national laws, regulations and administrative provisions must be assessed in the light of the interpretation given to them by national courts,[27] the European Court held that the Commission had failed to refer to any national judicial decision which interpreted section 4(1)(e) (the national law) as inconsistent with Article 7(e) (the Directive provision). However, to give the Commission its due, there was always a legitimate fear that this issue would only be triable in a case involving the discoverability of unforeseeable or undiscoverable defects, often of medicinal products, which would take several years to come to trial in the UK. If such a case were to be decided on this issue, the development risk defence in its section 4(1)(e) form might operate to deny liability in circumstances where the Article 7(e) definition might accept liability.

Fifthly, the European Court held that nothing in the material submitted to the Court suggested that the UK courts, if called upon to interpret section 4(1)(e), would not do so in the light of the wording and purpose of the Directive, as required by Article 189 of the EC Treaty. Moreover, section 1(1) of the Act imposed such an obligation on the national courts.[28]

The one clear situation in which the need for regard to the Directive is apparent is where the legislation is *ambiguous*. Since the legislation in section 4(1)(e) *is* ambiguous in its drafting, regard should be had to the Directive. However, the UK remains protected from an allegation of failure to implement under Article 169 since the Directive will assist in the interpretation of section 4(1)(e). Only if section 4(1)(e) had been *unambiguous* would there have been a strong argument that the legislation should have clearly enforced the Directive. The UK therefore seems to have benefited from the ambiguous way in which section 4(1)(e) has been drafted.

It is clear from the Directive that Member States are at liberty to choose whether to adopt or to derogate from the development risk defence.[29] All Member States with the exception of France have adopted national legislation implementing the Directive. All Member States except Luxembourg and

[25] [1943] AC 448, at 457.
[26] Emphasis added.
[27] See Case C–382/192 *Commission* v. *United Kingdom* [1994] ECR I–2435, para. 36.
[28] Case C–300/95 *EC Commission* v. *United Kingdom* [1997] ECR I–2649, paras. 34–40.
[29] Art. 15 of Dir. 85/374/EEC.

Finland are adopting the development risk defence and Germany has adopted the defence, except with regard to pharmaceuticals. Spain has adopted the defence, except in respect of medicines, food or food products intended for human consumption.[30]

It has been argued that the Directive focuses upon a state of knowledge enabling discovery of a defect, while the Act stresses the conduct of producers.[31] However, it has been convincingly reasoned that HM Government's interpretation is correct.[32] First, when an assessment of the relevant state of scientific and technical knowledge takes place, it will not require the defendant to prove "a worldwide absence of knowledge of the defect". In practice, the defence will operate when the defendant shows that there is no prior knowledge of the defect in the field with which he is expected to be familiar. Secondly, the plaintiff could expose information which revealed the defect but which could not reasonably be expected to be known to the producer. If such unrelated knowledge denied the defence's operation, the search for evidence would be "haphazard and wasteful".[33]

The section 4(1)(e) definition is satisfactory for the Association of the British Pharmaceutical Industry (ABPI) in its capacity of representing the interests of the pharmaceutical industry.[34] Nevertheless, it is submitted that the words "a producer of products of the same description as the product in question" cloud the definition with inherent complications. For example, does "a producer of products of the same description as the product in question" refer to all producers of drugs of the same therapeutic class (the author's submitted view) or does the definition embrace a more comprehensive group of drugs? Perhaps courts will return to the Directive, in accordance with section 1(1) of the Act, and to case law for an answer to these problems.

In considering the European Commission's comparatively uncontroversial proposal to extend the EC Product Liability Directive to cover primary agricultural products and game,[35] the European Parliament's Committee on the Environment, Public Health and Consumer Protection has sparked some controversy by proposing several significant changes to the Directive, including abolition of the development risk defence. The Committee has stated that producers which enjoy the profits of putting a successful innovative product on the market should bear its risks.[36] However, on 7 December 1998, the proposed

[30] EC Commission. *First Report on the Application of Council Directive on the Approximation of Laws, Regulations and Administrative Provisions of the Member States Concerning Liability for Defective Products (85/374/EEC) Brussels*, 13 Dec. 1995, COM(95)617 final, 4.

[31] Clark, n. 3 above, 153.

[32] Newdick, n. 3 above, 459, 460.

[33] *Ibid.*, 465.

[34] See Association of the British Pharmaceutical Industry, *ABPI Briefing on the Consumer Protection Bill* (London, ABPI, 6th Mar. 1987).

[35] Proposal for a European Parliament and Council Dir. amending Council Dir. 85/374/EEC on the approximation of the laws, regulations and administrative provisions of the Member States concerning liability for defective products: COM(97)0478 final—COD 97/0244 [1997] OJ C 337, 07.11.97.

[36] *Draft Report of the European Parliament Committee on the Environment, Public Health and Consumer Protection*, 3 Mar. 1998.

changes to be Directive were voted down by the European Parliament, which decided to take the matter no further.[37]

3. DEFECTS WHICH MIGHT BE EXPECTED TO BE DISCOVERED

(i) Discoverability and Economic Feasibility

In terms of medicinal product defects, the pre-clinical animal test stage will screen out drugs which are too dangerous and the commoner forms of adverse drug reactions will be detected at the pre-marketing stage of clinical trials. However, the only way that one can detect the rarer forms of adverse reactions to drugs is by large-scale usage involving widespread marketing. The Directive makes no reference to the practicability of the measures enabling a defect to be discovered.[38] But in the pharmaceutical field a distinction can be made between defects that are economically feasible to detect at the pre-clinical and clinical trial stages and those that are not.[39] Given that "any narrow interpretation would remove the utility of the defence for the innovative medicinal product manufacturer", it has been suggested that there is a strong case for saying discoverability should incorporate a consideration of economic feasibility.[40] Because of economic considerations, some US pharmaceutical companies have moved out of high-risk areas such as vaccines and contraception.[41] Moreover, HM Government stated in a minute of the Council of Ministers that it interpreted the defence as incorporating some consideration of what is reasonable to expect a manufacturer to discover. Contrastingly, the French minute was to the effect that economics have no relevance to the scientific issue of whether a defect is discoverable.[42] However, in the Commission's recent application against the UK for failing to implement the Directive correctly in respect of Article 7(e), Advocate General Tesauro stated in his opinion that "the practicability and expense of measures suitable for eliminating the defect from the product" are outside the scope of Article 7(e).[43] The Advocate General's view is arguably unrealistic given the inevitable bearing of economics on design, manufacture and marketing of medicinal products.

[37] Personal communication from Christopher J. S. Hodges, Cameron McKenna, Solicitors, London, 8 Dec. 1998.

[38] Dodds-Smith and Spencer, "Product Liability for Medicinal Products" in Powers and Harris (eds), *Medical Negligence* (2nd edn., London: Butterworths, 1994), 523.

[39] Dodds-Smith, "The Implications of Strict Liability for Medicinal Products Under the Consumer Protection Act 1987" in Mann (ed.), *Risk and Consent to Risk in Medicine* (Carnforth, Parthenon, 1989), 124.

[40] Dodds-Smith and Spencer, n. 38 above, 384; Griffiths, "Defectiveness in EEC Product Liability" [1987] *JBL* 222, 225, 226.

[41] Dodds-Smith and Spencer, n. 38 above, 525.

[42] *Ibid.*

[43] Case C–300/95 *EC Commission* v. *United Kingdom*, [1997] ECR I–2649, para. 20.

(ii) Discoverability of Unknown and Unknowable Defects

US jurisdictions have been divided over the issue of discoverability of unknowable defects affecting strict liability.[44] In *Beshada* v. *Johns-Manville Products Corporation* NJ,[45] the court held[46] that "state-of-the-art [was] a negligence defence" and that unknowability of the dangers of asbestos was irrelevant in a strict liability claim, and hence not a defence. On the other hand, in the medicinal product liability case of *Feldman* v. *Lederle Laboratories*[47] Schreiber J said[48] that "[i]f *Beshada* were deemed to hold generally or in all cases, particularly with respect to a situation like the present one involving drugs vital to health, that in a warning context knowledge of the unknowable is irrelevant in determining the applicability of strict liability, we would not agree".

The application of strict liability to unknown and unknowable defects in the context of medicinal products was rejected in *Brown* v. *Superior Court (Abbott Laboratories)*,[49] where the court held that all prescription drugs are unavoidably unsafe products in terms of Comment K of section 402 A of the *Restatement (Second) of Torts* (1965), and that a drug manufacturer should not be strictly liable for failure to warn of defects inherent in a drug of which it neither knew nor could have known by the application of scientific knowledge available at the time of distribution.[50] The upshot of this appears to be that "[s]trict liability for prescription pharmaceuticals now appears to be applicable if at all, only in classic manufacturing defect cases".[51]

In synopsis, the US position appears to have moved towards a negligence test for unknowable design defects in pharmaceuticals. It is submitted that discoverability of unknowable medicinal product defects under the Act will be decided in a manner probably identical to the requirements under negligence, reflecting the producer's inability to discover unknowable defects.[52] This is particularly poignant in relation to medicinal products, an area where there is often rapid innovative development outstripping relevant safety research leading to a heavy onus on the manufacturer to discover what aspects of a medicinal product are harmful. For example, insulin can now be manufactured with the use of

[44] Clark, "The Consumer Protection Act 1987" (1987) 50 *MLR* 614 at 620; Clark, n. 3 above, 166–80.

[45] 447 A 2d 539 (1982).

[46] *Ibid.*, at 546.

[47] 479 A 2d 374 (1984).

[48] *Ibid.*, at 387.

[49] 751 P 2d 470 (Cal 1988).

[50] *Ibid.*, at 479–82. See now, below, § 6(c) of the new *American Law Institute Restatement of the Law (Third) Torts: Products Liability* (Philadelphia, Penn., American Law Institute, 1998).

[51] Industry Attorney Geoffrey Smith in the *Pharmaceutical Manufacturers Association Newsletter*, vol. 30, no. 14, 11 Apr. 1988.

[52] It seems that the producer's ability to discover defects is not a subjective issue but an objective one: Tesauro AG's opinion in Case C–300/95 *EC Commission* v. *United Kingdom* [1997] ECR I–2649, *per* Tesauro AG, para. 26. This has been affirmed by the ECJ's judgment: *ibid.*, para. 36. See above.

organisms by a process of genetic engineering. The traditional technique is by extraction from bovine or porcine pancreatic glands.[53] The new multi-stage technique, involving genetic engineering, is complicated and involves additional stages and hazards. The implications of this submitted negligence approach are the requirements of more careful search for hitherto unknowable defects.

(iii) Known or Foreseeable Defects Yet Undiscoverable in Practice

(a) Extra-sensitive Persons with Allergic or Idiosyncratic Reactions

If a medicinal product is safe for the majority of users but is dangerous for a smaller number and cannot be made to a higher standard or be given a more specific warning of dangers, the question arises whether the defence is applicable. The majority of known or foreseeable injuries suffered will be looked at in the context of whether the product is defective from the position of the public in general under section 3 of the Act. It is possible, when looked at from the perspective of the individual rather than that of the public, that the product has not provided the safety that persons generally are entitled to expect. It is thus defective, and once a *prima facie* case of a defect is made out, the defence could be operable where the user at risk could not be identified.[54]

A possible example of a drug which could be regarded as being safe for the majority, but foreseeably dangerous for a minority, is chloramphenicol. The adverse reaction of aplastic anaemia due to bone marrow depression by chloramphenicol was discovered in 1955.[55] This antibiotic had been previously used to treat a whole number of infections successfully and the reported incidence of bone-marrow depression caused by chloramphenicol varied from one in 10,000 to one in 50,000.[56] Such a danger was foreseeable, since the metabolic action of antibiotics could have been perceived to have an effect on bone marrow cells, but it was certainly not discoverable, as it was impossible to show a sufficient statistical incidence of patients suffering from such a reaction prior to widespread marketing. In *Sharpe* v. *Pugh*[57] a doctor was held liable in negligence in 1967 for inappropriately prescribing chloramphenicol to a child who later died of aplastic anaemia and failing to warn the child's parents of possible or probable injurious effects.

[53] Lawrence and Bennett, *Clinical Pharmacology* (6th edn., Edinburgh, London and New York, Churchill Livingstone, 1987), 666.

[54] Newdick, n. 3 above, 467–9.

[55] D'Arcy and Griffin, *Iatrogenic Diseases* (2nd edn., Oxford, Oxford University Press, 1981), 3.

[56] Horler, "Blood Disorders" in Davies (ed.), *Textbook of Adverse Drug Reactions* (3rd edn., Oxford, Oxford University Press, 1985), 580.

[57] 155 SE 2d 108 (1967).

(b) Quality Control and Pharmaceuticals

It has been suggested that the defence should not be extended to cover problems of quality control[58] and that strict liability should apply for all such manufacturing defects, with only products "which public policy demands . . . outwith strict liability".[59] Such an exceptional group might be constituted by medicinal products with known but undiscoverable defects—for example, HIV-contaminated blood fractions prior to the discovery of the virus. Under these circumstances, sufferers of a disease through such a quality control defect could be left in an individious legal position.

(iv) **Defects Hidden from View by Limited Scientific and Technical Knowledge**

It is clear that medicinal products may be introduced to the market of which "complete understanding is impossible".[60] At the time of the thalidomide tragedy, drug companies were generally aware that a drug (the anti-cancer agent, aminopterin),[61] or maternal rubella (German measles), might cause teratogenesis. However, pharmaceutical science had not yet accepted the necessity for a routine screening process in experiments with animals to predict whether thalidomide could have such an effect.[62]

Diethylstilbestrol taken in pregnancy took up to 20 years to render cancer of the vagina detectable in the female offspring.[63] Practolol (Eraldin)[64] caused defects of the eye, skin and peritoneum which were detectable only after four years; the drug was the only one of a number of beta blockers to do so.[65] In the above examples the defence could conceivably be operable.

(v) **Defects Hidden from View by Limited General Knowledge**

Defects hidden from view by limited general knowledge are treated differently. Thus, a product defect may be unforeseen because of the "failure to put together obvious facts to appreciate and eliminate (or reduce) a risk".[66] It is difficult to

58 Newdick, n. 3 above, 472, 473.

59 Clark, n. 3 above, 166–8.

60 Newdick, n. 3 above, 461.

61 Davies (ed.), n. 56 above, 79.

62 Sneader, *Drug Discovery: The Evolution of Modern Medicines* (Chichester, New York, John Wiley & Sons, 1985), 32; Teff and Munro, *Thalidomide: The Legal Aftermath* (Farnborough, Saxon House, 1976), 32.

63 Herbst, Ulfelder and Poskanzer, "Adenocarcinoma of the Vagina: Association of Maternal Stilboestrol Therapy with Tumour Appearance in Young Women" [1971] *N Eng. J Med.* 878.

64 Lawrence and Bennett, n. 53 above, 501.

65 A. Goldberg, "Drug Regulation—A Global View"(1986) 5 *BIRA Journal*, 2–5.

66 P. S. Atiyah, *The Sale of Goods* (Adams, ed.) (9th edn., London, Pitman, 1995), 240.

relate such an example to medicinal products, but Professor Atiyah cites an example where limited general knowledge hides from view a possible defect. He states that child-proof medicine bottles are not inventions based on "scientific and technical knowledge" so that if the Act had been in force before their widespread use, a defendant supplying an ordinary medicine bottle could be held strictly liable on the ground that the bottle was defective.[67] However, in *Elsroth* v. *Johnson and Johnson*,[68] an unsuccessful claim on the existence of a design defect in cyanide-tampered extra-strength Tylenol capsules, the manufacturers (like those of most over-the-counter drugs) were given a timetable in which to take steps to improve product integrity by means of a tamper-resistant package. In recent cases of tampering, Sudafed was injected with cyanide poison,[69] and the existing FDA Tamper Resistant Packaging Regulations were updated in 1983, 1989 and 1990. All this suggests that tamper-resistant packaging is being sequentially improved with the state of scientific, and certainly technical, knowledge and that child-proof medicine bottles are indeed the product of technical knowledge. It thus seems that defects hidden from view by limited general knowledge is a category somewhat forced and difficult to justify in the context of medicinal products.

4. THE MEANING AND IMPLICATIONS OF SCIENTIFIC KNOWLEDGE

(i) When the Producer's Knowledge Arises

It has been said that "knowledge" arises when the acquisition of information reaches a stage where "a producer ought to take action to protect the consumer from danger".[70] This definition lends itself to ascertaining the problem of when knowledge arises in an innovative area where advances in scientific and technical knowledge are not clear cut.[71]

Guidance may be provided by the present law of negligence, where the courts have been imposing a high standard of care concerning the accuracy of product information of conceivable risks associated with normal use and possible foreseeable misuse, and they have been finding companies negligent where they have failed to exercise care in the research, design, manufacture, labelling or warning of products.

In *Wright* v. *Dunlop Rubber Co*,[72] ICI were held liable for the plaintiffs'

[67] P. S. Atiyah, *The Sale of Goods* (Adams, ed.) (9th edn., London, Pitman, 1995), 240.

[68] 700 F Supp. 151 (SDNY 1988).

[69] Food and Drug Administration Talk Papers of 3 and 4 Mar. 1991. US Department of Health and Human Services, Public Health Service, Maryland; remarks by President of Burroughs Wellcome Co on 7 Mar. 1991, reproduced in enclosure to NDMA's *Executive Newsletter*, 8 Mar. 1991, No. 10–91.

[70] Newdick n. 3 above, 466.

[71] *Ibid*., 464.

[72] (1972) 13 KIR 255.

contraction of cancer through being exposed to Nonox X from their commencing employment in Dunlop in 1946 and 1947 respectively, since they knew or ought to have realised in 1943 that the product was carcinogenic and should have taken appropriate steps to warn users.

In *Thompson* v. *Johnson and Johnson Pty. Ltd and Another*[73] the plaintiff sued the defendants, respectively distributors in Australia and manufacturers in New Zealand of tampons, for failing to warn her of the risk and symptoms of toxic shock syndrome. The plaintiff purchased some tampons no earlier than 1 November 1980. This potentially fatal condition had come to light over the previous year and a link with these tampons had been suggested. Prior to 5 October 1980 all reported cases of the illness had been confined to North America. On 5 October 1980 a case of toxic shock syndrome was reported in New Zealand, and this was confirmed on 14 October 1980. The victim had been using tampons manufactured by the second defendant and they were of a different type from those used in North America. The Supreme Court of Victoria stated[74] that "until the case occurred in New Zealand in October . . . the association of toxic shock syndrome with tampons had been shown to be only occurring in North America". The court held that the defendants did not breach their duty to the plaintiff in failing to advise the medical profession of toxic shock syndrome.

In *Buchan* v. *Ortho Pharmaceutical (Canada) Ltd*[75] the plaintiff sued a manufacturer of oral contraceptives for failing adequately to warn of the danger of stroke inherent in the use of the drug. The Ontario Court of Appeal held that the manufacturer had failed to discharge its duty. Robins JA stated:[76] "[w]hen additional dangerous or potentially dangerous side-effects from the drug's use are discovered, the manufacturer must make all reasonable efforts to communicate the information to prescribing physicians".

(ii) When Additional Knowledge First Appears to the Producer

A possible way of determining when the producer's additional knowledge of an adverse drug reaction (ADR) appears could be at the point in time when an ADR is defined. It has been stated[77] that "there are three main stages in the defining of an adverse drug reaction. First, the alerting message; second, the validation that such a suspicion truly associates a disease, syndrome, or symptom with a particular drug; and third, some evidence which provides a measure of the incidence of a particular ADR so that a proper judgment on the benefit-risk ratio may be taken". Scientific and technical knowledge would arise at stage two, a point in time when a definite association between a medicinal product

[73] (1991) Aust. Torts Reports 81–075, 68,587.
[74] *Ibid.*, at 68,603.
[75] (1986) 25 DLR (4th) 658.
[76] *Ibid.*, at 678.
[77] A. Goldberg, "Foreword to the Third Edition" in Davies (ed.), n. 56 above, p. xi.

and an adverse effect could be established either at the clinical trial stage or at the post-marketing stage. The scientific knowledge in question may for a time be restricted to the producer and the Committee on Safety of Medicines (CSM) and would then not be regarded as being part of knowledge yet in the public domain.[78]

(iii) When Additional Knowledge Appears in the General Domain

The European Court of Justice in *EC Commission* v. *United Kingdom*[79] observed that in order for the relevant scientific and technical knowledge to be successfully pleaded against the producer, such "knowledge must have been *accessible* at the time when the product in question was put into circulation".[80] Thus emphasis was placed on the need for scientific and technical knowledge to be accessible in discovering the defect.

It has been suggested that the most realistic point in deciding when knowledge is deemed to be thus available is once it has been published in a form that would come to the notice of the diligent producer, whether in a national or international professional journal.[81] A conceivable refinement to this would be the inclusion of a "conception period" for the product relating to the inevitable time delay between the initial discovery of a safer design and the time when implementation of it is feasible.[82]

(iv) The Constituents of Knowledge

Another difficulty with knowledge is what the state of scientific and technical knowledge consists of. It has been submitted[83] that the state of scientific and technical knowledge should include *present* and *constructive* knowledge. "Present knowledge" would be relevant when a medicinal product could not be tested for a certain effect as there was no basis for believing that it could have such an effect—for example, HIV-contaminated blood before the virus was isolated. But the "state of knowledge", it is suggested, can in some ways be best

[78] Exceptionally the CSM may communicate this information to all medical practitioners, thus rendering the information public.

[79] Case C–300/95 [1997] ECR I–2649, para. 29.

[80] Emphasis added.

[81] The state of knowledge "includes all data in the information circuit of the scientific community as a whole, bearing in mind, however, on the basis of a reasonableness test, the actual opportunities for the information to circulate": *per* Tesauro AG in Case C–300/95 *EC Commission* v. *United Kingdom* [1997] ECR I–2699, para. 24. However, as previously noted, there is clearly a need to take into consideration the instantaneous nature of modern scientific knowledge on CD Rom, the Internet and other data retrieval systems for scientific research.

[82] Griffiths, n. 40 above, 225.

[83] Whittaker, "The EEC Directive on Product Liability" (1995) 5 *Ybk. Eur. Law* 233, 257–8.

described as ignorance.[84] This proposition is derived from *IBA* v. *EMI Electronics and BICC Construction*,[85] where the House of Lords held that a television transmission mast designer (BICC) negligently failed to consider the possible yet unresearched effects of asymmetric ice loading on the stays of a cylindrical mast in conjunction with the effects of vortex shedding. To avoid the scenario where negligence law would be stricter than liability under the Act, "state of knowledge" should include "constructive knowledge"—"what the producer ought to have known at the relevant time".[86]

Powles[87] has emphasised that there should be no lessening of the knowledge that a pharmaceutical manufacturer would be expected to have to a standard of "all known measures to ensure the safety of the product", since his innovative research may require unique approaches.[88]

(v) When Knowledge Becomes Defined

The producer is to be judged with respect to the level of "knowledge . . . when he put the product into circulation",[89] i.e. normally when he "supplied the product to another".[90] What is envisaged is that a producer could well acquire in the post-marketing stage, but prior to delivery of the product into the distribution system, a knowledge of additional safety features—for example, further tests—which might or ought to have been incorporated in the product or in the literature pertaining to it. Hence the Directive and the Act seem to envisage continuous testing of pharmaceuticals as an essential for this defence.[91]

If the medicinal product is "supplied" when its dangerous propensities have not been foreseen, and then a few months later discovery is made before injury is actually caused, the development risk defence would be available but the producer would be required to act reasonably (in terms of the law of negligence) to reduce the harm that a product may cause in such a way as to protect the public from its danger—for example, by recalling the product or providing appropriate warnings.[92]

84 *Ibid.*, 258.

85 (1980) 14 Build LR 1.

86 Whittaker, n. 83 above, 258.

87 Powles, "Product Liability—A Novel Dimension in Scots Law" in Gamble (ed.), *Obligations in Context: Essays in Honour of Professor D. M. Walker* (Edinburgh, W. Green & Son, 1990), 58.

88 As noted above, the state of scientific knowledge is to be identified with "the most advanced level of research which has been carried out at a given time": *per* Tesauro AG in Case C–300/95 *EC Commission* v. *United Kingdom* [1997] ECR I–2649, para. 21. This has been affirmed by the ECJ's judgment: *ibid.*, para. 26.

89 Art. 7(e) of Dir. 85/374/EEC.

90 S. 4(2) of the Act: s. 46.

91 Finch, "Legislation on Product Liability" [1988] *Pharmaceutical Med.* 3, 15; Finch and Ranson, *Product Liability in Europe: What the New EEC Directive Will Mean for Pharmaceutical Companies* (Richmond, PJB Publications, 1986), 36.

92 *Walton* v *British Leyland (UK) Ltd* (unreported, 2 July 1978), in *Products Liability Casebook* (London, Lloyd's of London Press, 1984), 131.

5. REVERSAL OF THE BURDEN OF PROOF

Although under the law of negligence the burden is on the injured person to prove that the current state of scientific and technical knowledge was sufficient for a manufacturer to reveal a defect, under the Act the onus will fall on the producer to show that the defect could not reasonably be expected to have been discovered.[93] Thus, the burden of proof is reversed. The courts will undoubtedly "impose an exacting standard in respect of research and monitoring international literature".[94] This standard should be higher than the standard in negligence of *Bolam*[95] and *Hunter* v. *Hanley*.[96]

It has been argued that the new standard means that "no other producer in the field could be expected to have discovered the defect". If others exist whose research might have discovered the defect, the defence must fail.[97]

Newdick[98] cites the example of thalidomide as a drug whose scientific evidence would have effectively failed the requirements of the reversal of the burden of proof test. He states:

> "In the early 1950s tests for teratogenicity were not routinely carried out in the pharmaceutical industry. On the other hand, there were a number [*sic*] of companies that did so. The manufacturers of thalidomide did not . . . [A]nother producer could have conducted tests for teratogenicity and have discovered the defect in the drug . . . [T]he standard . . . under the development risk defence may be that of the highest common factor of opinion in the industry."

I am inclined to disagree, since there was no evidence to suggest that a producer of products of the same description as the product in question, i.e. sedative/hypnotics, was in fact using *routine* tests for teratogenicity. Although a few companies had been beginning to use such a test, there was no evidence that such testing amounted to a "standard" against which conduct was to be based;

93 S. 4(1) of the Act; HL Debates, vol. 482, col. 1056 (8.12.1986) *per* the Parliamentary Under-Secretary of State, Department of Trade and Industry. According to Tesauro AG, the reversal of the burden of proof onto the producer clearly shows that the UK was not introducing a system of liability based on negligence under the Act: Case C–300/95 *EC Commission* v. *United Kingdom* [1997] ECR 1–2649, *per* Tesauro AG, para. 27. Although technically true, the nature of the defence itself appears to have been constructed in a manner which reflects the requirements of negligence, particularly when it stresses the conduct of producers and whether they may be expected to discover the defect. As previously noted, the ECJ cited the reversal of the burden of proof onto the producer as being one factor which tended to show that the Commission had failed to make out its allegation that s. 4(1)(e) clearly conflicted with Art. 7(e): Case *ibid.*, para. 34.

94 Dodds-Smith and Spencer, n. 38 above, 381.

95 *Bolam* v. *Friern Hospital Management Committee* [1957] 1 WLR 582, *per* McNair J at 586–7. For the impact of the HL decision in *Bolitho* v. *City & Hackney HA* [1998] AC 232 on the application of the *Bolam* test, see Chap. 4, n. 61. See also *Roe* v. *Minister of Health* [1954] 2 QB 66, *per* Denning LJ at 84, 86, and *Thompson and Others* v. *Smith Shiprepairers (North Shields) Ltd* [1984] 1 QB 405, *per* Mustill J at 415–16, 422.

96 1955 SC 200, *per* Lord President Clyde at 295; *Moyes* v. *Lothian Health Board*, 1990 SLT 444, *per* Lord Caplan at 449; Anon, "Medical Negligence: *Hunter* v. *Hanley* 35 Years On", 1990 SLT (News) 325.

97 Newdick, n. 3 above, 474.

98 *Ibid.*, 474, 475.

nor were the tests of such a required sophistication that they could with any certainty have detected the teratogenicity.[99]

Stapleton observes that in respect of testing for teratogenicity at the time of the thalidomide disaster, the "testing of pharmaceuticals on animals was known and the relevant species did in fact exist".[100] Only the idea of applying them to the task of screening thalidomide for safety purposes was lacking.[101] However, she concedes that "no one had yet suggested testing pregnancy drugs on pregnant animals from the species which would have manifested birth defects".[102] It would thus seem clear that such testing did not amount to a standard against which the ability to discover the teratogenic nature of thalidomide could be assessed.

The question is, as Stapleton notes, should the technical ability to find and "eventually characterize the risk be enough to justify liability before such determinations have been . . . widely accepted".[103] In her view, there is a need for "consensus" about how specific the discovery must be to overcome the burden in respect of the defence and about how certain the scientist must be.[104] It seems, therefore, that there needs to be a general acceptance by the relevant scientific community of the testing in question. In such circumstances, the producers of thalidomide would be likely to overcome the burden of proof.

6. STAPLETON'S CLASSIFICATION OF PRODUCT DEFECTS AND THEIR INTERACTION WITH THE DEFENCE

Stapleton has argued that "[i]f the development risk defence is so wide that it excludes liability for all except those defects which were reasonably foreseeable to the defendant manufacturer, the latter's liability under the Directive is no greater than in negligence".[105]

She classifies product defects into three types and attempts to postulate whether the defendant would be liable in each characterised situation under the law of negligence and under the Directive.[106] The three types of product defects are classified according to whether at the relevant time the defect was:

(i) undiscoverable given the state of the art;
(ii) discoverable but only by extraordinary means;
(iii) discoverable by ordinary or reasonable means.[107]

[99] Sneader, n. 62 above, 32. Teratogenicity tests did not form part of a standard screening procedure in 1958: Teff and Munro, n. 62 above, 32. For the arguments both for and against liability in negligence in the thalidomide disaster, see Teff and Munro, above, 32–5.
[100] Stapleton, *Product Liability* (London, Butterworths, 1994), 240.
[101] *Ibid.*
[102] *Ibid.*
[103] *Ibid.*
[104] *Ibid.*, 24.
[105] *Ibid.*, 239.
[106] *Ibid.*
[107] *Ibid.*

Classification (i) reflects the situation where adverse drug reactions are manifest only in humans and affect only the user's offspring or further generations, and no way exists of detecting the defect until the first member of the second generation is born. Here there would be no liability under both negligence and the Directive.[108]

In respect of classification (ii), discoverable but only by extraordinary means, Stapleton states that under negligence the defendant would not be liable, and that the only way liability would be wider than negligence is if it refuses the defence here, and that the number of cases in this category is significant. However, Stapleton postulates that there is arguably no meaningful line to be drawn between (ii) and (iii).[109] Those who believe that there is a meaningful line which is "intelligible and workable", and that the Directive's liability is wider than negligence, must argue that Article 7(e) will be refused where technical tools and mechanisms exist for discovering the defect,[110] although it is my view that there is no such dividing line between (ii) and (iii). It is submitted that there is an identifiable and concrete "gold standard" of what is discoverable in practice and what is not.

The argument that the defence of Article 7(e) will be refused where technical tools and mechanisms exist for discovering the defect seems partially to accord with the view of Advocate General Tesauro in his opinion in *EC Commission* v. *United Kingdom*,[111] when he stated that the "practicability and expense of measures suitable for eliminating the defect from the product" are outside the scope of Article 7(e).[112] The European Court of Justice did not affirm him on this point and it has been consistently argued that discoverability should incorporate a consideration of economic feasibility.[113] It seems that, in practice, time and costs would have to be weighed against the benefits associated with the drug in question and the seriousness of the patient's illness.[114]

In cases involving medicinal products, whose very production is predicated upon economic considerations, it seems to be inevitable that discoverability should entail an element of economic feasibility. Thus the only distinguishing feature between the defence and negligence appears to be the reversal of the

108 Stapleton, *Product Liability* (London, Butterworths, 1994), 239. But note the increase in sophistication of genetic and chromosomal testing may rapidly change the scientific ability to discover such defects: see Chap. 2 above.

109 Stapleton, n. 100 above, 240–1.

110 *Ibid.*, 240.

111 Case C–300/95, [1997] ECR I–2649.

112 *Ibid.*, 20.

113 See above.

114 It has been argued that Art. 7(e) would provide a defence in category (i) only, but s. 4(1)(e) would provide a defence in cases falling within (i) and (ii): Spink, "The Consumer Protection Act 1987—the State of the Art Defence" (1997) 42 *JLSS* 416, 418. It is submitted that much will depend on whether discoverability will entail an element of economic feasibility in applying the defence: see above.

burden of proof, and that arguably seems to be a less than convincing distinction.[115]

7. THE CONTRAST BETWEEN CAUSATION IN NEGLIGENCE AND THE DEVELOPMENT RISK DEFENCE

An interesting comparison can be made between the position surrounding the admissibility of scientific evidence for the establishment of causation in negligence in medicinal product liability cases involving the novel sciences, where the burden of proof is on the plaintiff, and the acceptability of scientific evidence in assessing the discoverability of unknown and unknowable defects in terms of the development risk defence, where the burden of proof is on the defendant.

In the former situation, it appears that English law recognises that minority views in a profession can be accepted in the English courts, such methods being unsupported by peer review or publication.[116] Arguably, this reflects a close alignment with the post-*Daubert* v. *Merrell-Dow Pharmaceuticals Inc.*[117] position in the USA, which rejected the rule in *Frye* v. *United States*[118] that expert opinion based on scientific technique was inadmissible unless the technique was "generally accepted" as reliable in the relevant scientific community. It has been previously noted in Chapter 3 that a positive justification for a rejection of the *Frye* test was that not all scientific opinions, especially in medicine, are "generally accepted" in the *Frye* sense of these words. Another reason could also be the fact that the burden of proof remains on the plaintiff, which sufficiently favours the defendant in the sense that it is the plaintiff who must overcome the onus by the obtaining of scientific evidence relating to causation. It seems only just that the plaintiff should be entitled to present evidence in any case involving the novel sciences which, though not generally accepted, is both relevant and reliable, and sufficient to overcome the burden of proof of causation.

By contrast, in respect of the development risk defence, the burden of proof is on the defendant. Since the burden is an extremely exacting one, it might also seem just that any evidence to be used in assessing the discoverability of unknown or unknowable defects should be generally accepted scientific evidence, reflecting the fact that the difficulties in proving a negative (i.e. that the state of scientific and technical knowledge was not such that a producer of products of the same description might be expected to discover the defect) are arguably greater than those in proving a positive. There thus seems to be a need for a "consensus of views" from the relevant scientific community where there

115 See, *per contra*, Case C–300/95 *EC Commission* v. *United Kingdom* [1997] ECR I–2649, *per* Tesauro AG at para. 25 and *per* the ECJ at para. 34.

116 *R.* v. *Robb* (1991) 93 Cr. App Rep. 161 at 165–6, *per* Bingham LJ.

117 125 L Ed. 2d 469 (1993).

118 293 F 1013 at 1014. (DC Cir 1923).

is a disagreement on the existence of "knowledge" of a defect in a medicinal product.[119]

8. CONCLUSION

The development risk defence is arguably one of the main obstacles to the achievement of strict liability under the Act, since discoverability by the manufacturer of unknowable defects of medicinal products will be decided in a manner likely to be identical to the requirements of negligence.[120] Nevertheless, it could be argued that the defence is of conceivable assistance to therapeutic innovation and development within the pharmaceutical industry.[121]

Yet there seems to be a reasoned argument for saying that it fails to take account of the very victims of innovation when therapeutic medicines may cause severe adverse effects. Indeed, the Pearson Commission recommended that, in introducing a system of strict liability for defective products, the "producer should not be allowed a defence of development risk"[122] despite arguments that the cost of insurance might affect new product development. The dismissal of the defence was based on the premise that to include it "would be to leave a gap in the compensation cover, through which, for example, the victims of

[119] Newdick, "Risk, Uncertainty and 'Knowledge' in the Development Risk Defence" [1991] *Anglo-American Law Review* 127, 141. Newdick's view is that knowledge in respect of development risks has a "relative quality" since scientific knowledge is dependent on the opinions of others, verification of such knowledge and peer approval. However, it is also arguable that knowledge to enable a producer to discover a defect in a product, particularly a medicinal product, may first only appear to the producer himself. Such knowledge may be indigenous to the producer but would still be regarded as "knowledge". Such knowledge would not have to be present in the public domain to be regarded as knowledge for the purposes of the development risk defence. Nevertheless, any evidence in the public domain would necessarily have to satisfy the "generally accepted" standard to be regarded as "knowledge" for the purposes of s. 4(1)(e).

[120] Note that the *Restatement (Third) of Torts: Products Liability* has adopted a standard at least as negligence-orientated as our development risk defence, in that in § 6(c) it imposes liability only where the design of a prescription drug or prescription product poses sufficiently large foreseeable risks compared to its foreseeable therapeutic benefits that "reasonable health care providers, knowing of such foreseeable risks and therapeutic benefits, would not prescribe the drug or medicinal device for any class of patients": American Law Institute, *Restatement of the Law Third, Torts: Products Liability* (Philadelphia, Penn., American Law Institute, 1998). In essence, the plaintiff has to prove that the drug or device should not have been on the market at all. Arguably this is a kind of "super" negligence standard and one that may be higher than that under s. 4(1)(e) of the Act: see Schwartz, "The Impact of the New Products Liability Restatement on Prescription Products" (1995) 50 *Food and Drug Law Journal* 399, 407.

[121] There is considerable support both for excluding and including liability for development risks under strict liability: see Fleming, "Drug Injury Compensation Plans" (1982) 30 *Am. J Comp. L* 297, 308–9. Compensation for development risks may be desirable for reason of compensating the injured from a "deeper pocket". However, it is unjustifiable on the grounds of inefficient resource allocation since development risks "are unavoidable and preventable only by incurring socially undesirable costs" (e.g. longer testing): *ibid.*, 312–13.

[122] Royal Commission on Civil Liability and Compensation for Personal Injury, Cmnd 7054–1/1978, para. 1259. The Law Commission had similarly rejected the defence: Liability for Defective Products, Law Com. No.82, Cmnd 6831/1977, para. 105.

another thalidomide disaster might easily slip".[123] Similar concerns were raised before the defence's introduction into UK law.[124] However, in the European Commission's *First Report on the Application of the Product Liability Directive*, the Commission has "not considere[d] it necessary, at this stage, to submit any proposals for" the Directive's amendment,[125] and the future of the defence, given the current absence of cases under the Directive, seems fairly secure.[126]

In respect of the European Court of Justice decision, although it has generated some certainty over the issue whether section 4(1)(e) properly implemented Article 7(e) of the Product Liability Directive, it has arguably raised more questions than answers. Whatever the views of the European Court, it seems that, since the section 4(1)(e) version of the defence has been constructed in a way which places emphasis upon the conduct of producers, it has been formulated in a manner which reflects the requirements of negligence. Secondly, it appears that national courts will consider the issue of discoverability of a defect with, at the very least, a subjective element in their overall approach. Thirdly, the discoverability and accessibility of scientific and technical knowledge are more restrictive than the European Court's decision would suggest. It is also arguable that the UK has benefited from the ambiguous way in which section 4(1)(e) has been drafted. The apparent aborted outcome of the deliberations concerning the proposals of the European Parliament's Committee on the Environment, Public Health and Consumer Protection would appear to be a disappointment to consumer and patient interest groups, particularly in respect of the abolition of the development risk defence.

In the light of these discussions on the development risk defence, we now turn to addressing the question of the economic consequences of our reanalysis of causation.

123 *Ibid.*

124 Forte, "Medical Products Liability" in McLean (ed.), *Legal Issues in Medicine* (Aldershot: Gower, 1981), 76; P. Cane, *Atiyah's Accidents Compensation and the Law* (4th edn., London, Weidenfeld & Nicolson, 1987), 145. See also the view of Miller that those who support the existence of the defence "are saying in effect that liability for design or composition defects continue to be based on negligence or fault" and that although "[t]his is a perfectly tenable point of view", it is inconsistent with purporting to introduce strict liability along the lines of the Pearson Commission's or the Law Commission's proposals: Miller, *Product Liability and Safety Encyclopædia* (London, Butterworths, 1997), Division III, para. 131.

125 EC Commission, n. 30 above, 2.

126 See Hodges, *Report for the Commission of the European Communities on the Application of Directive 851/374/EEC on the Liability for Defective Products* (London, McKenna & Co., 1994), 26, para. 77.

8

Possible Economic Consequences of Probabilistic Approaches to Determining Causation

1. INTRODUCTION

Chapter 6 attempted to show how the uncertainties in proving causation in respect of medicinal products created an inefficient liability system generating inappropriate and misperceived incentives, as well as inconsistent judicial decisions. Uncertainty in proving injury causation resulted in unusually large liability costs in respect of litigation concerning vaccines, intra-uterine devices and the drug Bendectin.

A probabilistic approach to causation, based primarily on pharmaco-epidemiology and use of the Bayes' Theorem in the refinement of statistical data to specific cases has been mooted as a means of promoting economic efficiency.

A question that remains to be answered concerns the economic consequences of the author's analysis of causation; *viz.* whether the introduction of an epidemiological approach to drug causality will in fact reduce or increase the injury costs[1] of medicinal product litigation. This question will be considered in view of our findings on the restriction of liability caused by the introduction of the development risk defence of the Consumer Protection Act 1987, as adumbrated in Chapter 7.

2. POSSIBLE CONSEQUENCES

It seems that much will depend on the nature of the drug in question and the kind of scenario that our new reanalysis will be presented with.

A series of scenarios could be postulated.

[1] Other than injury costs, further consideration might be given to the costs involved in the organisation of pharmacoepidemiological studies which would result in an epidemiological database essential for the operation of the new approach. This would involve the costs of increased staffing and statisticians, technical assistance and equipment. At present, such studies are carried out by industry (through the Association of the British Pharmaceutical Industry (ABPI)) and by government (by the Medicines Control Agency (MCA)). There is a need for the consolidation of all these sources of essential information. The fact that causation requires detailed investigation to establish liability necessarily results in transaction costs: Fleming, "Drug Injury Compensation Plans" (1982) 30 *Am. J Comp. L* 297, 315.

(i) Scenario One: The Absence of any Epidemiological Link between Drug and Adverse Effect

The scenario contemplated here is that illustrated by the scientific evidence in the Bendectin litigation. In the event of no epidemiological link being established, any plaintiffs bringing a claim in respect of injuries from such a medicinal product would be entitled to no compensation. Injury costs could therefore be curtailed as a result.

(ii) Scenario Two: The Existence of an Unequivocal Epidemiological Link between Drug and Adverse Effect

The scenario suggested here is illustrated by the thalidomide litigation, where a clear statistical association existed between thalidomide and phocomelia. Any plaintiffs bringing a claim in respect of injuries from such a medicinal product would, *prima facie*, be able to establish causal link, unless the individual plaintiff had a pre-existing genetic propensity to suffer from such an effect.

However, assuming the drug was defective,[2] the individual plaintiff's likelihood of compensation would be conditional upon the operation of the development risk defence of section 4(1)(e) of the Consumer Protection Act 1987,[3] a consideration that will be examined below.

(iii) Scenario Three: The Existence of a Possible Epidemiological Link between Drug and Adverse Effect

This scenario is illustrated by the possible association between pertussis vaccine and brain damage, where children have experienced a serious acute neurologic illness within eight or nine days of receiving DTP vaccine. It will be recalled that the Committee to Study New Research on Vaccines, which reported in 1994, concluded "that the *balance of evidence [was] consistent with* a causal relation between DTP and . . . chronic nervous-system dysfunction . . . in those children who experience[d] a serious acute neurologic illness within seven days after receiving DTP vaccine".[4] Here the Bayes' Theorem would be an important aid to the reduction of causal uncertainty. By reducing such causal uncertainty, the likelihood of possible compensation being awarded could be probabilistically ascertained, and the question whether compensation could be proffered to the plaintiffs answered.

[2] In terms of s. 2(1), (3) of the Consumer Protection Act 1987, hereafter CPA.

[3] See below.

[4] Stratton, Howe and Johston (eds.), *Institute of Medicine, DTP Vaccine and Chronic Nervous System Dysfunction: A New Analysis* (Washington, DC, National Academy Press, 1994), 2–3, 15.

We must still tackle the problem of ascertaining the level at which evidence of probabilistic causation would indicate a causal connection. Rules of epidemiology require evidential proof on a balance of probabilities of at least 95 per cent that the association was not due to chance to establish causation. It is submitted that this standard may be difficult to satisfy for the provision of compensation to plaintiffs. Nevertheless, the use of this standard, when coupled with the refined statistical analysis of the Bayes' Theorem, would be the most equitable way of quantifying the problem of causation in such cases. The amount of compensation awarded would depend on the epidemiological evidence and the level of statistical significance in each case. The greater the level of statistical significance, the higher the compensation awarded. If there was no statistically significant association, no compensation could be awarded to any plaintiff.

In the event of a causal association being established between a drug and an alleged adverse event, the problem will remain whether such injury costs as would have been awarded would be negated by the existence of the development risk defence ("the defence") of the Consumer Protection Act 1987.[5] As previously indicated, this denies strict liability for defective products where the defendant is able to establish that the state of scientific and technical knowledge was not such as to enable a producer of products of the same description as the product in question to discover the defect.[6]

In the light of our analysis of the defence in Chapter 7 it seems that, in the cases of thalidomide, DES and practolol, even if causation were to be established through the use of epidemiological evidence, the development risk defence could conceivably operate to deny liability. If a medicinal product satisfies the requirements of defectiveness,[7] causation[8] and the development risk defence[9] in terms of the Consumer Protection Act 1987, liability of the producer would be established. Only then would an award of compensation result in injury costs to the manufacturer of the product.

The chapter now proceeds with a proposed analysis of how such costs would be sustained by a pharmaceutical company, while at the same time protecting its ability to innovate, particularly in areas involving the manufacture of medicinal products with high risk of adverse effects.

3. POSSIBLE SOLUTIONS TO THE PROBLEM OF INCREASED INJURY COSTS: THE ROLE OF INTELLECTUAL PROPERTY RIGHTS

In circumstances where the hurdles of causation, defectiveness and the development risk defence have been overcome in favour of the plaintiff, pharmaceutical

[5] CPA, s. 4(1)(e).
[6] *Ibid.*
[7] Ss. 2(1), 3.
[8] S. 2(1).
[9] S. 4(1)(e).

companies will need to utilise insurance and self-insurance mechanisms in order to cover any overwhelming liability costs ensuing from a drug disaster. It is arguable, nevertheless, that insurance premiums cannot be expected to resolve the problem of untoward injury costs in high-risk and innovative areas involving medicinal products. It could be submitted that in order to protect innovation in such areas, an increase in effective patent life[10] of such drugs might be justifiable.

In January 1993, the European Community introduced a regulation establishing the so-called "supplementary protection certificate" ("SPC") to address the problem of patent life erosion caused by the testing and authorisation requirements of new medicinal products.[11]

The SPC is a *sui generis* form of intellectual property right which supplements the marketing authorisation of a product issued in accordance with drug regulatory requirements[12] and was designed to assist in the purpose of patent

[10] Effective patent life is the period from the date of market introduction to patent expiry: Redwood, *Pharmaceutical Patent Term Restoration for the 1990s* (Felixstowe, Oldwicks Press, 1990), 18.

[11] Reg. 1768/92 concerning the creation of a supplementary protection certificate for medicinal products: [1992] OJ L182/1. A resulting series of SIs has helped establish the administrative procedures necessary for the SPC in the UK. These are: Patents (Supplementary Protection Certificate for Medicinal Products) Regs. 1992 (SI No. 3091); Patents (Supplementary Protection Certificate for Medicinal Products) Rules 1997 (SI No. 64). A similar reg. has extended the SPC to agrochemicals which also have problems of patent life erosion due to testing and authorisation requirements: Reg. 1610/96 concerning the creation of a supplementary protection certificate for plant protection products: [1996] OJ L198/30. The Reg. for medicinal products establishes a five-year maximum period of the SPC's duration, with 15 years' maximum effective monopoly: Reg. 1768/92, Art. 13. It had previously been proposed by the EC Commission that the maximum period of the SPC's duration be 10 years, with 16 years' maximum effective monopoly (see Proposal for Council Reg. (EEC) concerning creation of a supplementary protection certificate for medicinal products COM(90)101 final—SYN 255 Brussels, 11 Apr. 1990, Art. 8.1, 2; Whaite and Jones, "Pharmaceutical Patent Term Restoration" [1990] 5 *EIPR* 179), but political compromise and hostility from both patient groups and generic drug companies led to this period being reduced to 5 years and 15 years' maximum effective monopoly (see Whaite and Jones, "Pharmaceutical Patent Term Restoration: The European Commission's Regulation" [1992] 9 *EIPR* 324, 325, and W. R. Cornish, *Intellectual Property* (3rd edn., London, Sweet & Maxwell, 1996), 135). The original proposal was described by the Common Law Institute of Intellectual Property as "less than generous" and that "an effective life of sixteen years or less [was] not tolerable" (Common Law Institute of Intellectual Property (CLIP) Report, *Supplementary Protection Certificates* (London, CLIP, 1991), 21–3), so it would seem that the compromise adopted an even less satisfactory position than the proposal.

[12] Kunz-Hallstein, "The Compatibility of a Community 'Certificate for the Restoration of Protection'" [1990] 6 *EIPR* 209, 213–14. It has also been suggested that SPCs create a new intellectual property right from patents since the link between investment and innovation is *indirect*, whereas SPCs *directly* protect the successful investment, since SPCs are only applied for in respect of successful products. Cf Holyoak and Torremans, who disagree with the view that SPCs protect only successful inventions. They consider that patented inventions are successful by fulfilment of the patentability requirements and that the pharmaceutical industry often finds lucrative opportunities even for patented products which are not granted marketing authorisations as medicinal products. They say that the real tests for success are the drugs' sales figures: Holyoak and Torremans, *Intellectual Property* (London, Butterworths, 1995), 139. It is submitted that a marketing authorisation is a *sine qua non* for a medicinal product's success, and that without such authorisations, a pharmaceutical product cannot properly be exploited. It appears, therefore, that CLIP's observations are correct.

restoration for pharmaceuticals, *viz.* to help "underpin its resolve" to take the considerable risk of producing new drugs which would cope with serious gaps in therapy, particularly those arising from chronic diseases in the ageing population.[13] SPCs are now recognised as "essential to the survival of a European R & D-based pharmaceutical industry".[14]

It has thus been observed that the rationale behind patent restoration and the emergence of the SPC has been the erosion of patent life, due to the time taken for a drug to receive its marketing authorisation. On closer examination, it could be argued that the real link is not solely between drug regulation and patent law but also between drug disasters, product liability and patent law. The emergence of an increase in the time for testing medicinal products seems to be linked to the occurrence of major untoward incidents associated with such products. After the problems associated with non-steroid anti-inflammatory drugs (NSAIDs) in the early 1980s, e.g. Opren (benoxaprofen), a corresponding increase took place in the period of time taken for testing drugs before they received their marketing authorisations. Thus it seems that increasing testing has emerged, partly as a result of increased pharmacovigilance, but also as a result of the extensive product liability litigation which has been associated with certain drugs.

It is conceivable that increasing patent restoration or marketing exclusivity (the period of effective monopoly of a patented medicinal product) could be justified by several factors other than the erosion of patent life, which might affect the costs sustained by pharmaceutical companies. Such factors could include the type of patient, the type of disease being treated and the nature of the drug, where product liability litigation has affected innovation of similar drug structures.

Such developments remain possible,[15] but will be contingent upon future evidence of whether product liability litigation will result in an increase or decrease in costs to pharmaceutical companies.

[13] Redwood, n. 10 above, 1. Ironically, it seems that the upper limit for the duration of the SPC of five years has penalised medicinal products with a development time greater than 10 years by awarding them a shorter effective patent life, thus prejudicing products for the treatment of chronic diseases, where chronic toxicity tests, carcinogenicity tests and long-term efficacy tests necessarily result in longer testing-periods and development times: von Morzé and Hanna, "Critical and Practical Observations Regarding Pharmaceutical Patent Term Restoration in the European Communities" (1995) 77 *JPTOS* 479, 518.

[14] Adams, "Supplementary Protection Certificates: The Challenge to EC Regulation 1768/92" [1994] 8 *EIPR* 323, 326.

[15] Any further proposals to increase patent restoration or marketing exclusivity would need to consider the possibility of an overreaction to the strengthening of such intellectual property rights. Indeed, Prof. Cornish has cautioned about extensions of a patent generally without "most careful consideration": Cornish, n. 11 above, 113.

4. CONCLUSION

This chapter has attempted to address the question whether the introduction of an epidemiological approach to causation and medicinal products would have the effect of a reduction or increase in injury costs of product liability litigation.

It seems that the answer to this question is contingent on the nature of the drug used and the degree of epidemiological evidence establishing a causal link between drug and adverse effect, ranging from no evidence to unequivocal evidence of such an association.

In the event of a causal association being established, the problem of the negation of injury costs by the development risk defence has been addressed. Even if causation was established through epidemiological evidence, the development risk defence might operate to deny liability. In the cases of thalidomide, DES and practolol, this could have been a conceivable result.

The chapter finally addressed the scenario where the hurdles of causation, defectiveness and the development risk defence have been overcome in favour of the plaintiff. In addition to the use of insurance, the possibility has been mooted of increasing patent protection or marketing exclusivity in circumstances where certain factors may affect the costs of pharmaceutical companies, e.g. where product liability litigation has affected innovation of similar drug structures for diseases of exceptional community need, such as AIDS, or pioneering approaches to therapeutics, including gene therapy.[16] Such intellectual property developments will be dependent upon whether product liability litigation will produce a significant increase in costs to pharmaceutical companies in the future. Indeed, other unforeseeable factors may affect such costs. It may then be prudent to reconsider the possible option of increasing patent protection or marketing exclusivity.

[16] These advanced techniques have the potential of resulting in product liability litigation in the 21st century, yet in gene therapy we have a probable way of dealing with congenital disease, cancer and infections of worldwide significance.

9

Conclusion

This book has attempted to address the relationship between causation, risk and scientific evidence in medicinal product liability litigation. Several propositions have emerged from this work.

Chapter 1 examined the role of causation and medicinal products from a legal and probability perspective. Three propositions have emerged from this study: first, that the established legal approaches to causation, both traditional and alternative, are inadequate when complex issues of drug causality fail to respond to non-numerical solutions; secondly, despite its limitations, it seems that an epidemiological approach to dealing with medicinal products and the cause of adverse reactions is the most effective since it is a quantitative approach and one which should promote more certainty in judicial decision-making—it is submitted that this approach will in the long term lead to greater efficiency within the reformed civil justice system; thirdly, that the need to refine epidemiological statistics to reflect the personal circumstances of a particular drug administered to a particular patient is best served by the Bayes' Theorem. Although not embraced by the criminal courts, the theorem is potentially useful as a tool to refine statistics in order to establish the most accurate probability of a specific causal link between a drug and an injury in civil litigation, where proof of causation operates on a lesser standard than criminal law, i.e. that of a balance of probabilities.

Chapter 2 examined the relationship between Diethylstilbestrol (DES) and causation. Three propositions can be demonstrated by this chapter. First, the spectrum of adverse effects of DES, potentially spanning three generations, illustrates the range of levels of difficulty in proving a causal link between an adverse reaction and a drug. Compounded with that problem lies the difficulty in identifying the particular manufacturer of the product which caused the injury. There are no English or Scottish equivalents to the US and Dutch solutions of market share and alternative causation liability respectively which, while admirable in their pursuit of compensation and deterrence objectives, are ultimately blighted by operational and definitional problems. Secondly, the difficulty of establishing causation seems inherently to be related to the problem of establishing pre-conception tort liability since third-generation DES injuries appear to be beyond the contemplation of the courts as being actionable in the United States and possibly in the United Kingdom on policy grounds; such third-generation injuries are probably in causation terms the most formidable to prove. Thirdly, the law of negligence, the Congenital Disabilities (Civil Liability) Act 1976 and the Consumer

Protection Act 1987 continue to present great problems in resolving the DES causation question in the UK.

Chapter 3 addressed the importance of scientific evidence and expert witnesses in the elucidation of causation which emerged from a case study of the Bendectin (Debendox) Litigation. The exquisite sensitivity associated with drugs used in pregnancy is well illustrated by this work. Three propositions have emerged from this study. First, the fundamental lesson of the Bendectin litigation has been the vulnerability of effective drugs of this nature and their possible exclusion from the therapeutic armamentarium on the basis of tenuous and inadequate evidence of causation based on scientific evidence. Secondly, the study has tried to show the extent to which American jury trials in favour of plaintiffs in this area have been forcibly reversed by the use of a plurality of American procedural responses and has suggested ways of attempting to overcome the distortion of scientific evidence through the use of science panels, court experts and the bifurcation of trials. The study argues that such procedural responses are equally applicable to a trial by judge alone in the UK. Thirdly, it is submitted that a possible lesson for English courts from the study is that they should continue to exercise a discretion against jury trials in personal injury cases. It also seems evident that Scottish courts should not seek to have the types of action heard by civil juries extended to embrace questions of liability and causation in personal injury cases.

Social and legal issues of causation were then addressed in a comparative study of vaccine damage and causation in Chapter 4. Three propositions have emerged from this chapter. First, it seems that both the common law and statutory bases of vaccine damage and causation are affected by severe problems, principally due to the lack of scientific knowledge establishing general causation between a vaccine and an adverse reaction and also due to the lack of proof establishing specific causation in the individual. This has resulted in either the strict approach of the UK or Canadian courts, leading to a denial of liability in all cases that have come to trial, on the one hand, or the pragmatic but scientifically flawed casuistry of some American courts, particularly in the face of contrary epidemiological evidence. Secondly, the US National Childhood Vaccine Injury Act 1986 sails as close to the wind as possible in eliminating causation. However, a valid bone of contention is that compensation may be awarded under the Act in some cases where there is no real causal link between the vaccine and the injury, but where the Act's and the Table's requirements are satisfied. This is perhaps overshadowed by the Act's potential for providing the majority with an efficient compensation programme. Thirdly, it is submitted that the UK's Vaccine Damage Payments Act 1979 does nothing to ameliorate the causation problem, as is witnessed by the universally poor success rates at Tribunal level.

Attention was then focused in Chapter 5 on the ongoing studies into the possible effects of medicinal products on veterans of the Gulf War. The most important proposition to emerge from this case study is that the use of epidemiological approaches has proved vital in addressing these problems in the USA and in the UK, and it supports the book's attempt to encourage the appropriate use of such scientific evidence in the resolution of legal controversies.

In Chapter 6, an economic analysis was made of causation and medicinal products. The proposition which has emerged from this study is that the use of probabilistic evidence in the ascertainment of causal link in cases involving medicinal products may promote the efficiency theory of law and economics.

Chapter 7 then addressed the issue of liability for undiscoverable defects, distinguishing probabilistic risk from development risk and examining the impact of the development risk defence of the Consumer Protection Act 1987. The proposition which emerged from this study is that the development risk defence may deny liability, irrespective of causation.

Chapter 8 has tried to address the question whether the introduction of an epidemiological approach to causation and medicinal products would have the effect of a reduction or increase in injury costs of product liability litigation. Three propositions have emerged from this research. First, the answer to the question is contingent on the nature of the drug used and the degree of epidemiological evidence establishing a causal link between drug and adverse effect, ranging from no evidence to unequivocal evidence of such an association. Secondly, even if causation was established through epidemiological evidence, the development risk defence might operate to deny liability. Thirdly, in the event of the hurdles of causation, defectiveness and the development risk defence being overcome in favour of the plaintiff and of consequent product liability costs becoming so severe as to affect the production of innovative drugs, the possibility has been suggested of increasing patent protection or marketing exclusivity where certain factors may affect the costs of pharmaceutical companies. Such factors include the situation where product liability litigation has affected innovation of similar drug structures for diseases of exceptional community need. However, such intellectual property developments will be contingent upon whether product liability litigation will produce an increase in costs to pharmaceutical companies in the future.

It seems, therefore, in the light of the book's discussion and the propositions which have emerged from it, that an epidemiological approach to the ascertainment of causation and medicinal products could increase economic efficiency and produce more certainty in cases where the determination of causation through non-numerical solutions has proved elusive.

Laws should respond to the developments in science, and in pharmaceutical medicine in particular. Epidemiological approaches to resolving causation problems could help narrow the divide between science and law in this increasingly complex medical and legal area.

Index